The Global History of Black Girlhood

THE GLOBAL HISTORY OF Black Girlhood

EDITED BY

Corinne T. Field and LaKisha Michelle Simmons

UNIVERSITY OF ILLINOIS PRESS
Urbana, Chicago, and Springfield

Publication of this book was supported by the
Graduate School of Arts and Sciences and the
Department of Women, Gender & Sexuality,
University of Virginia.

1 2 3 4 5 C P 5 4 3 2 1
∞ This book is printed on acid-free paper.

Cataloging data available from the Library of Congress
ISBN 9780252044625 (hardcover)
ISBN 9780252086694 (paperback)
ISBN 9780252053634 (ebook)

For Black girls

Contents

Acknowledgments

At a roundtable we put together in 2015, "The History of Black Girlhood: Recent Innovations and Future Directions," Abosede George, author of *Making Modern Girls: A History of Girlhood, Labor, and Social Development in 20th Century Colonial Lagos,* pointed to the various ways in which blackness operated in different locales, and asked if the frameworks for Black girls' studies could be applied throughout the globe. In a published version of our roundtable, George wrote, "In colonial Lagos, which was neither a settler society nor a post-plantation society, racial difference or the blackness of black girlhood was somewhat secondary to gender, generational, and class differences . . . Black girlhood in more racially differentiated spaces would be articulated quite differently. In all contexts, a central starting point could be to denaturalize the categories of black, girl, and girlhood so as to trace or historicize the mechanisms by which these social constructs become assigned particular meanings and become assigned to certain bodies."[1] George's words became our primary inspiration for thinking more deeply about what a global history of Black girlhood might look like.

Inspired by this question, we organized the Global History of Black Girlhood Conference, held at the University of Virginia, March 17 and 18, 2017, which became the impetus for this book. We would like to thank the programs, departments, and individuals at the University of Virginia who provided funding for that event, including the Page Barbour Fund, the Center for Global Inquiry and Innovation, and Clay Endowment for the Humanities, and the Department of Women, Gender, and Sexuality among others, as well as at Harvard University, the Hutchins Center for African and African American Research and the Schlesinger Library on the History of Women in America, Radcliffe Institute for Advanced Study. The Radcliffe Institute also generously funded the editors' further collaboration as they drafted the introduction to this volume. At the University of Michigan, the Eisenberg Institute for Historical Studies, Center for the Education of Women+, the Institute for Research on Women and Gender, the Women's and Gender Studies Department, and the Penny W. STAMPS School of Art and Design supported the Narrating Black Girls' Lives Conference, February 26, 2019. Thanks to participants, especially Saidiya Hartman, for opening up new possibilities for understanding the history of Black girlhood.

Other conferences that fundamentally shaped our thinking included the Black Girl Movement Conference, planned by Farah Jasmine Griffin, Camille Brown, Aimee Meredith Cox, Kyra Guant, Carla Shedd, Cidra Sebastien, Joanne Smith, Salamishah Tillet, and Scheherazade Tillet, held at the Institute for Research in African-American Studies, Columbia University, April 7–9, 2016; Know Her Truths: Advancing Justice for Women and Girls of Color Conference, April 29, 2016, sponsored by the Collaborative to Advance Equity Through Research and held at the Anna Julia Cooper Center, Wake Forest University; and On/By Black Women/Girls: A Symposium, organized by Oneka LaBennett through the Minority, Indigenous, and Third World Studies Research Group at Cornell University, April 21–22, 2017.

This project would not have been possible without the many participants in the Global History of Black Girlhood Research Network who encouraged, guided, and contributed to this research, including but not limited to Abosede George, Renee Sentilles, Marcia Chatelain, Rhian Keyse, Tammy Owens, Kyra Gaunt, Laura Lovett, Katherine Sanchez-Eppler, Robin Bernstein, Catherine Jones, Anette Joseph-Gabriel, Kelly Duke Bryant, Emily Bridger, Alexandria Smith, Corrie Decker, Kai M. Green, Sonya Donaldson, Nicole Burrowes, Michele Mitchell, Oneka LaBennet, Lynn M. Thomas, Habiba Ibrahim, Wilma King, Colleen Vasconcellos, Ashleigh Wade, and Aria Halliday. Thank you to Lisa Wolfork and Tayari Jones. A special thank you to Tanisha Ford, Reighan Gillam, and Casidy Campbell, whose work has inspired our reading of key moments of Black girlhood.

Kathryn Vaggalis and Jennifer F. Hamer invited a special issue of *Women, Gender, and Families of Color* on Black girlhood and kinship. Undergraduate students at both the University of Michigan and the University of Virginia participated in a jointly coordinated seminar on the Global History of Black Girlhood, and we thank them for their energy, insights, and creative collaboration. Students also had an opportunity to curate a 2017 exhibition on "The Sounds and Silences of Black Girlhood" at the Albert and Shirley Small Special Collections Library, University of Virginia, and we thank the students and the library staff, especially Molly Schwartzburg and Holly Robertson.

We want to thank Zulaikha Patel and Reabetswe Mabilo for their photographs and the inspiration of their activism. We also thank Janaé E. Bonsu, Beverley Palesa Ditsie, Phindile Kunene, and Denise Oliver-Velez for sharing their stories with us. Special thanks to Tiffany Ball for copy editing the manuscript and Venessa Nielson for transcribing the panel discussion. We are grateful to the team at University of Illinois Press, especially Dawn Durante for encouraging the project at an early stage; Allison Syring Bassford, Dominque Moore, and Ellie Hinton for seeing the volume into print; and the two anonymous reviewers for their formative suggestions.

Thank you, Layla Young, for being the beautiful Black girl you are.

As always, we thank our families and friends for their love and support.

Note

1. Corinne T. Field, Tammy-Charelle Owens, Marcia Chatelain, LaKisha Simmons, Abosede George, and Rhian Keyse, "The History of Black Girlhood: Recent Innovations and Future Directions," *The Journal of the History of Childhood and Youth* 9, no, 3 (Fall 2016), 396.

The Global History of Black Girlhood

INTRODUCTION

Looking for Black Girls in History

CORINNE T. FIELD AND
LAKISHA MICHELLE SIMMONS

In 2016, images of teenaged Black girls with huge afros, braids, and locs, circulated on social media under the hashtag #StopRacismAtPretoriaGirlsHigh. More than one hundred South African girls protested their school's institutionalized racism, which they saw manifested in the school's ban on natural hairstyles. With the slogan, "Fists Up, Fros Out!" girls took to the street on August 26, 2016. A day later, they were threatened with arrests.[1] This school protest, led by girls and informed by their concerns, represents an important moment in Black history. Often, scholars and students alike do not think of children as significant historical actors. The purpose of this book is to help us think about history from Black girls' perspectives. How do we find stories that help us understand Black girls' lives? What type of source materials do girls leave behind, teaching us about how they saw the world? The South African students at Pretoria High School for Girls produced primary source documents for us to think about Black girls' lives and struggles at school. From social media posts to posters made at marches, and interviews with reporters, the girls' words will be forever remembered. Historians can use these sources to reconstruct and tell stories about the past.

Pretoria High School for Girls, formerly a whites-only girls' school, integrated in 1994. Nearly twenty-five years later, thirteen-year-old Zulaikha Patel's huge afro, teased out and as commanding as the young girl with her raised fist, became a symbol for Black girls' frustration with Eurocentric beauty standards and the disciplining of so-called "unruly" hair. Patel is part of a "post-1994" generation of South Africans—born after freedom fighter Nelson Mandela became the first Black president of South Africa. A month after the 2016 protests began, Patel met seventy-two-year-old American activist Angela Davis, a global icon of Black power style during the 1960s.

Figure 1. In August 2016, girls march together to protest institutionalized racism at their school, Pretoria High School for Girls. Photograph by Reabetswe Mabilo, who was a grade 11 student at the time. Image courtesy of Reabetswe Mabilo (photographer) and Zulaikha Patel.

Photographs of the two activists and their perfect afros circulated worldwide. As girls in South Africa protested school policies, Black girls in the United States challenged discriminatory hair rules at their schools—girls in Ohio (Horizon Science Academy), Kentucky (Butler Traditional High School), and North Carolina (The School for Creative Studies) insisted that their natural hair was not a problem but a joy. Today, Black girls continue to fight for freedom of expression through hair, dress, and fashion.[2]

The Pretoria High School for Girls' ban on natural hair represented a moment of transnational racial identification. Black schoolgirls in the United States could clearly understand the dilemma of Black schoolgirls in South Africa; they were fighting the same battles. Schoolgirls on both sides of the Atlantic articulated the problem of loving their natural hair and redefining beauty in societies that stifled Black articulations of self. During this time, Black girls were also struggling to understand the long histories of racism that

Figure 2. On August 27, 2016, Zulaikha Patel and the other protesters were threatened with arrest. Image courtesy of Reabetswe Mabilo (photographer) and Zulaikha Patel'

deeply affected their everyday lives even though they were growing up after civil rights and anti-apartheid movements. In a 2016 interview, Tiisetso Phetla, a recent graduate of Pretoria High School for Girls, was asked if she wore her hair natural since graduating from the exclusive school. Phetla replied, "All the time. I wear it with so much pride because my afro is my crown. I am an African queen. Why am I fighting to be African in Africa? If you can't be Black in Africa, where are we expected to be Black? Where can we be Black?"[3]

The transnational conversations created by Zulaikha Patel and her friends offer the perfect opening for a book about global Black girls' history. *The Global History of Black Girlhood* explores how scholars, artists, and activists think and write about Black girls' pasts. By confronting racist school policy, the South African schoolgirls' protests engaged in debates over the past, present, and future. Angela Davis explained, "Legacies of past struggles are not static. When past struggles are taken up by the new generation, they reveal unfulfilled promises."[4] Today, Black girls continue to be at the forefront of protests for Black Lives Matter, organizing marches with friends and pushing for change.

In some ways, this is nothing new. Black girls and young women often voice their frustration with sexism, racism, colorism, and economic inequality; yet until recently, historians have paid little attention to Black girls' opinions. The writers in this volume all believe that Black girls are worthy of historical study. What does history look like when we listen to Black girls, when we tell *their* stories? Some fundamental assumptions begin to shift. For example, simplistic distinctions between freedom and constraint turn to more nuanced analyses of how Black girls create arenas for self-expression while also answering to both adult and white supremacist authority. Black girls' creative self-fashionings reveal how young people reach back to the past to create new futures, and particularly how the significance of African ancestry has been continually refigured both on the continent and in far-flung regions of the world. Distinguishing stages of girlhood—early childhood, adolescence, young womanhood—reveals how each generation first learns about race, gender, and class domination in their families, friend groups, neighborhoods, and cities. These lessons make girls experts on the private dimensions of inequality and center issues such as colorism, access to leisure, and household work. The very questions of who counts as girl and what it means to be a girl take center stage as Black children often find themselves thrust into adult responsibilities sooner than others. As girls approach adolescence, youth emerges as a powerful means to gain public voice by representing the new, rebelling against elders, and articulating a generational identity. But, at the same time, youth remains a barrier to civic participation, a reason to delay speaking out, claiming rights, or defining an agenda. Sometimes never fully recognized as girls by dominant society, and facing a future of uncertain access to womanhood, Black girls hone a critical perspective on the social structures in which they live and imagine how they might live otherwise, launching themselves into the future not as qualified versions of white women or Black men, and certainly not as social problems, sexual objects, or surplus labor, but as "beautiful experiments" in new ways of living "as if they were free."[5]

The interdisciplinary field of Black girls' studies is an ethical orientation and a political praxis as well as a theoretical framework, a way of seeing the world *with* and *for* Black girls. This way of thinking rejects frameworks that construe Black girls as a problem and instead recognizes them as practitioners of creative genius.[6] Community-based Black women scholars have innovated participatory research methodologies that create space for Black girl brilliance and honor the integrity of their whole identities.[7] Saving Our Lives, Hear Our Truths (SOLHOT), founded by Ruth Nicole Brown in Urbana,

Illinois, in 2006, provides one influential model for how grown "homegirls" can work with middle-school-aged Black girls, not to control or correct them, but to create space for "Black girlhood celebration."[8] History is integral to this process, as a Black girlhood celebration participant, Nikky Finney, insists when she asks of Black girls' truthmaking: "What does it mean to have a twenty-first century sacred place for their 400-year-old, my-mother-was-not-inferior-and-I-am-not-inferior-either attitude?"[9]

What does it mean, as Finney suggests, to see this "I-am-not-inferior attitude" as a 400-year project of Black girlhood? One place to begin the story is with Phillis Wheatley. Wheatley was a young girl—only seven or eight—when traders in humans stole her from her home in West Africa. After the horrifying transatlantic journey across the sea, she landed in New England. She was a young, enslaved teenager when she published her first poem in a newspaper, and a teenager still, when she traveled to London in search of a benefactor for her writing career. At the age of nineteen or twenty, in 1773, Wheatley published her *Poems on Various Subjects, Religious and Moral.* Recognizing Wheatley as a transnational Black girl writer, who faced the trauma of the transatlantic slave trade and enslavement, sought freedom in her own writing, and traveled to England for her career, demonstrates that the creative genius of Black girlhood is nothing new. More than adding age to the familiar list of identity categories based on gender, race, and class, Black girls' studies is an epistemological revolution that demands a new understanding of who can produce knowledge and what counts as truth—and this revolution has been going on for a long time.[10]

Thus far, Black girls' studies has focused most centrally on African American girls living in the United States. Many of the theoretical frameworks for understanding Black girls' lives have been developed with American girls in mind. Concepts like "adultification," "the school-to-prison pipeline," and "stolen childhood" clarify the intersecting dynamics of race, gender, and age in the contexts of U.S. slavery, settler colonialism, Jim Crow segregation, and the dismantling of the U.S. welfare state.[11] It remains an open question whether these theoretical frameworks clarify or obscure Black girls' social positioning in other parts of the globe. What is the implication of "adultification"—the tendency to regard young Black girls as more "adult-like" than other children—for Black girls living in France, or for Black immigrant girls growing up in Italy? When girls in Jamaica or Nigeria get pushed out of school and into the criminal justice system, how should we conceive of this "school-to-prison" pipeline in majority Black contexts where social class may be more salient than racial difference? Given that understandings of age and life stage differed in Africa, does it make sense to think of girls enslaved on the continent as being robbed of their "childhood"? For Black Muslim girls, are there distinctly Islamic understandings of girlhood and womanhood to which we must attend, and do these differ in Africa, Europe, and North America? This book begins to answer some of these questions, but new frameworks and ways of thinking transnationally will develop in the coming years as scholars look to expand Black girls' studies. This volume seeks to advance the development of global frameworks through a comparative approach that brings together cutting-edge research on Black girls' pasts in different regions and time periods, testing how foundational concepts such as girlhood and blackness operate in different geographical and temporal contexts.

The history of Black girlhood is a subfield within Black girls' studies that employs a methodology rooted in archival research. Looking for Black girls in the past is difficult because we must turn to documents never meant to understand or preserve their truths. As Saidiya Hartman argues in her now iconic essay on the "violence of the archive," "Venus in Two Acts" (2008), the records produced by enslavers and colonizers preserve traces of Black girls' lives only at moments of violence, dispossession, and death. Asking how we can narrate these girls' stories from "the obscene descriptions that first introduced them to us" without reproducing that violence, Hartman posits informed speculation as a necessary methodology; her approach not only requires rich contextual knowledge about the past but also opens space for expressing "doubts, wishes, and possibilities" about what Black girls might have done, felt, seen, and desired before being disposed of in archival records.[12] Taking up this challenge, historians of Black girlhood have scoured archives for fragments of Black girls' lives, looked closely at visual and material culture for evidence of their embodied practices, reread experts who misconstrued but also preserved their words, and taken Black women's fiction seriously as a window on the facts of Black girls' experiences.[13] Local archivists and museum curators have enabled these efforts by re-cataloguing their collections to make Black girls' lives visible and self-consciously working to collect material produced by and for Black girls. Black girls themselves have joined these efforts, often by using digital platforms to preserve their political and cultural projects.

Searching for Black girls' stories can be hard. But sometimes finding their stories means coming to the archive with a radical vision that sees girls as *girls*—and employs age and generation as categories of analysis. When we start considering the age of our protagonists, for example, we notice that many of the icons of Black women's history were once girls themselves. For example, two iconic texts often used to teach African American women's history—Harriet Jacobs's *Incidents in the Life of a Slave Girl*, and Anne Moody's *Coming of Age in Mississippi*—are about girls and girlhood in ways that their authors emphasize but many readers overlook.[14] Jacobs and Moody rewrite the history of slavery and civil rights through their coming-of-age experiences, revealing not only how gender, race, and age intersect to endanger and constrain Black girls but also how Black girls' critical perspectives open up revolutionary possibilities for reconfiguring public and private life so that Black girls can be seen, heard, and valued in all their creative brilliance. It is not just African American texts that have sought to make visible Black girls' rich and complicated worlds. Afro-German writer Ika Hügel-Marshall dealt with the question of Black girl invisibility head on when she published *Invisible Woman: Growing up Black in Germany* in 1998. Writing about her life as a Black biracial girl living in Germany after World War II, Hügel-Marshall narrated a story of rejection and of finding her communities.[15] Many other key texts, some fiction, others "biomythographies,"[16] detail Black girlhood in its transnational contours. Caribbean writers such as Évelyne Trouillot weave archival research and fictional imaginings into the genre of "neo-slave narratives" that envision what the early years of the transatlantic slave trade might have meant for the West African and Creole girls who never had the chance to document their own stories.[17] Black women artists take up the visual archives of slavery, colonialism, and segregation to prompt new questions about how Black girls' pasts shape the present, as for example when African-American photographer Carrie Mae Weems repurposes archival images of the Hampton Institute, or South African photographer Z'étoile Imma creates representations of lesbian and trans youth that unsettle legacies of colonial violence and push back against outsiders' misrepresentation of LGBTI people in Africa as "victims rather than victors."[18] Interdisciplinary at its core, Black girls' history insists on using creative methodologies to understand the limits of archival evidence and consider how informed speculation, memoir, fiction, and visual art can access traces of the past missing from the documentary record but nonetheless surviving in social structures, memories, and cultural forms that carry the imprint of the past within the present. What unifies these various methods into a distinct field is a commitment to understanding the lives of Black girls as different from Black women, Black boys, or white children. Scholars have begun to map how the history of childhood, colonialism, slavery, and emancipation shift when considered from the standpoint of Black girls, findings that we survey in the remainder of this introduction before pointing out directions for future research.

Black Girls Disrupting the History of Girlhood

Rather than trying to shoehorn Black girls into histories that universalize the experience of other girls, historians have recently shifted to analyzing how distinctions within the category "girl" function to sustain and naturalize large-scale projects of racialization, colonialism, and economic inequality.

When European traders in humans first transported Africans to the Americas, a "girl" was a servant of any age. Additionally, many European cultures emphasized that all children were born sinful in need of salvation. But by the late eighteenth century when democratic revolutions spread across the Atlantic world, the definition of "girl" had changed. In this new definition, a young girl child needed protection because of her innocence—but for Anglo-Americans and white Europeans, this girl was usually construed as white or, in some colonial contexts, the mixed-race daughter of a white father.[19] In Europe and North America, enlightenment educators and Romantics celebrated the innocence of childhood by idealizing young, white girls.[20] As historian Robin Bernstein points out, the white, Victorian ideal of the tender and vulnerable white child—most often pictured as a little blonde and blue-eyed girl—split off from the slanderous caricature of the Black "pickaninny" comically impervious to pain. These white supremacist cultural scripts allowed for the violent exploitation of Black children, while naturalizing whiteness as the embodiment of innocence.[21] This racial distinction took shape within families and households, as enslavers and colonizers assigned young Black girls the tasks of caring for, and sometimes playing with, more privileged girls in the same household.[22]

Those protected girls, most often white, became schoolgirls by the late nineteenth century as propertied families focused on their daughters' education through their late teenage years.[23] A global movement to protect adolescent girls mobilized to raise the age of consent for sex and marriage while the category of the "delinquent" or "wayward" girl emerged to identify those whose purported lack of chastity, often the result of sexual abuse or highly constrained choices, justified incarceration. The creation of juvenile justice granted Black girls and other girls of color some recognition as children, distinct from adults, but at the same time rendered them vulnerable to new forms of state-sponsored violence. As parole programs channeled Black girls into domestic service, Black girls again found themselves answering to other girls who functioned, along with their mothers, as agents of state-sponsored segregation and violence.[24]

The spread of youth culture in the late nineteenth and early twentieth century offered new possibilities and new forms of exclusion as "the teenager" came to be associated with consumption, cheap amusements, and, sometimes, rebellion against adult authority. Peer culture replaced protection as the hallmark of girlhood, but whiteness remained as central to the teen girl as it had been to the angelic child. As images of the "modern girl" with her independent spirit, painted lips, and bobbed hair circulated around the globe in the 1920s and 1930s, marketers sold skin lighteners and hair straighteners to nonwhite women who hoped to approximate this new ideal. In response,

Black girls honed new skills for navigating color hierarchies within families and communities.[25] After the second World War, as marketers divided girlhood into ever narrower slices of tween, teen, and YA, their target audience remained largely white or proximate to whiteness. Black girls watched their own sense of style get repackaged for other people's profit, a dynamic that intensified with digitally circulating girlhoods in the twenty-first century. Black girls used digital media to express themselves and build community.[26] Even as democracies around the world committed to supposedly post-racial futures, Black girls learned early in life that racism and colorism remained powerful forces with which they would have to contend.[27] In short, as the meaning of girlhood changed from the sixteenth century to the present, a persistent anti-blackness remained fundamental to the category, requiring Black girls, and often other girls of color, to disrupt girlhood in order to be seen as girls. Black girls' attempts to be seen as girls requires fighting against racist definitions of who counts as innocent, as young, as worthy of protection.

To find Black girls' articulations of self, historians search for archival evidence that reveals how Black girls, often with the collaboration of Black women, turned constraint into possibility and expressed their own ideas about what it meant to be a girl. Historians have employed various frameworks including the social history of work and kinship, the cultural and political history of respectability, the importance of pleasure, and the possibilities for recognizing queer childhoods. Taking the first approach, Wilma King helped found the field of Black childhood studies as a problem of *Stolen Childhood*. She documented how enslavers and employers in the nineteenth-century United States forced Black children to work at young ages, denied them education, and separated them from their families, but also how Black children and their enslaved communities created spaces for nurturance and play, forestalling adult responsibilities as long as possible.[28] Building on King's insights, historians detailed distinct life stages under slavery, documenting how enslaved children and their kin sometimes managed to delay the onset of adult responsibilities, creating spaces for play and nurturance during the early and mid-years of childhood, before the teen years brought heightened threats of sale, sexual violence, and exploitation.[29] These historians provide a broad context for understanding the life stages Harriet Jacobs narrated in *Incidents in the Life of a Slave Girl*, particularly her often-quoted remembrance: "I now entered on my fifteenth year—a sad epoch in the life of a slave girl."[30] Antislavery activists mobilized this "prematurely knowing" enslaved girl as a rallying cry for abolishing slavery in order to protect girls from violation.[31]

Looking to the Caribbean, historians identify how high mortality rates intensified reproductive pressures on teenaged girls, truncating their girlhood while also increasing enslavers' investments in their health and cathecting the maternal-child bond with the potential for both exploitation and resistance.[32] In majority Black contexts, both on Caribbean islands and in cities such as New Orleans, the mixed-race daughters of planters could sometimes use white kinship bonds to gain protection, access education, control property, and travel, but they also found that prejudice within white families intensified racial difference, especially around questions of whom they could marry and what they could inherit.[33]

Black girls growing up free in the midst of slavery faced intense pressures to model an ideal comportment that would demonstrate fitness for full citizenship despite economic pressures that forced them to work early in life and often limited their employment options to domestic service.[34] Harriet Wilson's *Our Nig* (1859) revealed how white women in supposedly free households imposed racial violence upon Black and mixed-race girls left to nurture themselves into womanhood.[35]

Worldwide, the abolition of chattel slavery—which proceeded through fits and starts over the long course of the nineteenth century—exposed Black girls to new forms of coerced labor while also creating new possibilities for negotiating freedom. Whether in United States or French Soudan, indentured servitude, guardianship, and marriage functioned to control girls' labor after the end of slavery.[36] The ways girls navigated these coercive demands, choosing whom to obey, reveal uncomfortable links between the history of slavery and girlhood as states of unfreedom that can also authorize forms of consent. The demands that kinfolk made on girls' labor could resemble slavery.[37] Freedom never meant simple autonomy for young girls who longed for relational forms of dependence that would enable them to be treasured, nurtured, and protected, in other words, to be recognized as girls.[38] Girls working as domestic servants often found themselves forced to play with more privileged girls, navigating demands that they be both carefree children and full-time workers.[39]

Studies of slavery, emancipation, and segregated labor thus reveal the historical roots of what contemporary sociologists refer to as "adultification," that is, the tendency of adults to see Black girls as older and less innocent than other girls their age.[40] These histories also document how Black girls made sense of and reconfigured these misunderstandings, tracing a genealogy of "what girls know," which is that *they* are not the problem—inequality, discrimination, and exploitation are problems—and they are *girls*, though girls on their own terms.

Attending to the history of Black girls' self-expression also reveals that many want to be adults, not the exploitative "adultification" imposed upon them, to be sure, but the desire to be grown, to answer to nobody but themselves, to explore the world, express their sexualities, and create their own futures. Black girls often insist on their difference from Black women at precisely the moment they want to define themselves as young women and no longer be seen as girls. Historians have explored generational rebellion in relation to the "politics of respectability," through which Black women fought to distinguish their self-worth from racist stereotypes and claim equal citizenship.[41] African American adults invested in Black children as the future of the race, and especially in Black girls as potential mothers.[42] As LaKisha Simmons found in her study of Black girls coming of age in Jim Crow New Orleans, Black girls lived within a "double bind" between white supremacy, enforced by white people's insults and potential for sexualized violence, and respectability, imposed by Black adults hoping for a better future. Girls' subjectivity—their self-making, their feelings, their dreams for the future—formed between these two poles as girls found spaces to play, read, write, and express their fantasies, privately or in public spaces such as the YMCA or a Mardi Gras parade.[43] Similarly, Black girls moving to Chicago during the Great Migration recognized themselves in their elders hopes and fears, but also sampled new forms of consumer culture, employment, and religious expression through which they claimed their own rights as "child citizens . . . and critiqued the failure of adults to guide them."[44]

Ideas of respectability and delinquency traveled through colonial networks to Africa and the Caribbean, but expressed themselves differently in majority Black contexts where class was often more salient than race. As Abosede George demonstrates in her history of *Making Modern Girls* in Lagos, Nigeria, western-educated native women at the turn of the twentieth-century wanted to "save" working class Black girls by keeping them in school, even as girl hawkers continued labor practices that they and their families understood as fundamental to girlhood.[45] In colonial Mombasa, Kenya, it was mission-educated fathers who sought to keep their daughters in school, while mothers and grandmothers pressed initiation into womanhood and marriage.[46] In these regions, as in other parts of the world, Black girls responded to multiple ideas about what a proper girl should do even as the categories of "Black" and "girl" continued to disrupt each other.

The global civil rights, Black Power, and anti-apartheid movements opened up new possibilities for Black girls to redefine respectability through political activism. In the United States, the fight to desegregate public schools turned Black girls into symbols and agents of social change. Black youth in general, and girls in particular, used their aspirations for the future to present themselves as more capable of solving racial problems than adults, and often pushed for more militant tactics.[47] As girls joined social movements, they developed their capacities to resist state-sponsored violence and sexual harassment, developing a new sense of their own power.[48] Girls coming of age at the turn of the twenty-first century drew on these icons of militant Black girlhood to help craft new forms of political expression on emerging digital platforms, circulating distinctly Black expressive practices that envisioned what empowerment looked like for girls who wanted to be fully in control of their own bodies but did not yet want to be seen as women.[49] As anthropologist Aimee Meredith Cox documents in her work at the Fresh Start Shelter in Detroit, Black girls "shapeshift" through complex choreographies that reconfigure narratives of "problem" Black girls to clarify that they are inherently valuable, care worthy, and creative citizens, and as Savannah Shange argues, girls' everyday acts of willful defiance work to disrupt pervasive antiblackness that structures even progressive school settings.[50]

Recently, historians have challenged respectability frameworks, and looked beyond the violence, coercion, and incarceration so well documented in the history of Black childhood, to focus on Black girls' pleasures. Informed by Hip Hop feminism but rooted in archival research, these historians recover Black girls' ordinary joys, friendships, and play.[51] These pleasures might include the erotic, but neither begin nor end with sexual experience.[52] Whether in colonial New England or twentieth-century Johannesburg, Black girls found pleasure in friendships, fashion, reading, daydreaming, and fooling around.[53] As Kyra Gaunt insightfully argues, the "games Black girls play," such as double-dutch and clapping rhythms, enabled girls to toy with both respectable and transgressive embodiments of Black womanhood.[54]

Sometimes the self-inventions of Black girlhood lead not to Black womanhood but to Black manhood or a gender nonconforming identity. Historians looking to identify the gender-fluid practices of Black girls in the past have only just begun to fill in a picture of Black girlhood that does not depend upon a binary opposition between girls and boys or the assumption that Black girls are always future women. As C. Riley Snorton asserts, we still need to "find a vocabulary for Black and trans life." Asking what pasts have been erased to separate the histories of blackness and transness, Snorton opens up a more expansive recognition of how Black girls bring their full humanity into being.[55] Anya Wallace urges us to recognize that kin networks built on Black women's love for each other offer an underappreciated resource too often left out of Black girl memoirs, while Savannah Shange makes visible how "Black queer common sense" gets passed down from older women to Black girls.[56] Accounting for queer childhoods in Africa, meanwhile, requires recognizing how categories of gender and sexuality operate differently in diverse indigenous cultures and in post-colonial government regulations.[57] Centering histories of queer childhood on Black subjects suggests that reproductive heterosexuality is far from the only framework for understanding how adults value children or how children imagine themselves.[58]

Whether through their labor, kin relations, comportment, pleasures, or queerness, Black girls have disrupted assumptions about girlhood throughout the history of slavery, colonialism, and postcolonialism. Black girls have long honed what educator Charlotte E. Jacobs refers to as "Black girl critical literacies," that is they used their "competencies to recognize, process, and respond to messages that they receive connected to their status as Black adolescent girls . . . while simultaneously crafting their own sense of Black girl identities."[59] By adopting a comparative historical framework, this volume provides nuanced contextual histories that track how Black girls responded to changing definitions of girlhood and how they drew upon local resources to express their own understandings of what girls are and what they need.

Girling Blackness

If Black girls disrupt girlhood, they also raise persistent questions about what it means to be Black. Before the Black Power movement of the 1960s, many girls with African ancestry thought of themselves not as Black but as colored or Negro. Some emphasized their mixed-race ancestry or saw their familial, religious, ethnic, or national identity as more important than an abstract racial category. Black girls got told they were too Black or not Black enough. Retrospectively uniting such girls under the rubric of blackness risks misreading their experience. Yet, uniting them around a shared history proves worth the risk as it reveals how girls in different times and places make sense of ancestral connections to Africa, position themselves within the African diaspora, and confront global anti-blackness. Blackness functions as a political framework that identifies common threads of lived experience, shared self-identifications, and allied struggles against racism and colonialism.[60] At the same time, historians need to understand the particular identities forged by girls who thought of themselves in other terms and why many girls resisted or remixed globally circulating definitions of blackness. Stories of the past must trace moments of girls' racial belonging in the Black diaspora, pay attention to moments of transnational "misunderstanding," and locate moments where Black girls cannot or do not see themselves in a global framework.[61]

Key questions are the following: *when* and *how* did girls realize they were Black, or Negro, or colored, or whatever term circulated in their communities? In Zora Neale Hurston's novel *Their Eyes Were Watching God* (1937), Janie Crawford, age six, sees a photograph of herself with white classmates and realizes that she is Black.[62] Aoua Kéita, a political activist in the French colony of Soudan (now Mali), also understood her race in relationship to the other girls at her school. In her autobiography, *Femme d'Afrique: la vie*

Aoua Keïta racontée pare elle-même, Kéita explains that despite having two African parents (one from Guinea, the other from the Ivory Coast), she attended a school reserved for the "mixed raced" daughters of French colonial men. Kéita experienced teasing and violence, particularly because she was the top student.[63] Other girls learn that they are Black when mothers, grandmothers, and aunts instill a spirit of self-love and the skills necessary for self-expression. Some learn of their blackness from non-Black family members who see them as different.[64] By attending to when and how girls acquire such knowledge, Black girls' histories contribute to our understanding of how blackness takes shape over time.

For Black girls, color hierarchies within the Black community and within families often loomed as large as the question of blackness itself. Daughters whose color, hair, and features differed from their mothers or their sisters learned early in life that fine-grained distinctions within blackness could determine how others reacted and required distinct rituals for self-care and self-presentation. Girls' experiences reveal how racial identity forms not only through large-scale practices of segregation, state-sponsored violence, and racialized capitalism, but also at kitchen tables where mothers comb hair, in the laps of grandmothers who tell family stories, and on playgrounds where children tease and treasure each other. If feminists argue that the personal is political, and womanists add a spiritual dimension, as Porshé Garner argues, then Black girls offer a particular expertise on the private registers of political and spiritual survival. They also demonstrate the intergenerational dynamics that fuel historical change, or as Angela Davis put it to the girls at Pretoria High School: "When past struggles are taken up by the new generation, they reveal unfulfilled promises."[65]

The Question of Age

While focusing on age and generation as categories of analysis, the history of Black girlhood requires that we discard predetermined age thresholds and look at local contexts. Activists, NGOs, and girls themselves find chronological age useful for political purposes, but age categories fall apart as archival research turns up laws and regulatory mechanisms pinpointing the end of girlhood anywhere between age twelve to twenty-four or when indigenous cultures emphasize non-numeric understandings of age. The idea that girlhood ends at a specified age simply does not hold up in the archives. Better, historians find, to consider the meaning of chronological age in particular contexts alongside other metrics for measuring maturity such as life-cycle transitions (getting married, leaving school), bodily changes (menarche, childbirth), kin relationships (being a daughter or a ward), and peer cultures (shared intimacies and interests).[66]

When chronological age does matter to Black girls, historians must understand why, noting that chronological age itself has a history, one intertwined with the expansion of colonial power, the financing of the transatlantic slave trade, and Black people's struggle for democratic rights and national self-determination.[67] Black girls often had age imposed upon them, but they also took up age as a means of claiming protections, rights, and opportunities. Especially in the wake of legal emancipation, Black girls around the globe employed chronological age as a means of determining their own labor contracts, choosing marital partners, or demanding protections from guardians, social service providers, and government officials.[68] Chronological age thresholds around six and fifteen took on particular significance. The first could be used to define a stage of middle childhood when undifferentiated infants become boys or girls. The second could serve as a proxy for when puberty begins and turns girls into adolescents, teens, or young women.[69] Though responding to biological processes of human growth, these categories also derive meaning from the work of scientific experts. Doctors and social scientists, most of them white men, used normative stages of growth to idealize white masculinity as the standard while posing questions about whether females and nonwhite people matured too early, too late, or not at all.[70] In colonial encounters, different methods for recognizing and understanding female puberty proved a particularly rich site for controversy as fathers, mothers, daughters, local elites, and foreign colonizers all jockeyed for the power to determine how and when girls should properly become women. Meanwhile, bodies themselves varied as the age of menarche differed for individuals and under different historical conditions.[71] Far from being a neutral or universal category, chronological age offers a paradigmatic example of how people impose abstract categories upon the variable experience of individual lives and how those categories always remain incomplete and ripe for transformation.

A full understanding of "girl" as a category also requires attending to how mature women—mothers with children, even aged grandmothers—often define themselves as girls to create spaces of freedom and intimacy that they associate with girlishness. "Girl," "girlfriend," "homegirl," even "baby," call out relationships of mutuality, trust, and affection that do not depend upon chronological age or generational standing.[72] Unfortunately, "girl" can also be a hostile demand imposed by white people or more privileged people who refuse to recognize Black women as women. We must reckon with this contradictory and slippery language if we seek to understand what it means to be a girl.

Making Space for Black Girls in the History of Black Feminism

Defending, nurturing, and valuing Black girls has inspired Black feminist organizing around the world. In the United States, for example, concern for girls inspired African American women from Maria Stewart in the 1830s, through the National Association of Colored Women's Clubs in the 1890s, to civil rights and Black power activists in the 1960s. Leading Black feminists often found their voice in advocating for girls, such as when Anna Julia Cooper challenged Black male ministers to insist that more resources be invested in "the *Colored Girls* of the South."[73] This long history of Black women working for and with Black girls is an integral legacy of Black feminist thought and praxis. Clarifying the global history of Black girlhood, however, requires recognizing moments when the interests of Black girls are not the same as those of Black women and when girls develop forms of self-expression that force adult Black feminists to change their ideas of what liberation looks like and how it can be achieved.

Many Black feminists come to their own self-consciousness as activists and theorists in their girlhood. Zulaikha Patel continues to self-identify as an activist, and two years after organizing protests against her schools' hair policy, she co-organized anti-rape protests with other teens at the Magistrate Court in Pretoria, South Africa, alongside activist Boitumelo Thage. In social media posts, at talks, and in organizations, Patel continues to advocate for other Black girls. On Instagram she posted, "Black girl, spill your impossible scripture. Black girl rewrite those pages you were erased from. Liberate us."[74]

Making space for Black girlhood within the history of Black feminism is complicated but worthwhile. Black girls create visions of the future that differ from those of Black women, assert generational identities that revolutionize institutions and intimate relationships, and insist that age matters as a category of identity. When Black girls grow up to be Black men or genderqueer people, space opens up within Black feminism to embrace queer lives in new ways. Girlhood becomes a shared site of feminist organizing that does not rely on an unquestioned assumption that girls are women in the making, that women are always former girls, or that girls are all assigned the label "girl" at birth.

Distinguishing girls from adults is a theoretical challenge for Black feminists and also a more mundane methodological challenge for historians seeking to identify archival materials. The tendency to mistake Black girls for mature women shapes archives as well as social policy, with many sources about Black girls hidden by the keyword "women" and searches for "girls" turning up representations of young women, often overtly sexualized by pornographic meanings of the word girl.[75] The shifting language of race also presents a challenge. Entering the phrase "Black" in an archival search engine will miss sources that archivists catalogued as "negro," "colored," "African," or "slave." Finding Black girls in archives thus requires patience, a willingness to employ numerous categories, and the curiosity to look in unexpected places.

The "In-Between" Space of Black Girlhood

In her study of *Black Girlhood in the Nineteenth Century*, Nazera Wright argues that African American girls existed in an in-between space, a state of not quite belonging, because of life stage and the history of blackness: "As raced, gendered, and youthful figures, Black girls occupy a space of in-betweenness . . . not yet citizens and not yet women."[76] Black girls come of age within a matrix of domination that targets their blackness, their gender, and their youth.[77] This standpoint at the intersection of multiple oppressions renders them vulnerable to exploitation and violence, but also opens up possibilities for critiquing and reimagining how girlhood functions to anchor notions of ideal citizenship and reproductive heterosexuality. The in-between space of not white girls and not-yet Black women provides a standpoint for imagining new futures, demanding justice, living wholeness, and loving in new ways.[78] Black girls' "ability to use their states of ambiguity and renewal to unsettle traditions and alter preconceived notions," Wright argues, "is but one example of their latent power."[79]

Black feminist theorist Hortense Spillers provides a methodology for analyzing the vulnerabilities and revolutionary potential of Black girls when she argues that five hundred years of slavery and discrimination functioned as an "ungendering" process that removed people of African descent from the "grammar book" of American gender categories premised on mother/father, daughter/son. Stolen from their families and forced into the holds of ships, Africans lost their names and their status in kinship networks. Enslavers reduced them to undifferentiated "flesh," turning men, women, and children into "Negroes" or "Slaves." Once they embarked to the New World, these Black women and their daughters never had unreserved claims to womanhood, Spillers argues. Blackness placed Black women "*out* of the traditional symbolics of female gender." Clearing away misperceptions of Black womanhood, Spillers argues, requires that we be "less interested in joining the ranks of gendered femaleness than gaining the *insurgent* ground as female social subject."[80] This "insurgent ground" offers the revolutionary potential for Black women to name their own experience not as akin to white women, but as their whole, fully human selves. By focusing on youth, Wright adds that Black girls contribute an intensified investment in imagining new futures because of their age-based sense of becoming women and their awareness that the standard "grammar" will never apply to them.

If Black people were "ungendered" by processes of slavery, capitalism, and modernity, then we might also understand how these same processes placed Black children "out of time" or without specific age. Habiba Ibrahim develops the idea of Black age—a timeframe that is out-of-step with dominant Western notions of time, history, and age-categories. Following the work of Black feminists of the 1970s, Ibrahim explains that "racial capitalism distorts black gendered age into something untimely, and thus inhuman."[81] For Ibrahim, "untimely" means thinking about how Black age is "unrecognized, undervalued, or disavowed residue" by white social structures.[82] Like Spillers, Ibrahim sees revolutionary potential in probing what lies in the space of the undervalued. She wonders what we might find without sticking to "hegemonic categories of gender and life stages" and we instead seek new ways of relating to one another across gender and generations.[83]

In this book, we argue that seeing the revolutionary potential of Black girls requires recognizing their desires as sometimes distinct from those of Black women. Spillers focused on adult Black women's sexuality, finding in blues singers one example of mature Black women's "being for self." Watching Bessie Smith perform, Spillers saw her disrupt the "sexual universe" in which Black women remained "unvoiced, misseen, not doing, awaiting *their* verb." Smith conveyed the attitude that, for Black women, "sexuality is precisely the physical expression of the highest self-regard."[84] But what of Black girls who might want to be seen as *not yet* sexual, as having self-regard rooted in peer friendships, learning new things, and being nurtured by others? How do they express "being for self"? Spillers places her hope for articulating the truth of Black womanhood in contextualized histories that analyze Black women's subject formation not in relation to white women, but to other women of color around the world.[85] Surely adding girls to this project offers a resource for Black feminism and for girls themselves. As Zulaikha Patel learned when told not to wear her natural hair at a girls' school, expressing blackness requires disrupting girlhood and creating communities for affirming Black girls in spaces built to exclude them. In the process, Black girls reconfigure for every generation what it means to be a girl and what it means to be Black.

Adopting a global framework for the history of Black girlhood also shifts attention to contexts where class, ethnicity, and religious affiliation sometimes matter more than race in creating normative categories of girlhood. In majority Black contexts, access to a protected girlhood dedicated to a future of idealized motherhood depends upon middle-class status, access to colonial or missionary schools, and membership in a privileged racial group that is not necessarily white.[86] By positioning the category of Black girlhood in relation to "girl of color" configurations, as well as to the better-known ideals of white girlhood that emerged from Northern Europe and North America, historians and Black feminists can better appreciate how girlhood functions to shore up ideas of racial difference, social class, and national identity around the world, and how Black girls disrupt categories of girlhood both by affiliating with other girls and insisting on the distinctiveness of their blackness. As Black girls in Africa, Europe, and the Americas imagine themselves into a global category of Black girlhood, they create a diasporic space of in-betweenness that is both everywhere and nowhere. This is the in-betweenness that fueled Tiisetso Phetla's searing question: "If you can't be Black in Africa . . . Where can we be Black?"[87]

This anthology builds on existing histories of Black girlhood to prompt greater attention to the questions of who counts as a girl, how girls define blackness, and how girls imagine their place in a global African diaspora. Whereas many historians of Black girlhood have narrowed their topic with predefined parameters based on age and gender, these essays open up definitions of girlhood to include Black women who call each other girls; girls who work full time but want to be protected or to participate in teen culture; girls and grown women who contest the meaning of play; and girls who grow up to be men. To understand how girls define blackness, contributors consider mixed-race girls in the colonial period navigating transnational kin networks; African American schoolgirls after the Civil War creating interracial friendships; Progressive Era girls testing the limits of segregated juvenile justice; and the children of Black GIs and German mothers searching for belonging in the aftermath of World War II. How girls imagined the African diaspora becomes apparent when Black girls stage a play about the Haitian Revolution; when girls in Jamaican reform schools confront Black adults with colonial attitudes toward race; when high school students in the Black Power Era look to Africa for new beauty standards; and when activists from the United States and South Africa reflect together on how girlhood shaped their commitment to Black liberation. By bringing histories focused on different regions and time periods to bear on a shared theme, this anthology aims to prompt a deeper understanding of what Black girls share across time and space and what does not translate from one context to another.

To date, the history of Black girlhood has developed through focused study on particular times and places, a method necessitated by the difficulty of finding Black girls in archival sources. This volume begins to move beyond this local approach to prompt more thinking about continuity and change, the local and the global. Contributors to this anthology engage in a conversation across disciplines and historical subfields to consider three key questions posed by Black girls' history: What does it mean to be a girl? What is the meaning of blackness when seen from girls' perspectives, in different times and places? And, how have Black girls imagined themselves as part of a global African diaspora? Each section begins with a short introduction that highlights the creative knowledge practices of contemporary Black girls and then asks how historical inquiry offers a resource for understanding the issues these girls raise. By considering both the local and the global, this anthology offers new possibilities for understanding how Black girls create themselves by making history. The work gathered here is only a beginning. Our hope is that this anthology opens up new possibilities for understanding the past from the perspective of Black girls who lived long ago and offers a useful tool to Black girls in the present who want to take up the challenge of researching and reinterpreting Black girls' history.

Notes

1. Zulaikha Patel, email message to author, February 14, 2021.

2. Tanisha Ford, *Liberated Threads: Black Women, Style and the Global Politics of Soul* (Chapel Hill: University of North Carolina Press, 2015).

3. "Girls At South African High School Protesting Hair and Language Bans," transcript, in *Weekend Edition*, NPR, September 4, 2016, accessed May 30, 2017, http://www.npr.org/2016/09/04/492599435/girls-at-south-african-high-school-protesting-hair-and-language-bans.

4. Loyiso Sidimba, "Zulaikha Patel Impresses Angela Davis," *Sowetan LIVE*, September 12, 2016, accessed May 30, 2017, http://www.sowetanlive.co.za/news/2016/09/12/zulaikha-patel-impresses-angela-davis.

5. Saidiya Hartman, *Wayward Lives, Beautiful Experiments: Intimate Histories of Social Upheaval* (New York: W. W. Norton, 2019), xiii.

6. Tammy C. Owens, Durell M. Callier, Jessica L. Robinson, and Porshé R. Garner, "Towards an Interdisciplinary Field of Black Girlhood Studies," *Departures in Critical Qualitative Research* 6, no. 3 (Fall 2017): 116–132; Julia S. Jordan-Zachery and Duchess Harris, *Black Girl Magic Beyond the Hashtag: Twenty-First Century Acts of Self-Definition* (Tucson: University of Arizona Press, 2019).

7. Treva B. Lindsey, "Let Me Blow Your Mind: Hip Hop Feminist Futures in Theory and Praxis," *Urban Education* 50, no. 1 (2015): 52–77; see for example, Joyce Ladner, "Tomorrow's Tomorrow: A Twenty-Five-Year Retrospective," in *Tomorrow's Tomorrow: The Black Woman*, reprint ed. (1971; Lincoln: University of Nebraska Press, 1995); Rebecca Carroll, *Sugar in the Raw: Voices of Young Black Girls in America* (New York: Three Rivers Press, 1997); Kyra D. Gaunt, *The Games Black Girls Play: Learning the Ropes from Double-Dutch to Hip-Hop* (New York: New York University Press, 2006); Oneka LaBennett, *She's Mad Real: Popular Culture and West Indian Girls in Brooklyn* (New York: New York University Press, 2011); Bettina L. Love, *Hip Hop's Li'l Sistas*

Speak: Negotiating Hip-Hop Identities and Politics in the New South (New York: Peter Lang, 2012); Aimee Meredith Cox, *Shapeshifters: Black Girls and the Choreography of Citizenship* (Durham: Duke University Press, 2015).

8. "SOLHOT," Ruth Nicole Brown, accessed April 24, 2020, https://www.ruthnicolebrown.com/solhot. Ruth Nicole Brown, *Hear Our Truths: The Creative Potential of Black Girlhood* (Urbana: University of Illinois Press, 2014); Ruth Nicole Brown, *Black Girlhood Celebration: Toward a Hip-Hop Feminist Pedagogy* (New York: Peter Lang, 2009); Ruth Nicole Brown and Chamara Jewl Kwakye, *Wish to Live: The Hip-Hop Feminism Pedagogy Reader* (New York: Peter Lang, 2012).

9. Nikky Finney, "Pinky Swear," *Black Girlhood Celebration*, accessed April 24, 2020, https://www.solhot.com

10. Crystal Lynn Webster, "The History of Black Girls and the Field of Black Girl Studies: At the Forefront of Academic Scholarship," *American Historian* (March 2020). For non-U.S. sources, see the writings of Chimamanda Ngozi Adichie, Évelyne Trouillot, Edwidge Danticat, and the Afro-German anthology *Farbe Bekennen* (1986), translated as *Showing Our Colors*, among many others.

11. Rebecca Epstein, Jamilia J. Blake, and Thalia González, "Girlhood Interrupted: The Erasure of Black Girls' Childhood," (Washington, D.C.: Georgetown Law Center on Poverty and Inequality, 2017). https://www.law.georgetown.edu/poverty-inequality-center/wp-content/uploads/sites/14/2017/08/girlhood-interrupted.pdf; Monique Morris, *Pushout: The Criminalization of Black Girls in Schools* (New York: The New Press, 2016); Wilma King, *Stolen Childhood: Slave Youth in Nineteenth-Century America*, 2nd ed. (Bloomington: Indiana University Press, 2011).

12. Saidiya Hartman, "Venus in Two Acts," *Small Axe* 12, no. 2 (June 2008): 1–14.

13. LaKisha Michelle Simmons, *Crescent City Girls: The Lives of Young Black Women in Segregated New Orleans* (Chapel Hill: University of North Carolina Press, 2015); Paula Austin, *Coming of Age in Jim Crow DC: Navigating the Politics of Everyday Life* (New York: New York University, 2019); Robin Bernstein, *Racial Innocence: Performing American Childhood from Slavery to Civil Rights* (New York: New York University Press, 2011); Nazera Wright, *Black Girlhood in the Nineteenth Century* (Urbana: University of Illinois Press, 2016); Maria W. Stewart and Eric Gardner, "Two Texts on Children and Christian Education," *PMLA* 123, no. 1 (January 2008): 156–65.

14. Harriet Jacobs, *Incidents in the Life of a Slave Girl: Written by Herself*, ed. Jean Fagan Yellin (Cambridge: Harvard University Press, 1987); Anne Moody, *Coming of Age in Mississippi* (New York: Bantam Dell, 1968).

15. Sonya Donaldson, "'How Does it Feel to Be a Problem?': Black German Girlhood and the Historical Entanglements of Nation," *Women, Gender, and Families of Color* 7.1 (2019): 12–36.

16. Audre Lorde calls her autobiography a "biomythography," a narrative built from myth, history, and autobiographical writing. See Lorde, *Zami: A New Spelling of My Name* (New York: Random House, 1982). Other writers who have written coming-of-age stories that combine the autobiographical and fictional include Zora Neal Hurston, Maryse Condé, and Nella Larsen.

17. Évelyne Trouillot, *The Infamous Rosalie* (Lincoln: University of Nebraska Press, 2013); Ashraf H. A. Rushdy, *Neo-slave Narratives: Studies in the Social Logic of a Literary Form* (New York: Oxford University Press, 1999).

18. http://carriemaeweems.net/; Zanele Muholi, *Faces and Phases* (London: Prestel, 2010); Z'étoile Imma, "(Re)visualizing Black Lesbian Lives, (Trans)masculinity, and Township Space in the Documentary Work of Zanele Muholi," *Journal of Lesbian Studies* 21, no. 2 (2017): 228.

19. Daniel Livesay, *Children of Uncertain Fortune: Mixed-Race Jamaicans in Britain and the Atlantic Family, 1733–1833* (Chapel Hill: Omohundro Institute, University of North Carolina Press, 2018); Jennifer Palmer, *Intimate Bonds: Family and Slavery in the French Atlantic* (Philadelphia: University of Pennsylvania Press, 2016).

20. Miriam Forman-Brunell and Leslie Paris, eds., *The Girls' History and Culture Reader: The Nineteenth Century* (Urbana: University of Illinois Press, 2011); Steven Mintz, *Huck's Raft: A History of American Childhood* (Cambridge: Belknap, 2004); Jennifer Helgren and Colleen Vasconcellos, eds., *Girlhood: A Global History*, (Rutgers: Rutgers University Press, 2010).

21. Bernstein, *Racial Innocence*, Chapter 1.

22. Stephanie Jones-Rogers, *They were Her Property: White Women as Slave Owners in the American South* (New Haven: Yale University Press, 2019), 1–24; King, *Stolen Childhood*; Jonathan Blagbrough and Cary Craig, "'When I Play with the Master's Children, I Must Always Let Them Win': Child Domestic Labor," in *Child Slavery Before and After Emancipation: An Argument for Child-Centered Slavery Studies*, ed. Anna Mae Duane (New York: Cambridge University Press, 2017), 251–69.

23. Jane Hunter, *How Young Ladies Became Girls* (New Haven: Yale University Press, 2002); Corrie Decker, "Fathers, Daughters, and Institutions: Coming of Age in Mombasa's Colonial Schools," in *Girlhood: A Global History*, 268–88.

24. Michele Mitchell, *Righteous Propagation: African Americans and the Politics of Racial Destiny After Reconstruction* (Chapel Hill: University of North Carolina Press, 2004); Laura Lovett, *Conceiving the Future: Pronatalism, Reproduction, and the Family in the United States, 1890–1938* (Chapel Hill: University of North Carolina Press, 2007); Abosede George, *Making Modern Girls: A History of Childhood, Labor, and Social Development in Colonial Lagos* (Athens, OH: Ohio University Press, 2014); Lindsey Elizabeth Jones, "'The Most Unprotected of All Human Beings': Black Girls, State Violence, and the Limits of Protection in Jim Crow Virginia," *Souls: A Critical Journal of Black Politics, Culture, and Society* 20, no. 1 (January-March 2018): 14–37; Tera Eva Agyepong, *The Criminalization of Black Children: Race, Gender, and Delinquency in Chicago's Juvenile Justice System, 1899–1945* (Chapel Hill: University of North Carolina Press, 2018); Ashwini Tambe, *Defining Girlhood in India: A Transnational History of Sexual Maturity Laws* (Chicago: University of Illinois Press, 2019).

25. Alys Eve Weinbaum, Lynn M. Thomas, Priti Ramamurthy, Uta G. Poiger, Madeleine Yue Dong, and Tani E. Barlow, eds., *The Modern Girl Around the World: Consumption, Modernity, and Globalization* (Durham: Duke University Press, 2008); Simmons, *Crescent City Girls*; Treva B. Lindsey, *Colored No More: Reinventing Black Womanhood in Washington, D.C.* (Urbana: University of Illinois Press, 2017).

26. Kyra Gaunt, "YouTube, Twerking & You: Context Collapse and the Handheld Co-Presence of Black Girls and Miley Cyrus," *Journal of Popular Music Studies* 27, no. 3 (2015): 244–73.

27. Patricia Hill Collins, *Black Feminist Thought: Knowledge, Consciousness, and the Politics of Empowerment,* 2nd ed. (1990; New York: Routledge, 2000), 91–93; Habiba Ibrahim, *Troubling the Family: The Promise of Personhood and the Rise of Multiracialism* (Minneapolis: University of Minnesota Press, 2012); Lori L. Tharps, *Same Family Different Colors: Confronting Colorism in America's Diverse Families* (Boston: Beacon, 2016).

28. King, *Stolen Childhood.*

29. Marie Jenkins Schwartz, *Born in Bondage: Growing up Enslaved in the Antebellum South* (Cambridge, MA: Harvard University Press, 2000); Daina Ramey Berry, *The Price for Their Pound of Flesh: The Value of the Enslaved, from Womb to Grave, in the Building of a Nation* (Boston: Beacon Press, 2017).

30. Jacobs, *Incidents in the Life of a Slave Girl, 27.*

31. Wright, *Black Girlhood,* 10–14; Wilma King, "'Prematurely Knowing of Evil Things': The Sexual Abuse of African American Girls and Young Women in Slavery and Freedom," *The Journal of African-American History* 99, no. 3 (2014): 173–96.

32. Colleen Vasconcellos *Slavery, Childhood, and Abolition in Jamaica, 1788–1838* (Athens: University of Georgia Press, 2015).

33. Livesay, *Children of Uncertain Fortune.*

34. Wright, *Black Girlhood*; Hilary J. Moss, *Schooling Citizens: The Struggle for African American Education in Antebellum America* (Chicago: University of Chicago Press, 2009); Kabria Baumgartner, *In Pursuit of Knowledge: Black Women and Educational Activism in Antebellum America* (New York: New York University Press, 2019).

35. Harriet E. Wilson, *Our Nig: or, Sketches from the Life of a Free Black*, ed. Gabrielle Foreman (New York: Penguin, 2009).

36. Sharon Sundue, "'Beyond the Time of White Children': African American Emancipation, Age, and Ascribed Neoteny in Early National Pennsylvania," in *Age in America: The Colonial Era to the Present,* edited by Corinne T. Field and Nicholas Syrett (New York: New York University Press, 2015), 47–65; Catherine Jones, Intimate Reconstructions: Children in Postemancipation Virginia (Charlottesville: University of Virginia Press, 2015); Marie Rodet, "'Under the Guise of Guardianship and Marriage': Mobilizing Juvenile and Female Labor in the Aftermath of Slavery in Kayes, French Soudan, 1900–1939," in *Trafficking in Slavery's Wake: Law and the Experience of Women and Children*, eds., Benjamin N. Lawrance and Richard L. Roberts (Bloomington: Ohio University Press, 2012), 86–100; Kelly M. Duke Bryant, "Changing Childhood: 'Liberated Minors,' Guardianship, and the Colonial State in Senegal, 1895–1911," *Journal of African History* 60, no. 2 (2019): 1–20; Kelly M. Duke Bryant, "Runaways, Dutiful Daughters, and Brides: Family Strategies of Formerly Enslaved Girls in Senegal, 1895–1911," *Women, Gender, and Families of Color* 7, no. 1 (Spring 2019): 37–55.

37. Anna Mae Duane, ed., *Child Slavery Before and After Emancipation: An Ar-*

gument for Child-Centered Slavery Studies (New York: Cambridge University Press, 2017).

38. Sarah L. H. Gronningsater, "Born Free in the Master's House: Children and Gradual Emancipation in the Early American North," in *Child Slavery Before and After Emancipation: An Argument for Child-Centered Slavery Studies,* ed. Anna Mae Duane (New York: Cambridge University Press, 2017), 123–49.

39. Blagbrough and Craig, "When I Play"; and for a comparison focused on India, Tambe, *Defining Girlhood.*

40. Epstein, Blake, and González, "Girlhood Interrupted."

41. Evelyn Brooks Higginbotham, *Righteous Discontent: The Women's Movement in the Black Baptist Church, 1880–1920* (Cambridge: Harvard University Press, 1994).

42. Mary Niall Mitchell, *Raising Freedom's Child: Black Children and Visions of the Future After Slavery* (New York: New York University Press, 2010); Mitchell, *Righteous Propagation*; Wright, *Black Girlhood.*

43. Simmons, *Crescent City Girls.*

44. Marcia Chatelain, *South Side Girls: Growing Up in the Great Migration* (Durham: Duke University Press, 2015), 132.

45. George, *Making Modern Girls*, 7, 12.

46. Decker, "Fathers, Daughters, and Institutions."

47. Rebecca de Schweinitz, *If We Could Change the World: Young People and America's Long Struggle for Racial Equality* (Chapel Hill: University of North Carolina Press, 2009); Katherine Capshaw, *Civil Rights Childhood: Picturing Liberation in African American Photobooks* (Minneapolis: University of Minnesota Press, 2014); Rachel Devlin, *A Girl Stands at the Door: The Generation of Young Women who Desegregated America's Schools* (New York: Basic Books, 2018). For more on gender relations in the Black Power movement, see Robyn Spencer, *The Revolution Has Come: Black Power, Gender, and the Black Panther Party in Oakland* (Durham: Duke University Press, 2016) and Ashley Farmer, *Remaking Black Power: How Black Women Transformed an Era* (Chapel Hill: The University of North Carolina Press, 2017).

48. Emily Bridger, "Functions and Failures of Transnational Activism: Discourses of Children's Resistance and Repression in Global Anti-Apartheid Networks," *Journal of World History* 26, no. 4 (December 2015): 856–87.

49. Treva B. Lindsey, "'One Time for My Girls': African American Girlhood, Empowerment, and Popular Visual Culture," *Journal of African American Studies* 17 (2013): 22–34; Tiera Chantè Tanksley, "Education, Representation, and Resistance: Black Girls in Popular Instagram Memes," in *The Intersectional Internet: Race, Sex, Class, and Culture Online*, eds. Saifya Umoja Noble and Brendesha M. Tynes (New York: Peter Lang, 2016), 229–42; Carla Stokes, "Representin' in Cyberspace: Sexual Scripts, Self-Definition, and Hip-Hop Culture in Black American Adolescent Girls' Home Pages." *Culture, Health, and Sexuality* 9 (2017): 169–84; Ashleigh Wade, "When Social Media Yields More than 'Likes': Black Girls' Digital Kinship Formations," *Women, Gender, and Families of Color* 7, no. 1 (Spring 2019): 80–97.

50. Aimee Meredith Cox, *Shapeshifters: Black Girls and the Choreography of Citizenship* (Durham: Duke University Press, 2015); Savannah Shange, *Progressive*

Dystopia: Abolition, AntiBlackness, and Schooling in San Francisco (Durham: Duke University Press, 2019).

51. Tara Bynum, "Phillis Wheatley's Pleasures," *Common Place* 11.1 (October 2010); Tara Bynum, "Phillis Wheatley on Friendship," *Legacy: A Journal of American Women Writers* 31, no. 1 (2014): 42–51; Simmons, *Crescent City Girls*; Joan Morgan, "Why We Get Off: Moving Towards a Black Feminist Politics of Pleasure," *The Black Scholar*, special issue: *On the Future of Black Feminism* 45, no. 4 (Winter 2015): 36–46.

52. Porshé R. Garner, Dominique C. Hill, Jessica L. Robinson, and Durell M. Callier, "Uncovering Black Girlhood(s): Black Girl Pleasures as Anti-respectability Methodology," *American Quarterly* 71, no. 1 (March 2019): 191–97.

53. Lynn M. Thomas, "The Modern Girl and Racial Respectability in 1930s South Africa," in *The Modern Girl Around the World: Consumption, Modernity, and Globalization*, ed. Alys Eve Weinbaum, et. al (Durham: Duke University Press, 2008), 96–119; Simmons, *Crescent City Girls*; Lindsey, *Colored No More*.

54. Gaunt, *The Games Black Girls Play*.

55. C. Riley Snorton, *Black on Both Sides: A Racial History of Trans Identity* (Minneapolis: University of Minnesota Press, 2017), xiv.

56. Anya Wallace, "Sour Apple Green: A Queer Memoir of Black Family," *Callaloo* 37, no. 5 (Fall 2014), 1042–50; Savannah Shange, "Play Aunties and Dyke Bitches: Gender, Generation, and the Ethic of Black Queer Kinship," *The Black Scholar* 49, no. 1 (2019): 40–54.

57. Sokari Ekine and Hakima Abbas, "Introduction," in *The Queer African Reader*, eds. Sokari Ekine and Hakima Abbas (Dakar: Pambazuka Press, 2103), 1–5; Zethu Matebeni, Surya Monro, and Vasu Reddy, eds., *Queer in Africa: LGBTQI Identities, Citizenship, and Activism* (New York: Routledge, 2018); Zethu Matebeni, "Intimacy, Queerness, Race," *Cultural Studies* 27, no. 3 (2013): 404–17; Brenna M. Munro, "States of Emergence: Writing African Female Same-Sex Sexuality," *Journal of Lesbian Studies* 21, no. 2 (2016): 186–203.

58. Kai M. Green, "In the Life: On Black Queer Kinship," *Women, Gender, and Families of Color* 7, no. 1 (Spring 2019): 98–101.

59. Charlotte E. Jacobs, "Identity in Formation: Black Girl Literacies in Independent Schools," in *Black Girl Magic*, ed. Julia S. Jordan-Zachery, Janell Duchess Harris, Janell Hobson, and Tammy Owens (Tucson: University of Arizona Press, 2019), 80–104.

60. See for example, Black Youth Project, "Anti-Blackness," http://Blackyouthproject.com/tag/anti-Blackness/

61. Brent Edwards, *The Practice of Diaspora: Literature, Translation, and the Rise of Black Internationalism* (Cambridge: Harvard University Press, 2003), 14.

62. Wright, *Black Girlhood*, 14.

63. Annette K. Joseph-Gabriel, *Reimagining Liberation: How Black Women Transformed Citizenship in the French Empire* (Urbana: University of Illinois Press, 2020), 143–144.

64. Donaldson, "'How Does it Feel to Be a Problem?"; Ibrahim, *Troubling the Family*; Tharps, *Same Family Different Colors*.

65. Sidimba, "Zulaikha Patel Impresses Angela Davis."

66. Corinne T. Field and Nicholas L. Syrett, eds., "AHR Roundtable: Chronological Age: A Useful Category of Analysis," *American Historical Review* 125, no. 2 (April 2020): 371–459; Audra Abbe Diptee, "Imperial Ideas, Colonial Realities: Enslaved Children in Jamaica, 1775–1834," in *Children in Colonial America*, ed., James Marten (New York: New York University Press, 2007), 48–60; Schwartz, *Born in Bondage*.

67. Holly Brewer, *By Birth or Consent: Children, Law, and the Anglo-American Revolution in Authority* (Chapel Hill: University of North Carolina Press, 2005); Field and Syrett, "AHR Roundtable."

68. Corrie Decker, "AHR Roundtable: A Feminist Methodology of Age-Grading and History in Africa," *American Historical Review* 125, no. 2 (April 2020): 418–26.

69. Wright, *Girlhood*, 12.

70. Tambe, *Defining Girlhood in India*; Crista DeLuzio, *Female Adolescence in American Scientific Thought, 1830–1930* (Baltimore: Johns Hopkins University Press, 2007).

71. Joan Jacobs Brumberg, *The Body Project: An Intimate History of American Girls* (New York: Vintage Books, 1997).

72. Jordan-Zachery and Harris, *Black Girl Magic*, 14–16; Brown, *Black Girlhood Celebration*.

73. Anna Julia Cooper, *A Voice from the South*, in *The Voice of Anna Julia Cooper*, eds. Charles Lemert and Esme Bhan (New York: Rowman and Littlefield, 1998), 60–61, 63.

74. Protest took place in 2018. Zulaikha Patel (@zulaikhapatel_), "Black Girl Spill," Instagram, July 14, 2019. https://www.instagram.com/p/Bz6t0Q6p3cb/; See also poster for "Silent Protest" organized by Patel and Thage, Zulaikha Patel (@zulaikha patel_), "Young Women Against GBV-Rape-Abuse" Instagram, November 28, 2018, https://www.instagram.com/p/Bqt8owNgNdG/ and also Boitumelo Thage, "We are Here to Stay," July 11, 2020, https://boitumelothage.wordpress.com/2020/06/16/youth-day-piece/.

75. Safiyia Noble, "Searching for Black Girls," in *Algorithms of Oppression: How Search Engines Reinforce Racism* (New York: New York University Press, 2018); Safiyia Noble, "Google Search: Hyper-Visibility as a Means of Rendering Black Women and Girls Invisible," *Invisible Culture: An Electronic Journal for Visual Culture* (29 October 2013), http://ivc.lib.rochester.edu/google-search-hyper-visibility-as-a-means-of-rendering-Black-women-and-girls-invisible/.

76. Wright, *Black Girlhood*, 10–11.

77. Kimberlé Crenshaw, "Demarginalizing the Intersection of Race and Sex: A Black Feminist Critique of Antidiscrimination Doctrine, Feminist Theory and Antiracist Politics," *University of Chicago Legal Forum* 140: 139–68; Collins, *Black Feminist Thought*; Kimberlé Crenshaw, Priscilla Ocen, and Jyoti Nanda, *Black Girls Matter: Pushed Out, Overpoliced, and Underprotected* (African American Policy Forum, 2015).

78. Saidiya Hartman, *Beautiful Experiments*.

79. Wright, *Black Girlhood*, 10–11.

80. Hortense Spillers, "Mama's Baby, Papa's Maybe: An American Grammar Book," in *Black, White, and In Color: Essays on American Literature and Culture,* ed. Hortense Spillers (1987; Chicago: University of Chicago Press, 2003), 228–29.

81. Habiba Ibrahim, *Black Age: Oceanic Lifespans and the Time of Black Life* (New York: New York University Press, 2021), 20.

82. Ibrahim, 29.

83. Ibrahim, 41.

84. Hortense Spillers, "Interstices: A Small Drama of Words" (1984), in *Black, White, and In Color,* 152–3, 156, 167.

85. Spillers, "Interstices," 175.

86. George, *Making Modern Girls*; S. E. [Sarah] Duff, "The Jam and Matchstick Problem: Working-Class Girlhood in Late Nineteenth-Century Cape Town," in *Colonial Girlhood in Literature, Culture and History, 1840–1950*, ed. Kirstine Moruzi and Michelle Smith (Basingstoke: Palgrave Macmillan, 2014), 124–40.

87. "Girls At South African High School Protesting Hair and Language Bans."

INTERLUDE

Black Girlhood as an Analytical Framework for Doing History

CRYSTAL LYNN WEBSTER

"That the term 'colored girl' is almost a term of reproach in the social life of America is all too true; she is not known and hence not believed in."
—Fannie Barrier Williams[1]

Historical scholarship has been enriched by approaches to history which deploy analytical categories with theoretical rigor. In 1986, Joan Scott made a convincing call for historians to consider gender as a category of analysis beyond its "literal" application to gender difference toward a more theoretical understanding of how "gender" informs social structures, economic and political organization, and hegemony.[2] Black feminist theorists and scholars have long advocated for the inclusion of race to the "woman question."

Kimberlé Crenshaw's groundbreaking theory of *intersectionality* has become mainstream for understanding the intersecting experiences of Black women's racial and gender oppression.[3] And Childhood Studies has led scholarship on childhood and age, arguing that childhood too is socially constructed and that age is an analytical category which reveals much of power, agency, dependency, and subjugation. These analytical categories are often treated as though they are discrete—they are not. They are profoundly and intrinsically connected. Combined categories of analysis hold incredible theoretical and conceptual power. As Kimberlé Crenshaw, Joan Scott, and Black feminist theorists have done for the field of history, a strong theoretical foundation based on the standpoint of Black girls has the power to transform historical analyses and expand categories of analysis to race, gender, *and* age. The general inability of scholars to use the terms "child" or "girl" when referring to Black girls is representative of the categorical and metaphysical dilemma of Black girlhood. Scholars will more readily list chronological ages or refer to Black girls as teens or "youth." Scholars have particular trouble working with Black girls who have been sexualized or impregnated, and struggle with referring to these girls as children *and* mothers. Centering Black girls *as* children deepens critical analysis and reveals how historical, social, and political movements, as well as systemic and institutionalized structures of power, are tied to ideas about age, gender, and Black girlhood.

Researching Black girlhood requires theoretical sophistication. Any historical analysis that fails to consider age, race, and gender also misses many of the fundamental dimensions of a time period. The material circumstances and social dynamics experienced by Black girls encapsulate the complexity of both the human experience and structures of power. Black girls are the primary subjects through which to examine the function and purpose of such forces of hegemony. They encounter what I refer to as a metaphysical dilemma—Black girls have and continue to move through the world as Black children and girls while white hegemonic society fails to recognize them. White dominant society defined childhood in ways that actively excluded Black children—it was "raced white."[4] Black girls were rejected further from social recognition as children. They exist at the extreme margins of archival representation and social categorization and their experiences are therefore not "believed."[5] They elude historical representation for these very reasons and, therefore, require new theoretical frameworks. This essay demonstrates how Black feminist theory can be used as a foundational framework to study Black girlhood. It also reveals the hidden history and historical dynamics of the experiences of Black girls within significant historical periods and social phenomenon such as slavery, emancipation, and the carceral state.

Black feminists have long considered the gendered dynamics of the Black experience. However, they have done so with little distinction between the girlhood experience and that of Black womanhood and motherhood. Beginning with some of the earliest articulations of the specific experience of Black girlhood in slavery by those such as Harriet Jacobs who lived it, Black feminist theories produced by bell hooks, Angela Davis, Hazel Carby, and others have built upon the long tradition of Black women's scholarship. In doing so, they contributed frameworks which allow for inclusion of Black girls in scholarly analysis.[6] For many Black feminist scholars, Jacobs and her 1861 autobiography *Incidents in the Life of a Slave Girl* are foundational elements of Black feminist theory. However, Jacobs' powerful articulation of Black girlhood has been overlooked and undertheorized. Scholars have focused on her claim, "Slavery is terrible for men; but it is far more terrible for women."[7] From this claim, Black feminists produce analyses of Black women. Jacobs' experiences of abuse, sexualization, and motherhood were foundational for Black feminist theories of the gendered struggles of enslaved Black women.

The significant distinction between enslaved men and women—the vulnerability of Black women to sexual assault and rape—propelled Black feminist thinking. Drawing on Harriet Jacobs, bell hooks points out how the enslaved Black woman's experience was one in which enslavers attempted to assert complete domination as a means of maintaining the "white imperialistic order."[8] Angela Davis also draws upon the sexual assault and rape of enslaved Black women and argues that enslavers committed such acts as a means of "subjecting [women] to the most elemental form of terrorism." Davis identifies how this terror would be used to force enslaved women into a "ransom system of sorts," which included punishments for refusal such as family separation, physical punishment, and the withdrawal of food.[9] Hazel Carby's analysis of violence against enslaved Black women exposes their erasure in scholarship and aptly claims, "The institutionalized rape of black women has never been as powerful a symbol of black oppression as the spectacle of lynching."[10] Because of the terror of sexual assault, Black women lived the categorical challenge of being women and Black.

Although it has not been identified as such, the plight of Black girls is fundamental to Black feminist thought. Scholars have failed to understand that, when Jacobs wrote that slavery was "far more terrible for women," she reflected on the experience of giving birth to a baby girl. In that moment, she realized her child would endure the specifically gendered trauma and terror of slavery that she had experienced at a young age. In her biography, she elaborated on this experience in her chapter, "Trials of Girlhood," in which the enslaver Dr. Flint sexually corrupted her with words and perhaps, though unwritten, actions. Jacobs made clear the particular dilemma of gendered slavery for children because it is Black *girls* who were abused when they were in their "extreme youth."[11] Jacobs's sexual corruption alienated her from her grandmother, who she feared would perceive her differently if she revealed the experience. The enslaver's ability to assert sexual power and domination over African Americans functioned not only as a means of disrupting bonds between a man and a woman, or to keep mothers from their children, but also specifically targeted Black girls *as* children in order to corrupt their childhoods as a form of terror and dehumanization. Black girls like Harriet Jacobs faced suspicion, guilt, and blame in three intersecting ways: as *children* whose age and dependency alienated them from experiences of adulthood; as *girls* whose gender disbarred them from public social recognition; and as enslaved "chattel." Black girls faced even more socially constructive dilemmas as society was unable to recognize them *as* children. This is a persistent paradoxical and metaphysical dilemma that Black girls continually encounter.

The reach of the metaphysical dilemma of Black girlhood extends to the historical archive. On the one hand, as an extremely marginalized historical subject, the historical archive sidelines Black girls. The U.S. archive itself offers relatively few clear documentations of Black girlhood, both in its colonialist design and as a preservation of white supremacy.[12] On the other hand, however, conventional scholarship on various historical topics, particularly Black women's history, includes the experience of Black girls but without critical analysis of their experiences *as* children. Some scholars dismiss Black girls' experiences due to the ways in which childhood has been historically and socially constructed—around whiteness. A common response of researchers to the treatment and subjectivity of Black girls is that they would not have been considered girls "in that time," or that they were too old or too young to warrant historical attention. On the contrary, analyzing the age of historical subjects alongside critical understandings of ideas of childhood clearly reveal that Black girls are not only visible in the historical archive, but they are also essential to the ways in which ideas of race, childhood, freedom, criminality, citizenship, and humanity developed. Their history transforms understandings of American history, African American history, and the history of childhood.

Multidimensional analyses of subjects enhance historical research. This is especially so for scholarship on the history of slavery, violence/sexual assault, and criminalization. Black girlhood provides a necessary analysis to these areas that is not only additive but also transformative. The interrelated dynamics of gender and age reveal much about the history of slavery. For instance, scholars building upon Hazel Carby's analysis of sexual assault and lynching, note that the history of rape and deadly violence against Black girls deserves serious attention. Carceral studies emphasizes the experiences of Black men and boys. However, the history of incarceration requires critical analysis of the role of age and gender, and attention to the phenomenon of incarcerated Black girls who comprised a sizeable portion of imprisoned populations in specific historical periods. Taken together, the exploration of Black girls in each of these areas serves as a model for how to research, analyze, and communicate about history with critical attention to age, race, and gender. The implications of this research complicate traditional historical analysis of violence and incarceration, and elucidate how age, race, and gender impact past and contemporary Black girls through their social adultification and the institutionalization of racism in schools and juvenile reformatories.

The enslaved experience was marked by age. Enslavers used and exploited age as part of the institution of slavery. Enslavers disrupted enslaved people's relationship to age and development as part of the maintenance and enforcement of slavery and white supremacy. From the moment of capture to birth into enslavement, Black children's experience was singular and significant. Historian Sasha Turner explicates the experience of Black girls in the transatlantic slave trade in her study of pronatalism and abolitionism in the Caribbean. She explores the 1791 incident in which a young captive African girl who was just fifteen years of age was hung and flogged, naked, on a slave ship belonging to Captain Kimber. She died days later. British abolitionists used this as part of their campaign to end slavery, using her "age and sexual innocence" as part of a strategy to evoke sympathy.[13] Abolitionists and enslavers imposed ideas of childhood and adulthood onto the captive girl and claimed she was an innocent child, a virgin girl, and a laboring woman when it was politically and economically expedient. Black girls were a categorical paradox. Similarly, Sowande' Mustakeem describes how Black children and girls had unique experiences during slavery. She recounts the inconceivable violence they endured as part of a process of "unmaking" in which enslavers obscured the experience of Black girls' experience in the Middle Passage. Enslavers categorized the enslaved as captives along binary terms of either men or women: "Infant, prepubescent, teenage, and elderly captives fell outside of prevailing socioeconomic desires and are therefore unaccounted for in contemporary slave trade discussions." Nevertheless, Mustakeem's attention to age reveals that young children and girls were aboard slave ships.[14] Similarly, Wilma King identifies the particular agency and resistance of Black children and points out that captive boys and girls moved with relatively more freedom on the slave ship and "often walked about the decks unfettered." Space was not allocated for children below deck as they were forced to rest on shipping containers. One enslaver commented, "It is no wonder . . . we loose [*sic*] them so fast."[15]

Hortense Spillers describes the paradox of the dehumanization of enslaved bodies who endured simultaneous "naming and valuation" alongside a dehumanization process which removed familial, gendered meaning:

> A female body strung from a tree limb, or bleeding from the breast on any given day of field work . . . adds a lexical and living dimension to the narratives of women in culture and society. This materialized scene of unprotected female flesh—of female flesh "ungendered"—offers a praxis and a theory, a text of living and dying, and a method of reading both their diverse mediations.[16]

Reading Spillers with attention to age, she demonstrates how enslavers removed and disrupted the social significance and meaning of age, childhood, and girlhood for Black girls. The work of Turner, Mustakeem, King, and Spillers make clear that the transatlantic slave trade blurred categories and binaries of age and gender in ways that merit further consideration.

North American slavery, through the birth, sale, and subjugation of enslaved children, devalued Black childhood in social terms. Black girls' experiences reveal many new contours to the capture, enslavement, and escape of African Americans. Daina Ramey Berry's careful attention to age exposes previously unexamined dynamics of the enslaved experience, including differential treatment once enslaved children reached age ten: "This milestone in their development as property was important because it marked the moment that gender differences emerged." Berry also discovered differential treatment at even early ages. For example, legislation that prohibited separation of young children from their parents did not apply to incarcerated mothers enslaved in Louisiana whose infants were sold by prison officials. Berry identifies distinctions between enslaved boys' and girls' treatment through their clothing. Older boys wore pants and older girls wore dresses. Berry's attention to age, therefore, contradicts earlier scholarship that argued against gender as a marker of difference for enslaved children.[17]

These scholars demonstrate that despite assumptions in conventional scholarship, Black children and girls *are* represented in the historical archives of slavery, and these archives clearly marked age and gender in records of enslavement including plantation records, bills of sale, and advertisements for fugitives. In many ways, these are some of the richest archives for locating Black girls, yet they are rarely examined with close attention to age and gender.

Other records of categorization which similarly include race, gender, and age emerge in the post-emancipation South through systems of imprisonment and convict-lease. Black girls' incarcerated experiences trouble legal and social categorization of girlhood and blackness. Close attention to prison records challenges traditional scholarship by revealing how black girls are represented disproportionately in prisons when compared to white children and adults. Sarah Haley's research on incarcerated Black women and girls provides insight into the lives of the incarcerated in Jim Crow–era Georgia. Her work produces a theoretical vision of the power of the carceral state as a means of producing gendered and racialized terror. In the convict camps of the period, Black women were beat, raped, and isolated. This produced a phenomenon of "gendered racial terror as a particularized instrument of state attack against black women and as a mechanism through which gender was constructed in historical, cultural, and political context." The performance of violence on the physical bodies and flesh of Black women excluded them from the social category and protection of "woman." This violence then "reified, normative, mutually constitutive, gendered and racial social categories." Haley and other scholars identify ages of imprisoned Black females, but often do not differentiate between the experience of Black girls and women. Nevertheless, they demonstrate that girls as young as twelve were incarcerated and some were sent to convict camps. Scholars also presume Black children and girls were present in prisons as infants. They suggest that their relative absence in prison records is, in part, because they were considered "'things' but not 'convicts,'" and thus, Black children and girls "were only documented in relation to their mothers through the reports of childbirth." Haley writes these infants have been "erased and disregarded" and remain only as "spectral presences, making visible the social violence so consistently denied."[18] Incarcerated Black girls and those born into prisons experienced racialized, gendered, and age-based violence. Gendered violence othered Black women from womanness; similarly, carceral violence ensured that Black girls were not afforded protection as women or as children.[19]

The violence enacted against Black children in prison spaces was appalling and for many people, unimaginable. The perpetrators of this violence and the scholars who study it have both intentionally and/or defensively obscured it. Similarly, Americans have failed to reckon with the history of rape and the murder of Black girls. In her examination of sexual violence against Black girls in South Carolina, Cynthia Greenlee explains the public's inability to see the rape of Black girls as the rape of children. Instead, scholars have "grouped together black women and girls as 'women,'" which then "flattens possible age difference in black girls and women's vulnerability to assault and legal treatment." Black girls' sexual violence has been concealed due to their identities "as children, dependents, workers whose labor was typically folded into household economies, females, and African Americans."[20] LaKisha Simmons has similarly remarked on the inability of scholars to recognize the violence enacted against Black girls in the Jim Crow South. She argues that U.S. society has an "incomplete understanding of how racial violence functioned," in part due to the ways in which "gendered experience of Jim Crow coming-of-age cannot be fully expressed or even conceptualized."[21] Nevertheless, Black girls experienced sexual and physical violence throughout the South.

Black girls also experienced physical violence as victims of lynchings. Although scholars have unpacked the gendered dynamics of lynching, particularly in relation to Black men who were accused of raping white women, they have not analyzed the role of age and gender in the lynching of Black children and girls. While Black girls who were lynched do not account for a particularly numerous proportion of documented lynchings, their very existence troubles how we understand the function of such violent racial terror. Within the documented lynchings between 1880 and 1930, 130 of them were Black women. However, within this category, several were under the age of eighteen, meaning Black girls were, indeed, lynched in the Jim Crow South. Though ages are available for analysis and documented in lynching archives, the unique experience of Black girls has not been researched. For example, in South Carolina, Julia Brandt was lynched at just fifteen years old, alongside two other boys aged eighteen and sixteen (one was her brother) for the murder of a white woman. As Crystal Feimster has argued, for Black women, these lynchings served to portray "white women as innocent, white men as avenging protectors, and black men and women as violent beasts."[22] Sometimes, Black children were lynched alongside Black women. Alma House, aged sixteen, was lynched with her sister Maggie House in 1918, Mississippi.[23] Black children were also forced to observe their parents' lynchings in order "to serve as a violent lesson to all blacks, young and old, male and female, who dared to challenge white authority," as a reminder that "no one, not even a mother, was safe from the lynch mob."[24] Indeed, not even a female child. That this racial terror operated not only in order to dehumanize Black women, but also to target Black girls in extreme and specific ways is significant.

While temporal specificity is required, it is clear that white children were almost exclusively referred to as children when of the same age as Black girls under similar contexts. Furthermore, whites and African Americans themselves used these terms to describe their own children during these periods. After all, if Harriet Jacobs passionately pleaded for her audience to treat her as a child when she wrote, " I was a poor slave girl, only fifteen years old," scholars do a grave disservice when they fail to do so.[25] The inability to categorize Black girls as children is, therefore, also a contemporary problem—one based in a cognitive dissonance scholars encounter as a result of how the construction of childhood has been racialized. This failure of categorization subjugates Black children and Black girls.[26]

While girlhood does not possess the same power differential and constitutive influence as that of race and gender, age offers a further layer of critical analysis for the historical context and material conditions of blackness. Studies of Black girlhood offer ways to engage creatively with theoretical and research methods for historical analysis, which reveal deeper levels of subjugation by those who used age and girlhood vulnerability as a means to reinforce hierarchies of race and gender. In similar ways as Black feminist scholars have pointed out the racialized gender differences between Black men and women, further analysis of Black girls provides new understanding and imaginative possibilities for the field of history. This essay demonstrates how scholars can do the history of Black girlhood and gestures to further areas of study which deserve scholarly research and critical questions. How does the enslaved girlhood experience transform our understanding of subjugation, negotiation, and resistance? What constitutive forces did the incarceration of Black girls have in the rise of mass incarceration? How was the motivation and racial violence of lynching different for Black girls? These questions and new approaches to history and African American studies hold the potential to transform not only ways in which we understand the history of Black girls, but also its impact on the institutionalization of racism in its current form.

Notes

1. Fannie Barrier Williams, "The Colored Girl," *Voice of the Negro*, no. 2 (June 1905): 402–3.

2. Joan W. Scott, "Gender: A Useful Category of Historical Analysis," *The American Historical Review* 91, no. 5 (1986): 1053–75.

3. Kimberlé Crenshaw, "Demarginalizing the Intersection of Race and Sex: A Black Feminist Critique of Antidiscrimination Doctrine, Feminist Theory and Antiracist Politics," *The University of Chicago Legal Forum* 140 (1989): 139–67.

4. Robin Bernstein, *Racial Innocence: Performing American Childhood from Slavery to Civil Rights, America and the Long 19th Century* (New York: New York University Press, 2011), 8.

5. Crystal Webster, "Beyond the Boundaries of Childhood: Northern African American Children's Cultural and Political Resistance, 1780–1861," (PhD diss., University of Massachusetts Amherst, 2017), 1071.

6. See bell hooks, *Ain't I a Woman: Black Women and Feminism*, 2nd ed. (London: Routledge Ltd, 2015); Angela Davis, "Reflections on the Black Woman's Role in the Community of Slaves," *The Massachusetts Review* 13, no. 1/2 (1972): 81–100; Hazel V. Carby, *Reconstructing Womanhood: The Emergence of the Afro-American Woman Novelist* (New York: Oxford University Press, 1988).

7. Harriet Jacobs, *Incidents in the Life of a Slave Girl: Written by Herself* (1861; Chapel Hill: University of North Carolina, n.d.), 119, http://docsouth.unc.edu/fpn/jacobs/jacobs.html, 119.

8. hooks, *Ain't I a Woman*, 27

9. Angela Davis, "Reflections on the Black Woman's Role in the Community of Slaves," 96.

10. Carby, *Reconstructing Womanhood*, 39.

11. Jacobs, *Incidents in the Life of a Slave Girl*, 44.

12. Marisa J. Fuentes, *Dispossessed Lives: Enslaved Women, Violence, and the Archive*, 1st ed., Early American Studies (Philadelphia: University of Pennsylvania Press, 2016).

13. Sasha Turner, *Contested Bodies: Pregnancy, Childrearing, and Slavery in Jamaica*, 1st ed., Early American Studies (Philadelphia: University of Pennsylvania Press, 2017), 3–4.

14. Sowande' M. Mustakeem, *Slavery at Sea: Terror, Sex, and Sickness in the Middle Passage*, The New Black Studies Series (Urbana: University of Illinois Press, 2016), 42.

15. Wilma King, *Stolen Childhood: Slave Youth in Nineteenth-Century America*, 2nd ed, Blacks in the Diaspora (Bloomington: Indiana University Press, 2011), 3,15.

16. Hortense J. Spillers, "Mama's Baby, Papa's Maybe: An American Grammar Book," *Diacritics* 17, no. 2 (1987): 65–81, 68.

17. Daina Ramey Berry, *The Price for Their Pound of Flesh: The Value of the Enslaved, from Womb to Grave, in the Building of a Nation* (United States: Random House Inc, 2018), 47, 48.

18. Sarah Haley, *No Mercy Here: Gender, Punishment, and the Making of Jim Crow Modernity*, Justice, Power, and Politics (Chapel Hill: The University of North Carolina Press, 2016), 111, 113.

19. See also, Kali N. Gross, *Colored Amazons: Crime, Violence, and Black Women in the City of Brotherly Love, 1880–1910*, Politics, History, and Culture (Durham: Duke University Press, 2006); Talitha L. LeFlouria, *Chained in Silence: Black Women and Convict Labor in the New South*, Justice, Power, and Politics (Chapel Hill: The University of North Carolina Press, 2015); Lindsey Elizabeth Jones, "'The Most Unprotected of All Human Beings': Black Girls, State Violence, and the Limits of Protection in Jim Crow Virginia," *Souls* 20, no. 1 (January 2, 2018): 14–37.

20. Cynthia Greenlee, "Due to Her Tender Age: Black Girls and Childhood on Trial in South Carolina, 1885–1920" (PhD diss., Duke University, 2014), 41, 45, 47, 2, https://hdl.handle.net/10161/9115.

21. LaKisha Michelle Simmons, *Crescent City Girls: The Lives of Young Black Women in Segregated New Orleans*, (Chapel Hill: University of North Carolina Press, 2015), 3.

22. Crystal Nicole Feimster, *Southern Horrors: Women and the Politics of Rape and Lynching* (Cambridge: Harvard Univ. Press, 2009), 159, 161.

23. Jason Morgan Ward, *Hanging Bridge: Racial Violence and America's Civil Rights Century* (New York: Oxford University Press, 2016), 26.

24. Feimster, *Southern Horrors*, 169.

25. Jacobs, *Incidents in the Life of a Slave Girl*, 84.

26. See Bernstein, *Racial Innocence*.

PART I

Girlhood

CORINNE T. FIELD AND
LAKISHA MICHELLE SIMMONS

Introduction: What Is the Meaning of Girl?

"I came up with #BlackGirlMagic the year I turned 40," CaShawn Thompson reflected in her contribution to *Black History Untold*, a web series that uses personal memoir to explore the Black past. In her untold history, Thompson elevated the life of Gloria Richardson, who led the 1963 Cambridge Movement for civil rights in Dorchester County, Maryland. Thompson found inspiration in a famous photograph of Richardson standing up to police violence. What struck Thompson most was Richardson's age. Although many of the civil rights workers were young college-aged students, Richardson was forty years old when she stepped forward, her self-assurance reflected in the photograph where she pushes a white policeman's bayonet out of her face. "It sticks with me," Thompson explained, "and makes me think about how you can make an impact anytime in your life, and also how it is imperative that women in my age bracket not be afraid to step out there and accompany our nieces, our daughters, our granddaughters, and push back against this cop that keeps coming towards us all the time."[1] By hailing Richardson as an exemplar of #BlackGirlMagic, Thompson emphasized the power of "Black girl" as a category of shared affinity across generations of Black women, a way of marking the bonds through which ancestors and elders created possibilities for middle-aged women who, in turn, sustained girls and future generations. Black girl functions here not as an age category but as a means to celebrate intergenerational community and reconfigure how we understand history.

"The term *girl* . . . serves as a means of intragroup communication," Julia Jordan-Zachery and Duchess Harris explain in their anthology, *Black Girl Magic Beyond the Hashtag: Twenty-First Century Acts of Self-Definition*. The girl invoked by #BlackGirlMagic "is not bound by chronological age or society's conceptualization of moving into adulthood. Instead, the term often deployed colloquially as 'gurl,' 'homegirl,' 'sista-girl,' etc., represents a way of acknowledging commonalities among Black femmes, girls, and women." *Girl* in this sense is not an identity category bound by age, but part of the "call-and-response mechanisms used by Black femmes, girls, and women to suggest relatedness to one another." Blackness is integral to this call for mutual support "in the face of hostility." But age and gender assigned at birth are not. "The fluidity embedded in the term *girl* is an important aspect of #BlackGirlMagic," Jordan-Zachery and Harris explain. #BlackGirlMagic offers an expansive strategy for Black feminism because it binds "Black femmes, girls, and women" in a shared project of self-definition and self-valuation.[2]

But what about when Black girls want to define themselves as distinct from Black women? What about the moments when they push back against their elders or celebrate themselves as a new generation in rebellion against the past? Can these moments when Black girls want to be recognized as *not yet women* only undermine Black feminism, or can they strengthen it by deepening appreciation for what women can learn when they listen to girls, rather than just speaking for girls or attempting to protect girls? Age, as much as gender, sexuality, race, class, ability, national origin, and other aspects of identity shape lived realities and political possibilities. What makes age different than other categories is that people move through age categories over time, thus linking Black girlhood to Black womanhood. Even when Black girls most want to be seen as definitively young, they are always in the process of growing older. This question of the shifting relations among Black girls and women are ones that Black feminists have long explored but that often drop out of theoretical approaches and political projects premised on the easy conjunction of Black women, transwomen, femme folks *with* girls and gender queer youth. The contributors to this section use history to pose new questions about when Black girls can be girls and how that girlhood relies on hailing support from Black women.

Part of why intergenerational bonds fuel Black feminism is because Black girls and women have never been able to lay uncontested claim to their status as girls or women. Both categories, historically, have been pinned to whiteness. As contributors to this section reveal, the mainstream meaning of girlhood has changed over time from a status accorded to white, legitimate daughters in the eighteenth century, through an ideal of white childhood innocence in the nineteenth, to the shared consumption patterns forged through white teen culture since World War II. With anti-blackness remaining a foundational component of girlhood in all its modern forms, Black girls turned to Black women for support and validation as girls, but they also struggled against Black women to assert their own understandings of girlhood. To better understand how and why they did this, and more broadly to understand how Black girlhood fits within the history of Black feminism, we need to revisit archives with a focus on Black girls' efforts to define what it means to be a girl.

Rather than presuming a universal definition of girlhood, historical inquiry needs to ask when the concept of girlhood reveals new information about the past and when it conceals what needs to be made clear. Girls themselves, and the scholars that study their lives, often ask: What makes someone a *girl*? What is the stuff of *girlhood*? Who counts as a girl, and when does girlhood end for Black girls? These are not simple questions. Some girls must begin working at young ages, bringing home money to help their families survive. Other girls find themselves alone, perhaps kicked out of the house, living with friends or on the streets. And as we know, Black girls are often seen as adults at very young ages—as without youthful innocence.[3]

When describing the coming of age of young Edna Thomas in Harlem at the turn of the twentieth century, Saidiya Hartman reflects, "There were few memories of her childhood she could recollect with any pleasure. It would not be wrong to say that she had never been a child, or at least, she had never been a happy child. Are precocious children ever happy? To learn about the world or to blossom too early was dangerous."[4] As a child, Edna faced a difficult world all around her. She encountered racism, and the men around her beat and abused the women in her family. In her scholarship, Hartman questions where a child/young woman like Edna would ever find a space for pleasure. By claiming childhood for themselves, Black girls sometimes try to catch that happiness or pleasure that young Edna found so elusive.

Edna eventually sought pleasure by escaping childhood. She married at sixteen and then built a career as an actress, finding on stage the power to express the beauty and pleasure that drew so many young, modern, Black women to urban dance halls and theaters, not only in New York but in cities around the world, such as in Paris and Johannesburg.[5] Catching these types of pleasures often meant defying parents and social reformers who insisted that girls—especially Black girls—must pursue more respectable life choices. Those who snuck out, ran away, or defied their elders risked confinement in a home for wayward girls. As a married woman, no longer a girl, Edna could risk desires beyond the bounds of respectability. In midlife, she partnered with a white British aristocrat, Lady Olivia Wyndham, and the two grew old together. "Late love and a successful career" enabled Edna to create a future for herself that would have been difficult to imagine as a young girl.[6] Her story underlines the complexity of Black girlhood as something that Black girls may at times be eager to claim and defend; at other times, girlishness may be exactly what they want to leave behind in order to have access to more control over their lives. In the process, they can revolutionize institutions, such as marriage and intimate relations, and change who counts as beautiful, in order to create new possibilities for what it means to be a Black woman. Affiliations that cross racial boundaries and national divides can help Black girls grow into self-defined Black women. Appreciating these strategies requires that historians pay attention to age, gender, and race as analytical categories while adopting a "bifocal" vision that identifies the local resources immediately at hand and the global circuits of culture that can also be accessed.[7] This is the project that contributors to this section undertake, focusing on particular regions and time periods to explore the question of how Black girls themselves understand girlhood and how these understandings create what Hortense Spillers refers to as an "insurgent ground" for embodying wholistic selves outside of normative assumptions.[8] This is indeed a form of magic, as expressed in CaShawn Thompson's creative hashtag, but it is one that must sometimes be recognized as the creative property of Black girls who might ally with older Black women, but might who might also insist on making their own way in the world even when—perhaps especially if—there is no map upon which they can rely.

Literary critic Tara Bynum begins this section by exploring the close friendship between two married Black women in eighteenth-century Rhode Island. Proof of their loyalty to each other appears only in a brief notation left in an account book, a line that indicates the two women traveled together from Newport to Bristol on a summer day in 1768. By lingering over this fragment in the context of other evidence—Sarah's obituary, her husband's trade networks, the writings of her contemporary Phillis Wheatley—Bynum glimpses the possibility of a lifelong friendship between two enslaved women, a facet of lived experience that would have enriched their girlhoods in ways hidden by histories that stress only the dehumanization of slavery or rely on white people's perspectives. Bynum's creative methodology introduces the challenges faced by those seeking to recover Black girls' self-defined identities from fragmentary records written by other people and for other purposes. Her strategy also reveals how theoretical debates within Black feminism, in this case the importance of pleasure, can inform new questions about the past, such as how enslaved girls and women must have left some record of the pleasures they enjoyed and the deep, lifelong friendships they created with other women.

S.E. Duff focuses on the global dimensions of teen culture in the 1950s and asks how working-class Black girls in South Africa accessed these new forms of consumption, leisure, and self-assertion even as they had to fulfill distinct responsibilities (such as earning money and completing household chores for their families) and navigate the rigid racial segregation of Apartheid. The category of the teenager was capacious enough, Duff argues, that both white schoolgirls and Black servant girls could claim new pleasures as modern teens. Even as global marketing campaigns advertised products that remained out of reach to cash-strapped Black girls, *Drum* magazine printed stories that fueled their dreams and offered an advice column where they could pose questions about their identity as modern teenagers. In the process, they forged a distinct sense of what it meant to be a teenage girl.

Anasa Hicks traces how Black girls in early twentieth-century Cuba navigated local racial categories premised on the defense of honor. Court cases reveal that working-class Black girls tried to protect themselves from sexually predatory white men by claiming protection as girls, but they faced a judicial system more concerned with defending white male honor. In these cases, white men claim a presumption of innocence denied to Black girls. The ideal of an innocent, protected girlhood remained out of reach for Black, working-class Cuban girls as it did for Black girls elsewhere, though this case is particularly rooted in Spanish colonial understandings of honor. Hicks thus demonstrates the importance of looking to both local context and global circuits of power in order to make the lived experience of Black girls visible.

Lindsey Jones untangles the complicated collaborations and conflicts through which Black women worked to create spaces where Black girls could enjoy the protected and carefree girlhoods idealized in mainstream culture only to find that these girls often wanted other things, on the one hand, while white people remained eager to exploit their labor, on the other. At the Virginia Industrial School for Girls, founded and run by Black women in the 1920s, superintendent Janie Porter Barrett created what Jones terms a "pedagogy of respectability" centered on wholesome forms of recreation. Barrett believed that by teaching resident girls to "play in the right way," she could both create a space of protected innocence and demonstrate Black girls' capacity for reform. By reading records of girls' behavior, Jones recovers girls' varied responses to the tension between play and discipline in Barrett's program. Rereading archival sources previously used to understand the emergence of juvenile justice, Jones poses new questions about the relationship between freedom and constraint in intergenerational relationships among Black women and girls.

Sometimes navigating the pleasures and challenges of Black girlhood leads not to womanhood, but to manhood or to nonbinary identities; yet, as SA Smythe reveals, girlhood still "remains" as part of a fully realized adulthood. Through personal reflection on how a "trans-temporal and transnational Black girlhood persists" in the self-understanding, kin networks, and creative possibilities of living as a "transmasculine/nonbinary person," Smythe defines how Black girl friendships, Black girl culture, and the specific demands placed upon Black girls persist later in life and without any necessary relationship to Black womanhood. The important question, Smythe points out is not just what is Black girlhood, but "when is it"?

Notes

1. CaShawn Thompson, "CaShawn," *Black History Untold*, accessed April 16, 2020, https://www.blkhistoryuntold.com/herstory/cashawn.

2. Julia S. Jordan-Zachery and Duchess Harris, eds., "Introduction: We Are Magic and We are Real," *Black Girl Magic Beyond the Hashtag: Twenty-First Century Acts of Self-Definition* (Tucson: University of Arizona Press, 2019), 12, 15–16.

3. Robin Bernstein, *Racial Innocence: Performing American Childhood from Slavery to Civil Rights* (New York: New York University Press, 2011); Aimee Meredith Cox, *Shapeshifters: Black Girls and the Choreography of Citizenship* (Durham: Duke University Press, 2015).

4. Saidiya Hartman, *Wayward Lives, Beautiful Experiments: Intimate Histories of Social Upheaval* (New York: W. W. Norton, 2019), 205.

5. Hartman, *Wayward Lives*, 210–11; Alys Eve Weinbaum, Lynn M. Thomas, Priti Ramamurthy, Uta G. Poiger, Madeleine Yue Dong, and Tani E. Barlow, eds., *The Modern Girl Around the World: Consumption, Modernity, and Globalization* (Durham: Duke University Press, 2008).

6. Hartman, *Wayward Lives*, 214.

7. Ashwini Tambe, *Defining Girlhood in India: A Transnational History of Sexual Maturity Laws* (Chicago: University of Illinois Press, 2019), 6.

8. Hortense Spillers, "Mama's Baby, Papa's Maybe: An American Grammar Book," in *Black, White, and In Color: Essays on American Literature and Culture*, ed. Hortense Spillers (Chicago: University of Chicago Press, 2003), 228–29.

CHAPTER 1

Sarah and Bess

An Accounting of Two Black Girl-Friends

TARA A. BYNUM

> Variously named Harriot, Phibba, Sara, Joanna, Rachel, Linda, and Sally. She is found everywhere in the Atlantic world. The barracoon, the hollow of the slave ship, the pest-house, the brothel, the cage, the surgeon's laboratory, the prison, the cane-field, the kitchen, the master's bedroom—turn out to be exactly the same place and in all of them she is called Venus.[1]

Their names are not Venus. They are not the "*dead girl*," as Saidiya Hartman writes, "named in a legal indictment against a slave ship captain tried for the murder of two Negro girls."[2] They are Sarah Searing and Bess Thurston, and they have first and last names. They are likely friends. Both women share and make time together—in the way of "girl-friends" or "home-girls"—while living in almost-revolutionary-era Newport, Rhode Island;[3] I mean to use these words—albeit, anachronistically—to name the familiarity, belonging, and intimacy (though not always sexual) between women-friends. This is what the addition of "girl" to the words, "friend" or "home" suggests. It's not diminutive but rather, it admits to a tenderness and care for someone; not everyone can take on this title. Not everyone deserves to be called "girl" or "friend" or "girl-friend." But it seems to me that Sarah and Bess do share this sort of familiarity and care for one another. Even though Sarah and Bess may be enslaved just like Venus, I do find them and their eighteenth-century friendship. They are not dead in slavery's archive or in the hollows of a slave ship, a brothel, or even in their master's bedroom. They are very much alive in 1768 and on a day's journey, of about fifteen or so miles, to Bristol.

I read their names in an account book just like the many ledgers, daybooks, and journals that gather the names of living or dead, enslaved women. This account book lists all sorts of things—sow pigs, pickled lobsters, leather "breeches"—and people too. Even though it is a familiar eighteenth-century form, what makes this particular accounting different and a bit curious is that it belongs to Sarah's husband, Cesar Lyndon, enslaved to one-time colonial governor, Josias Lyndon.[4] Lyndon's account book is not the work of slave master, trader, learned white man, or "failed witness" who has no regard for the lives or humanity of enslaved women.[5] These are his lists of persons, events, and numbers. In fact, Sarah's husband remembers them and records a trip that she and Bess take on a summer's day:

> Tuesday July 5th 1768, Sarah Searing and Bess Thurston went away on a journey for Bristol between the hours of 3 & 4 o'clock afternoon.[6]

Cesar Lyndon writes of their hours-long journey from Newport (on Aquidneck Island) to Bristol, over land and across a waterway. They leave on a Tuesday afternoon and for an unspoken number of days. It's the fifth day of July, eight years before the American colonies would declare their independence from the metropole. Sarah and Bess must have traveled by boat—maybe, by way of the Bristol ferry—after riding or walking eleven or so of those fifteen miles. They may be in Bristol for any number of reasons: to help birth a baby, to see about a friend, to collect something on behalf of an unnamed someone. Lyndon doesn't seem to concern himself with those details of their living that I really want to know because I have an argument to make and a particular story to tell about enslaved women's friendships. He withholds how they travel, where they are going in Bristol and for what reason, and how long they've been friends. Instead, he leaves behind a sentence with only a date, a town, and the names of his wife and her friend. I am left to wonder not only what to do with their living or how long they've been friends but also what it means to account for a sentence-worth of friendship, of girl-friends amidst the lists of numbers, persons, and the itemized slaughter of livestock.

What I know for sure is that they go together to Bristol. They make time for one another on this summer's day, and it's a trip that is important for Sarah's husband to remember. It may not be their first trip with one another; they may have traveled together before. Bess might show up again—as Prince Thurston's unnamed wife—in the account book of Sarah's husband on a Tuesday in 1766. On this August day, Sarah and Bess go eight miles north to Portsmouth for a summertime pig roast; this time, Sarah and Bess don't go alone but instead journey with a group: Boston Vose; Neptune Sisson and his wife; Sarah and Cesar; Prince and Bess; Zingo Stevens; and Phylis Lyndon. Because it is to be a "pleasant ride out to Portsmouth," Lyndon secures—for him and his fellow travelers—a "house room," plenty of rum and limes for punch and of course, a hefty-sized "pigg [*sic*] to roast." Sarah and Bess seem to be so much a part of each other's lives that Lyndon must make note of it.

Every one of Lyndon's entries invites us to ask: How do we read this living even when the story of these women is told by a faithful witness and not a slave master? I still can't say with certainty who Sarah and Bess are, what they like, or how many children they have. But, it seems their trip, their friendship—at the very least Lyndon's mention of it—asks us to read about them with an expectation for their living rather than their death. There is living in their journey, and because of this living, there are extant lessons for those of us who are looking for them, their friends, and peers in Rhode Island or elsewhere. First, enslaved women befriend each other all the time, even in the eighteenth century; second, Sarah and Bess aren't the only friends with extant stories (Phillis Wheatley and Obour Tanner will trade letters, just a few years later, about their faith, travels, and the sale of Wheatley's *Poems on Various Subjects, Religious and Moral*);[7] third, we must learn to read closely for those glimpses of familiarity and belonging that evidence just how Black women and girls have lived and have made friends. Sarah's and Bess's friendship offers a way of reading their trip and maybe, their relationship to each other. Because, their stories are there to read, and in no more than a sentence, Sarah's husband tells a brief story about his wife and her friend who must go to Bristol on a Tuesday afternoon.

Lyndon notes the trip of Sarah and Bess on an easy-to-miss bit of paper in between his itemized debits, credits, and mentions of the everyday activities of the town's slave traders as well as its free and enslaved persons. In what remains extant—from 1761 to 1771—he inventories the sale and acquisition of goods and services from regional and international locales, as far off as Surinam and Jamaica. He logs the inflow and outflow of tradesmen, merchants, and also his wife and his friends. He notes the merchant class and their wives with prefixes, such as Capt., Ms., Mrs. or Mr. He doesn't always worry with any of these titles for his friends, business partners, or even himself. Instead, he assumes familiarity, and they are named without a title; take as examples Sarah and Bess.[8] With every mention of a person, place, or salable good, he transacts slavery's business as an enslaved accountant and as a sort of shopkeeper. Lyndon, in this position, has the unexpected power to remember, to write down, and in so doing, to make a thing or a person have meaning. He seemingly wields his power—to name, to number or value, and to make lists—to collect or tell stories. I find myself reading for the enslaved women, in particular, because their names are there as part of Lyndon's accounting, and they are living. Lyndon's archive isn't a "tomb" or a "death sentence" even though he keeps for himself those stories that are presently "predicated upon impossibility."[9] What is impossible, of course, is the certainty of knowing exactly who these enslaved women are. Yet they are there.

There are Sarah and Bess. And Lyndon names a few other women, and they are living too. There's Phylis Lyndon who, in the afternoon, is married to Zingo Stevens by the pastor of Newport's Baptist church. Phyllis Mowatt is listed on "Sunday morning Nov. 8th 1767" when she "went away from Mrs. Searing onboard of Capn. Ingraham for a passage to New London abt. 1/2 after 6 o'clock in of morning."[10] Another Phillis—without the specificity of a last name—"had her gown" on 28 November 1766, and Lyndon values it at about £30.[11] Each woman is offered a sentence-worth of description, and it seems to suggest that Lyndon has an interest in these women's lives. Even though he doesn't say why Phyllis Mowatt went away from Mrs. Searing's house to New London, Connecticut, and he doesn't mention legal restrictions on certain activities—to include, a seemingly, unsupervised weekday boat trip—what he does is gather lists and numbers that help him remember what and who are most important to him. And I suspect Sarah, Bess, and every Phylis or Phyllis are important to his and his wife's story.

Even though I want those details—who, what, when, where, why—that help make for a good story, I am reading Lyndon's account book just as it is because that's all any of us can do. It is his way to organize what he knows and to make what he knows mean something to him. He can and does take for granted those details that make for good archival recovery. For Lyndon, the certainty of enslavement and freedom are just as normal as the ongoing political conflicts with England; it's also as certain as his wife's friendships. He has little concern for our archival angst, fevers, or disappointments because he hasn't lost his or his wife's story, and he doesn't need to find it. He knows that his wife is enslaved to the family of the late Rev. James Searing, former pastor of First Congregational Church and that her friend is owned by one of Rhode Island's oldest merchant families. I suspect Lyndon doesn't need to remember to whom Sarah and Bess belong or how they meet. He doesn't need to recall if Bess might have been there to console his family after the loss of their baby boy, Pompey, in 1765. He knows for sure how he and Sarah felt about the Sugar Act of 1764 or the Stamp Act of 1765 and its continued effect on his business. He is likely not surprised by what we might call their "agency" or even his ability to keep a literate and numerate accounting of his daily life. Instead, what Lyndon records in his ledger is an everyday kind of life that he shares with many: Sarah and Bess, the members of Newport's Free African Union Society—Prince Thurston, Boston Vose, Neptune Sisson, Zingo Stevens. He catalogues the mundanity that gives life its meaning: the birth of Phyllis Mowatt's baby girl; the death of his baby boy; his wedding to Sarah on an October evening in 1767; a pig roast and gathering in neighboring

Portsmouth; his collection of silver buckles. Lyndon understands what we may have missed: that this living isn't impossible even if there are unanswered questions. Their living isn't simply a burden for those of us who scavenge in archives to lament. Sarah and Bess are alive and living despite the limits of the so-called "archive," its silences, and our present-day expectations that the enslaved must accept their dehumanization or, worse yet, believe what white people or even American history have said about them.

Nearly sixty years after this trip to Bristol, Sarah (Searing) Lyndon dies at the age of ninety-four. She is eulogized in the *Rhode Island Republican* on February 9, 1826. She is remembered as

> one of the few survivors of that old race of domestic servants, which was educated in the excellent school of our fathers, and who were the best models in this or any other country of the estimable qualities we seek, in that class of community.[12]

The obituary celebrates her deceased husband, too, even though Cesar Lyndon has died thirty years before; it says of him that he was "well known in this town as a man of color of remarkable attainments, having actually officiated as Secretary to his master."[13] It offers fewer details about Sarah's servitude, family history, or even her life story in favor of a memorialization of her respectable character. It's Sarah's husband who remembers those compelling details of her story—her whitewashed bedroom, the mention of her friend, Bess Thurston, and a summer pig roast. There is still more to wonder at—for example, whether or not Bess outlives her or if she has any more children after the death of Pompey and, of course, what brings them to Bristol on a July day in 1768.

The story of Sarah and Bess asks questions and has few, if any, answers. I can't provide the simplest details of their trip or even explain why Lyndon might have written about their trip on the backside of a eulogy for his son. There are no extant birthdates or family histories. And yet, Sarah and Bess are living; they are there to be remembered as girl-friends. They are two women who share and make time together. What they share as girl-friends is theirs to know and to remember. It seems to me that's what makes them girl-friends too; time makes stories, and some stories aren't meant to be shared among those who wouldn't be called "girl," in a casual sense, or referred to as a "friend." Lyndon is the enslaved man who remembers them, and maybe we can too if we read for what's there—in the so-called "archive" or in the account book—instead of for what's not there. There is a friendship between two enslaved women. There is a trip to Bristol.

There is an uncertainty too. But, I know the uncertainty is mine; it belongs to the reader, and it's uncomfortable. Lyndon is certain about his reason for noting this trip. It's a meaningful trip for Lyndon because he writes it down. Sarah and Bess know where they are, where they are going, and to whom they belong. They know what person, event, or idea prompts their travel. The uncertainty is the burden of the reader who can't know because time and its remains keep secrets. There is a lesson in this uncertainty. Firstly, uncertainty is a valid kind of knowing. Secondly, every story carries its meaning in whatever is left of it—a name, a line item, a sentence, or any other kind of reference.

It can have meaning for us too if we're willing to read their names—Sarah Searing and Bess Thurston—and listen for what's said and what's left unsaid in their living.

• • •

Acknowledgments: Special thanks are owed to the following persons and institutions for their gracious support of this project: Keith Stokes; Dr. Tammy Owens; Dr. Dominique Hill; Hampshire College's Dean of Faculty Summer Research Grant and NEH Challenge Grant; NEH Summer 2015 Institute at the Rhode Island Historical Society, Drs. Elyssa Tardif and Suzanne McCormack; Library Company of Philadelphia's Program in African American History; Washington College's CV Starr Center for the American Experience, the John Carter Brown Library, and the Hodson Trust-John Carter Brown Library 2018–2019 Fellowship; Dr. Susan Brown, Dr. Kim Martin and the University of Guelph THINC Lab 2018–2019 Fellowship.

Notes

1. Saidiya Hartman, "Venus in Two Acts," *small axe* 26 (June 2008): 1. For a greater discussion of the archive, see the following: Laura Helton, Justin Leroy, Max A. Mishler, Samantha Seeley and Shauna Sweeney, eds., "The Question of Recovery: Slavery, Freedom, and the Archive," a special issue of *Social Text* 33.4, no. 125 (December 2015); Marisa J. Fuentes, *Dispossessed Lives: Enslaved Women, Violence, and the Archive* (Philadelphia: University of Pennsylvania Press, 2016); Paul Erickson, "Where the Evidence Is; Or, Willie Sutton Visits the Library," *J19: The Journal of Nineteenth-Century Americanists* 2, no. 1 (Spring 2014): 186–194; Frances Smith Foster, "Forgotten Manuscripts: How Do You Solve a Problem like Theresa?" *African American Review* 40.4 (Winter 2006): 631–645; Lois Brown, "Death-Defying Testimony: Women's Private Lives and the Politics of Public Documents," *Legacy* 27, no. 1 (2010): 130–139.

2. Hartman, "Venus in Two Acts," 1.

3. For more on Rhode Island see, Christy Clark-Pujara, *Dark Work: The Business of Slavery in Rhode Island* (New York: NYU Press, 2016); Akeia Benard, "The Free African American Cultural Landscape: Newport, RI, 1774–1826,"(PhD diss., University of Connecticut, 2008); Sarah Deutsch, "The Elusive Guineamen: Newport

Slavers, 1735–1774," *The New England Quarterly* 55, no. 2 (June 1982): 229–253; Ann Tashjian, and Dickran Tashjian, "The Afro-American Section of Newport, Rhode Island's Common Burying Ground," in *Cemeteries Gravemarkers*, ed. Richard E. Meyer (Boulder: University Press of Colorado, Urban Institute, 1989), 164–196; William D. Johnston, "Slavery in Rhode Island, 1775–1776," *The Publications of the Rhode Island Historical Society*, 2.2 (July 1894): 113–164.

4. Lyndon's account book is housed at the Rhode Island Historical Society. For more on Lyndon's account book see, Tara Byum, "Cesar Lyndon's Lists, Letters, and a Pig Roast: *A Sundry Account Book*," *Early American Literature* 53, no. 3 (2018): 839–849. For more on using account books as source material, see Peter A. Coclanis, "Bookkeeping in the Eighteenth-Century South: Evidence from Newspaper Advertisements," *The South Carolina Historical Magazine* 91, no. 1 (January 1990): 23–31; Christopher Densmore, "Understanding and Using Early Nineteenth Century Account Books," *Archival Issues* 25.1/2 (2000): 77–89.

5. Hartman, "Venus in Two Acts," 2.

6. Lyndon, *Sundry Account Book*, MSS 9004, Box V10, Folder 81. Rhode Island Historical Society, Providence, Rhode Island. Lyndon writes about this trip on an unnumbered page.

7. For an extended discussion of Phillis Wheatley's friendship with Obour Tanner, see Vincent Carretta, *Phillis Wheatley: A Biography of a Genius in Bondage* (Athens: University of Georgia Press, 2011); Katherine Clay Bassard, *Spiritual Interrogations: Culture, Gender and Community in Early American Women's Writing* (Princeton: Princeton University Press, 1999); Dwight McBride, *Impossible Witness: Truth, Abolitionism, and Slave Testimony* (New York: New York University Press, 2001); Tara Bynum, "Phillis Wheatley on Friendship," *Legacy: A Journal of American Women* 31, no. 1 (Spring 2014): 42–51 and "Phillis Wheatley's Pleasures: Reading Good Feeling in Phillis Wheatley's *Poems* and Letters," *Common-Place: The Interactive Journal of Early American Life* 11, no. 1 (October 2010).

8. There is one instance in which Lyndon provides a friend with an honorific. He logs the marriage of his friend, Zingo Stevens and Phylis Lyndon. And he writes, "Mr. Zingo Stevens and Ms. Phylis Lyndon." He's forgotten the "Ms." and includes it as a superscript just before Phylis Lyndon's name (vol. 10, p.84C).

9. Hartman, "Venus in Two Acts," 3.

10. Lyndon, vol. 10, p. 83C.

11. Lyndon, vol. 10, p. 83B.

12. "Sarah Lyndon," obituary, *Rhode Island Republican*, 26 February 1826, 3.

13. "Sarah Lyndon," 3.

CHAPTER 2

Youth, Girls, Teenagers

On the Intersections of Race, Gender, and Age Categories in Twentieth-Century South Africa

S. E. DUFF

What did it mean to be a Black teenage girl in apartheid South Africa? In April 1958, *Drum*, a magazine with a Black readership, published: "This is my life, by teenager Sharon Davis." It begins:

> Gee, but it's sure grand to be alive, especially if you're a modern miss! Like me! I'm not very particular about conventions or about what gossips and other "people who don't matter" think.
>
> For instance, I enjoy walking barefooted in the rain through the middle of town, and sitting on the kerb singing while waiting for a tram or bus.[1]

Apartheid had been imposed precisely a decade before this article appeared. A system designed to shore up white supremacy through the classification of all South Africans into race categories that determined each person's full life trajectory, from birth to death; apartheid was an all-pervasive feature of everyday life. For the working-class author of this article, her choices as to what kind of education she could receive or career she could pursue were constrained precisely by the racial identity into which she had been classified, as well as by her gender and the relative poverty of her family. And yet—despite being triply disadvantaged within this system—her account of an ordinary day in her life is emphatically hopeful, shot through with ambition, and absolutely insistent on her ability to shape her future according to her own dreams.

To be sure, historians of South Africa have available to them a number of accounts of girlhood produced by Black and multiracial girls themselves. The correspondence collected by the historian Shula Marks and published as *Not Either an Experimental Doll* describes the tense relationship between a young Black woman in her teens (dubbed 'Lily Moya' by Marks, in an attempt to protect her privacy), the educationalist Mabel Palmer, and the social worker and activist Sibusisiwe Makhanya in the 1940s and 1950s.[2] Several memoirs by Black women devote a great deal of space to an evocation of girlhoods over the course of the twentieth century, from activist Ellen Kuzwayo's *Call Me Woman* (1985) to, more recently, *Endings and Beginnings: A Story of Healing* by the journalist Redi Tlhabi (2012). But what is striking about Davis's article is her description of herself as a teenager—a term which links her to the worlds inhabited by Black teenage girls around the world. Her article is, indeed, an account of life under apartheid by someone who occupied a marginalized position within South African society. It also opens up the possibility of writing a history of teenage girls—and specifically Black teenage girls—in apartheid South Africa. Davis redefines what it means to be a teenager in the 1950s by considering this age category in its specific social and political context in apartheid South Africa. While her article opens with a description of the characteristics associated globally with being a teenager—impulsiveness, rebelliousness, a refusal to accept convention—the piece goes into some detail about the aspects of Davis's life which would have been unfamiliar to many white, middle-class teenagers in the United States. For instance, she earns a wage; she shares a house with her parents and six younger siblings; she cooks, cleans, and assists with the running of a large household sustained by low pay. The category of teenager was elastic enough to include all of these experiences.

This chapter addresses historians' neglect of the category of "teenager" in South African history. It uses the popular publication *Drum* as an archive for investigating not only how teenagers were constructed in the minds of adults—*Drum* was read by people across Africa—but also how teenagers perceived themselves and their problems. The chapter positions Black South African girls within a broader, global youth culture of which they were aware through reporting on fashion, music and film, and internationally circulating dance crazes. But it also recognizes the specificities of local definitions of who counted as a "teenager."

How do we write the history of teenage girls in apartheid South Africa? There are a number of ways to approach this question. First, and perhaps most obviously, there is the rich scholarship on histories of youth in Africa. Dealing with questions of generational conflict, political protest and violence, labor, slavery, and youth culture and subcultures, this body of work tends to emphasize the agency—the ability of people to effect change in the world—of young people in negotiating the complex worlds of colonial and postcolonial Africa.[3] Yet when historian Abosede George argues for the "girling" of the subject of African youth history, she draws attention to the fact that, for historians as well as other scholars, African "youth" have been almost invariably defined as male. The historical scholarship has tended to privilege the experiences of boys and young men, those who have left traces in the archives, and whose work or political activity fall easily within conventional definitions of agency as resistance to authority.[4] This definition of youth reflects colonial and postcolonial politics on the continent, as groups of men who were young both in years and in social terms—who were unable to accrue the markers of manhood (marriage and property ownership, for instance) as a result of generational conflict and colonial policy—entered into political life as "youth."[5] But this narrow definition of "youth" excludes more than it includes. As Jean and John Comaroff note, although "youth" is a capacious signifier—"youth stands for many things at once"—in writing on Africa, "youth" has long been used to denote a specific group of people: "In the final years of struggle against apartheid, the category of youth expanded to include diverse classes of freedom fighters: students, workers, even criminals. In this story, it is true, not all young Blacks are youth. But all youth are Black. Also overwhelmingly, if not exclusively, male. And if some people never become youth, others seem unable to outgrow the label, even in middle age."[6] The point is not to dismiss this scholarship, which is urgently relevant to contemporary African politics, but rather to draw attention to how age categories are historically constructed and to make the category of youth capacious enough to include girls, younger children, young people not involved in conventional political action, and other racial and ethnic groups.[7]

Second, there is a growing literature on international girlhoods which considers broader questions relating to agency. Research on the global phenomenon of the Modern Girl shows how twentieth-century modernity, pop culture, and consumerism allowed for the emergence of new feminine identities that were at once a response to intensely local developments as well as part of a set of international trends and debates. As the authors of *The Modern Girl Around the World: Consumption, Modernity, and Globalization* (2008) note, the Modern Girl requires a reassessment of how historians have defined and identified agency in the past. If Modern Girls were marked out by their ability to buy consumer goods, instead of judging the degree to which "Modern Girls were dupes or resistors of consumer capitalism," scholars should pay attention to "how Modern Girl commodities [such as make-up, fashionable clothes, magazines, and sanitary towels] functioned pedagogically and as technologies of the self." Put another way, how did Modern Girls make themselves? How were they inducted into "the 'cultural practices of modernity?'"[8] Developing this recalibration of definitions of agency, Lynn M. Thomas has argued for a more nuanced approach to questions of agency in African history, especially for writing histories of women in Africa. She argues for historicizing agency, to understand it as "a concept that people in the past have defined and deployed in quite different, and sometimes disorienting, ways."[9] In this way, agency is no longer defined simply as resistance to the political or social order: it describes the multiple ways people have chosen to make sense of and navigate complicated situations.[10]

Thomas's argument echoes those made by historians of childhood and girlhood, who warn against falling into the "agency trap." Mona Gleason makes the point that writing histories of childhood agency that seek out children's autonomy and resistance will produce a very narrow scholarship.[11] Moreover, as historians identify new tools for excavating histories of children and youth that use an expansive definition of agency—one which is attentive to the many ways in which children can exercise change in the world, either consciously or not—they need to subject children's voices and contributions to critical scrutiny. This is to avoid overrepresenting the views of privileged children—whose words are more likely to be recorded and archived—and also to recognize the contexts that shape how children speak about themselves or others.[12]

Refocusing on Black teenage girls, rather than on "youth," requires a wider definition of agency, to understand how these young women, who were marginalized by South Africa's overlapping patriarchal systems on the grounds of their gender, race, and class,[13] made use of an increasing array of consumer goods and international popular culture to make themselves and to fashion their futures self-consciously. This expansive interpretation of agency does not suggest that the Black girls in this chapter accepted or gave in to the apartheid system. Rather, my aim is to recognize how apartheid worked itself into the fabric of ordinary existence—how girls navigated apartheid while buying nail polish or reading a magazine at a bus stop—and how girls found ways of getting by in a violent system. Importantly, although the girls in this chapter were shaped by their experience of apartheid, they were aware of Black girls abroad—particularly in the United States—and of an increasingly global, post-1945 youth culture. The strategies they employed to make themselves and their futures were similar to those used by Black girls internationally.[14]

It is worth noting briefly the differences in racial terminology and categorization between South Africa and the United States. There are important overlaps in the two countries' histories of segregation. For instance, white South African social scientists studied segregation and white poverty in the United States and vice versa, especially in the interwar period. But there are as significant differences. In South Africa, the term "Black," while often used interchangeably with "African," can also refer to all people who experienced discrimination under apartheid on the grounds of their racial identity, a designation developed by the Black Consciousness Movement in the late 1960s and 1970s. As a result, people of multiracial and South Asian descent—like Sharon Davis, the author quoted at the beginning of this essay—can fall under this category too. While it was certainly true that Indian and multiracial ("colored" in South African terminology) communities did receive more preferential treatment than Africans under apartheid, they experienced, regardless, the full brunt of a white supremacist political system. Here, though, I have tended to use Black to denote African, to echo usage in the United States. I have also noted, wherever necessary, the racial identities of the teenage girls who appear in this essay.

Age as a Category of Historical Analysis: Young Ladies to Teenagers

All age categories refer both to chronological time as well as to the shifting social and cultural expectations associated with those ages. While there are clear psychological, physical, and intellectual differences between a two-month-old, an eighteen-year-old, and a seventy-year-old, the meanings attached to those ages and to their attendant age categories—toddler, teenager, pensioner—are subject to change over both time and place. Their meanings are inflected by race, class, and gender. In late nineteenth-century South Africa, for instance, the same household could include two young women of precisely the same age, but who were regarded, respectively, as child and adult. The white, middle-class fifteen-year-old daughter of the house would have attended school, worn short skirts, and had her hair down her back; she was, in the eyes of her parents and the society around her, a girl. In contrast, a Black, working-class fifteen-year-old domestic servant would have been treated as an adult and expected to perform the work of an adult while wearing long skirts and pinned-up hair.[15] Historians can use age as an analytical category, much as they use gender, to understand the dynamic workings and negotiations of power within families and other institutions, as well as within society more generally. But age is also useful for thinking about change over time through the body, its aging, and through life spans and life cycles.[16]

The idea of the "teenager" developed in the United States in the 1930s and 1940s came to reflect how Americans and, later, elsewhere in the West defined what it meant to be an adolescent at that time.[17] (The psychologist G. Stanley Hall coined the term "adolescence" in 1900, although he was describing a phenomenon—a longer, leisure- and education-filled period of youth between childhood and fully independent adulthood—which had surfaced in industrialized states and colonies since the mid-nineteenth century.)[18] Middle-class prosperity and, after 1945, more extensive state spending on welfare and education further lengthened young people's emotional and financial dependence on their parents: teenagers stayed at home and in education for longer than ever before. They were also conceptualized from the beginning as consumers. Like the Modern Girl, primarily white, middle-class teenagers in prosperous post-war America had pocket money and, thus, spending power. At the same time, scholarly research on children by psychologists, educationalists, sociologists, and medical professionals began to shape popular perceptions of childhood and youth. Drawing on this Child Study Movement, adults began to see "teenagers" as hormonal, emotional, and unsteady not-quite-children and not-quite-adults in need of parents' and teachers' guidance and attention. Of course, the popularization of the category of teenager coincided with the sexual revolution of the 1960s, and, partly as a result of this, teenagers were also conceptualized as sexually dangerous.

But despite the fact that teenagers were produced by a set of economic, social, intellectual, and cultural circumstances specific to the midcentury United States, the idea of the teenager has proven to be flexible; people across the globe call themselves teenagers, revising and redefining the meaning of the word in the process. Even in the United States, this category differed across locations. Race determined who was allowed to be a carefree teenager and who was not. The category was also gendered. Although "teenager" referred to both girls and to boys, being a "teenage girl" accrued its own meanings. This is not unusual: other gender-specific age categories have also changed over time. The historian Jane Hunter, for instance, demonstrates that the idea of the "girl" emerged in the nineteenth century to describe middle-class young women between childhood and adulthood who, particularly after the 1870s, attended school until almost marriageable age. There they worked in academically competitive environments, which allowed them to explore identities and ways of being previously off-limits to young ladies educated at home by governesses and private tutors.[19] These "girls" became the New Women, the Modern Girls, and the teenage girls of the twentieth century. Girlhood was a global and a profoundly modern category.

"It's sure grand to be alive": Teenage Girls in *Drum* Magazine

The author of the article quoted at the beginning of this chapter was Zubeida (or "Juby") Mayet (1937–2019), writing under the *nom de plume* Sharon Davis. She was one of only a handful of women employed by *Drum*. Founded by the white, British-born publisher and writer Jim Bailey in 1951, *Drum* was by 1956 the bestselling periodical in Africa, with editions printed in South Africa as well as in east and west Africa. Until at least 1966, when the apartheid government "banned" many of *Drum*'s star writers (meaning that they were not allowed to work as journalists in South Africa), the magazine was a significant literary force as well as the unparalleled chronicler of urban African life on the continent. Alongside serious reporting on politics and social crises, the magazine attracted its large readership with what its second editor Anthony Sampson described as "cheesecake": sensational crime stories; coverage of beauty pageants, boxing, and other sports; articles on film stars, musicals, and fashion; and advice columns.[20] As Kenda Mutongi notes, *Drum* had "a little something to offer" to its broad readership, which sold up to 300,000 copies a month to English-speaking readers.[21] *Drum* was similar to many newspapers and periodicals aimed at Black readers in the United States in its mingling of serious news coverage, much of it sharply critical of apartheid, and sexual scandal. Editors had to sell newspapers, and readers were as drawn to *Drum*'s cover story celebrating Ghana's independence from Britain in 1957 as they were to salacious tales about popular singers and actors. Moreover, Black audiences were always multiple, and debates circulated within them—both in South Africa and the United States—about political tactics and what constituted "respectability."[22]

Drum addressed, then, an audience that was largely urban but that included middle- and working-class readers, men and women across the age spectrum, who held a range of politics. Priding itself on being outward looking and bringing international trends to local readers, it is little wonder that *Drum* printed some of the earliest references to teenagers in South Africa. Its treatment of the category—and particularly of teenage girls—reflects the diversity of its readership's worldviews.

Mayet's article describes behavior that the readers of *Drum* would have associated with being typical of a teenage girl. She was disorganized, referring to the chaos of her bedroom, with clothes strewn everywhere, and she implied that she spent a lot of time at work flirting with her male colleagues: "Fr'instance, I order coffee for the chaps, distract some of the boys from doing their work properly, phone my current boy friend."[23] In fact, Mayet, according to her article, spent a lot of time with boys, particularly on Saturdays when she liked to go "jiving."[24] Her definition of herself as a teenager was echoed by other articles published in *Drum* from the period, which described teenagers embracing jiving and other dance crazes, as well as fashions intended specifically for teenagers, like pedal pusher pants or miniskirts. But Mayet was also profoundly unconventional. Not only did she work instead of attending school full-time, but she also chose to work as a journalist when most professional Black women trained to be teachers, social workers, or nurses. She wrote:

> You know, I was supposed to become a teacher—in fact, I am a qualified teacher—but I'm not teaching. Why? Because teaching struck me as being too conventional a way of earning a living.
>
> So, I became a journalist instead. Not [that] journalism is such an unconventional way of earning a living, but it is certainly not an ordinary thing, especially for a Non-White girl—and that in South Africa![25]

She added that in addition to her very unusual choice of career, she was studying for her final school examination on her own and at night, with the intention of enrolling for a BA degree at a university. From an Indian family, and self-identifying as Black, Mayet was one of only a miniscule number of women journalists of color to continue to write for newspapers during this period, often under extraordinarily dangerous conditions.[26] Her access to higher education was far more limited than it was for white women. But in other ways, Mayet was typical of adolescent girls from her class in South Africa. She lived in Fietas—a working-class, multiracial suburb slightly to the east of the Johannesburg's inner city, which was bulldozed in the 1970s to make way for a suburb zoned "white." Her mother required her to cook on Sundays. She lamented that she "can't sleep till later than 10.30 because [she has] to do the cooking"—and she was still firmly under parental control: another reason she disliked Sundays was because "mummy wants me to dress up" while she would prefer "to slop around in any old thing."[27]

So Mayet was not exceptional. Aware of the meanings associated with being a "teenager," her experience of the category was shaped by her racial and class positions, and it was also gendered. For all her insistence on her unwillingness to marry and her belief in the equality of men and women, her article emphasizes her coquettishness. Her girlishness allowed her license to behave in ways not necessarily deemed appropriate for older women.

Drum also provides insight into the lives of other teenage Black and African girls through a lens provided by Mayet. She was—alongside Dolly Hassim, another rare woman journalist of Indian origin—one of the South African edition's two "Agony Aunts" who provided advice to an apparently endless stream of worried readers.[28] Titled initially "Heartbreaks" and later "Dear Dolly," these advice columns centered on questions relating to love, relationships, and sex. The questions posed by readers suggest at least some of the complexities of coming of age for young Black women in their teens in apartheid South Africa during the 1950s and 1960s. An overwhelming number of questions relate to choices between education and marriage, and the Agony Aunts, writing as both "Priscilla" and "Dolly," remained remarkably consistent in their view that adolescent girls should stay in school, regardless of the views of their boyfriends. In a typical exchange in March 1960, Priscilla advised nineteen-year-old Noluthando from Humansdorp not to drop out of school, where she was studying for her Junior Certificate (her final high school qualification), in order to marry her boyfriend: "You must complete your studies before you can think of marrying him. You must make him realize that this is for the future good of both of you."[29] Priscilla answered nineteen-year-old Dorothy from Umtali's question if she and her boyfriend should both drop out of school to marry in a similar fashion: "Tell your boy not to leave school but to carry on with his lessons. Education is very important these days if one is to become a success in life."[30] Another reader wrote: "I am a 17-year-old high school girl and in love with a boy of the same age. He is good-looking and loves me madly, but my mother doesn't want him. I can't stay away from him because I made him a promise. What should I do?"

Dolly was firm: "Perhaps your mother merely wants to discourage you from making love promises while you are still at school. Take her advice. You can make promises about your future when you are older and have finished schooling."[31] These young women—all of them Black, most of them from working- or lower-middle-class families—had narrow pathways to forms of financial independence, mainly through education. As noted earlier, nursing, teaching, and social work were all available to Black women throughout the apartheid period, but as readers of *Drum* knew, while these professions allowed Black women some upward social mobility, this success was precarious. *Drum* may have given voice to young Black women anxious about how to plan for the future, but the Agony Aunt columns reveal that these women faced not only the difficulties of navigating their own patriarchal families, but also the limitations imposed on them by the apartheid state.

Drum was suffused with anxiety about teenage girls' sexuality. Perhaps one of the best-known covers of *Drum* is from February 1957. It depicts a schoolgirl in a gymslip, lobbing a netball across a court, her frilly knickers titillatingly revealed as she jumps. The article connected to the cover is not actually, as the illustration would suggest, about teenage girls themselves but, rather, about the threat posed to them by sexually predatory teachers. It is titled "Stop These School Lovers, Says an Ex-Teacher." Yet as the cover implies, the article suggests that girls themselves were complicit in their teachers' efforts to seduce them. The author of the article recounts an episode relating to a teacher called "Richard" who was "a teacher with real finesse": "Elegantly dressed . . . a whiff of perfume lingering alluringly about him, he was the heart-throb of most of the teenagers at his school." This was not, though, an innocent flirtation. Richard took full advantage of the girls' attraction to him, despite being "a married man": "Young Ethel from Boksburg was a petite little, very neat and tidy, the kind of school accident that was strangely allowed to come to school with plaited made-up hair and nylon stockings. She had a child-like face and well-behaved manner that disguised an impertinent attitude to life as society has chosen to organize it. She and Richard just fell for each other." When Ethel, "crazed" by their "not so secret love affair," decided to "taunt Richard's wife" with a "very impertinent letter," the wife "went to the school and gave Ethel a thorough tongue-lashing." The article lays much blame at the feet of parents for being too trusting of teachers: "The irony is that many parents have an unquestioning confidence in Richard. If he goes to ask the parents' permission to take a girl student to a concert or a dance, he gets their ready agreement. Then he uses these chances for taking the girls into the bush."[32]

The article rehearses a familiar trope about sexually precocious teenage girls allowed to grow up too quickly by their easily duped and credulous parents. Its point is that while young male teachers do certainly pose a threat to their teenage pupils—and the story goes on to describe a number of unplanned pregnancies—the girls who fall for their teachers are at fault too. They are the agents of their own misfortune, even if the author agrees that this misfortune is undeserved. *Drum*'s interest in teenage girls' sexuality was shared by publications intended for Black audiences across Africa and in the United States, but South African circumstances shaped the question of the sexual behavior of Black teenage girls in urban areas. Rapid youth urbanization in the 1920s and 1930s—as young Black men and women left an increasingly impoverished countryside for better pay and, to some degree, more freedom from the constraints of traditional African society, particularly for women—was subject to intense scrutiny from white politicians, clergy, and social scientists, as well as a small Black middle-class. The Black elite's investment in a politics of respectability echoed similar anxieties in the United States. In South Africa, though, discussion in the pages of *Drum* went back and forth on the salience of "traditional" values, those associated with pre- or early colonial African societies, and modernity. Many readers and authors of articles on teenage pregnancy recommended sex education for Black youth in urban areas, as had been part of processes of socialization of young adults in the countryside before colonial conquest. At the same time though, a 1960 article titled "What Shall We Do with our Unmarried Mothers and Their Babies?" blamed teenage pregnancies on outmoded traditions like *lobola* (or "bride price," paid to the bride's family from the groom to compensate for the loss of her labor after marriage) as well as on ignorance about sex. As social worker Joseph Zulu argued, "None of our girls know what they ought to know."[33]

Even if the author of "Stop these School Lovers" was suspicious of some of the symbols of modernity (stockings, a new hairstyle), *Drum* came down firmly on the side of modernity. Across its advice columns, editorial pages, and correspondence, its journalists and readers argued consistently for the embrace of modernity and for the relinquishing of "tradition" to facilitate upward social mobility. In fact, as the Agony Aunts suggested, modern lovers would probably be happier lovers too: knowledge of sex made for healthier and more equal relationships, they wrote. Nowhere are the virtues of modernity more evident than in the bright, colorful advertisements spread across *Drum*'s pages. While many of them are for products that can be found in considerably more staid publications, such as tonics to promote good health, in *Drum*, readers were enticed by a growing range of consumer products, from bicycles and batteries for torches and radios, to the latest fashions in men's underwear and baking powder guaranteed to raise cakes reliably. Each edition of *Drum* in the 1950s and 1960s also featured advertisements for menstrual technologies, specifically for tampons.

All over the world, learning to cope with menstruation was part of a broader process of becoming modern.[34] In a series of advertisements for Tampax in *Drum*, readers were presented with photographs of poised, smiling, fashionably dressed and coiffed, light-skinned Black women, describing their conversion to Tampax. They refer to Tampax as hygienic and modern, its use signifying women's cosmopolitanism and embrace of science and progress. One advertisement from 1957 asserted not only that a "doctor made it" but also that in "America and all over the world, modern and educated women use TAMPAX." Readers were urged to write to the distributor, asking for "the booklet 'For Modern Women Only,'" which explained how to use the tampons.[35] Tampax also guaranteed women's "freedom." Another advertisement depicting a woman wearing a white swimsuit assured readers that, as "millions of smart educated women" would attest, "TAMPAX brings you such wonderful new freedom, you'll jump for joy all month long." It is the "modern way" and "chases away all your monthly worries, makes you feel smart, free and easy."[36] Crucially, and unlike the belts and thick pads worn by most women while menstruating, tampons allowed women to hide the fact of their periods:

> There are no belts, no pins, with Tampax. Tampax stops odor from forming, it doesn't chafe, and there are no disposal problems. It's so dainty, your hands need not touch the Tampax. Both Tampax and the handy hygienic applicator are easily disposed of. Tampax is so small, so inconspicuous, so easy to carry, that a whole month's supply goes into your handbag.[37]

This emphasis on Tampax being safe, comfortable, hygienic, and the choice of educated, modern women was intended to overcome readers' wariness of the product, specifically consumer's concerns about its price, which was far more expensive than homemade sanitary towels, and the suspicion that tampons were not for morally respectable women. Importantly, these advertisements implied that tampons allowed women—even Black women and teenagers—to enter the public sphere on more equal terms with men, no longer hindered by menstruation and inadequate, homemade, and "unhygienic" technologies. For Black women and girls, Tampax facilitated their shift to becoming fully modern subjects, reliant on medicine and "expert" advice. Quite clearly, though, modernity was associated with whiteness and depended on the full transformation of Black women and girls: not only should they wear deodorant to mask the odor of perspiration, but they were supposed to straighten their hair and use skin lightening creams. Using tampons, similarly, signified that they had embraced a subjectivity which identified them as modern, respectable, and educated.

What these examples attest to are the multiple constraints placed on Black teenage girls in apartheid South Africa. Of course, the worlds evoked by Tampax and other advertising would have been out of reach for the majority of Black teenagers, and indeed adult Black women, at the time. As the articles about teenage pregnancy and harassment at school demonstrate, girls acted within a tightly patriarchal system. Their questions to Dolly and Priscilla provide a glimpse of how those young women attempted to navigate this world, with such tenuous paths available to relative degrees of financial security (if not full independence). Girls were also subject to their parents' and other adults' respectability politics. They were subject to a debate over the virtues of "tradition" while many longed to be "modern." And yet, as Juby Mayet's defiantly hopeful article gestures to, these Black teenage girls looked beyond the often-limited horizons of apartheid South Africa through *Drum*. As Tanisha C. Ford has observed, fashion, dance, and listening to popular music looped Black girls into a global project of making a Black politics through aesthetics. Deciding to wear African prints or not straightening their hair—as modeled by the singer Miriam Makeba, who figured frequently as a cover star on *Drum*—was part of a process of asserting an alternative way of living in the world. Moreover, in an increasingly culturally isolated South Africa, listening to American pop and jazz and dancing to international dance crazes was, to some degree, an assertion of a cosmopolitanism against apartheid.[38]

Conclusion

While "teenagers" were first described in the United States in the 1930s, the age category gained powerful social and economic meaning in the West after 1945 as a generation of largely white and middle-class youth came of age in a context where adolescence was transformed into a carefree period, which adults recognized should be devoted to adolescents' self-discovery and self-making. With spending power and leisure time, teenagers became a significant economic force as consumers of popular culture. Yet even though Black South African adolescents may not have possessed the same resources as their American contemporaries, the category of the teenager proved to be remarkably flexible. The Black teenage girls in the pages of *Drum*, for instance, were employed in full-time work and supported themselves and often their families financially. But they read similar magazines, listened to similar music, and danced the same dances as teenage girls elsewhere.

In paying attention to the choices that teenage girls were faced with, this chapter assembles the complicated circumstances in which Black teenage girls found themselves. Should they stay in school, or marry? Should they stay in school despite the potential sexual harassment they might face? Should they have sex with their partners and risk pregnancies that would put an end to their ambitions to become teachers or nurses? Could they become the modern women of the TAMPAX advertisements? Caught between girlhood and adulthood, they were at once in a position to attempt to make themselves into modern subjects, but were also constrained by the strictures imposed by apartheid and South Africa's patriarchies.

Notes

1. "This Is My Life, by Teenager Sharon Davis," *Drum*, April 1958, 64.

2. As Marks reveals in the epilogue, Moya had struggled with mental illness throughout her life, a fact Marks discovered after stumbling across the correspondence in an archive. For more on the compilation of the book, see Shula Marks, 'Changing History, Changing Histories: Separations and Connections in the Lives of South African Women,' *Journal of African Cultural Studies* 13, no. 1 (2000): 94–106.

3. See for instance Abosede George, *Making Modern Girls: A History of Girlhood, Labor, and Social Development in Twentieth-Century Colonial Lagos* (Athens, OH: Ohio University Press, 2014); Saheed Aderinto, "'O! Sir I Do Not Know Either to Kill Myself or to Stay': Childhood Emotion, Poverty, and Literary Culture in Nigeria, 1900–1960," *Journal of the History of Childhood and Youth* 8, no. 2 (2015): 273–294; Corrie Decker, *Mobilizing Zanzibari Women: The Struggle for Respectability and Self-Reliance in Colonial East Africa* (New York: Palgrave Macmillan, 2014); Paul Ocobock, "'Joy Rides for Juveniles': Vagrant Youth and Colonial Control in Nairobi, Kenya, 1901–1952," *Social History* 31, no. 1 (February 2006): 39–59; Beverly Grier, *Invisible Hands: Child Labor and the State in Colonial Zimbabwe, 1890–1965* (Portsmouth, NH: Heinemann, 2005); Kathleen Vongsathorn, "Teaching, Learning, and Adapting Emotions in Uganda's Child Leprosy Settlement, c.1930–1962," in *Childhood, Youth and Emotions in Modern History: National, Colonial, and Global Perspectives*, ed. Stephanie Olson (London: Palgrave, 2015), 56–75.

4. George, *Making Modern Girls*.

5. Colin Bundy, "Street Sociology and Pavement Politics: Aspects of Youth and

Student Resistance in Cape Town, 1985," *Journal of Southern African Studies* 13, no. 3 (April 1987): 304–305.

6. Jean and John Comaroff, "Reflections on Youth, from the Past to the Postcolony," in *Frontiers of Capital: Ethnographic Reflections on the New Economy*, eds. Melissa S. Fisher and Greg Downey (Durham, NC: Duke University Press, 2006), 274.

7. Clive Glaser's *Bo-Tsotsi: The Youth Gangs of Soweto, 1935–1976* (London: James Currey, 2000) is a particularly good example of a nuanced reading of Black youth politics in twentieth-century South Africa. See also Katie Mooney, "'Ducktails, Flick-Knives and Pugnacity': Subcultural and Hegemonic Masculinities in South Africa, 1948–1960," *Journal of Southern African Studies*, special issue on masculinities in Southern Africa 24, no. 4 (December 1998): 753–774.

8. The Modern Girl around the World Research Group (Alys Eve Weinbaum, Lynn M. Thomas, Priti Ramamurthy, Uta G. Poiger, Madeleine Yue Dong, Tani E. Barlow), "The Modern Girl as Heuristic Device: Collaboration, Connective Comparison, Multidirectional Citation," in *The Modern Girl Around the World: Consumption, Modernity, and Globalization*, ed. the Modern Girl around the World Research Group (Durham, NC: Duke University Press, 2008), 22.

9. Lynn M. Thomas, "Historicizing Agency," *Gender & History* 28, no.2 (August 2016): 335.

10. See also Frederick Cooper, "Conflict and Connection: Rethinking Colonial African History," *The American Historical Review* 99, no. 5 (December 1994): 1516–45.

11. Mona Gleason, "Avoiding the Agency Trap: Caveats for Historians of Children, Youth, and Education," *History of Education* 45, no. 4 (2016): 446–59.

12. See Allison James, "Giving Voice to Children's Voices: Practices and Problems, Pitfalls and Potentials", *American Anthropologist* 109, no. 2 (June 2007): 261–72; Kristine Alexander, "Can the Girl Guide Speak? The Perils and Pleasures of Looking for Children's Voices in Archival Research," *Jeunesse: Young People, Texts, Cultures* 4, no. 1 (2012): 132–45.

13. My thinking here is shaped by Belinda Bozzoli's notion of the "patchwork quilt" of patriarchies at work in South Africa. See Belinda Bozzoli, "Marxism, Feminism and South African Studies," *Journal of Southern African Studies* 9, no. 2 (April 1983): 149–55.

14. On histories of Black girlhood in the United States, see particularly LaKisha Michelle Simmons, *Crescent City Girls: The Lives of Young Black Women in Segregated New Orleans* (Chapel Hill, NC: University of North Carolina Press, 2015); Marcia Chatelain, *South Side Girls: Growing Up in the Great Migration* (Durham, NC: Duke University Press, 2015); and Nazera Sadiq Wright, *Black Girlhood in the Nineteenth Century* (Chicago: University of Illinois, 2016).

15. This example is inspired by a similar passage in Leonore Davidoff, Megan Doolittle, Janet Fink, and Katherine Holden, *The Family Story: Blood, Contract, and Intimacy, 1830–1960* (London and New York: Longman, 1999), 168–69.

16. Steven Mintz, "Reflections on Age as a Category of Historical Analysis," *Journal of the History of Childhood and Youth* 1, no. 1 (Winter 2008): 91–92.

17. There is a large historical scholarship on teenagers, although much of this writing does not approach the racial politics of this age category. See, for instance, Grace Palladino, *Teenagers: An American History* (New York: Basic Books, 1996); Steven Mintz, *Huck's Raft: A History of American Childhood* (Cambridge, MA: Harvard University Press, 2004), 252–53; Catherine Driscoll, *Girls: Feminine Adolescence in Popular Culture and Cultural Theory* (New York, NY: Columbia University Press, 2002); Miriam Forman-Brunell, *Babysitter: An American History* (New York: New York University Press, 2009); Kelly Schrum, *Some Wore Bobby Sox: The Emergence of Teenage Girls' Culture, 1920–1945* (New York: Palgrave, 2004); Ilana Nash, *American Sweethearts: Teenage Girls in Twentieth-Century Popular Culture* (Bloomington and Indianapolis: Indiana University Press, 2005).

18. Jeffrey P. Moran, *Teaching Sex: The Shaping of Adolescence in the 20th Century* (Cambridge, MA: Harvard University Press, 2000), 95.

19. Jane Hunter, *How Young Ladies Became Girls: The Victorian Origins of American Girlhood* (New Haven: Yale University Press, 2002).

20. Colette Guldimann, "'A Symbol of the New African': *Drum* Magazine, Popular Culture, and the Formation of Black Urban Subjectivity in 1950s South Africa," (PhD diss., Queen Mary, University of London, 2003), 6–7; Lindsay Clowes, "'Are You Going to be MISS (or MR) Africa?' Contesting Masculinity in *Drum* Magazine 1951–1953," *Gender & History* 13, no. 1 (April 2001), 3–4.

21. Kenda Mutongi, "'Dear Dolly's' Advice: Representations of Youth, Courtship, and Sexualities in Africa, 1960–1980," in *Love in Africa*, eds. Jennifer Cole and Lynn M. Thomas (Chicago and London: University of Chicago Press, 2009), 84.

22. See particularly Kim Gallon, *Pleasure in the News: African American Readership and Sexuality in the Black Press* (Chicago: University of Illinois Press, 2020).

23. "This is my life, by teenager Sharon Davis," 68.

24. "This is my life, by teenager Sharon Davis," 68.

25. "This is my life, by teenager Sharon Davis," 64.

26. For more on Juby Mayet's pioneering and exceptionally difficult career as a journalist and political prisoner, see Gaele Sobott-Mogwe, "Interview with Juby Mayet, Johannesburg, 29 July 1993," *Journal of Gender Studies* 3, no. 3 (1994): 347–350.

27. "This is my life, by teenager Sharon Davis," 68.

28. Lindsay Clowes, "A Modernized Man? Changing Constructions of Masculinity in *Drum Magazine*, 1951–1984" (PhD diss., University of Cape Town, 2002), 36; Gaele Sobott-Mogwe, "Interview with Juby Mayet, Johannesburg, 29 July 1993," *Journal of Gender Studies* 3, no. 3 (1994): 348. The only study dealing specifically with the Dolly advice column looks exclusively at the west and east African editions of *Drum*: Mutongi, "'Dear Dolly's' Advice:" 83–108.

29. "Priscilla Asks: 'Have You a Love Worry?'" *Drum*, March 1960, 53.

30. "Priscilla Asks: 'Have You a Love Worry?'" *Drum*, October 1960, 73.

31. "Dear Dolly," *Drum*, July 1954, 43.

32. "Stop these School Lovers, Says an Ex-Teacher," *Drum*, Feb. 1957, 28.

33. "What Shall We Do with Our Unmarried Mothers and their Babies?" 51.

34. This linking of menstrual technologies and modernity was by no means unique to South Africa. See, for instance, Tani E. Barlow, "Buying In: Advertising and the Sexy Modern Girl Icon in Shanghai in the 1920s and 1930s," in *The Modern Girl around the World: Consumption, Modernity, and Globalization*, eds. The Modern Girl around the World Research Group, Alys Eve Weinbaum, Lynn M. Thomas, Priti Ramamurthy, Uta G. Poiger, Madeleine Yue Dong, and Tani E. Barlow (Durham, NC: Duke University Press, 2008), 288–316.

35. "Nobody knows I'm wearing TAMPAX," *Drum*, January 1957, 8.

36. "New Freedom for You Too!" *Drum*, October 1957, 36.

37. "I'm Telling You as a Friend . . . !" *Drum*, July 1958, 36.

38. Tanisha C. Ford, *Liberated Threads: Black Women, Style, and the Global Politics of Soul* (Chapel Hill, NC: University of North Carolina Press, 2017).

CHAPTER 3

Dubious Victimhood

Labor, Race, Age, and Honor in Republican Cuban Courts

ANASA HICKS

In a different context, the girls might have been friends. Celia was the oldest, born in 1892. Regla María was nine years behind, born in 1901. Reyita was born along with the new Cuban nation in 1902. But these girls almost certainly never met. Only the documentary evidence they left behind in Cuba, the island of their birth, connects them. Of the three, it is Reyita who offers us the most detail about her history through the testimonial she dictated late in life to her daughter. Her first memories are not her own but those of her grandmother: she recalls, almost as though it happened to her, her grandmother's upbringing in modern-day Angola. European soldiers stormed the village where they grew manioc and coffee, murdered those Africans who could not be put to work, and kidnapped the rest, including Reyita's grandmother Antonia. In Cuba, one of Antonia's masters raped her, and she gave birth to a girl named Isabel. Isabel was a child when Spain abolished slavery in Cuba, and her father exerted paternity over her so that she could continue working as a maid in his home. Later, he kicked her out when she became pregnant by one of his sons-in-law. During the war for independence, Isabel began a relationship with a rebel soldier named Carlos Castillo Duharte. That was Reyita's father.[1]

Celia and Regla María were girls like Reyita, likely with similar lineages of forced movement from Africa and slavery in Cuba. But little of their personal histories emerge in the documents available about them. What emerges from the archives is their survival of violence: in the first decade of the twentieth century, both girls accused men of rape and pursued criminal cases against their assailants. Reyita could tell her own story at the end of her life, but the Cuban archives have distilled the lives of Celia and Regla María into slim files, light on narrative. Still, this essay uses what narratives emerge to answer the question: What of Black girls in Cuba, born along with the twentieth century as the colonial past gave way to a democratic future?

The singular manner in which Cuba obtained independence from Spain, and the United States' role in the process, wound itself around notions of female innocence and vulnerability. In the last few years of the nineteenth century, Americans regularly consumed salacious photographs and stories from reconcentration camps in Cuba that featured sick and wasting women and children. *Reconcentrados* were people whom the Spanish colonial government had forced off their rural land and into makeshift camps to starve the Cuban Rebel Army of supporters. Their welfare was a huge point of interest for domestic and international followers of the Cuban independence struggle.[2] Political cartoons from the era portrayed the island as a young damsel in distress, seeking protection from both the evil Spaniards *and* the barbaric Cubans fighting for national independence.

Men like José Martí and Antonio Maceo envisioned *cubanidad* as raceless and imagined an independent Cuba as a nation based on brotherhood that was blind to racial difference, but the importance of racial difference for turn-of-the-century media consumers was obvious even as the war raged.[3] American newspapers and magazines coded *reconcentrados* as white for their audiences. The damsel in distress that represented Cuba was always white too. In reality, however, significant numbers of formerly enslaved and freed African-descended women and children numbered among those orphaned or abandoned by the chaos of war. Reyita's mother Isabel spent the years between 1898 and 1902 following Castillo Duharte from rebel camp to rebel camp. Four of the six children to whom she'd given birth died.[4]

Independence came not exactly as expected once Spain finally surrendered not to Cuba but to the United States in August of 1898. The 1901 Cuban Constitution, while it included the almost-universally hated Platt Amendment, granted citizenship to a far wider swath of Cubans than the U.S. occupiers might have preferred. North American occupiers did not leave Cuba until 1902.

The first challenge to Cuba's democracy came in 1906, when Liberals took up arms against President Tomás Estrada Palma's fraudulent reelection. In 1906, Reyita was four years old. She remembers: living with her mother on a sugar plantation in Guantánamo, being cared for by a Haitian woman living there. She remembers: being left with her great-aunt Casilda, who tied her to the leg of her kitchen table while she went to work in the fields. She remembers: leaving Casilda to reunite with her mother and father in the countryside, where her childhood was filled with the tasks of survival. She remembers: moving from family member to family member, always enduring some level of abuse, some expression of hard labor.

In the last decades of the nineteenth century and the first decade of the twentieth, things changed in Cuba. Men fought each other over national independence; then, they debated each other in person and in newspapers about the shape their new nation might take. But political turmoil and transformation overlaid some constant pains. Reyita's mother's experience during the war and Reyita's memories of her early childhood highlight this chapter's argument: to be a Black girl in early republican Cuba was to be vulnerable in a way that Black girls always had been vulnerable. Abolition changed the categories into which Black Cubans fell, and independence granted them citizenship, but the intersecting identities of race, gender, and age combined to render Black girls less protected than they could have been. Girls of African descent navigated racist and discriminatory perceptions that the new Cuban nation was supposed to have erased.

The collision of honor, a colonial ideal, and citizenship, a republican standard, contributed to Black girls' vulnerability. Honor is a slippery term that has to do with race, gender, and sex, specifically female virginity. Often a family's honor was dependent on the preserved chastity of its women. Race affected honor; elites automatically assumed that people of African descent had less honor than their white counterparts, but African-descended communities had their own internal standards of honor as well.[5]

Notions of citizenship in Cuba emerged in the late nineteenth century as the island began its independence struggle in earnest. Supposedly, citizenship was a more grounded concept than honor. In independent Cuba, it had to do with who could claim the rights to legal protection by the state. Women could not vote in Cuba until 1934, but the 1901 Constitution guaranteed all people the ability to make claims before the government. The court cases in this chapter demonstrate that women and girls of African descent did have access to Cuban courts and made use of them, but the limits of their citizenship were rooted in assumptions about their (lack of) honor. When Black girls pursued legal cases against assaulters, colonial and national categories of legitimacy worked together not to silence them, but to dismiss their claims. Racialized notions of honor rendered them sexually promiscuous; tropes of honor embedded in notions of citizenship rendered them liars, undeserving of the benefits of a criminal justice system.

Across Latin America, not just in Cuba but in places like Colombia, Puerto Rico, and Brazil, standards of "respectable" female behavior had material impacts on women's and girls' lives.[6] Those standards varied across racial and class differences, but often poor and non-white women, failing to attain sufficient standards of "respectability," suffered when they advocated for themselves in court. Other Latin American scholars have paired discourse about nation-building and legal theory with such court cases to show that women's sexuality was a useful touchstone for the male-dominated political sphere. In the Cuban case, my focus on two specific court cases further demonstrates how racial and gendered discrimination can flourish under distinct governmental systems.[7] Democracy does not necessarily bring justice.

Even after Cuba abolished slavery, sloughed off its colonial status under Spain, and enacted a constitution which guaranteed cross-racial male suffrage, categories that had been of the utmost importance in the colonial era persisted. The Cuban Liberation Army fought for independence because they wanted a raceless nation, and indeed, racial categories in Cuba are more fluid than they are in the U.S. Historically, Cubans have allowed for more racial distinctions than just "Black" and "white." But flexibility within racial categories should not be confused with erasure of racial hierarchy. The fluidity of white supremacy made it all the more insidious for people who existed at the bottom of those power structures.

That fluidity played out in Black girls' lives at the turn of the twentieth century, as the colonial past and republican present confronted each other. Celia and Regla María's rape cases tested the limits of Cuba's expansive definition of citizenship. While Cuba's republican courts did take seriously violence against Black girls, the outcomes of their cases revealed the limits of their willingness to combine childhood, blackness, and female respectability.

At the turn of the century, some Cubans' concern for children and for childhood made them advocates against child labor. Poor Cuban families often had little choice but to send their children out as apprentices to help support their families. Apprenticeship in workshops or with one master artisan has a long and venerated tradition in the Caribbean and Latin America, and the practice was widespread in Cuba. But frequently, enterprising Cubans hired children not as apprentices per se, but as what one journalist called "voluntary slaves." In a 1905 article in the Afro-Cuban newspaper *El Nuevo Criollo,* reporter A.M. de J. González railed against the insidious practice of "hiring" small children for jobs for which they were ill-equipped. He took specific issue with the use of young children as domestic servants, writing that this above all other labors "reduced and humiliated children." González excoriated the parents of children who sent their young ones out into the predatory control of men who "filled with clumsy appetites, don't respect the young age of their servant."[8] A sexual undertone lurked within the practice González so abhorred; he feared for the sexual innocence of children who left their own homes to serve adult men.

Celia Alfonso y Díaz was on the cusp of adulthood when she entered a home to work as a servant, but what happened to her contained echoes of González's worries about the loss of sexual innocence. Described as *negra* (Black) in official records, Celia was eight years old in May of 1900 when she entered the Orphan Asylum in Güines, a small town about thirty-one miles southeast of Havana. She was an orphan of the wars for independence that ended in 1898. The Red Cross, the American organization that ran the asylum, had no information about her parentage or background even though she lived at the orphanage for seven years.[9] At a similar orphanage in Madruga, just thirteen miles from Güines, girls took sewing and dressmaking classes. Celia might have been enrolled in similar classes and trained in the domestic arts.[10]

By far, the most important area of labor for African-descended Cuban girls at the turn of the twentieth century was domestic service. Eighty-three percent of Black girls under the age of fifteen who worked did so as domestics.[11] Domestic service, defined broadly, is the paid labor that sustains households and families: it can encompass both domestic labor (like cleaning and cooking) and reproductive labor (like childcare).[12] Up until the 1959 Cuban Revolution, domestic service was the largest employer of working women in Cuba, so it is not surprising that it predominated among young working women of color.

When Celia was fifteen years old, Señora María Teresa Toscano hired her to work as a domestic in her home in Guanabacoa, a Havana township about twenty-six miles away from her orphanage in Güines. One year into her position with Señora Toscano, Celia began to complain of dizziness and fatigue. Her employer took her to the doctor, who told Celia and Señora Toscano that Celia was pregnant. Confused and disturbed, Toscano tried to return Celia to the asylum, but the secretary of the orphanage convinced her to keep Celia and take care of her. However, Toscano said, Celia became uncooperative and truculent, refusing to talk to Toscano about the pregnancy or about anything else. By mid-December of 1907, she had returned Celia to the asylum.[13]

This was obviously not the desired outcome for graduates of Cuba's newly organized asylum system. The American Red Cross had opened the orphanage that Celia entered when the agency arrived in Cuba in October 1898 in order to help *reconcentrados* and soldiers toward the end of the war for independence. The Spanish-American War, as Americans called it, was the Red Cross's first opportunity to demonstrate its own viability as an aid organization. One visitor had this to say about the state of the asylum when the Red Cross arrived:

> The children were in a ruinous and pestilent building that had been a stable for the Spanish horses; and the adults in a barrack of wood made for the quarantining of people with contagious diseases.
>
> Some existed in the rooms in the most miserable and moving state: the children nude or covered with tattered rags. All were horribly bloated, pale

as wax, filled with scabies, repugnant ulcerations and disgusting parasites, their chronic hunger and desperation reflected in their cadaverous facial expressions. Almost all had chronic diarrhea, and as they could barely move for lack of strength, lived in a veritable manure heap.[14]

First-person narratives of the state of Cuban buildings and human beings *before* the Red Cross's arrival, such as the one above, and observations about the transformations that the Red Cross was able to achieve were consistent in their focus on the plight of children. Red Cross nurses turned terrified, smelly, sometimes catatonic war survivors back into their ideal of a child—happy, energetic, innocent. The effectiveness of the Red Cross effort was a synecdoche for the effectiveness of the United States as a colonial force, more modern and more compassionate than its Spanish predecessor. Children and childhood were central to this narrative. The children had to be, and could be, saved.

Celia was one such child, and her tracking into a life of domestic service was not uncommon in Cuba or in the rest of Latin America. In the early twentieth century, training for jobs in domestic service was a popular solution for the "problem" of impoverished girls and women. Nara Milanich has shown that in Chile in the late nineteenth and early twentieth century, orphanages essentially functioned as hiring houses for middle- and upper-class Chileans desirous of cheap domestic labor. Her work also illustrates how domestic service reproduced itself in impoverished social networks. When poor women had to leave their own children in orphanages so that they could work as domestics elsewhere, those children were then often hired out to be domestics themselves. In Brazil, too, elites and lawmakers saw a useful connection between poverty, youth, and domestic service. Escola Nossa Senhora de Amparo opened in the late nineteenth century as a school for poor young women to be trained in the domestic arts. Elite families whose contributions supported the institution would then hire those girls to work in their own homes.[15]

In Brazil, in Chile, and in Cuba, poor girls could become useful members of society if they entered and stayed on the right track. In Cuba the problem was especially acute because of the newness of the country and its concern with modernity and civilization. If the right path for young girls who lacked familial and/or financial support was state- or charity-funded housing (along with vocational training), the *wrong* path was just as clear: premarital sex. The author of *The Red Cross in Cuba* noted that in Madruga, where girls were enrolled in sewing and dressmaking classes, the orphanage housed "sixty children of both sexes whom the reconcentration had put at the doors of death and on the path of corruption."[16] Orphans were not only vulnerable to death but also to sex work. This was an extremely common theme and popular concern in Cuba at the end of the war: so many men had died, leaving behind so many women and children unable to support themselves with anything but their bodies.

Despite such fear, census data reveals that children did engage in wage labor in significant numbers after the war ended. An 1899 census found that in Cuba, one-fourth of children between ten and fifteen years of age were engaged in gainful occupation, which was three times the number for children in the same age range as the United States.[17] The census also found that 2,053 children, less than one-third of one percent, under the age of ten were gainfully employed, although the census attributed that data point to mistakes on the part of enumerators.[18] Two percent of girls under fifteen worked, and 17 percent of boys under fifteen worked. More finely detailed data illustrates the racial divide in labor among young people: while almost 10 percent of women of color under the age of fifteen worked, just under 3 percent of native white women under fifteen and 4 percent of foreign-born white women under fifteen worked.[19]

After Toscano returned Celia to the asylum, authorities relocated Celia once more to a correctional school on the outskirts of Havana. There, she was far more forthcoming with one of the nuns at the school than she had been with her employer. She testified that she'd had "amorous relations" with a twenty-year-old *mestizo* (mixed) day worker named Ricardo Daumil, who was building a house across the street from where she lived with Toscano. Celia testified that Daumil had deceived her, promising her marriage in exchange for sex. Then, apparently, he had disappeared. Prosecutors charged Ricardo Daumil with statutory rape on March 28, 1908. Daumil was difficult to find. By April 22, he was still on the lam, and by the end of June 1908, the Havana police had given up on finding him. But by a stroke of luck, Daumil was apprehended and imprisoned on August 17 awaiting his trial. For all that trouble, the court found him innocent of any wrongdoing because the court could not verify whether he had actually deceived Celia. There is no record of what happened to Celia or to her baby after the trial.[20]

A precise definition for *estupro* (statutory rape) is "carnal access with a person older than twelve years but younger than sixteen, gotten with deceit."[21] According to the Spanish Penal Code for Cuba and Puerto Rico, published some twenty-five years before Celia's case, seduction by fraud of a person between the ages of twelve and twenty-three was punishable by anywhere from one to four months in prison.[22] Sexual misconduct was fairly common in the Spanish colonies and even in early modern Spain. When so much of a family's honor and prestige depended on securing good marriages and because women's virginity was so highly valued, scandal was rampant. In his study of sex crimes in early modern Spain, Renato Barahona found that seduction, meaning the fraudulent promise of marriage in exchange for sex, was a last resort for men who had already spent copious amounts of time pursuing their would-be wives in culturally acceptable ways. These culturally acceptable ways were public: courting the young woman at her home, inviting her to dances, and negotiating with her family.[23]

Daumil did none of this. According to Celia, he only promised *her* marriage, privately: there were no parents for him to court, and she had no community to witness his behavior. His defense was that Celia was a willing sexual partner and that he had not promised her anything. In the court cases Barahona perused, the suits for compensation or recognition of wrongdoing were family affairs: fathers, mothers, sisters, and neighbors defended the damaged honor of the female victim.[24] In Celia's case, there was no word but her own. Because she was alone, Daumil could seduce her alone, in secret. On an immediate level, her vulnerability was due to her age, race, and gender; on a societal level, the recent upheavals in Cuba' political economy were to blame.

Whether Daumil had committed statutory rape depended on whether he had deceived Celia. The court tasked itself with determining whether Daumil had, in fact, promised Celia marriage when he had no intention of following through. It also undertook determining whether Celia herself was telling the truth about Daumil's promises. Since there were no other helpful witnesses—Celia's employer denied that any sexual relationship had occurred under her watch—the court system had to weigh Celia's word against Daumil's. Effectively, the Cuban court found Celia to be the duplicitous party and found her honor to be lacking.

Scholars of colonial Latin America have effectively demonstrated that honor, defined by historian Steve Stern as "personal virtue or merit and . . . as social precedence," was materially important, perhaps especially in working-class environments where a challenge to one's honor could result in a loss of a job opportunity, an advantageous marriage, or credit.[25] Honesty and the value of one's word was an important component of honor. Celia's honor was found lacking in two related ways: her sexual honor and the value of her word, since the courts found her to be dishonest. Sueann Caulfield, in her study of deflowering cases in early twentieth-century Brazil, found that honor was relational and corresponded to skin color: courts were more likely to find in favor of a female plaintiff if she was lighter-skinned than the male defendant who deflowered her.[26] This single case in Cuba tracks with that finding, as Celia was identified as *negra* and Daumil as *mestizo*. Surely, Celia's gender and her race contributed to the court's decision not to believe her narrative over Daumil's.

However, it was the actions of the new republican government itself which put Celia in the vulnerable situation that led to her pregnancy. As a little girl, she had been the burden of the U.S. neocolonial charitable operation. Then, she had been hired as a servant in a home miles away from the orphanage where she'd grown up, likely removed from any social networks she might have had previously. Her life to that point represented the hopes and failures of the new republic; the court's decision demonstrated the limits of institutions' capacity to uplift the neediest of new Cuban citizens.

At least officially, honor was not a category that had legal importance when the criminal case against Daumil was moving forward, but citizenship was. Because of the nature of Cuba's independence struggle and the 1901 Constitution, Celia was a Cuban citizen, even as a young woman of color. While stereotypes based on her race, gender, and class likely affected the outcome of her *estupro* case, the fact that the case moved forward at all is suggestive of the power of citizenship. Celia's case demonstrates the nexus at which notions of citizenship and honor intersected at the turn of the twentieth century. Her rights as a citizen allowed for the criminal case; her deficient honor allowed for Daumil's acquittal.

While the court document outlining the case in March of 1908 noted that the Red Cross knew nothing about Celia's parentage or relatives, Celia told nuns at her asylum exactly who her parents were. Her father was José Alfonso of Güines and her mother was María Díaz of Havana. She did not know where either of them were, but she certainly knew them as her parents. It begs the question why the Red Cross did not have this information. Did they not ask, or not care? It was all too easy a narrative to believe that a young Black girl had no parents, no lineage to go back to. Perhaps it was too easy to believe, as well, that a young Black domestic worker would agree to sex with full knowledge of the possible consequences.[27]

Seven years after Celia's ordeal, another rape case suggested once more that court systems rarely believed girls of African descent. Teresa Sánchez Castaño washed clothes for people in her Guanabacoa home. Sánchez often sent her daughter, thirteen-year-old *mestiza* Regla María Sánchez, to deliver clean clothes to her clients. One client was a forty-nine-year-old *mestizo* tobacco factory worker named Enrique Guerrero y Ruiz. In June of 1914, Regla María and her cousin, twelve-year-old Elena Bentancourt y Sánchez, went to Guerrero's apartment to deliver the clothes Regla María's mother had washed. According to Elena and Regla María, after they'd given Guerrero his clothes and were standing in the doorway, waiting for payment, Guerrero grabbed Regla María by the arm, slammed the door shut, threw her on his bed and raped her. He threatened that if she told anyone, she and her cousin would be sent to prison. The prosecution recommended that for his crime,

Guerrero receive fourteen years in prison and a fine of 2,000 *pesos*, and that he take financial responsibility for any offspring that might result from his attack on Regla María.[28]

Speaking on Guerrero's behalf, his lawyer denied the story wholesale. Guerrero maintained that the transaction was unremarkable: Regla María and Elena had dropped off his clean laundry, he had paid the girls, and they had promptly left. There were no witnesses. Guerrero's only neighbor who was home at the time of the alleged rape was a deaf man, so it did not mean very much that he heard no screams from Regla María.[29]

Like Celia, Regla María was subject to standards of both honor and citizenship even though she was a child—that the court saw her as a child is evident in her identification as "la menor" (the minor) in the title of the court case. That the prosecution pursued this case at all was a signal that despite being of African descent and working-class, Regla María was possessed of an honorable reputation. A doctor who examined Regla María days after Guerrero raped her confirmed that she had only lost her virginity several days prior. One of Regla María's teachers, to whom the investigating police spoke in their efforts to investigate her character, said that Regla María behaved well in class, had an earnest demeanor, and made a very good impression.[30] The confirmation of both her prior status as a virgin and her good behavior in school were apparently enough for the police to believe that Guerrero had, in fact, raped her.

The court prosecuted Guerrero to punish him and prevent him from raping again. However, the additional assertion that he bear financial responsibility for Regla María's potential child indicates another goal, common in rape and deflowering cases across Latin America: the maintenance of the patriarchal order. I mean "patriarchy" in its most literal sense; that is, the power that men and fathers wield over their families. Even while seeking to punish him as a rapist, the prosecutors in this case also wanted to ensure that Guerrero would fulfill any fatherly duties that might arise from his attack. He was responsible for the child he might have produced, and *he,* not the Cuban government, would take care of him or her.

Regla María and her mother might have welcomed such a requirement. Around the same time in Brazil, many of the court cases accusing men of seduction or deflowering were suits for marriage. The families of girls who had been deflowered wanted the perpetrators to marry their daughters, to rehabilitate the honor lost, and to provide financially for potential children.[31] In Celia's case, which hinged on the issue of deceit and not forcible violence, lawyers also pushed for the defendant to take financial responsibility for the victim's offspring.

Guerrero's lawyer attempted to cast doubt on the teenager's good reputation and her narration of what, exactly, had happened that day at Guerrero's apartment. In a list of questions that he submitted to the Audiencia, he asked Teresa whether she ever had an inkling that Guerrero was "in love with" her daughter; how it was possible that she did not notice anything wrong with Elena or Regla María on the day in question; and precisely which symptoms Regla María displayed which made Teresa think she had been deflowered. He asked Elena, Regla María's twelve-year-old cousin, why, if she knew that Regla María was in grave danger, she did not cry out for help. He asked Regla María herself with what, precisely, Guerrero covered her mouth if his hands were busy closing the door; why she did not scream for help when Guerrero removed his hands from her mouth to close the door; and about Guerrero's precise actions as he raped her. The lawyer had sixteen questions for Regla, most of which asked her to explain in minute detail why, if she was truly raped, she did not "resist" at every possible second. His final question for Regla María was whether "it required a lot of effort on Guerrero's part to deflower her; or if, on the contrary, he succeeded in doing so with ease."[32]

His strategy worked: Guerrero was acquitted on all charges. The prosecution appealed, arguing that Regla María's delay in reporting the attack was not due to its nonexistence but instead to her fear; but the Court denied the appeal, upholding Guerrero's innocence. The line of questioning that Regla María endured demonstrated that even girls as young as thirteen could fall under suspicion of sexual impropriety. Regla María's race and class made her all the more vulnerable to such suspicion.

Teresa, Regla María, and Elena were without a patriarch to vouch for their honor and respectability. As in Celia's case and so many cases involving sexual violence, the case came down to he said/she said. Guerrero y Ruiz was a mixed-race working-class man, but he *was* a man. Teresa Sánchez y Castaño was single, apparently, and enlisted her young daughter and niece to help her with domestic work. A relatively progressive model of citizenship in Cuba ensured that this case moved beyond accusations, but the still-relevant ideals of honor and male authority loomed large over proceedings. These two court cases show that people of African descent and working-class people were welcome to take advantage of Cuba's court system, and that Cuban courts identified the importance of childhood, but it did not mean that their cases would be decided in their favor.

Early twentieth-century literature and commentary often pointed to the sexual vulnerability of children, especially children of African descent. The 1924 novel *La Raza Triste* (*The Tragic Race*) was a melodramatic commentary on the state of Cuban race relations in Bayamo, an eastern Cuban town that set the city center on fire rather than submit to Spanish forces during the independence war. The main character, a *mulato* doctor, meets a woman called La Larga, who works as both a laundress and a prostitute. Her daughter works as a maid in the house of Don Pancho, one of the town's elders—until he rapes her and pays off La Larga to avoid conflict. The author, Jesús Masdeu, describes Don Pancho's strategy thusly:

> Librada, the youngest, had been caught twice in compromising positions with older men. Don Pancho had incited her in this perversion, as he had initiated other girls between eight and twelve years old. Seated in the porch of his house, Don Pancho watched his victims walk by . . . he talked to their parents. He placed the chosen girl in his house as a maid, and, late at night, he committed the crime.[33]

In the novel the town of Bayamo is well aware of Don Pancho's pedophilia and the strategies he employs to trap his victims. But he is so wealthy, and his victims so powerless, that very few people try to stop him. Fiction, of course, cannot replace historical documents. But Masdeu wrote a sprawling novel that attempted to critique early republican Cuba, and the way that he chose to portray the most powerful man in Bayamo was as a rapist of young, Black, domestic servants. By virtue of their class position, Black girls were vulnerable.

This chapter has explored the trajectories of some of Cuba's most vulnerable citizens just after the island's revolutionary independence movement. Famously, Cuba had another revolution in 1959, resulting in some thirty years of radical socialist transformations. Much post-1959 policy targeted institutional racism, and women became involved in statecraft to an unprecedented degree.[34] But since the Soviet Union's collapse in 1991, racial inequalities that the government banished in the early years of the revolution have returned. Especially in the tourism sector and in the sectors that benefit directly from tourism, it is impossible to ignore that white Cubans are benefiting at hugely disproportionate rates from Cuba's opening.[35]

If Cuba continues to open itself up to global market forces and to chip away at the socialism that has defined it for the past fifty years, thinking about the pre-revolutionary past can only help to think about the future: What lessons are there to draw from the experiences of Black girls at a previous period of radical change? However, the meaning of Black girlhood in Cuba is not only important as a bellwether for a deeper understanding of Cuba's past and future. The meaning is important because Black lives matter, because young Black lives matter. In the early twentieth century, to be a Black girl in Cuba meant that while you nominally had access to most trappings of citizenship, deeply rooted and effectively dispersed patriarchal norms endangered you and circumvented justice. Black girlhood, while acknowledged as separate from adulthood, was training for Black womanhood, with its dangers and injustices.

Notes

1. María de los Reyes Castillo Bueno, *Reyita: The Life of a Black Cuban Woman in the Twentieth Century,* trans. Anne McLean (Durham: Duke University Press, 2000).

2. Guadalupe García, "Urban *Guajiros*: Colonial Reconcentración, Rural Displacement, and Criminalization in Western Cuba, 1895–1902," *Journal of Latin American Studies* 43, no. 2 (August 2011): 209–235.

3. Ada Ferrer, *Insurgent Cuba: Race, Nation, and Revolution* (Chapel Hill: University of North Carolina Press, 1999).

4. Castillo Bueno, *Reyita,* 34.

5. Steve J. Stern, *The Secret History of Gender: Women, Men, and Power in Late Colonial Mexico* (Chapel Hill: University of North Carolina Press, 1995); Lyman Johnson and Sonya Lipsett-Rivera, ed., *The Faces of Honor: Sex, Shame, and Violence in Colonial Latin America* (Albuquerque: University of New Mexico Press, 1998); Ann Twinam, *Public Lives, Private Secrets: Gender, Honor, Sexuality, and Illegitimacy in Colonial Spanish America* (Stanford: Stanford University Press, 1999).

6. Eileen Findlay, *Imposing Decency: The Politics of Sexuality and Race in Puerto Rico, 1870–1920* (Durham: Duke University Press, 2011).

7. Sueann Caulfield, "Interracial Courtship in the Rio de Janeiro Courts, 1918–1940," in *Race and Nation in Modern Latin America,* eds. Nancy P. Applebaum, Anne S. Macpherson, and Karin Alejandra Rosemblatt (Chapel Hill: University of North Carolina Press, 2003) 163–186; Henrique Espada Lima, "Wages of Intimacy: Domestic Workers Disputing Wages in the Higher Courts of Nineteenth-Century Brazil," *International Labor and Working-Class History* 88 (Fall 2015): 11–29.

8. A.M. de J. Gonzalez, "Esclavos voluntarios," *El Nuevo Criollo,* 19 August 1905.

9. "Causa formada por Estupro a virtud de querella del Ministerio Fiscal, 25 May 1908," Audiencia de la Habana, Legajo 459 Num. 2, ANC.

10. Red Cross (Cuba), *La cruz roja en Cuba* (Washington: Red Cross, 1900).

11. U.S. War Department, *Report on the Census of Cuba* (Washington: Government Printing Office, 1900), 439.

12. Nara Milanich, "Women, Children, and the Social Organization of Domestic Labor in Chile," *Hispanic American Historical Review* 91, no. 1 (2011): 32.

13. "Causa formada por Estupro a virtud de querella del Ministerio Fiscal, 25 May 1908," Audiencia de la Habana, Legajo 459 Num. 2, ANC.

14. "Los ninos estaban en un ruinoso y pestilente edificio que había sido cuartel de la caballeria española; y los adultos en una barraca de madera fabricada por subscripción popular para epidemias contagiosas.

Unos y otros yacían en los suelos en el más miserable y conmovedor estado: los niños desnudos, o cubiertos con andrajosos harapos. Todos esataban horiblemente hinchados, pálidos como cera, llenos de sarna, ulceraciones repugnantes y parásitos asquerosos, reflejando en el semblante cadavérico el hambre crónica y la desesperación. Casi todos tenían diarrea, y como apeanas podían moverse por falta de fuerzas, vivían en un verdadero estercolero" (Red Cross, *La cruz roja en Cuba,* 1900).

15. Olivia Gomes da Cunha, trans. Micol Sigal, "Learning to Serve: Intimacy, Morality, and Violence," *Hispanic American Historical Review* 88 no. 3 (2008): 455–91.

16. *The Red Cross in Cuba,* 27.

17. U.S. War Department, *Report on the Census of Cuba,* 160.

18. U.S. War Department, 155.

19. U.S. War Department, 165.

20. "Causa formada por Estupro a virtud de querella del Ministerio Fiscal, 25 May 1908," Audiencia de la Habana, Legajo 459 Num. 2, ANC.

21. Real Academia Española, *Diccionario de la Lengua Española* (Madrid: Editorial Espasa Calpe, 1922), 923.

22. Divisions of Customs and Insular Affairs, War Department. *Translation of the Penal Code in force in Cuba and Porto Rico* (Washington: Government Printing Office, 1900), 158.

23. Renato Barahona, *Sex Crimes, Honour, and the Law in Early Modern Spain: Vizcaya, 1528–1735* (Toronto: University of Toronto Press, 2003).

24. Barahona, *Sex Crimes.*

25. Stern, *The Secret History of Gender,* 14.

26. Sueann Caulfield, "Interracial Courtship in the Rio de Janeiro Courts, 1918–1940," 177.

27. "Causa formada por Estupro a virtud de querella del Ministerio Fiscal, 25 May 1908," Audiencia de la Habana, Legajo 459 Num. 2, Archivos Nacionales de Cuba (ANC).

28. "Violación de la menor Regla María Sánchez," Audiencia de la Habana, Legajo 492 Num 4, ANC.

29. "Violación de la menor Regla María Sánchez."

30. "Violación de la menor Regla María Sánchez."

31. Sueann Caulfield, "Interracial Courtship in the Rio de Janeiro Courts, 1918–1940," 168.

32. "Violación de la menor Regla María Sánchez," Audiencia de la Habana, Legajo 492 Num 4, ANC.

33. Jesús Masdeu, *La Raza Rriste* (La Habana: Imprenta y Papelería Rambla y Bouza, 1924).

34. Michelle Chase, *Revolution within the Revolution: Women and Gender Politics in Cuba, 1952–1962* (Chapel Hill: University of North Carolina Press, 2015); Devyn Spence-Benson, *Antiracism in Cuba: The Unfinished Revolution* (Chapel Hill: University of North Carolina Press, 2016).

35. Alejandro de la Fuente, *A Nation for All: Race, Inequality, and Politics in Twentieth-Century Cuba* (Chapel Hill: University of North Carolina Press, 2001), Chapter 8.

CHAPTER 4

"How to Play in the Right Way"

Recreation and Respectability at the Virginia Industrial School for Colored Girls, 1915–1940

LINDSEY ELIZABETH JONES

At the dawn of the twentieth century, organized African American women in the Commonwealth of Virginia identified a crisis threatening the well-being of African American girls and the stability of society at large. They alerted local and national networks of potential supporters to the disgraceful situation: across the Commonwealth, hundreds of "wayward" Black girls sat alongside adults in local jails because they, unlike white boys, white girls, and Black boys, did not have access to a juvenile reformatory. When Black girls' crimes, adolescent misbehaviors, and acts of sexual self-determination were met with legal sanction, local courts—most of which had limited resources available to supervise African American juvenile probationers—had no other option but to send them to jail. Beginning with its founding in 1907, the Virginia State Federation of Colored Women's Clubs worked to create awareness of the lack of a reformatory for Black girls, obtain support for the project from sympathetic whites, and raise the funds necessary to build a school. While local Black women's clubs had frequently worked to secure alternative placements for Black girls who would otherwise be jailed with adults, the new statewide organization represented an opportunity to centralize and formalize efforts on behalf of an estimated "300 colored girls in different parts of Virginia who could be saved from lives of immorality and shame if given a chance to reform in the proper environment with suitable training."[1] Their efforts reveal Black clubwomen's strong conviction that Black girls needed to be recognized and treated as girls, not adults. Virginia State Federation President Janie Porter Barrett and her supporters successfully leveraged the juvenile justice reforms of the progressive era to create a protected space for

Black girls; however, their efforts also subjected these inmates to new forms of control and surveillance. The tightly managed recreation program at the school, especially when contrasted with the commercial amusements available to teenagers in the early twentieth century, imposed an understanding of girlish playfulness that many of these young people would likely have rejected if left to their own devices. This pedagogy of play raises persistent questions about who has the power to determine what counts as girlish pleasures.

State officials expressed relief and enthusiasm as they learned about the efforts of Black women to create a reformatory for wayward colored girls. This institution would complete Virginia's modern, race- and sex-segregated system of juvenile corrections—a system which, although subsidized by public monies, relied primarily on private initiative and private funding. With the blessing of state social welfare officials, the support of white social reformers, some state appropriations, and the financial support of hundreds of African American small-dollar donors, the Virginia Industrial School for Colored Girls opened in January of 1915 in rural Hanover County, Virginia.

Janie Porter Barrett, founding president of the Virginia State Federation of Colored Women's Clubs and superintendent of the Virginia Industrial School for Colored Girls (VISCG), believed that recreation had pedagogical import for the VISCG's student-inmates and for observers of the institution. As an outward-facing tool of propaganda, VISCG superintendent Barrett's description of play created a pedagogy of respectability that countered notions of Black female sexual deviance and instead illustrated wayward Black girls' capacity for moral redirection. For the student-inmates of the VISCG, the activities she described were pedagogies of respectability meant to teach them proper forms of amusement—alternatives to the kinds of entertainment which frequently led adolescents down the path of delinquency. The recreational program illustrates how Black clubwomen's discourses and practices of respectability worked alongside state conceptions of delinquency to discipline the working-class Black girls committed to the VISCG, a population subject to the overlapping reform agendas of Black adults and a white-controlled state.

Paranoia about adolescent female sexuality and stereotypical images of Black female sexual deviance worked in tandem to create the conditions precipitating the reform project of the VISCG. Even as reformers fought negative stereotypes, data communicated by the institution itself threatened to confirm racist notions of Black female sexual impropriety. Barrett turned to recreation as a means of proving the girls' youthfulness and potential to reform. Through structured play, Barrett and her colleagues tried to reshape girls' sensibilities around amusement, redirecting them from morally questionable to respectable modes of entertainment. In addition to state-enforced confinement, Black girls committed to the VISCG also experienced the attempted disciplining of their minds and bodies at the hands of the women who were their fiercest advocates. Barrett and her staff delivered the lesson that play should not be considered synonymous with unrestrained pleasure; rather, play offered an opportunity to practice and demonstrate the self-mastery required of a respectable young woman.

Defining Delinquency and Countering Stereotypes

Virginia's state legislature established the State Board of Charities and Corrections in 1908 to supervise private charities, local jails, the state penitentiary, and other state institutions. Its leadership almost immediately decided to tackle the problem of children in local jails, and in 1910, their lobbying efforts secured a law providing that "no court should commit or sentence a child under seventeen years of age to jail."[2] In 1914, Virginia's General Assembly passed a "Juvenile Law," which raised by one year the age under which an individual should be considered a juvenile; prohibited the sentencing of any child under eighteen to a police station, jail, or the penitentiary ("unless the offense is aggravated"); and prohibited making any child appear before a grand jury. This legislation also authorized the establishment of Juvenile and Domestic Relations Courts in cities with a population of over 50,000 and defined juvenile delinquency for the first time in the state's history. The definition read as follows:

> The term "delinquent child" shall include a child under eighteen years of age who—
>
> 1. violates a law of this State or a city or town ordinance; or
> 2. who is incorrigible; or
> 3. who is a persistent truant from school; or
> 4. who associates with criminals or reputed criminals, or vicious or immoral persons;
> 5. or who is growing up in idleness or crime; or
> 6. who wanders about the streets in the nighttime; or
> 7. who uses intoxicating liquor as a beverage, or who uses opium, cocaine, morphine, or other similar drug, without the direction of a competent physician; or
> 8. who frequents, visits, or is found in a disorderly house, house of ill-fame, saloon, barroom or a place where intoxicating liquors are sold, exchanged or given away; or
> 9. who patronizes, visits, or is found in a gambling-house or place

where a gambling-device is operated, or in a billiard hall or pool room; or

10. who uses vile, obscene, vulgar, profane or indecent language, or is guilty of dissolute or immoral conduct.[3]

At the same time that the 1914 Juvenile Law provided much-needed clarity to Virginia reformers seeking solutions to the problem of children in jails by adding the category of juvenile delinquency to the state's code, it also left room for ambiguity in its application. While this law contained no explicit differentiation by gender, Virginians applied different definitions of delinquency to boys than to girls, as did Americans in general during the Progressive Era. In the context of rapid urbanization, industrialization, and immigration, juvenile reform workers obsessed over the so-called "girl problem" plaguing urban America, defined by historian Susan Cahn as the nexus of three interrelated concerns: pervasive economic and sexual exploitation of girls and young women in cities, intergenerational conflict stemming from girls' acts of sexual and reproductive self-determination, and shifting legal and social definitions of girlhood and womanhood. The solution to the "girl problem," in the eyes of many Progressive reformers, was to "protect adolescent women from the perceived hazards of modern city life and their own youthful inclinations" by using courts, probation officers, and state institutions as instruments of surveillance and mechanisms of behavioral control.[4]

Virginians shared in the national concern about adolescent female behavior, particularly the sexual choices of urban girls. Girls regularly appeared before the state's first Juvenile and Domestic Relations Court for status offenses—charges such as "immoral," "ungovernable," "incorrigible," "runaway," "disorderly," and "delinquent" that encompassed various rebellious behaviors but especially indexed sexual activity when applied to girls.[5] In 1916, the first year that the court reported juvenile statistics, a total of 93 white girls and 176 colored girls appeared before the court. Among white girls, the court charged one-third (thirty-one) with status offenses.[6] For Black girls, this proportion rose to 54 percent. The ninety-five Black female status offenders faced charges of behaving disorderly (forty-two) or incorrigible (thirty-five), or committing offenses against morality (eighteen).[7] While many Richmond girls ended up on probation, some found themselves in one of the state's two segregated female juvenile reformatories. Of the 161 girls committed to the VISCG between 1915 and 1920, Richmond's Juvenile and Domestic Relations court sentenced sixty-nine.[8] Girls committed to the VISCG between 1915 and 1920 were on average 14.6 years old. Most of these girls lived in population-dense areas of the state, including the Central Virginia cities of Richmond and Petersburg, the Southwestern city of Roanoke, and the coastal cities of Portsmouth, Norfolk, Newport News, and Hampton. Department of Juvenile Justice records yield few details about specific offenses inmates committed during this period, but given their ages, primarily urban backgrounds, and the fact that many carried the catch-all term "delinquent," these girls likely landed in the VISCG as a result of status offenses relating to disobedience and sexual activity at least as frequently as for criminal offenses.[9]

Barrett, along with organized Black women in general, detested both the sexual double standard and the particular ways in which white supremacy and racialized sexual violence compounded its impacts upon Black girls. In a 1911 speech before the Virginia Child Welfare Conference, she asserted, in thinly veiled terms, that the African American "girl problem" did not originate with any inborn predisposition toward delinquency. Rather, Black girls' problematic behaviors were the logical result of their hypervulnerability to sexual violence for which courts rarely held their attackers accountable. As Barrett told her audience, "The negro girl because of previous conditions, I suppose, has no rights that any man, white or Black, feels bound to respect. No indignity or crime heaped upon her offends society, and in very few cases does it offend the law; so beyond a doubt she is the most unprotected of all human beings. When we find her running the wayward girl record high, indeed, we can't expect any more."[10]

As much as she detested the sexual double standard and the special vulnerabilities it created for Black girls, the reformatory that Barrett hoped to open was not meant primarily to be an intervention into the sociolegal structures that determined the definitions of juvenile delinquency and unfairly stigmatized Black girls for their sexual experiences. Rather, it was meant to be a site that would intervene in the lives of *individual* Black girls who would otherwise have been destined for jail or the state penitentiary, nurturing and disciplining their minds and bodies rather than merely punishing them for their misdeeds. By giving them "the love and sympathy they need," as Barrett told the group of reformers and state officials who ultimately supported the Virginia State Federation's plan to construct a reformatory, she and her colleagues hoped to "[make] these girls into respectable, useful women."[11]

Barrett's desire to cultivate "respectable" women indexes a specific strategy of racial uplift that historian Evelyn Brooks Higginbotham famously characterized as the "politics of respectability": organized Black Baptist women's rejection of wealth and social status as determinants of one's inherent value and their creation of an alternative, manners-and-morals-based hierarchy that any ordinary African American woman could climb.[12] The strategy of respectability, per Higginbotham, rested upon the belief that Black individuals', especially Black women's, public behavior—their "temperance, cleanliness of person and property, thrift, polite manners, and sexual purity"—would "[determine] the collective fate of African Americans." Black efforts toward "behavioral self-regulation and self-improvement along moral, educational, and economic lines" would both demonstrate the illogical nature of African Americans' social subordination and shield Black women from pervasive slanderous attacks on their individual and collective sexual identities.[13]

As Higginbotham and others have demonstrated, the politics of respectability was a strategy that was not particular only to Black Baptist women at the turn of the century; rather, it animated the work of overlapping groups of organized Black club and church women and informed Black public life in general during and after this time period.[14] The pitfalls of respectability as a political tool, therefore, impacted more than just Black Baptist women. Higginbotham argues that respectability's "emphasis on individual behavior served inevitably to blame Blacks for their victimization and, worse yet, to place an inordinate amount of blame on Black women," who were expected to hew especially close to proper gender roles in order to be regarded as worthy of respect. For Higginbotham, "This conservative and moralistic dimension tended to privatize racial discrimination—thus rendering it outside the authority of government regulation."[15]

Bearing in mind Higginbotham's claim that the politics of respectability was a strategy motivated in large part to defend Black women and girls against attacks based on their sexuality, a brief look at girls' paths to the VISCG illustrates the high stakes for the women of the Virginia State Federation both of transforming student-inmates into respectable women and of convincing the public that wayward Black girls were even capable of making such a transformation. While records often fail to record explicitly the specific offenses of the girls committed to the VISCG, the codes used to document their paths to the school illustrate the raced and gendered construction of juvenile delinquency. The Virginia Department of Juvenile Justice's individual records for many of these girls simply include the disposition "delinquent" to describe why girls were ordered by courts to the school. The most common comment accompanying this disposition was "incorrigible," a term literally meaning "uncorrectable" and evoking rebellion and sexual misbehavior when applied to adolescent girls. Rarely, one finds more colorful explanations that elaborate further upon the meaning of "delinquency" for individual girls. For instance, a fourteen-year-old girl committed to the VISCG from Richmond in 1925 was described as "immoral, pregnant and keeps late hours, has been on probation." A comment regarding a sixteen-year-old Richmond girl committed in 1924 indicated that she "keeps bad company, contracted venereal diseases." Similarly, a fifteen-year-old Suffolk City girl's juvenile index card (committed in 1925) described her as "indiscreet in conduct—has V.D."[16] While such comments appear infrequently in the record, they point to the relative prevalence of status offenders—girls whose age was the primary legal justification for criminalizing their sexual behavior—among the VISCG student population.

In her intake interviews with newly committed girls, and in the course of developing relationships with them during their time at the institution, Barrett surely learned in some detail the stories that were subsumed under the category of "delinquency" for the VISCG's student-inmates, and these stories likely evoked sympathy and compassion rather than pure judgment when she heard them. Outside observers of this widely publicized institution, however, did not have the benefit of this insight. In Barrett's early discourse about the VISCG, particularly the annual reports of the school that circulated nationally among Black and white readers, she declined to comment with any specificity about the experiences of trauma and abuse that might have led girls down a path of sexual delinquency. Even while pleading for resources to build quarantine space for venereal cases at the institution, Barrett attributed the contagion to the fact that "these girls coming from the jails are often diseased" but did not go the further step to explicitly link girls' incarceration to venereal disease.[17] To straightforwardly address the sexual nature of the criminalization of Black girls by pointing directly to consensual and unwanted sexual experiences before or during incarceration would add evidence, she likely believed, to widespread charges of Black women's and girls' promiscuity and immorality. Barrett therefore remained reticent until forced to do otherwise, embodying what Darlene Clark Hine has termed the "culture of dissemblance": a set of practices meant to shield Black women's individual and collective sexuality from the uncharitable gaze of white Americans.[18] In order to gain recognition of their sexual morality and protection against sexual exploitation, and to demonstrate that negative sexual stereotypes were false, many Black women of Barrett's generation were driven to "downplay, even deny, sexual expression"—their own and that of other Black women.[19] By avoiding public discourse about sexual matters, Black women refused to lend ammunition to white supremacist attacks on their individual and collective image.

In the context of describing the lives and experiences of criminalized Black girls, the consequences of inadvertently fueling negative sexual stereotypes would likely be injurious to the project of reinforcing distinctions between Black girls and Black women. As the 1912 execution of Virginia Christian (two weeks after her seventeenth birthday) and the widespread incarceration of other Black girls in adult facilities demonstrated, Black girls in the Commonwealth of Virginia had long experienced legal "age compression."[20] Providing information about their sexual experiences would likely have fueled this phenomenon rather than evoking compassion for the plight of wayward

Black girls. Barrett therefore downplayed the sexual nature of girls' paths to the VISCG in her public discourse—until she was forced to circulate this information directly to the widespread readership of her annual reports.

Beginning in 1920, when the Virginia State Federation of Colored Women's Clubs (along with the private organizations in charge of the other youth reformatories) transferred ownership of the VISCG to the Commonwealth of Virginia, the institution was required to relay health statistics for its student-inmates in its annual reports and to report syphilis tests and their results to the Virginia State Department of Health. These aggregate health statistics, like girls' individual records, point to girls' sexual behavior as a factor in their commitment to the school. While in prior years Barrett had referred vaguely to the need to segregate "diseased" girls and new admits from the school's general population in order to halt the spread of contagious diseases, annual reports beginning in 1922 presented numbers that described the problem in more detail. The number of Wasserman tests administered to diagnose syphilis, number of girls treated for syphilis and gonorrhea, number of intravenous, intramuscular, intracervical, and surgical treatments, and the various medicines involved were all recorded in the VISCG's annual reports.

In the first year of health reporting at the Virginia Industrial School, March 1921 through March 1922, there were 105 girls living at the school. Thirty-three girls were treated for syphilis, twenty-three for gonorrhea.[21] In the next year, forty girls were treated for gonorrhea, twenty-two for syphilis.[22] In the 1924–1925 reporting year, fifty-three girls were treated for syphilis and forty-two treated for gonorrhea.[23] These high numbers of venereal infections were a constant through all of the years of Barrett's superintendence, until 1940.

In each annual report after 1920, Barrett was forced to communicate to her audience a quantitative illustration of the extent of the girls' sexualization. Reporting these numbers alone, without the benefit of being able to convey the stories of adolescent sexual exploration, economic deprivation, or sexual victimization that gave rise to instances of venereal disease, risked reinforcing images of Black girls as sexually precocious and of loose moral character. Barrett's detailed reporting on the school's program of recreation, in which she emphasized the capacity of wayward Black girls to become respectable women, was one way to counteract the potential harm of publishing these decontextualized statistics about venereal disease.

Recreation as a Pedagogy of Respectability

In her study examining the lives of Black girls and young women in segregated New Orleans, LaKisha Simmons articulates a "double bind": Black girls' sense that "they saw themselves through the eyes of whites but also through the eyes of middle-class Blacks who attempted to regulate their behaviors, bodies, and sexuality."[24] Examining public discourse on "wayward girls," who were "marked as delinquent through their sexuality and bodies," Simmons illustrates how Black girls were policed and disciplined both by the state and by the middle class African Americans who wrote about and intervened in the problem of Black female juvenile delinquency.[25] Within the double bind, discourses of respectability worked alongside systemic racism to constrain the daily lives of Black girls and young women. Wayward Black girls committed to the VISCG can also be said to have experienced this double bind. Sexist enforcement of juvenile laws, compounded by white supremacist notions of Black female criminality and hypersexuality, shaped Black girls' paths to the VISCG.[26] However, once they arrived in the institution, it was middle-class Black women who structured these girls' daily lives according to their own ideas about respectability.

Recreation and play were important elements of institutional life at the VISCG. Barrett's educational philosophy and theory of rehabilitation held that structured, supervised play was as important to the reclamation of delinquent Black girls as the academic, industrial, and religious lessons that also comprised her curriculum. In 1916, reflecting on the school's first year of operation, Barrett wrote:

> The girls appreciate the least thing done for their pleasure. We are always glad of an excuse to give any kind of party; it gives them something to look forward to and something to talk about after it is over and it gives also very valuable training in how to play in the right way. I know of nothing they need to be taught more. All the trouble they get into is during their play time and simply because they do not know how to play.[27]

Barrett refers here not just to the behaviors she saw in the girls committed to her institution, but also to challenges posed by urbanization that she believed to be influential factors in girls' paths to the VISCG. Black and white members of Virginia's juvenile reform community found fault with the fact that young Black children in Virginia's urban areas did not have easy access to segregated playgrounds and sports fields. Without spaces for wholesome outdoor play, children were prone to loitering on city streets and getting into trouble. Moreover, cheap urban amusements like dance halls, movie theaters, and bowling alleys proliferated in the early twentieth century, and reformers in Virginia and across the nation saw these as unwholesome activities for adolescents. These activities, which working class girls could readily access using their own money or that of a male companion, took place at night, in heterosocial spaces, and without responsible adult supervision—conditions which reformers believed led straight to delinquency.[28] "Learning to play in the right way" was in large part about working-class Black girls learning to enjoy the outdoor activities and homosocial amusements that middle class Black women like Barrett thought appropriate for the development of respectable young women.

"Learning to play in the right way" was also about incorporating recreation into the school's curriculum and institutional culture in systematic ways rather than expecting or encouraging play to happen organically. Play times were written into the school's daily schedule. For Barrett, play was key to behavioral management. Reporting in 1919 on the school's relatively low number of disciplinary issues, she wrote, "I think the secret of our discipline is keeping them busy with an evenly balanced program of work, play, study, rest, and something of interest ahead to look forward to occasionally."[29] The girls' schedule that year, therefore, included "school a part of each day, work a part of each day, with supervised play thrown in at the noon hour and between supper and the study hour."[30] The enduring plan, in her words, was to "have [the] recreation program serve a threefold purpose: to provide pleasure; to improve health; and to build character."[31] She stated that "leisure and relaxation, so necessary to well-rounded development, may prove worse than disastrous to a group like ours if allowed to degenerate into mere idleness."[32] For Barrett, proper "leisure and relaxation" meant alternative forms of entertainment to those which girls' families disapproved of and the Commonwealth defined as delinquent—for instance, drinking "intoxicating liquor" or using "opium, cocaine, morphine, or other similar drug, without the direction of a competent physician"; visiting places such as a "disorderly house, house of ill-fame, saloon, barroom or a place where intoxicating liquors are sold, exchanged or given away," or a "gambling-house," "billiard hall," or "pool room"; "wandering the streets at night"; joyriding in automobiles; and engaging in sexual activity.[33] She designed a recreational program that was purposed to develop self-control by teaching girls to channel their youthful energy into wholesome and productive activities such as parlor games, athletics, folk dances, and "regular Field Days at which time there are relay races, potato races, three-legged races, obstacle races, stilt races, and any others we can think of."[34]

Barrett kept recreation tightly linked, in a bidirectional fashion, to discipline. For instance, she stated in one annual report: "Play night is looked forward to with great pleasure by the girls and it is a real punishment to miss it. No girl who has not measured up to our standards, especially in conduct, is allowed to play on play night."[35] Even though recreation was a regular part of daily life at the school, there were certain special amusements, such as evening programs and off-campus trips, where each girl's participation was contingent upon her conduct.

While girls' conduct in other areas could impact their participation in special amusements, their conduct while playing was also subject to assessment, with merits and demerits assigned according to the quality of their behavior at play. Barrett reported that "the girls are making rapid progress in learning how to play, since they lose their per cent for not playing just as they lose it for not doing their work."[36] She also described what it looked like for girls to self-regulate during play. She noted, "The relentless rule about never allowing squabbling at games or on play night has worked wonders. It matters not what the cause is, if squabbling begins everything stops immediately without any explanation. If it is at night they go to bed; if it is in the daytime they go to work, and they miss several chances to play before the privilege is granted again." Failure to play in the right way could therefore mean that girls *both* earned demerits *and* lost the privilege of playing in the future. Moreover, play was an opportunity for girls to demonstrate self-control and share responsibility for the surveillance of their fellow students' behavior. "We seldom have to call off games or play now," Barrett recorded in 1921, "because the girls have learned to keep watch on themselves and their neighbors too, and the improvement has been wonderful."[37]

A look at the structure of a typical "play night" at the VISCG demonstrates the extent to which the program of recreation involved direct instruction in how to enjoy properly supervised, highly structured, homosocial amusement:

> Upon their arrival . . . the girls take seats around the sides of the room. The first number is a progressive conversation. A chord on the piano is a signal for each girl to begin conversing with the girl nearest to her. They must all talk, whether they wish to or not, and they *must* say something pleasant. At a second signal they change their seats so that each will have an opportunity to talk with someone else. This is repeated until every girl has exchanged a few pleasant words with all the other girls in the room. A few bars of a lively march are played on the piano to announce a grand march. All girls must take part in this, thus doing away with "wall flowers," and by the time the march is over the spirit of play is on. The march lasts long enough to make them glad to be seated and listen with interest to selections, first from the quartet of Federation Cottage and then from that of Virginia Cottage. . . . When the singing is over impromptu conversation is indulged in as long as it seems wise, then another game which consumes much energy is introduced—"Going to Jerusalem," "The Indian Game," and "Going to Paris" are excellent games for this purpose and the girls never seem to tire of them. After this game there may be some more singing . . . and sometimes a recitation. This is followed by folk games and then it is time to report to their cottages and retire for the night.[38]

Barrett relates a scene in which adolescent girls—an average age of about fifteen years—joyfully dance while a march is played on the piano and engage in a game of musical chairs (i.e., "Going to Jerusalem"). Whether they originated from urban or rural Virginia, one can speculate that these girls would not have been likely to enjoy such forms of amusement as "progressive conversation" or "The Indian Game" had they been free to choose their own entertainment. This and other descriptions of the recreational activities at the VISCG provide a window into what middle class Black women reformers thought constituted proper ways for Black adolescent girls to enjoy themselves. On a "play night" such as the one described above, girls engaged in activities meant both to engage the intellect and to permit an appropriate amount of physical activity.

Athletics also comprised part of the VISCG's recreational program. Through participating in sports, girls learned to channel their physical energy into structured forms of vigorous outdoor exercise rather than allowing ennui to draw them into the less-than-respectable forms of amusement that had caused many of them to be labeled "delinquent." Barrett narrated in great detail a typical game of baseball at the school:

> The girls are becoming more and more interested in athletics. They have two fine baseball teams, the "Red Sox" of Federation Cottage and the "Blue Sox" of Virginia Cottage. They have match games at special times and they play wonderfully well. They have bloomers, which I succeeded in getting for them just as the baseball season was closing, and it gave a new interest which has kept baseball popular the year round. I bought cheap white stockings which the "Red Sox" dyed red and the "Blue Sox" dyed blue. . . . When a game of ball is called all baseball regulations must be observed. Whenever a question arises it must be settled by the captains of the teams, the referee, and the officer in charge. If this rule is violated the game ends at once. When a match game is played, there is an officer in charge of each team and its rooters. All the girls who are not regular players or substitutes must root for their cottage team. Among the rooters are to be found the tin-pan division, the horn and whistle division, and the yelling division. Their aim seems not so much to cheer the players as to outroot the rooters on the other side. One cannot tell by the noise who is winning, for they cheer as vigorously for one who is put out on their side as they do when they make a home run. Since the fun for those not playing is in the rooting, I raise no objection as to when or how they do it; I simply insist that they root, since that is their part in the game.[39]

This description exemplifies the extent to which Barrett believed in the teachable nature of play. Girls could be taught to abide by all of the rules, regulations, codes of dress, and other customs of baseball as team players. They could also be explicitly taught the institution's specific conventions for sports spectatorship, including "divisions" responsible for providing the sonic backdrop (tin pans, horns, whistles, yelling) for the game. Spectators, rather than merely venting their excitement or disappointment in the process of *consuming* a game of baseball, were tasked with *producing* the game's festive atmosphere through the regimented (not organic) modes of "vigorous cheering" that constituted "their part in the game."

During the VISCG's play nights, inmates socialized with their cohorts, under the watchful eye of adults, in accordance with a predetermined schedule—criteria that were almost certainly missing from the typical amusements the girls would have enjoyed outside of the institution. During athletics matches, the girls exerted their bodies and raised their voices in intense but contextually appropriate ways. In these elements of the school's recreational program, girls practiced—and Barrett advertised their capacity to enjoy—self-controlled, respectable forms of entertainment.

Conclusion

In her role as superintendent of the Virginia Industrial School for Colored Girls, Barrett understood her task to be moral reclamation of Black girls who were stigmatized by the label of sexual delinquency. She therefore devised practices of recreation that aimed to discipline girls' bodies and minds according to Black middle-class ideas of respectability. As the primary interpreter of the institution's activities to the outside world, she also sought to convince her readership that it was the social and legal denial of a protected child status, rather than any inherent vice within Black girls themselves, that gave rise to the phenomenon of Black female sexual delinquency. She succeeded in creating a specialized rehabilitative space for Black girls that, as Anasa Hicks and Shani Roper explain, remained out of reach for Black girls who found themselves before the courts in Cuba or Jamaica at this time. Barrett's detailed descriptions of the VISCG's recreation practices also served a pedagogical function, attempting to resolve for outsiders a tension that was inherent within the reform project: that between Black clubwomen's assertion that Black girls should be considered morally perfectible children on the one hand, and the ways in which girls' diseased bodies threatened to confirm white supremacist ideas about Black female hypersexuality, regardless of age, on the other. By depicting scenes of girls at play, Barrett endeavored to persuade her readers that VISCG student-inmates were capable (and desirous) of becoming "respectable, useful women."

Notes

1. Virginia State Federation of Colored Women's Clubs, "Industrial Home School for Colored Girls Endorsements" (pamphlet, n.d., circa 1913).

2. See Arthur W. James, *Virginia's Social Awakening: The Contribution of Dr. Mastin and the Board of Charities and Corrections* (Richmond, Va.: Garrett and Massie, 1939), for details on the development of this agency under Mastin's leadership. In its first survey, the State Board of Charities and Corrections found an estimated 359 children in jails, 96 white and 263 colored.

3. Commonwealth of Virginia, *Acts of the General Assembly of the Commonwealth of Virginia* 1914, Ch. 350.

4. Susan K. Cahn, *Sexual Reckonings: Southern Girls in a Troubling Age* (Cambridge: Harvard University Press, 2012), 71.

5. Miroslava Chávez-García, "'The Crime of Precocious Sexuality' Celebrates Thirty Years: A Critical Appraisal," *The Journal of the History of Childhood and Youth* 2, no.1 (2009): 88.

6. Categories are as follows: offense against morality (14), incorrigible (12), and disorderly conduct (5). *First Annual Report of the Juvenile and Domestic Relations Court of Richmond, Virginia* (1916).

7. *First Annual Report of the Juvenile and Domestic Relations Court of Richmond, Virginia* (1916).

8. Virginia Industrial School for Colored Girls, *Admission and Discharge Register* (1915–1940).

9. Individual juvenile index cards record each juvenile's name, race, sex, and relevant dates, including when the juvenile was committed to the State Board of Charities and Corrections or placed in a state industrial school. However, many of these records (per Department of Juvenile Justice Staff and Library of Virginia archivists) have been destroyed pursuant to the retention schedule agreed upon by the Department of Juvenile Justice and the Library of Virginia. Personal communication with Janet P. Van Cuyk, Legislative and Research Manager, Virginia Department of Juvenile Justice (August 14, 2015).

10. Virginia Conference of Charities and Corrections, *Proceedings, Virginia Child Welfare Conference* (Richmond: Davis Bottom, Superintendent of Public Printing, 1911): 118. For an in-depth examination of the role of interpersonal and state violence in Black girls' experiences before and during incarceration at the VISCG, see Lindsey Elizabeth Jones, "'The most unprotected of all human beings': Black Girls, State Violence, and the Limits of Protection in Jim Crow Virginia," *Souls* 20, no. 1 (forthcoming).

11. Virginia Conference of Charities and Corrections, *Proceedings,* 118.

12. Evelyn Brooks Higginbotham, *Righteous Discontent: The Women's Movement in the Black Baptist Church, 1880–1920* (Cambridge: Harvard University Press, 1993), 191.

13. Higginbotham, *Righteous Discontent*, 193, 196.

14. See Kevin Kelly Gaines, *Uplifting the Race: Black Leadership, Politics, and Culture in the Twentieth Century* (Chapel Hill: University of North Carolina Press, 1996) and Deborah Gray White, *Too Heavy a Load: Black Women in Defense of Themselves, 1894–1994* (New York: W.W. Norton, 1999).

15. Higginbotham, *Righteous Discontent*, 202–3.

16. All quotations listed here are from individual girls' records in the Juvenile Index Card Files of the Virginia Dept. of Juvenile Justice, 1895–1987.

17. *First Annual Report of the Virginia Industrial School for Colored Girls* (1916).

18. Darlene Clark Hine, "Rape and the Inner Lives of Black Women in the Middle West: Preliminary Thoughts on the Culture of Dissemblance," *Signs* 14, no. 4 (1989): 916.

19. Hine, 916.

20. Per Monique Morris, "The assignment of more adultlike characteristics to the expressions of young Black girls is a form of age compression. Along this truncated age continuum, Black girls are likened more to adults than to children and are treated as if they are willfully engaging in behaviors typically expected of Black women—sexual involvement, parenting or primary caregiving, workforce participation, and other adult behaviors and responsibilities." Monique Morris, *Pushout: The Criminalization of Black Girls in Schools* (New York: The New Press, 2016), 34. On the case of Virginia Christian, see Lashawn Harris, "The 'Commonwealth of Virginia vs. Virginia Christian': Southern Black Women, Crime & Punishment in Progressive Era Virginia," *Journal of Social History* 47, no.4 (2014), 922–42, and Lindsey Elizabeth Jones, "Black Girls, State Violence, and the Limits of Protection in Jim Crow Virginia."

21. *Seventh Annual Report of the Virginia Industrial School for Colored Girls* (1922).

22. *Eighth Annual Report of the Virginia Industrial School for Colored Girls* (1923).

23. *Tenth Annual Report of the Virginia Industrial School for Colored Girls* (1925).

24. LaKisha Michelle Simmons, *Crescent City Girls: The Lives of Young Black Women in Segregated New Orleans* (Chapel Hill: University of North Carolina Press, 2015), 17.

25. Simmons, *Crescent City Girls*, 16.

26. Tera Agyepong, "Aberrant Sexualities and Racialised Masculinisation: Race, Gender and the Criminalization of African American Girls at the Illinois Training School for Girls at Geneva, 1893–1945," *Gender and History* 25, no. 2 (2013): 270–93; Cheryl Nelson Butler, "Blackness as Delinquency," *Washington University Law Review* 90, no. 5 (2013): 1335–97.

27. *First Annual Report of the Virginia Industrial School for Colored Girls* (1916).

28. See for instance Kathy Lee Peiss, *Cheap Amusements: Working Women and Leisure in Turn-of-the-Century New York* (Philadelphia: Temple University Press, 1986) and Cheryl D. Hicks, *Talk with You Like a Woman: African American Women, Justice, and Reform in New York, 1890–1935* (Chapel Hill: University of North Carolina Press, 2010).

29. *Fourth Annual Report of the Virginia Industrial School for Colored Girls* (1919).

30. *Fourth Annual Report of the Virginia Industrial School for Colored Girls* (1919).

31. *Twenty-Fourth Annual Report of the Virginia Industrial School for Colored Girls* (1939).

32. *Twentieth Annual Report of the Virginia Industrial School for Colored Girls* (1935).

33. *Acts of the General Assembly of the Commonwealth of Virginia* 1914, Ch. 350.

34. *Sixth Annual Report of the Virginia Industrial School for Colored Girls* (1921)
35. *Fifth Annual Report of the Virginia Industrial School for Colored Girls* (1920).
36. *Second Annual Report of the Virginia Industrial School for Colored Girls* (1917).
37. *Sixth Annual Report of the Virginia Industrial School for Colored Girls* (1921).
38. *Sixth Annual Report of the Virginia Industrial School for Colored Girls* (1921). Emphasis in original.
39. *Sixth Annual Report of the Virginia Industrial School for Colored Girls* (1921).

CHAPTER 5

Black Girlhood Remains

SA SMYTHE

my body is my body whether i like it or not.
my condition is believing my body could be mine.
—jayy dodd, "i am interested in the black condition"

Can a girl ever stand
far enough away
to see her mother
& not the edges
of a shadow bent
into her own?
Don't ask me
I'm not a girl
though I was
when I first saw her
body, doubled
& moving
down the hallway
beyond my door.
—Cameron Awkward-Rich, "Carve A
Space to Hold Our Mother"

Girlhood for the Black of Us

There is something unsettled about the object of girlhood and its studies. Girlhood as a process and an experience is non-natural, non-inevitable, and certainly not universal among those who have been or could be termed "girls" over the course of the term's West-inflected history. As socially constructed ideals and perceptions shift across time and space, the fact remains: there is a *where* and a *when* to all of our genders.[1] The attributes, assignations, and alignments of how we become named in relation to our sex, and how we are consolidated concerning a colonial (and thereby gendered) order issues meaning over and unto our bodies. This indicates our relative place in nation, in language, in history, in class, and in narrative time, rather than indicating material fact or actual evidence of gender's fixity. Thus, the object of girlhood cannot be said always to be or always to have been a girl.[2] So, too, must it be acknowledged that "girl" does not necessarily presume a female, femme, or feminine referent. Girlhood is a multi-referential container that holds a dynamic range of traits, qualities, skills, perceptions, embodiments, and yes, genders—as does boyhood. Common figures like "the tomboy" and "the sissy" point to the very porosity of those two supposedly binary categories, showing us that they are not discrete, even for normative subjects, or those who eventually grow up to align with the contours of cisheteronormativity.[3] Further, our genders are always racialized and inseparable from the co-constitutive idea of race.[4] The over-determinative presence of blackness and the subsequent production of Black gender explicitly casts those rendered Black as unthought and outside of a paradigm of normative (which again is to say colonial, white supremacist, and heteropatriarchal) gender. This means that the experience of being a girl is never fully analogous to being a Black girl, since the experience or process of being a Black girl—that is, accessing, enjoying, and enduring Black girlhood—is routinely out of time, out of sync with the normative status quo. It is useful to remember these entangled positions as foundational and to delink the social constructions of girlhood and boyhood from their coercive and linear goals of womanhood and manhood, respectively, as I reflect in this chapter on my personal, fugitive relationship between girlhood and masculinity.

What might girlhood mean to me as a Black transmasculine nonbinary adult? This essay offers a series of meditations about the pleasures, poetics, and possibilities inherent in the acknowledgment that, despite fraught implications, complex experiences, and dysphoric realities, Black girlhood remains. If girlhood is not—as the structural force of the West's hegemonic colonial order would have it—the de facto prerequisite to womanhood, what then are some political implications of girlhood *remaining*? The phrase "girlhood remains" can be at once a lament, a charge, and a recognition whose different connotations compose the body of this essay in four parts. The final section is a poem that both generates a further analysis and explores Black nonbinary reading practices as an expansive method, with a structure that reflects and refracts the previous sections.

This meditation is grounded in the work of teacher, writer, and community worker Toni Cade Bambara, specifically "On the Issue of Roles," a lecture excerpted from her autobiographical essay, *The Scattered Sopranos*.[5] In this lecture, delivered in 1969 to the Livingston College Black Women's Seminar, Bambara parsed out the difficulty she faced when tasked with speaking on "the Black Woman's Role in the Revolution" (101). She mostly took issue with the false and stereotypical hierarchies between men and women that were reinforced throughout the Black community, which she argued occluded and undermined Black liberation's ultimate struggle. Bambara was "not arguing the denial of manhood or womanhood, but rather a shifting of priorities, a call for Selfhood, Blackhood" (105). Bambara called on her listeners and readers to commit to this liberatory mode of being in relation to one another and to measure one's self and one's worth outside of consumptive and capitalist models of propriety and subjugation. In so doing, she offers us a way to "create from scratch" new models and practices of ethical relation and new collectivities that, as she would say, are worth checking out (109). Thinking capaciously about who and what girlhood's referents have been, are, and might be is a radical act of self-reflection for the Black of us, whether or not we have consistently aligned with the project of girlhood in our interior, embodied experiences. Bambara's polemic sought to move us toward a collective shift in priorities. Embracing that shift led me to resist disavowing my Black girlhood as a constitutive self-affirmation of my Black trans nonbinary adult present, especially in a world where all of those identitarian descriptors are dynamic and should not be taken for granted or as fixed.

I. Girlhood's Remains

***remains* (noun):** the portion or pieces of something left over or left behind after it has been destroyed; a euphemism for a dead body

When asserting that girlhood remains, I mean that it lingers, permeates, and persists. I am also speaking of girlhood's *remains*—that is, of the material remnants of a youth gendered female and their relational impact on what's to come and what's already here. I particularly mean to consider the remnants of girlhood for a transmasculine nonbinary person coercively assigned female at birth (AFAB), a Black person whose very relationship to gender was also coercively forged, found in the recesses of the gap of the symbolic order of Western thought.[6] Because of this lived experience of racialized gender, what remains is not, by any means, neutral. If gender is a product of colonial thought, then " girlhood remains" could be interpreted as a sign of defeat, of relinquishing self-definition to the imposition of those totalizing and antagonistic logics. And yet, Black nonbinary embodiment flouts the linear maxims of colonial determination while simultaneously embracing the genders of my individual and ancestral pasts. My gender is Black, and Black girlhood itself remains an integral part of the childhood I experienced. This assertion remains the case whether or not my gender is legible or coherently navigable through a normative lens that seeks to produce or define fully integrated, cisgender subjects in the present and project onto that self a fixed and (cis)gendered past.

My intention here is not to speak in any totalizing or totalitarian way about AFAB people as a class. Narrating this understanding has helped to name, agentially and personally, a willful connection to those experiences and processes that contribute to my constant becoming, and my desire for an otherwise more just, unbordered, and decolonized world. To be clear, even with the multivalent understandings of the gender(s) and (un)gendering of Black people, there is such a thing we may approach as girlhood, even if the material, linguistic, historical, and psychological peripheries around it are porous and ill-defined. The people self-identified as girls have and will continue to inhabit and shift that dynamic category. Black girls who shape the very terrain of (their) girlhood, and Black women who reflect back on the girlhood they experienced, deserve to name themselves, deserve to have their voices heard and elevated as they agitate for autonomy and a recognition of their own worth via the recollection and constitution of their experiences. However, the lingering trace of Black girlhood does not explicitly characterize the experiences of, say, a Black trans woman whose girlhood was deferred or someone who was coerced into aligning with normative gender, which prevented them from fully experiencing a gender-expansive childhood, as with some trans, nonbinary, agender, and intersex folks who otherwise have nonlinear experiences of gender identity. Thinking about those who were made to align with and were regulated in relation to the container of girlhood against their wishes—some trans boys, trans men, nonbinary, or intersex people, for example—can also help us to shift those categories into their multi-referential and noncoercive outer limits. To speak of girlhood's remains is to name that many of us who have been girls, have been moved to bury or leave behind some aspects of girlhood, to obliquely or to directly disavow femininity, to ossify the parts of ourselves that may once have been soft under the guise of self-affirmation or becoming "true" selves. This often means adopting a rigid view of the masculine as femininity's bordered and binary opposite. Still, some of us never had access to those qualities; our blackness was always fated to meet a world that would have us be either stillborn or fully grown and nothing else between these two modes of the long-since-been and the never-to-be.[7]

Black girlhood populates my present with seeds from my past, germinating and rendering Western time at once thick and immaterial. "Happy birthday, princess," my uncle purrs through the phone year after year, on the same bittersweet September day, somehow always around noon no matter my time zone. His calls used to come collect or via a Jamaican phone card; but, in the last year or two, it comes through the free Voice over IP (VoIP)

WhatsApp widely used throughout the Caribbean and broader diaspora in places where landlines are less common or reliable. The dialogue is fixed no matter the medium. *Heyyyy princess*, my uncle drawls as we retrace our semi-scripted routine. *How you do? All right. Yuh truck still a work? Mhmm. Miss Pearl all right? Yeh man, she aright. Good, good. Mi just call fi she happy birth-day. Mi love you, you nuh. Gwan mek us proud. You too, Uncle. Mi love unno so till. Come visit we nuh? We long fi see you. Maybe next year, uncle. Soon come, aright? Aright.* My mother's favorite brother, the Rasta with dreads down to his backside, the black sheep of my mother's generation and man of relatively few words, does not believe in the monarchy or anything regal. Nevertheless, since I was an infant, my uncle always afforded me the role of "princess." Judging from family photo albums, this was probably facilitated by how I was always covered from head to toe—socks included—in garments adorned with the most ornate frills and reams of lace.

I've told this story before and people invariably cringe or chuckle nervously on my behalf. Many of the people who've heard the account have only known me as a trans person who goes by they/them pronouns. Most of them have been sensitive to and considerate of the epistemic violence that trans, nonbinary, and gender nonconforming people routinely face, often at the hands and tongues of biological kin or other families of origin. I've readily grasped how easy, how *logical* it might seem for some to lodge a complaint of obliviousness or misgendering onto this narrative scene. But the tender complexity that lingers whenever I return to this, or any other encounter with my uncle, is such that terms like "misgendering" —and perhaps more accurately, gender misrecognition—feel inadequate at best. These terms are too superficial to describe those sporadic encounters, too flattened by the lens of colonial relation when I know that, in those moments, something in the ecology of kinship between my uncle and me protect us from its two-dimensional capture.

In truth, whatever my uncle did or did not learn about gender during his incomplete high school education or life pre- or post-deportation in Spanish Town, Jamaica, he surely knows about respect and love; I've always received both from him. It's worth noting, then, that I've never actually said, "Do not call me 'princess,' uncle." If I had, I feel certain he would apologize and honor the request regardless of his intent. Instead, I never have, nor has it ever occurred to me as an option, until recently, when sharing the story with others abroad.

And so, I would insist that there is something illegible at play when only considering colonial logics of racialized gender that trans nonbinary identity can get trapped back into, if we allow it. These logics point us toward linear time. They call on us to (re)produce and project a coherent and consistently identifiable subject and then demand that this newly coherent thing assert itself backward through time, that we retcon ourselves into a consumable and cognizable whole. For those of us who are trans, colonial logics demand a reinforcement of binary identification that can be recuperated back into a heteropatriarchal ideal. This suggests that the trans man must disavow any traces of femininity or female attributes, as a cis heterosexual man might. However, trans and/or nonbinary people can opt-out and wrest what remains of our past and future selves from the vice grip of normative thinking. These fleeting exchanges with my uncle, often timed to finite phone card minutes and work breaks, are as laconic as in-person reunions but no less warm. Between us there is something like unconditioned love—that is, love has not been conditioned in proximity and compliance to certain normative mores. There is also love unconditional, which is to say love without the prerequisites of gender antagonism, suspicion, or demands for legibility that undermine a dynamic relationship to familial intimacy. It is as though I am being received in relation to the *when* of the gender that I seemed to occupy, while openly touching and connecting with the *now* and *thence after* of the adulthood that I navigate physically away from home. Like Proust's madeleine, or the opening "Sth" of Toni Morrison's *Jazz*, my uncle's "hey, princess" triggers deep affective memory, in this case nostalgia for that sense of home, but also reminds me that I am more secure than I imagined in my attachments to place, and always capable of visitation. I dare not say "return" because I never really left. All of this feeling occurs in an ordinary instant; it feels at once too precious and too impossible to correct—not least because there is nothing "wrong" with the exchange, just the ungainly friction of multiple *whens* in one encounter.

I used to feel bemused, flushed, and not quite hailed in my uncle's refrain when initially coming to terms with my transmasculine adulthood. I've since come to understand it as my uncle tugging on the girl that I was in order to maintain a connection with the person I am. And I am, it has been said, a bit of a nonbinary princess to this day. So why resist what lovingly applies, and for whose sake? These exchanges belong to a mountain of reasons why I don't want to erase girlhood. My own experience of being a trans nonbinary person has not sprouted from the desire to erase what came before; that kind of erasure would mean burying significant aspects of my memory, my relationships, and myself. I would instead embrace the what's-to-come as the already-here. Contextualizing the phases of my life helps me orient toward what I think it means to be psychically and materially whole in a world of corrupt(ing) fragments. Rather than stepping over the remains of my girlhood and burying them deep, I linger over and commune with them. I carry them in my arms and tenderly lay them to rest each day. The remains of my girlhood need to be honored, scattered over the sea of my becoming.

II. Girlhood Remains

***remains* (verb):** to linger indefinitely in existence or in the same state; to continue to be in a place for a significant amount of time

My Black girlhood remains. But if you do not want it, it is not yours. I would never advocate for a coercively tethered relationship to the past. But really, I ask myself, prompted by the project of this anthology: What remains of this girlhood? What is girlhood, and when is it? When I think about the gendered childhood I experienced across Jamaica, Costa Rica, the UK, and the United States, I reflect on the transtemporal and translingual elements that persist and insist into the present moment. My transnational relationship to Black girlhood meaningfully grounds the construction of what I would narrate as a global "future-otherwise," something that has the potential and resilience of youth coupled with other diasporic knowledge.

My relationship to girlhood is self-evident, by which I mean "plain" or "obvious," and also understood primarily in relation to itself. This is not to say that it is singular, but rather that I cannot and do not require external proof to know that it exists. My relationship to Black girlhood is evident in its remains *qua* remains, which is to say, in what is left behind and what survives. The memories of Black girlhood that I carry are foundational; they physically and mentally constitute my present personhood. While my personal avowal does not bear the flawed markings of the "self-evident" truths like those performed in the U.S. Declaration of Independence, it is, ironically enough, an experience that I witness as evidencing my relationship to trans nonbinary embodiment.

I have come to know myself as nonbinary in a way that resists the type of negation that the medical industrial complex relies on, one that props itself up against narratives of the "wrong body" to access hormones and produce other physical alterations. My gender is Black, and thus can always capacitate itself: being Black is enough of a foundation to break from binary gender. That realization and subsequent reckoning have been enough for me to know myself as trans.

III. Trans Nonbinary Poesis, Or Remaking the Wor(l)d

When I think about what it means to be trans and nonbinary, and what that routinely presupposes about my relationship to masculinity, femininity, and the way I embody certain gender in a way that renders gender neither certifiable nor true, I am called to the idea of negation. This is not least because mainstream articulations of the rapidly developing category of nonbinary translate into both the "not-binary" and also "in between the binary," in the middle space along the spectrum of gender as "not-man" and "not-woman." But as in all things, I do not mean the kind of negation that occurs in this trite binary sense. I speak instead of positive refusal, of the kind of "negative capability" that English Romantic poet John Keats fleetingly called forth. As far as the public archive reveals, Keats wrote this phrase only once in a private letter to his brothers, recalling a conversation he had some time in December 1817. Thus, in the offhand and one-off mention with no further recorded clarification, Keats ushered forth a concept in a performatively capacious way, a fleeting gesture to imaginative being and aesthetic possibility that I find assuring and seductive:

> I had not a dispute but a disquisition with Dilke, upon various subjects; several things dove-tailed in my mind, and at once it struck me what quality went to form a Man of Achievement, especially in Literature, and which Shakespeare possessed so enormously—I mean Negative Capability, that is, when a man is capable of being in uncertainties, mysteries, doubts, without any irritable reaching after fact and reason—Coleridge, for instance, would let go by a fine isolated verisimilitude caught from the Penetralium of mystery, from being incapable of remaining content with half-knowledge. This pursued through volumes would perhaps take us no further than this, that with a great poet the sense of Beauty overcomes every other consideration, or rather obliterates all consideration.[8]

Thinking about this passage, I realize that poesis and poetics are precisely the aesthetic lens through which I experience Black girlhood. Etymologically, poesis is derived from the Greek verb ποιεῖν, which means "to make" or "to create." As such, it is the process of creativity and production, which canonical Western philosophy refers to as the activity in which someone brings something into being that had yet to be (as such) prior to its creation. What I'm narrating is coming to terms with trans nonbinary subjectivity as poesis. This is to identify trans nonbinary subjectivity as the capacity for the invention of one's own paradigms for existence, one's own relationship to being, belonging, and self-evidencing. As is common in a colonial Anglophone education, my first encounters with poetry were with English Romanticists who counted Keats among their ranks. His "negative capability" resonated with me a great deal. There continues to be something beautiful and emancipatory in the fact that the ability to opt out and capacitate one's self-determination with indeterminacy. Negative capability's antitheses include certainty and fact, but that makes it indeterminate, rather than uncertain. Indeterminacy is a key element of queer and trans thought, and Black nonbinary embodiment and method are instances of what it means not to be able to determine or define in relation to current modes of thought and metrics for understanding.

Black nonbinary methods would have us sustain a reading practice that rejects the either/or demands and regulations of cisheteropatriarchy and instead mobilize or manifest something otherwise. It refuses the very premise of binary gender but is not negation as such. It does not simply say "no" to this thing or that or any presently conceivable options. Rather, it builds a patchwork platform and cobbles together the grounds for other possible configurations and worlds, with options that don't require dispatching swaths of one's own life to make a shovel that will help you fashion a new "you" out of the graveyard of your former being. This Black nonbinary orientation rebuffs the competitive positioning of "who wore it best"—or rather *when* were you best, if we recall the aforementioned temporality of our genders, and gently places a sign above the door of gender's reverse garage sale: "Everything Must Stay." Or at least, that it can; the metaphor doesn't render all items the same in terms of our affective attachments or their use value. Our attachments and affections for our past selves may take on different meanings, different values, and differential modes of desire and recognition. However, they need not be discarded or fixed to our past in order to have a coherent present take shape. We can continue to return to ourselves and cobble together makeshift parts of our lives that might galvanize us into generously indeterminate futures.

The cento is a poetic form that primarily consists entirely of lines and verses from multiple other poets. It is a remix, a mashup that develops into the thesis of the cento-maker, that when quilted well, shows the multiplicity of voices that came before, a distinct and egalitarian chorus. It is also an exercise *par excellence* of reading as an extension of the act of creation—one cannot make a cento if one only has a limited reading sample. One poetic mode of Black nonbinary gender is the patchwork poem, the cento self-evident, refashioning the pieces that comprise a life—the traumas, the seductions, the joys, the hailing, the violence, the refuge—and saying here is something new. In this muddled and mysterious equation, Black girlhood remains. Woven in the patchwork, flowing through the archives, chafing against the cloth. It remains.

What follows is a cento comprised of lines found throughout this anthology. I followed the rules traditional to the cento form. Namely, I did not add any new words that were not in the source material. Given the source material consists of academic prose, I changed tenses where necessary to fit with the internal grammar of the poem (in this case, historical present tense and third-person point of view), discarding lines and phrases from one source and adding phrases from another to make one line. The lineation/enjambment of the cento is also clearly of my doing given the prose form of the sources. Technically, it is a found poem because it comes from multiple sources in this volume that are not poetry. A found poem takes existing texts and refashions them, reorders them, and presents them outside of the chrysalis of their new poetic form. What also remains (to be found, to be considered) is not just what's left of Black girlhood as it pertains to transtemporal embodiment. It is also the rest of the authors' sentences that I didn't use, our implicit and collective contexts that needed to be read. Spectered, dangling limbs of sentences both present and unsaid, like the girlhood I carry unresigned, ghost these pages and the ones to come.

IV. cento sustaining remnants of their girlhood

> 'We was girls together,' she said as though explaining something.
> —Toni Morrison, *Sula*

I.

to understand black girlhood
we must know we was girls & that doesn't explain a thing .

the protagonist is not a lone individual
but a community, not limited to
special vulnerabilities traces in the archives

no other person would go near the remains

how do we dream their lives?
common specter haunts
narratives—
reticent until forced otherwise —undertakes resistance
through a nighttime healing

mourn truncated futures,
time and its remains

after years of discipline
in a sweet environment
the situation remains
ambivalent
struggling
against divine (in)justice,

history, seemingly dormant
beneath the skin, keeps secrets

a presumption of innocence denied

II.

brave
the multitudes of the ^ nameless
leave such lasting
impressions we grapple
with the gulfs of time

conscious of being seen,

glimpse familiarity and belonging

how black women and girls have lived

the girls growing up in idleness who would otherwise be
jailed in the shadow
of the boys, embrace the shards
of history and memory that remain
cannot be afraid; vulnerable
freedom is deferred but remains
a possibility

obsessed over their joys
the certainty romance, tragedy,
of knowing comedy, satire
i will only later sow pigs, pickled lobsters,
be able to understand the so-called "girl problem"
leather "breeches" —and people too

III.

historically entrenched
they are not the "*dead girl*,"
but incorrigible, or,
in what remains extant,
capable—and desirous—
of becoming

imagining futures gone
pasts to come

innocence is dubious:
where would the future be?

the unexpected power
to remember,
to make a person have meaning

to root
a healing practice a discourse of love
can put you through hell and high water
dreams can be dishonest
the dynamic negotiations of power
as tenacious as the violence they seek to counter:
there is a lesson
in uncertainty
offering their body as script,
they locate themself
in the spiral towards freedom and
find
a little more happiness
down the
road

*The poem comprises selections from the works of several authors in this volume.

Acknowledgments: I would like to thank the generous editors, LaKisha Simmons and Corinne Field, for their patience and support in completing this piece, as well as my interlocutors and thinking partners C. Riley Snorton, Muriel Leung, Moya Bailey, and Airea D. Matthews for helping me to clarify my thoughts and continue to immerse myself toward the otherwise possibilities that continue to seduce and shape me daily.

Notes

1. My thinking around the "when and where of gender" references C. Riley Snorton's as-yet-unpublished work titled "The Gospel of Thon," which includes essays of nonbinary archives of Black being. Snorton has been a crucial interlocutor and friend to me in the ongoing struggle to clarify my own thinking around race, gender, and trans nonbinary matters.

2. Kathryn Bond Stockton, *The Queer Child, or Growing Sideways in the Twentieth Century* (Durham: Duke University Press, 2009).

3. The terms "cisheteronormativity" and "cisheteropatriarchy" are complex terms that I use informed by queer theory, trans theory, and feminist thought to respectively describe the fact that the perceived "norm" of Western society is a figure that is cisgender (one whose perception of their own gender identity corresponds with the sex they were assigned at birth) and heterosexual (one who is sexually or romantically attracted to a person of the opposite sex, which as a description presumes a binary system of two sexes, which are meant to correspond to two genders). Cisheteropatriarchy refers to a system of power based on the hegemonic (dominant) supremacy of cisheterosexual men through the exploitation and oppression of women and all other people who are not cisgender men. Since we are speaking of norms and things

like gender, we must also understand these concepts as colonial, in that they are produced from within and disseminated by the West across multiple cultures and nations, informing and erasing the way that people from those contexts relate to one another, even if it contradicts their own traditions.

4. This is a common tenet of much of Black feminist thought, but for a clear articulation of racialized gender, see Hortense Spillers, "Interstices: A Small Drama of Words," in *Black, White, and In Color*, ed. Hortense Spillers (Chicago: University of Chicago Press, 2003), 152–175.

5. Toni Cade Bambara, "On the Issue of Roles," in *The Black Woman*, ed. Toni Cade Bambara (New York: New American Library, 1970), 101–112.

6. Spillers, "Interstices."

7. Here, I am broadly addressing the topic of trans childhood, capaciously defined, as Jules Gill-Peterson has in *Histories of the Transgender Child* (Minneapolis: University of Minnesota, 2018), but also naming the violent force of a white supremacist world against Black life, especially in one of its most vulnerable forms: the Black child. This world is one that views Black children as sexually deviant (e.g., from Emmett Till to the exonerated and wrongfully accused teens hailed as Central Park Five) or otherwise to be treated as a threat, even while engaging in the typical childhood activity of play (Tamir Rice, Dajerria Becton), walking home after purchasing snacks (Trayvon Martin), or asleep (Ayana Jamieson). There are multiple other convergences with the law and multiple other modes of subjugation for Black children who are queer, disabled, poor, undocumented, etc. However, evidence from multiple centuries has shown us that anti-blackness is an inescapable bedrock of this current world order and can prevent Black childhood from being experienced or fully realized as it intersects other embodied and aesthetic categories.

8. John Keats's letter of December 1817 to George and Tom Keats in *The Letters of John Keats*, ed. Hyder E. Rollins (Cambridge, 1958), v. I, 193–19.

INTERLUDE

Conscious of Being Seen

NASTASSJA E. SWIFT

I'm too dark to be pretty. I don't speak Black enough.
I'm not Black enough. I just look Black enough.

My work is a reaction. To what I've experienced, the conversations I've had, things that I've read and what I notice taking place around me, as a child and as an adult. For much of my girlhood, I believed the thoughts above to be true. Uncomfortable with what I thought was my reality, I didn't voice it to anyone. With the transition into womanhood, I've found myself allowing art to be that voice for me.

At such a young age, I was unaware of the existence of the word "colorism" and its meaning. Nor had I realized that there were other little girls and boys of color who too were taunted for their complexion. I often thought, *what if I were just a little bit lighter?* In 2018, I googled the definition of the word "concealer." To mask dark spots on the skin. Those were the words that I read, and immediately I felt a bit uncomfortable thinking about what it feels like, and has felt like, to think of yourself as a dark spot in need of masking.

I then created the piece "Concealer," depicting Black faces with all white wool, interested in the global act of Black and brown people lightening their skin in the interest of ascending to Western standards of beauty. The multiplicity of faces was important, as it speaks to the span of colorism and to my realization that I wasn't alone in wanting to escape the realm of feeling like the "other" or the dark one. The ways in which we're conditioned to understand blackness as an afterthought filters into how we perceive ourselves and how we believe the world perceives us. As a darker-complexioned girl, I often compared myself to my lighter-toned companion. Thinking that her social life had to be more enjoyable than mine, that school had to be easier for her, I wanted to be her because "She Was Light Enough to Pass." Before making that series, I recalled reading *Passing* by Nella Larson in school and remembering how much I felt that book detailed some of my childhood feelings.

I thought that there was something to gain by having a lighter complexion, and speaking to that through dolls feels right because of how we're often introduced to that idea at an early age as Black girls.

If only my hair was straight like hers.

Hair. A topic often discussed among Black women, but equally relevant, and arguably more significant, within the context of girlhood. From my Barbie dolls (even with them being Black) to my mother's old straightening combs and Just For Me relaxers, there was a clear message that my kinks weren't preferred, manageable, weren't enough. Do I believe that it was directly from my mother? No. However, generational conditions often transfer when not transformed or challenged. "Before I Lay" existed first as a conversation between myself and my two younger sisters, Chloe and Kyndal. How do you feel about your hair? What constitutes "good hair"? How is beauty defined through your hair? These were some of the questions I posed for them to think about as I began sketching their portrait. As sisters, hair appears, very casually, within many of our conversations, and I wanted to know how or if they conceptualize Black hair and what it means to them. I began wearing extensions in middle school as a result of feeling like the hair growing out of my scalp was inadequate. After listening to my sisters, I admired their level of confidence within their hair and how they own that they wear extensions or braids because they can, disregarding any idea that their real hair isn't enough. Sharing that confidence in the form of painting through having them intimately posed with one another, vulnerably in their bonnets, I get to transition the conversation my work is offering, even for just a moment, from questioning to reassuring.

The little dark skin girl within myself that felt the need to hide how she felt, what she was thinking, and her perception of the world in which she exists is what drives the conceptual framework of my studio practice, thus encouraging me to consider how I create space for her. My work is my voice—constantly evolving, it challenges and questions me, provides clarity as well as additional questions for me to consider. My intention is to create a space for dialogue between myself and others, but most importantly between Black girls.

Figure 3. *Before I Lay*. Oil on panel, 36 × 36 × 2 inches, 2018.

Figure 4. *Now You Can Touch My Hair.* Synthetic hair, woven cotton, 9 × 12 × 2 inches, 2015.

Figure 5. *Concealer.* Merino wool, wire, 31 x 27 x 3 inches, 2016.

Figure 6. *But My Skin Was Always Darker.* Wool, wood, clay, cotton, 2016.

Figure 7. *Ode to Black Wombman*, Mask Scene—Philadelphia, video still. Performers: Sanchel Brown, Nastassja Swift, Dani Criss, Imani Shibazz, and Brittany Johnson, 2017.

Figure 8. *Ode to Black Wombman*, Mask Scene—Philadelphia, video still. Performers: Sanchel Brown, Nastassja Swift, Dani Criss, Imani Shibazz, and Brittany Johnson, 2017.

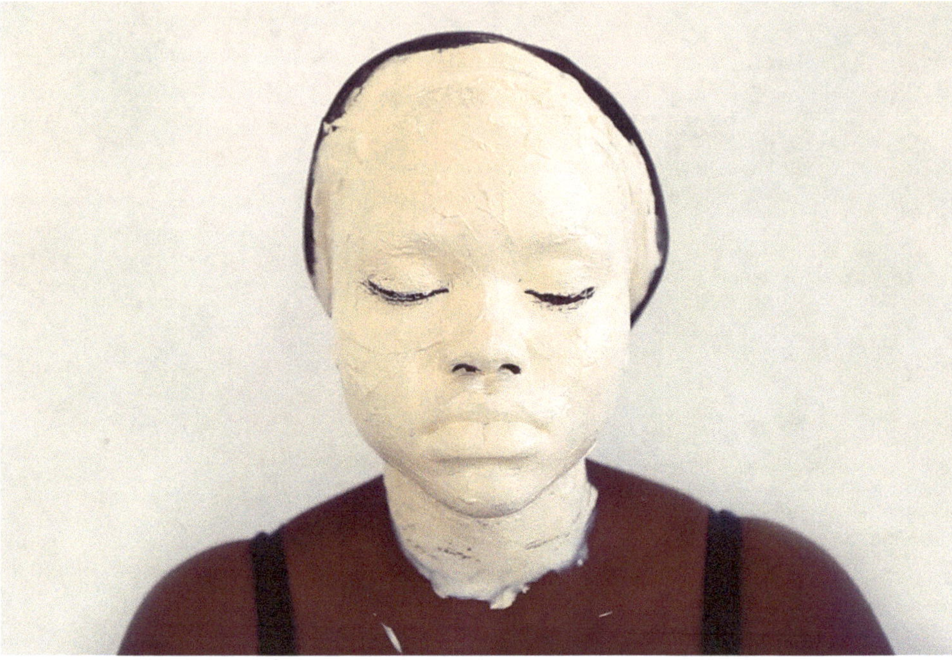

Figure 9. *Camouflaged*, Video Still. Video 20 seconds looped, 2016.

Figure 10. *Being Seen*. Oil on canvas, 42 x 30 x 2 inches, 2015.

PART II

Black

CORINNE T. FIELD AND
LAKISHA MICHELLE SIMMONS

Introduction: What Is the Meaning of "Black"?

MC Soffia is a hip-hop artist from Cotia, São Paulo, Brazil, and That Girl Lay Lay (Alaya High) is from Houston, Texas, United States. Analyzing these artists' songs and performances as "an embodied cultural act" that seeks to claim Black girlhood in the face of dispossession, we can think about what blackness means to them and how girls' creative claims to Black identity circulate globally through popular culture.[1] In 2016, at the age of twelve, Soffia released a video called "Menina Pretinha" ("Little Black Girl"), a song she had been performing for years. Known for conscious lyrics, activism, and messages of Afro-Brazilian empowerment, MC Soffia insists that Black girls should be proud of their dark skin and curly hair.[2] In the 2016 video, MC Soffia demonstrates that Afro-Brazilian girls deserve a beautiful childhood and all the pleasures that come with it. Preschool-aged girls surround MC Soffia as she raps. Performing the innocence of youth, the tiny girls cuddle and play with Black dolls half their size. MC Soffia functions as their older role model, rapping for and to them. The song focuses on reclaiming a specifically Black childhood: "Give me back my dolls / I want to play with them / My Black dolls, what did you do with them? / I'll have fun while I'm small." In close-ups of MC Soffia and the little girls, viewers see big bows in curly, natural hair, funky jewelry and sunglasses, with exaggerated makeup. It looks like the girls raided their mother's closet, play-acting and make-believing. MC Soffia's performance insists that Afro-Brazilan girls have a right to come of age slowly, even in the face of prejudice that would deem them unbeautiful and unimportant. The video ends with its main message, a quote in graffiti prominently behind MC Soffia: *crescendo e lindo feio e seu preconceito* (curly is beautiful, ugly is your prejudice).[3] Facing Brazil's colorism, MC Soffia works to redefine beauty as a celebration of Black girlhood.

That Girl Lay Lay's songs are not as overtly political. And yet, her 2018 viral videos of freestyle rapping in the family's car, with her father filming/producing, highlight her very different claims to membership in an African diasporic culture that values the blackness of Black girlhood. Steeped in the tradition of hip hop, with all the sonic signifiers of the best rappers, Lay Lay's performance is astounding because of the way she raps like a young adult, making use of the staples of hip hop: "collage, intertextuality, boasting, toasting, and signifying" along with the technology of social media.[4] Simultaneously, she plays with the poetry of everyday girlhood. Her lyrics—purposefully kept clean—point to the stuff of childhood: cooties, recess, school buses, honor roll, and teachers. In this way, Lay Lay produces her very own version of a girlish "sonic cool"[5]—a physical and sonic performance that emphasizes fresh dress, a relaxed pose, a femme aesthetic, and complex lyrics that all emphasize natural talent, skill, and leadership qualities. In her song "Taste," as the beat begins, she tells her dad: "Daddy, you can be kinda hype on this one." Taking charge of her own sound, she gives her dad permission to be the hype man; he dances (the car shakes) and laughs on cue in the background. But she also places herself in relation to her father—a child still using the endearment "daddy." Sitting in the passenger seat, Lay Lay raps: "It's time for me to fly out the nest / It's your girl Lay Lay got my hair re-pressed / I'm still here trying to be the best / you're still mad you're still depressed / 'cause I play with beats like it's recess."[6] In an interview with a Houston radio station, Lay Lay told the DJs, "Kids gotta keep it positive. Cause, on the way here, [you] weren't that kid friendly. I was listening." She then yelled, "So kids, we gotta take over!"[7]

That Girl Lay Lay is able to present herself as innocent child and part of Black diaspora in part because of her privileged background. When recording, she does so in her family's Mercedes Benz. Lay Lay also fits into acceptable beauty standards in the U.S.—light in color, with long, loose curly hair that she often wears pressed straight. She adorns herself in bracelets and earrings. Her gender performance, as a sweet 'girly-girly', allows her to embody a socially acceptable girlhood within the music industry and within the Black community.

This gender performance adds sugar to her spicy precociousness. MC Soffia, in contrast, makes claims to girlhood as an outsider to Brazilian beauty standards that center light skin and luxury fashions. Despite their various insider/outsider positions, both girls insist on expressing their desires, having fun, and celebrating their own sense of pride in their blackness. MC Soffia and That Girl Lay Lay demonstrate what Black feminist Daphne Brooks explains, that "Black women's musical practices are, in short, revolutionary because they are inextricably linked to the matter of Black life."[8]

Hip hop scholar and literary critic Regina Bradley explains that Black male rappers negotiate what it means to be Black and male "in the American public and popular imagination" in their songs.[9] Both MC Soffia and That Girl Lay Lay are negotiating what it means to be a *Black* girl; they contest and play within local (São Paulo versus U.S. Gulf South), national (Brazil versus United States), and global perceptions of blackness. They both persistently make claims to childhood and their own definitions of Black beauty in their songs. Because minors cannot vote or hold office, creating popular culture offers a powerful means for girls to gain public influence.[10] Girls who listen to and collect such music are not only consumers of popular culture but also archivists, critics, producers, and theorists.[11] In popular culture, they find not only pleasure but also the space to form their own identities, pushing against stereotypes and expressing their own sense of self and what blackness might mean to them.[12] In a world that claims to be post-racial but delivers potent messages to little girls about where they stand in hierarchies of color and social class, popular culture offers an opportunity to learn "ways of being" through musical play.[13] As the anthropologist Aimee Meredith Cox argues, Black girls in the U.S. engage with misrepresentations of their lives through "shape-shifting strategies" that speak their own truths. Insisting that they "are not the problem. Their lives do not need sanitizing, normalizing, rectifying, or translating so they can be deemed worthy of care and serious consideration."[14] As Black girls engage in an everyday creative choreography that expresses what it means to be young and Black, they often "mobilize history, whether officially documented or bricolaged through recall and desire."[15] How Black girls have imagined blackness in the past thus matters deeply to Black girls in the present and adds urgency to the project of recovering their own self-understandings from the misperceptions generated by anti-Black racism. Black girls are always navigating the politics of the past, intraracial tensions in the present, and their own visions for the future.

This section begins with the story of a girl who would not have understood herself as Black during her lifetime. Born in Saint-Domingue (now Haiti) in 1741, Marie-Jeanne Fleuriau Mandron was the daughter of a white planter and an enslaved Black woman. As she came of age, her family's freedom and wealth classified her in official records as a "free person of color" (*gen de couleur libre*). "*Nègre*," or "Black," was a term she would have used to refer to enslaved people. When she traveled with her father to France as an adolescent, her skin color mattered more as a mark of distinction in a primarily white town within an imperial nation intent on hardening racial boundaries between Black and white. By placing her narrative within a longer history of Black girlhood, Jennifer Palmer poses the central question addressed by other contributors to this section: What is Black?

Nazera Wright picks up the thread of relatively privileged Black girlhoods in the context of late-nineteenth-century Philadelphia, where two sisters, Miranda and Sallie Venning, kept autograph albums recording signatures and short sayings by their family, friends, and associates. Wright argues that these entries reveal tangible evidence of how the girls formed friendships, asserted freedom, and took advantage of opportunities within a tight-knit circle of family and friends who fought to provide them with a protected and extended girlhood. At the same time, these young women had to navigate increasingly rigid racial distinctions that placed even the most educated Black girls on the disadvantaged side of a sharply drawn color line. Questions of how Black girls like the Venning sisters should embody Black beauty and respectability became freighted with political import as striving adults looked to them to represent the future of the race.

The opportunities available to the Venning sisters remained out of reach for most African American girls who continued to find themselves forced to work, most often as domestic servants in other people's households. As southern states expanded the use of criminal justice to control Black labor, even as reformers worked to segregate children within a less punitive juvenile justice system, Black girls could find themselves caught in the crosshairs of a debate over what it meant to be both Black and a child. Cynthia Greenlee considers the debate sparked by South Carolina's 1892 decision to hang a teenaged Black girl, Milbry Brown, for the alleged crime of poisoning a white infant. Both defenders and critics of the execution mobilized understandings of girlhood to justify their views. The former insisted that Brown was too young to be held responsible for her crimes and should be given a chance to reform. The latter insisted that by committing a crime at such a young age, Brown proved herself irredeemable, likely because of her race. Though Brown received no salvation from the "child savers" constructing juvenile justice, the Black journalist Ida B. Wells used the case to illustrate the injustice of southern courts and call for further reform. Thus, in very different ways, both the Venning sisters and Brown carried the weight of representing what it meant to be Black and a girl in Progressive Era America.

The final chapter in this section traces the unique position of Afro-German women who used memoir to reflect on their experiences coming of age after the defeat of Nazism and during the early years of the Cold War. Drawing on several memoirs published by the children of African or African American fathers and white German mothers, Vanessa Plumly coins the term "kin(d)ship" to convey both how these girls assert their own kinship claims to white German family members and also how white Germans classified Afro-Germans as perpetual children, *Kinder*, unable to fully join the nation state. Plumly reads texts and images to reveal the heterogeneity and complexity of Afro-German identity.

Over the broad span of time and within the different regions explored in this section, Black girls honed expertise as critics of racist stereotypes and color-based hierarchies that shaped their lives from an early age. From kinfolk, friends, teachers, popular culture, and political rhetoric, they gathered evidence about what it meant to be Black and where they fit in social structures defined by race and color. And then they improvised, remixed, and created entirely new understandings of what blackness meant to them. Even when they could not escape the murderous slander of misperceptions intent on exploiting and cutting short their lives—as in the tragic case of Milbry Brown—the meaning of their blackness never remained fixed or stable as adults and girls themselves continually debated what it meant to be a Black girl. Though with a radically different sense of style and vocabulary than M. C. Sofia, and with different technologies at their disposal, Black girls in the past left behind a similar message: "Ugly is your prejudice."[16]

Notes

1. Daphne A. Brooks, "'All That You Can't Leave Behind': Black Female Soul Singing and the Politics of Surrogation in the Age of Catastrophe," *Meridians: Feminism, Race, Transnationalism* 8, no. 1 (2007): 183.

2. Reighan Gillam, "Representing Black Girlhood in Brazil: Culture and Strategies of Empowerment," *Communication, Culture and Critique* 10, no. 4 (December 1, 2017): 609–25, https://doi.org/10.1111/cccr.12176.

3. “MC Soffia-Menina Pretinha,” March 9, 2016, https://www.youtube.com/watch?v=cbOG2HS1WKo.

4. Tricia Rose, *Black Noise: Rap Music and Black Culture in Contemporary America* (Milldetown, Conn.:Wesleyan University Press, 1994), 63.

5. Regina Bradley, “Contextualizing Hip Hop Sonic Cool Pose in the Late Twentieth-and Twenty-first-Century Rap Music,” *Current Musicology* No. 93 (2012).

6. “That Girl Lay Lay- Taste (Freestyle),” August 2, 2018, https://www.youtube.com/watch?v=5e2QHouCiUM.

7. “That Girl Lay Lay Talks Being the Youngest Signed Female Rapper,” 979TheBox, December 3, 2018, https://www.youtube.com/watch?v=4ykM_vj1P5A.

8. Daphne A. Brooks, *Liner Notes for the Revolution: The Intellectual Life of Black Feminist Sound (Cambridge, Harvard University Press, 2021), 3.*

9. Bradley, 70.

10. Treva B. Lindsey, “‘One Time for My Girls’: African American Girlhood, Empowerment, and Popular Visual Culture,” *Journal of African American Studies* 17 (2013): 22–34; Kyra Gaunt, “YouTube, Twerking & You: Context Collapse and the Handheld Co-Presence of Black Girls and Miley Cyrus,” *Journal of Popular Music Studies* 27, no. 3 (2015): 244–73.

11. Ruth Nicole Brown and Chamara Jewl Kwakye, *Wish to Live: The Hip-Hop Feminism Pedagogy Reader* (New York: Peter Lang, 2012); Brooks, *Liner Notes for the Revolution: The Intellectual Life of Black Feminist Sound.*

12. Oneka LaBennett, *She's Mad Real: Popular Culture and West Indian Girls in Brooklyn* (New York: New York University Press, 2011).

13. Kyra D. Gaunt, *The Games Black Girls Play: Learning the Ropes from Double-Dutch to Hip-Hop* (New York: New York University Press, 2006), 13.

14. Aimee Meredith Cox, *Shapeshifters: Black Girls and the Choreography of Citizenship* (Durham: Duke University Press, 2015), 8.

15. Cox, *Shapeshifters*, 27.

16. “MC Soffia-Menina Pretinha,” March 9, 2016, YouTube video, https://www.youtube.com/watch?v=cbOG2HS1WKo.

CHAPTER 6

Compromised Independence

Mixed-Race Girlhood in the Eighteenth-Century French Atlantic

JENNIFER L. PALMER

Marie-Jeanne Fleuriau Mandron lived a life in between different races, places, and families. She was of mixed racial origin, a *mulâtresse* in contemporary parlance, daughter of a white planter and a Black woman who he likely at some point had owned. In her bifurcated girlhood as a mixed-race girl, she occupied an interstitial space between enslaved Blacks and free whites. She lived in two very different locations, first in the plantation society of Saint-Domingue (now Haiti), which had more enslaved people and more free people of color than any other contemporary plantation colony, and later in France, where the population was almost exclusively white. As Marie-Jeanne traveled from the Caribbean to Europe, she encountered a hardening of racial distinctions even as she benefited from her father's wealth. Her story reveals how the category of Black girlhood never remains stable, but instead shifts in different times and places, even in the course of single life.

I know only the sparse contours of her life, delineated by the dry documents produced at its boundaries: birth and death, her baptism, her registration in France as a person of color, and a will that she wrote outlining how she wished to distribute her belongings. As a member of a large and connected family, she also made appearances in family letters and account books.[1] The outlines of these sketchy details pose the temptation to fill them in with a romantic tale à la the 2013 Fox Searchlight movie *Belle*. It's easy to imagine her father's longing to give his children a better life in France, a touching separation from her mother, and romantic explanations for her life of celibacy: a lover left behind in Saint-Domingue (perhaps even a future revolutionary, as were her brothers), or a star-crossed match thwarted by a liberal-minded young man's racially rigid family. Such fantasies fit easily with

Disneyfied narratives of girlhood. But in the face of a paucity of traditional historical evidence, how can we understand the life of a girl—especially a *Black* girl—outside of these fictionalized constructs?

Archival sources reveal nothing about Marie-Jeanne's everyday life, how she saw the world, or her dreams and frustrations; we have nothing from her in her own words. We can, however, use what we know about the historical context to think creatively about possibilities, even in the absence of knowing for sure.[2] In this essay, I will productively explore archival gaps, approaching the contexts in which Marie-Jeanne lived and the experiences of Black, white, and mixed-race girls and women more generally to analyze her life and her choices. I reconceptualize the gaps as constructive spaces rather than lacks, interstices where a history of Marie-Jeanne's girlhood begins to emerge, a girlhood shaped by her race, her gender, her social status, her family connections, and her geographic place.

Marie-Jeanne was born in 1741 in the town of Croix-des-Bouquets, Saint-Domingue, a market town situated on the sugar-rich Cul-de-Sac Plain, not far from the colonial administrative center Port-au-Prince.[3] Marie-Jeanne would have grown up seeing people who looked and sounded like her (mixed-race Creoles) who owned land and slaves, ran businesses, and lived near and socialized with whites, their lives entwined socially, economically, and sexually.[4] In this colonial milieu, racial categorization and social status never neatly aligned. Many free people of color attained prosperity, although some, especially emancipated former slaves, lived on the economic margins. So too did some whites, especially recent migrants known as "*petits blancs*."

Marie-Jeanne would have noticed that white men outnumbered white women by a ratio of least two to one.[5] This meant that white men often had sexual relationships and even set up households with women of color. Many people, like Marie-Jeanne's own parents, lived outside the sanctified bonds of marriage, perhaps sometimes willingly but almost always in relationships characterized by force, hierarchy, and the brutality of colonial plantation societies. However, Marie-Jeanne also would have witnessed interracial marriages. In a colony flooded with white male migrants, daughters from well-established free-colored families or the illegitimate mixed-race offspring of wealthy white planters provided newcomers with an entrée into colonial society.[6] As a little girl who grew up in a plantation society, Marie-Jeanne likely realized that for a free woman of color, patriarchy, violence, force, constraints, and lack of options afflicted any intimate relationship with a man. She also would have noticed, though, the prevalence of free women of color as independent economic actors. They often ran market stalls, shops, inns, taverns, or rented out property or slaves. Because of expectations of white femininity and legal restrictions on white women, these options were not as possible for white women either in Saint-Domingue or in France. As a young girl, Marie-Jeanne thus might have envisioned three potential life paths that were shaped by her blackness: independent proprietress, as free women of color in towns often owned and ran small businesses; wife, to either a free man of color or a recent white arrival; or mistress, potentially to a white man on the higher end of the social spectrum in her small town.

Marie-Jeanne also would have interacted with people with similar skin color and features who were enslaved. While in Saint-Domingue most enslaved people were recent arrivals from Africa, enough were Creole (born in the colony) and enough were mixed-race that she certainly would have noticed the similarities. Her father could have had other children with enslaved women, children who he chose not to free, so she may have interacted on a daily basis with people who were her siblings but had a very different status. Yet she certainly would not have worried about becoming enslaved, or even being mistaken for an enslaved person. She had a certain security because of the social position of her father—his wealth and position, acknowledgment of his children, and long relationship with her mother—and perhaps more importantly because of the legal documents that recorded her freedom.[7] Even in everyday encounters, her physical carriage, body language, vocal intonations, dress, and how she interacted with others shaped her position in the community.[8] Everyone she encountered would have recognized her as free. Plantation society depended on hierarchy, and Marie-Jeanne, like all free people of color, had an interest in distancing herself from people who were enslaved. In the years leading up to the Haitian Revolution, elite free people of color, including her brothers, reinforced the differences between free and enslaved people as part of an effort to protect and extend their own privilege.

As a result of this complexity and ambiguity, Marie-Jeanne almost certainly would not have referred to herself as "Black," one of the organizing categories that structures this volume. Instead, her freedom and her family's status were much more important to her. For the purposes of official records, she would have been considered a "free person of color" ("*gen de couleur libre*"), a category that indicated African ancestry but also denoted liberty. Legally, socially, and culturally, free status was much more significant in Saint-Domingue than race. Furthermore, at this point, race was a flexible concept that changed both in France and in Saint-Domingue over the course of Marie-Jeanne's lifetime; only in the nineteenth century did it come to be understood as a firm and immutable category. She also might have used the term "mulatress" ("*mulâtresse*"), which implied mixed-racial ancestry but also indicated relatively high social status; in colonial Saint-Domingue, free people of color with high social and economic standing often were classified as "mulattos" regardless of their actual skin tone and sometimes were not identified by a racial descriptor at all.[9] But "*nègre*," or "Black," was a term she would have used to refer to enslaved people on her father's plantation in Saint-Domingue or perhaps the enslaved manservant Hardy whom her father brought with him to France.[10] Indeed, in all extant sources, when Marie-Jeanne was classified by race she was always called a "*mulâtresse*," while Hardy was always identified as a "*nègre*." Marie-Jeanne discovered, however, that her new neighbors in France did not understand the subtle gradations of race and status that were so well known in Saint-Domingue.

Marie-Jeanne was born second of the eight mixed-race children of Jeanne Guimbelot and Aimé-Benjamin Fleuriau. Her father had emigrated to Saint-Domingue around 1729 to seek his fortune, like thousands of other hopeful French men.[11] By the 1740s he had prospered enough to purchase his own sugar plantation on the Cul-de-Sac Plain. We don't know if Jeanne was free or enslaved when her sexual relationship with Fleuriau began. By the time of Marie-Jeanne's birth, however, she was identified as free, and Fleuriau acknowledged Marie-Jeanne and their subsequent children as free.[12] Two weeks after Marie-Jeanne's birth, she was baptized in the parish church of Croix-des-Bouquets.[13] In the French empire, baptism signified both the moment when an infant's soul entered the Catholic Church and when the state recognized civil personhood. In the context of the French Antilles, baptism gained further significance for free people of color because baptism records could also act as proof of freedom.[14] In Marie-Jeanne's case, the record identified her as the "illegitimate daughter of S[ieu]r Benjamin Fleuriau, merchant of this town, and of Marie Jeanne, free négresse."[15] While it was by no means obligatory for white men to acknowledge and free their mixed-race children, it was not unusual.[16] Fleuriau acknowledged all eight of the children he had by Jeanne as free from birth, and he also provided them with considerable financial support, both throughout his life and even after his death.

If Marie-Jeanne had stayed in Saint-Domingue, as Fleuriau's eldest daughter she could have anticipated making a good match, either with a white man (albeit one of lower social standing than her father) or a free man of color.[17] Upon her marriage she could have expected that her father would have given her money, land, enslaved people, or household goods. However, it turns out that any hopes she may have had for marriage vanished when she departed for France in 1755, at the age of fourteen. When Fleuriau left Saint-Domingue to return to France permanently, he took five of his mixed-race children with him: Marie-Jeanne, her brothers Joseph-Benjamin, Pierre-Paul, and Jean, and her sister Marie-Charlotte.[18]

Arriving in her father's natal town of La Rochelle, a prosperous port on the Atlantic coast of France, must have felt to Marie-Jeanne like entering a new world. Accustomed to small houses and shops built of wood, and dirt roads that turned to mud in the rainy season, she was faced instead with three- to five-story edifices of glowing golden sandstone and cobblestone streets crowded with carriages. The bustle of the busy port replaced the agricultural rhythms of plantation life. The cold of the North Atlantic winter would have seeped into her bones, very different from the Caribbean heat so humid that you never stopped sweating. Most jarring, perhaps, Marie-Jeanne would have seen hardly anyone, except for her brothers and sister, who looked like her, with dark skin and curly hair.[19] Of the few people of color who did reside in the city—probably only around one hundred in a city of about 10,000—most were or had been enslaved, forming part of a group that Marie-Jeanne and her siblings viewed as very different from themselves socially and economically.[20] In France, the whites she interacted with on a daily basis, both inside and outside her home, might have read her as "servile" because of her dark skin. The subtle distinctions of carriage, dress, body, diction, and social interactions that separated free people of color from the enslaved in Saint-Domingue would have meant nothing to most residents of the port city.[21] This lack of understanding of the complex interplay of race and status eviscerated the social and economic potential Marie-Jeanne had in Saint-Domingue. Her connections with her father may have elevated her in the drawing room, where her family and social status would have been evident, but not on the street, where people she passed may have formed their own opinions solely on her race.

In La Rochelle, then, Marie-Jeanne likely became more aware of her blackness than she ever would have in Saint-Domingue. Furthermore, as a girl, perceptions of her race would have shaped her experiences more than those of her brothers. While all five children might have gone to school or had tutors, families tended to privilege the education of sons (even illegitimate ones) over that of daughters, so her brothers were more likely to have school friends or associates of their own, outside the confines of their family. As the daughter of a planter whose colonial success had made him one of the wealthiest men in La Rochelle, might Marie-Jeanne have felt the need to hide or to conform, always reaching toward whiteness and hiding her own thoughts about her new world, as Nastassja Swift suggests? She had a toolkit of strategies that worked to make her privilege clear in Saint-Domingue. How did she attempt to translate that into this new context?

Soon her family circle increased when her father married a white woman, the daughter of a wealthy merchant.[22] Her father's marriage could not but transform Marie-Jeanne's home and family situation. While, as the oldest daughter, she may have run his household, the appearance of a new, young wife demoted her to the position of something more akin to a dependent, a hanger-on, a poor relation, or perhaps even a servant. The changes wrought by this marriage may have plagued Marie-Jeanne with questions and doubts. What did it mean for Jeanne, Marie-Jeanne's mother? Would Marie-Jeanne have resented her young stepmother? Would she and her sister have helped to take care of the three half-siblings who soon arrived? Would it have increased or limited her opportunities for independence?

In La Rochelle, even had she wanted to leave her father's house, there were few means for her to do so. Marriage was the principal path for girls of Marie-Jeanne's social status, but she never married and, as a result, her girlhood extended. On average, white women in Saint-Domingue married several years earlier than white French women, who married in their mid-twenties.[23] Unmarried women remained legal minors until the age of twenty-five. This meant that until her twenty-fifth birthday, Marie-Jeanne did not have the legal ability to make contracts, to buy, sell, or own anything, or even to make her own decisions; she remained completely under the patriarchal authority of her father and depended entirely on him economically.

Yet Marie-Jeanne was far from alone in remaining unmarried; up to twenty percent of the population did not marry in early modern Western Europe.[24] As with other women, her single status may have stemmed from a conscious desire to remain unwed, a lack of suitable husbandly candidates, or a status chosen for her by her family.[25] Marie-Jeanne's race would have played a role in all these scenarios, although exactly how large a role remains uncertain. Personal choice may have been a factor; we can understand her potential reluctance to live under the authority of a husband, especially a white man for whom her race might have evoked stereotypes and tropes of racial and sexual domination. Alternatively, Marie-Jeanne's white relatives may have had specific family reasons for not wanting her to marry. She may have fulfilled certain tasks to help with housekeeping, possibly seen as too much of a burden on her father's inexperienced wife, who was only a few years older than herself. Perhaps even in her girlhood she took care of her sister Charlotte, who later developed an incurable illness, and her brothers. Whatever position she filled in her white stepfamily, in France her illegitimacy and her mixed racial background compromised her marriageability in ways that they did not in Saint-Domingue. As the daughter of one of the wealthiest merchants in town, it seems likely that some white men would have viewed her as an attractive marriage prospect. However, any prospective suitors probably would not have been drawn from the social strata with which she customarily mixed. She may have dismissed them as transparent fortune hunters, or she may have been unwilling to marry down socially, thus giving up the comforts and independence she had under her father's protection.[26]

Her race also placed her in a vulnerable position because of the growing correlation between African ancestry and enslaved status in France. Slavery had long been a fraught legal issue in metropolitan France. The customary legal principle of "free soil" meant that for centuries anyone enslaved who set foot in France automatically became free.[27] This principle eroded in the early eighteenth century when white colonists brought those they enslaved with them on trips between France and the Antilles. Legal provisions allowed them to do so but preserved some of the spirit of the Free Soil Principle insofar as enslaved people not registered as such were automatically freed.[28]

While this trajectory seems clear enough, free people of color such as Marie-Jeanne and her siblings muddied the legal waters. In an effort to revise this earlier misapprehension, in 1762 authorities mandated that all people of color, enslaved or free, register with local officials.[29] Fleuriau made these registrations for his children and also for an enslaved man, Hardy, who had accompanied him from Saint-Domingue.[30] Thus, for the first time in their lives, these privileged children were classified alongside the enslaved by virtue of French understandings of their race. They were listed in an official document as "*mulâtres*" for the first time since their arrival in France. This is a significant moment that signals a broader shift in attitudes toward race in France that collapsed race and status, thereby associating even people of color who were born free with slavery. Race became simply a matter of Black and white. What would Marie-Jeanne have thought about a registration requirement that connected her in such tangible ways with enslaved people? Did she know about it? She knew very well how official documents could protect her freedom in Saint-Domingue. This register, in contrast, seemed to reduce her social status.

This change happened just as Marie-Jeanne reached the usual age of marriage for women in France; she was twenty-two when her name appeared on a list of all people of color, enslaved or free, who lived in La Rochelle. We can view her registration alongside people who were or had been enslaved as a turning point. While it might not immediately have been apparent either to her or her father, grouping her with enslaved people reduced her marriageability, thus foreclosing the future she thought she had. Marriage across racial lines was not illegal in France at this time—it did not become so until 1778—but her classification alongside the enslaved seemed to sound the death knell to any hopes Marie-Jeanne may have had to marry.[31]

By 1772, when Marie-Jeanne was about thirty-one, she and her sister Charlotte (one year younger) set up independent housekeeping. After the colonial economy had recovered from the dip occasioned by the Seven Years' War (1756–1763), their father purchased multiple properties in La Rochelle, and he allowed the sisters to live in one of them. The house, although far less grand in size, furnishings, or situation than the one their father occupied with his white family, was comfortable and well-furnished with the luxuries deemed important by bourgeois sensibilities.[32] On the one hand, this seems to mark an official end of the sisters' girlhood: they lived as independent women. On the other hand, they still depended on their father for their every need, and their roles continued to be both marginalized and gendered. By this point they alone remained of Fleuriau's mixed-race children in France. Two of their brothers had returned to Saint-Domingue for good in 1765, ten years after their initial arrival, and their youngest brother followed several years later.[33] Their return comes as no surprise; part of the point of bringing or sending mixed-race sons to France was so they could acquire education or training that would make them better plantation administrators, and this is exactly what Fleuriau's sons did when they returned to Saint-Domingue. (Their father might have been surprised, however, if he had ever learned of his son Paul's role in demanding rights for free men of color during the Haitian Revolution.[34])

Daughters occupied a different role. Rather than managing property, caregiving fell to their lot. According to their father, "Charlotte has been for a number of years attacked by a cold distemper sickness, and it has afflicted her sight, from which neither doctor nor surgeon has yet been able to cure her, and . . . her sister Marie is the only one who can care for her and monitor her in this distressing state that visibly will carry her to the tomb."[35] Marie-Jeanne cared for her sister in their own house until Charlotte died in 1773, when she was thirty years old.[36]

Yet ties from Marie-Jeanne's girlhood in Saint-Domingue continued to exert a pull. In 1783, ten years after her sister's death, her niece, the daughter of her younger brother, came to La Rochelle.[37] Marie died shortly after her arrival, but a few years later Marie-Jeanne's father communicated with his agent in Saint-Domingue about having another "daughter and a niece of Paul Mandron" [his son] come to La Rochelle.[38] Ultimately, the girls did not make the journey, as one of them fell ill right before their scheduled departure. These visits, tragically brief and unexpectedly aborted though they were, shed a different light on Marie-Jeanne's isolated youth. Her will, written in 1788, made clear that she maintained communication and connections with her siblings and their children in Saint-Domingue. Would she have encouraged the plan to send her nieces more than three thousand miles if she disapproved of the scheme and thought their prospects would be better if they remained in the Antilles?

This opens up questions about what Marie-Jeanne gained and what she lost when she left behind her childhood home, some of her siblings, and her mother upon her departure from Saint-Domingue at the age of fourteen. In leaving behind her past, she also left behind her expected future: getting married and having children. She also gave up the possibility of becoming an independent proprietor, as in France guild restrictions and contract laws rigidly regulated women's economic activity.[39] Her position as a mixed-race woman also shaped her experience. Mixed-race women in Saint-Domingue were viewed as lascivious sexual objects defined by carnal desire and sexual available to all, especially white men.[40] While she would not have been immune to such expectations in France (to a certain extent all women were defined by their sex) her simple removal from the colonial milieu may have spared her from the worst sexual harassment and abuse that would have been occasioned by her racial position.

Furthermore, while Marie-Jeanne and her siblings may have been subject to the whims of their father, it still seems likely that they had some say in their future or could at least voice an opinion. After all, if their father did not value their company, there was little reason for him to travel or live with his daughters. Marie-Jeanne was quite young when she initially arrived in France, but by the time her brothers returned to the colonies, she was older: twenty-four when the first two returned, and thirty-two when the youngest departed. Surely if she had desperately wanted to return to her birthplace she could have embarked with her brothers. Perhaps she chose to stay to take care of her sister, who, according to their father, was too ill to travel.[41] But perhaps she weighed the options and chose to stay for her own reasons. Her father had proven willing to support her, even, eventually, setting her up in her own comfortable household. He continued this support throughout his life, and upon his death left her an annual income of twelve hundred livres, enough for a single woman to live upon in considerable comfort.[42] She maintained relations with his white family, eventually appointing one of her white half-brothers as the executor of her will.[43] Marie-Jeanne remained in the same small house provided by her father for the rest of her life; she died when she was fifty-three, having passed most of her life in France, never returning to her place of birth, or seeing her brothers and sisters again.[44] Perhaps her peculiar state of independent dependence, indebted to her father for her support but thanks to his largesse able to live independently, was ultimately preferable to her to life as a wife, and her asexual position as an unmarriageable woman in France more desirable than being sexualized in Saint-Domingue.

For Marie-Jeanne, her blackness and, more specifically, her mixed racial ancestry shaped her life, the choices and experiences open to her, and her position in the world. But in her life, the meaning of race was inconstant and malleable. What mixed-race girlhood meant and how it was experienced varied across time, by location (even within the same empire), and by social position. It also was shaped by family relationships. For Marie-Jeanne, blackness, illegitimacy, family situation, and personal choices all entwined to shape her life path. In the end, the gaps in the historical record of Marie-Jeanne's life offer us a constructive space to think about one Black girl, her experiences, and her choices. They also open up the opportunity, however, to consider the category of Black girlhood and how it changes over time.

Notes

1. I have also written about this case in Jennifer L. Palmer, *Intimate Bonds: Family and Slavery in the French Atlantic* (Philadelphia: University of Pennsylvania Press, 2016), chapter 5.

2. Ann Stoler, *Race and the Education of Desire: Foucault's History of Sexuality and the Colonial Order of Things* (Durham, NC: Duke University Press, 1995); Saidiya Hartman, *Lose Your Mother: A Journey Along the Atlantic Slave Route* (New York: Farrar, Straus, and Giroux, 2008); Marisa Fuentes, *Dispossessed Lives: Enslaved Women, Violence, and the Archive* (Philadelphia: University of Pennsylvania Press, 2016); Tiya Miles, *Tales from the Haunted South: Dark Tourism and Memories of Slavery from the Civil War Era* (Chapel Hill: University of North Carolina Press, 2015).

3. Médéric-Louis-Élie Moreau de Saint-Méry, *Description topographique, physique, civile, politique, et historique de la partie française de l'isle Saint-Domingue*, Vol. 2 (Philadelphia: Moreau de Saint-Méry, 1798), 286–310; 292; Sue Peabody, "'A Dangerous Zeal': Catholic Missions to Slaves in the French Antilles, 1635–1800," *French Historical Studies* 25 (2002): 75.

4. Dominique Rogers, "Les libres de couleur dans les capitales de Saint-Domingue: Fortune, mentalités et intégration à la fin de l'Ancien Régime" (PhD diss., Université Michel de Montaigne, Bordeaux III, 1999).

5. Arlette Gautier, *Les Soeurs de Solitude: La condition féminine dans l'esclavage aux Antilles du XVIIe au XIX siècles* (Paris, Editions Caribéenes, 2010), 32–33.

6. Jacques Houdaille, "Trois paroisses de Saint-Domingue au xviiie siècle: Étude Démographique," *Population* 18 (1963): 93–110, 100.

7. Rebecca J. Scott and Jean M. Hébrard, *Freedom Papers: An Atlantic Odyssey in the Age of Emancipation* (Cambridge, MA: Harvard University Press, 2012).

8. Yvonne Fabella, "'An Empire Founded on Libertinage': The *Mulâtresse* and Colonial Anxiety in Saint Domingue," in *Gender, Race, and Religion in the Colonization of the Americas*, ed. Nora Jaffary (Burlington, VT: Ashgate, 2007), 109–24.

9. John Garrigus, *Before Haiti: Race and Citizenship in French Saint-Domingue* (New York: Palgrave Macmillan, 2006).

10. "Registre pour recevoir las déclarations des Nègres, Négresses, Mulâtres et Mulâtresses qui sont dans cette ville de La Rochelle, suivant les lettres de M. l'Intendant," 1763, 352–19, Archives municipales de La Rochelle, hereafter AMLR.

11. Jacques de Cauna, *L'Eldorado des Aquitains: Gascons, Basques et Bérnais aux Iles d'Amérique (XVIIe-XVIIIe siècles)* (Biarritz: Atlantica, 1998), 13.

12. To be precise, she was identified as "Marie Jeanne *negresse libre*" in Marie-Jeanne's baptism; "Jeanne dite Guimbelot *négresse libre*" in Marie-Charlotte's; "Jeanne *négresse libre*" in Joseph Benjamin's and Toinette's; and "Jeanne Guimbelot *négresse*

libre" in Pierre Paul's, Jean's, and Marie-Magdeline's. Etat Civil, Les Croix des Bouquets, Saint-Domingue, 85 MIOM 46 and 85 MIOM 47, Archives nationales d'outer mere, hereafter ANOM.

13. Baptism, "Fleuriau Marie Jeanne," 2 August 1742, parish records- Croix-des-Bouquets, ANOM.

14. "Arrêt en Règlement du Conseil du Cap, touchant la police des Esclaves," 7 April 1758, Moreau, *Loix et constitutions*, 4:225–9, Art. XIX.

15. Baptism, "Fleuriau Marie Jeanne," 2 August 1742, parish records- Croix-des-Bouquets, ANOM. Jeanne was identified slightly differently in the baptism records of all her children. See footnote 12.

16. Moreau de Saint-Méry, *La Description*, 1:85.

17. According to their father, Marie-Jeanne's younger brother Jean trained as a goldsmith. "Registre pour recevoir las déclarations des Nègres, Négresses, Mulâtres et Mulâtresses qui sont dans cette ville de La Rochelle, suivant les lettres de M. l'Intendant," 1763, 352–19, AMLR.

18. Ibid. The family likely arrived in 1755, although the precise date is unclear.

19. Historians generally agree that in the eighteenth century there were 4,000–5,000 enslaved people in France. There are no separate figures available for the population of free people of color because, except for a brief period from about 1762–1777, race was not a category used in French records. The most recent study that confirms these numbers is Erick Noël, *Etre noir en France au XVIIIe siècle* (Paris: Tallandier, 2006). My own research suggests that enslaved and free people of color were undercounted in official documents.

20. In 1763 only fifty-six people of color were recorded as living in La Rochelle, a town of about 10,000. "Registre pour recevoir les déclarations des Nègres, négresses, mulâtres, et mulâtresses qui sont dans cette ville de La Rochelle, suivant les lettres de M. l'Intendant," 1763, 352, AMLR.

21. Fabella, "'An Empire Founded on Libertinage,'"109–124.

22. At 22, Marie-Anne-Suzanne Liége was less than half Fleuriau's age. She was born in 1733. 1733, parish records, Saint-Barthélémy, GG 250, AMLR.

23. White women in Saint-Domingue tended to marry about four years earlier than their French counterparts. Houdaille, "Trois paroisses de Saint-Domingue," 99; Jean-Pierre Bardet, "Early Marriage in Pre-Modern France," *The History of the Family* 6, no. 3 (2001): 345–363.

24. Jacques Dupaquier, *La Population française au XVII et XVIIIe siècles* (Paris: Presses universitaires de France, 1979), 60–61.

25. Christine Adams, "A Choice Not to Wed? Unmarried Women in Eighteenth-Century France," *Journal of Social History* 29, no. 4 (Summer 1996): 883–894. Adams particularly warns against reading choice where there actually may have been very little on the part of the women involved.

26. In France, marrying far outside one's social status was called a *mésalliance*. In a colonial context, the term acquired a connotation of marrying someone of a different race.

27. Sue Peabody, "An Alternative Genealogy of the Origins of French Free Soil: Medieval Toulouse," *Slavery & Abolition* 32, no. 3 (September 2011): 341–362.

28. Sue Peabody, *"There are No Slaves in France": The Political Culture of Race and Slavery in the Ancien Régime* (New York: Oxford University Press, 1996), 72–75; Palmer, *Intimate Bonds*.

29. Ordinance of April 5, 1762, B 5592, ADCM. For further discussions on the Ordinance of 1762 and the legal case that brought it about, see Sue Peabody, "*There are No Slaves in France*," 72–75; Dwain Pruitt, "Nantes Noir: Living Race in the City of Slavers" (PhD diss., Emory University, 2005), 74–76.

30. "Registre pour recevoir las déclarations des Nègres, Négresses, Mulâtres et Mulâtresses qui sont dans cette ville de La Rochelle, suivant les lettres de M. l'Intendant," 1763, 352–19, AMLR.

31. The "Arrét du conseil portant defense de célébrer marriage entre les blancs, noirs, mulâtres et autres gens de couleur, et à tous notaires de passer aucun contrat entre eux" of 5 April 1778 prohibited interracial marriage, and also prohibited people of different races from making marriage contracts. In Isambert, Decrusy, and Taillandier, *Recueil général des anciennes lois françaises, depuis l'an 420 jusqu'á la Révolution de 1789*, 29 vols., vol. 25 (Paris: Belin-Leprieur, 1830), 257–258.

32. "Inventoire Fleuriau Mandron," 2 December 1793, archives of Notary Farjenel, 3 E 960, ADCM.

33. "Joseph and Paul Mandrox [sic]" were passengers on the ship the *Père de Famille*, which departed from La Rochelle 25 July 1765, bound for Saint Domingue. They were both identified as "natural sons of Sr. Fleuriau." Jean-Baptiste left France in 1773 on the ship the *Cérès*, Captain Nicolas Collett. "Passagers embarqués en France- La Rochelle," 1764–1765 and 1773, Colonies F 5B57, ANOM. Cauna refers to the sons' role in managing the plantation. Cauna, *Au temps des isles à sucre*, 5.

34. Jean Fouchard, *Les Marrons du syllabaire: Quelques aspects du problème de l'instruction et de l'éducation des esclaves et affranchis de Saint-Domingue* (Port-au-Prince: Editions Henri Deschamps, 1953); plates 34–37 are facsimile reproductions of this letter and its signatures. Paul Fleuriau's signature appears on plate 37. On relations between whites and free people of color in Mirebalais, see David Geggus, *Slavery, War, and Revolution: The British Occupation of Saint-Domingue, 1793–1798* (New York: Oxford University Press, 1982), 328–330. Also see Cauna, *Au temps des isles à sucre*, 55.

35. "Registre pour recevoir las déclarations des Nègres, Négresses, Mulâtres & Mulâtresses qui sont dans cette ville de La Rochelle, suivant les lettres de M. l'Intendant," 1763, 352–19, AMLR.

36. Parish records, Saint-Barthélémy, 1773, GG 313, AMLR.

37. Marie Mandroux, 20 September 1783, parish records, Saint-Barthélémy, GG 333, AMLR.

38. Michel-Joseph Leremboure to Aimé-Benjamin Fleuriau, 22 March 1787, in Papiers Châtillon. Cited in Cauna, *Au temps des isles à sucre*, 54.

39. Clare Haru Crowston, *Fabricating Women: The Seamstresses of Old Regime France, 1675–1791* (Durham, NC: Duke University Press, 2001); Daryl Hafter, "Female Masters in the Ribbonmaking Guild of Eighteenth-Century Rouen," *French Historical Studies* 20, no 1 (Winter 1997): 1–14. On legal restrictions on women's abil-

ity to make contracts, see Jérôme Luther Viret, "De l'exclusion coutumière à l'égalité révolutionnaire: Les Normandes et la légitime au XVIIIe siècle," *Revue historique de droit française et etranger*, 4 (October-December 2013): 707–724.

40. Fabella, "'An Empire Founded on Libertinage,'" 109–124; John Garrigus, "'Sons of the Same Father': Gender, Race, and Citizenship in French Saint-Domingue, 1760–1792," in *Visions and Revisions of Eighteenth-Century France*, ed. Jack R. Censer, Christine Adams, and Lisa Jane Graham (University Park, PA: Pennsylvania State University Press, 1997): 137–154; Marisa Fuentes, *Dispossessed Lives.*

41. "Registre pour recevoir las déclarations des Nègres, Négresses, Mulâtres et Mulâtresses qui sont dans cette ville de La Rochelle, suivant les lettres de M. l'Intendant," 1763, 352–19, AMLR.

42. "Dépôt du testament olographe de M Aimé Benjamin Fleuriau," 21 August 1787, in files of Notary Delavergne fils, 3 E 1698, ADCM.

43. "Dépôt du testament de la citoyenne Mandron Fleuriau," 24 November, 1793, records of Notary Farjenel, 3 E 960, ADCM. The will itself, written in Jeanne-Marie Fleuriau Mandron's own hand, was dated 24 May 1788, although it was not filed until her death five years later. On the continuing relationship among Marie-Jeanne and her white half-siblings, e.g., Michel-Joseph Leremboure to Aimé-Benjamin Fleuriau, May 22 and July 31, 1785, 1 Mi 259, ADCM.

44. Parish records, Saint-Barthélémy, 1793, GG 354, AMLR.

CHAPTER 7

Imagining Freedom

Black Girlhood in the Sanders-Venning Family, 1815–1890

NAZERA SADIQ WRIGHT

In this essay, I examine two autograph albums that belonged to two sisters, members of an elite African American family. Miranda Cogdell Venning, the oldest sister, was born in 1862. Her autograph album contains signatures from 1877 to 1886. Sallie Sanders Venning was born in 1872. Signatures in her album were written during 1886, the year she graduated from the eighth grade. The signatures and inscriptions in these Black girls' autograph albums offer a lens into one Black family's history of practicing freedom in the nineteenth century. Signatures reveal that Black girls were building alliances that would widen their networks, contribute to their intellectual development, and connect them to a Black elite. Black girls occupy a space of in-betweenness, like the figures Hortense Spillers labels 'not-yet' subjects: they are not yet citizens and not yet women.[1] Therefore, signatures and inscriptions in autograph albums convey everyday writing practices that inculcated Black girls into the citizenry and enabled them to secure belonging on their own terms. Each individual who signed the album would have touched the cover, flipped through its pages, read messages from others, and decided, carefully, on her own inscription. These autograph albums encourage us to think in recuperative, productive ways about intimacy among Black women and girls in ways that move beyond associations of touch with acts of sexualized violence in the antebellum era.

Figure 11. Miranda Cogdell Venning's Autograph Album. 1877–1886. Stevens-Cogdell/Sanders-Venning Collection, The Library Company of Philadelphia.

Figure 12. Sallie Venning's Autograph Album. Stevens-Cogdell/Sanders-Venning Collection, The Library Company of Philadelphia.

Freedom Denied: The Girlhood of Sarah Martha Sanders

This history of three generations of Black girlhood begins in 1815, the year Sarah Martha Sanders was born on a plantation in Mount Pleasant, across the inlet from Charleston, South Carolina.[2] During Sarah Martha's first twelve years, she lived with her mother, Juno, and her grandmother, Sarai, on a 500-acre plantation called White Hall.[3] Their owner, Sabina Hall, was an elderly widow in poor health. In 1821, when Sabina Hall was eighty-two, she sold White Hall and another plantation she owned to her stepson, a Charleston physician named Anthony Toomer, with the understanding that she would continue to live there until her death. That same year, Sabina Hall made her will.

Sarah Martha, who was six years old when Sabina Hall drew up her will, was Hall's particular favorite. She made a complex provision for Sarah Martha that was designed to protect her until she reached the age of twenty-one, giving her a girlhood that was as close to freedom as was possible. In 1820 the South Carolina legislature had passed a law that made it illegal for owners to emancipate slaves.[4] Because she was willing her entire estate to her stepson Anthony Toomer, all of her slaves would become his property upon her death. Sabina Hall did not want her stepson to hire out Sarah Martha's labor. Therefore she stipulated that Toomer should hire out five other slaves she owned, Phebe, Amy, Myrtilla, and Sukey and her son Peter, to earn money to support Sarah Martha. Her executor, a Charleston lawyer, was to collect their wages and pay Toomer $100 a year for the cost of supporting Sarah Martha until she turned twenty-one. The lawyer was to invest the rest of the wages of these five slaves in stock that would become Sarah Martha's property when she came of age.[5] This was an unrealistic will that had no means of legal enforcement.

Hall died on January 9, 1827 at the age of eighty-eight.[6] Thus, when Sarah Martha was twelve years old, her protected girlhood ended. All seven of Hall's slaves became part of Anthony Toomer's plantation empire of over 2,000 acres and joined the 122 slaves Toomer owned.[7] Toomer probably moved Sarah Martha, Juno, and Sarai into slave quarters. After years of living with a white woman who showed at least some desire to protect them, Sarah and her mother and grandmother became plantation slaves.

By the 1820s, the price of cotton had plummeted, and South Carolina plantation owners were scrambling to find marketable products.[8] Toomer frequently mortgaged land and slaves to meet his financial obligations.[9] Conditions were likely harsh; we know that at least one young man who had belonged to Sabina Hall ran away in 1830.[10] That year Toomer sold Sarah Martha. At the age of fifteen, she became the property of Richard Cogdell, a forty-three-year-old married bank clerk.[11] This time Sarah Martha's girlhood was truly over. She was ripped away from her mother and grandmother and placed in Cogdell's household in Charleston. Her family and the community she knew were nine-and-a-half miles away.

As an enslaved girl, Sarah Martha was likely sexually victimized repeatedly. Within ten months, young Sarah was pregnant with a child by Richard.[12] Over the next two decades, Sarah bore him nine more children. Only five survived beyond infancy. Richard set her up in a house on Tradd Street in Charleston, in a mixed neighborhood of whites, free Blacks, and slaves.[13] He made no effort to conceal his second family; his brother lived just a few houses away from Sarah Martha and her children.[14] Richard filled the house with the trappings of middle-class life: a set of fine china, a piano, and a machine for washing clothes.[15] Yet, whatever comforts and advantages Sarah and her children had could not mitigate the reality that they were slaves who belonged to Richard Cogdell. That legal fact could have torn the family apart at any moment. Although Richard worked for the Bank of the State of South Carolina, he lived mostly on money he had inherited from his father and an uncle.[16] If he had squandered his inheritance or gone into debt, the façade of freedom he had created could have come crashing down.

Sarah Martha died in 1850 at the age of thirty-five of puerperal fever, days after giving birth to her tenth child.[17] She named her baby Miranda. Richard buried them together. We know only a few details about Sarah as a person. She mourned the loss of her babies. In 1843, she paid on time for a gravestone for one of them.[18] When she died, the gravestone Richard erected for her said, "She was loved by all who knew her for her gentleness of character." Historian Amrita Chakrabarti Myers sees her as a woman who used "savvy tactics of negotiation" to obtain goods and advantages for her children.[19] I see Sarah Martha as a person who was denied girlhood. Sabina Hall's death deprived her of the protection Hall had tried to provide for her. Sarah Martha's story is a powerful illustration of the fact that good intentions by white owners counted for nothing in a global economy in which human beings were property that was vulnerable to the fluctuations of the marketplace.

Freedom Envisioned: The Girlhoods of Julia Sanders Venning and Cordelia Sanders Chew

Perhaps remembering the quasi-freedom she had had as a very young girl, Sarah Martha raised her children as virtually free. This was possible because of Richard's wealth.[20] The four older children gained an education at a time when it was illegal to educate slaves in South Carolina.[21] At least one of Sarah's daughters took piano lessons. The family likely worshipped at an Episcopalian church, perhaps even a white church.[22] When Sarah Martha Sanders died, Robert was eighteen, Julia was fifteen, Sarah Ann was eleven, Cordelia was nine, and Sophia Elizabeth was three. Young Julia suddenly became responsible for running the household and caring for her siblings. That same year, in 1850, the U.S. Congress passed the Fugitive Slave Act. With one stroke of a pen, the Sanders children became much more vulnerable. Robert, the oldest, had likely already acquired skill in tailoring, but it would have been very difficult for him to find work. In the 1850s, as the white population of Charleston overtook the Black and mulatto population, white laborers were becoming increasingly resentful of their African American competitors.[23] Sarah Martha's children were completely dependent on Richard for food, clothing, shelter, and, most important, protection from slavecatchers. And Richard was getting old.

In 1858, Richard Cogdell moved his five children from Charleston, South Carolina, to Philadelphia. He bought them a three-story brick house in the Third Ward of the rapidly growing city.[24] The address was 1116 Fitzwater Street. Robert was twenty-six, Julia was twenty-three, Sarah Ann was nineteen, Cordelia was seventeen, and Sophia was eleven. The neighborhood was mostly white, largely native born but a small percentage from Ireland and Germany. Most of the households were headed by men who were already participating in the industrialization of the North. They were merchants and manufacturers.[25] As they had in Charleston, the Sanders siblings lived with whites and moved in both the Black and white worlds.[26] An 1860 census record reveals Richard Cogdell also moved to Philadelphia, but he lived several blocks away from his children in a hotel called La Pierre House on the 100 Block of South Broad Street.[27]

This migration from South Carolina to Philadelphia marks the second generation of Sanders children who were born in slavery but worked to find freedom. Robert became the head of the household and began running a tailoring business from home. This choice of occupation provided employment for numerous family members for the rest of the century. The Sanders siblings immediately made contact with elite free Blacks in Philadelphia. This was easy for them to do; many Black people had migrated from Charleston to Philadelphia before the war. Almost as soon as the Sanders family arrived in Philadelphia, they began holding social gatherings in their home for friends with connections to Charleston. After one such gathering in the spring of 1858, Charlotte Forten, a native Philadelphian, remarked in her diary that "all were Southerners, save me."[28]

Forten was very impressed with seventeen-year-old Cordelia's imagination: "a great deal of freshness and originality," she wrote in her journal. Forten thought the entire Sanders family was "much more interesting than Southerners usually are." But the most revealing detail Forten observed is that the Sanders siblings did not see themselves as slaves and did not understand their connection to the abolitionist movement. Forten wrote that she would "*try hard* to convert them to anti-slavery."[29] Perhaps in their own minds, Sarah Martha's children were already free.

The next fifteen years were very eventful for the Sanders siblings. Julia married Edward Y. Venning in 1861. Cordelia likely continued her education at the normal school at the Institute for Colored Youth (ICY), which was just six blocks away from their home.[30] For most of the 1860s, she taught grades 4–6 in Colored School No. 1 in Brooklyn, New York.[31] In 1865, the youngest sibling, Sophia, died at the age of eighteen.[32] The next year, 1866, Richard died. He had managed to live long enough to protect his children until they were free. In 1870, Cordelia married William Chew. The next year, another sibling, Sarah Ann Sanders, died at the age of thirty-one.[33]

By 1871, only Robert, Julia, and Cordelia were left of the ten children Sarah Martha Sanders had borne. Her daughters had prepared for freedom in Charleston. They took advantage of every resource their wealthy white father could provide. By the time Richard moved them to Philadelphia in 1858, they were ready to join the city's elite circle of mixed-race community leaders. Regardless of what the law had to say about their status, Sarah Martha's daughters imagined themselves as free.

Practicing Freedom: The Girlhoods of Miranda and Sallie Venning

Sarah Martha's children mentored the next generation about freedom. By 1875, the next generation included Julia's children: Miranda (age thirteen), Julia (ten), Oliver (eleven), Sallie (three), and George (one). Cordelia was the mother of Richard Sanders Chew (four) and Charles Sanders Chew (one). These children were cherished by a circle of adult relatives. They learned what freedom meant from their mothers and the aunts and uncles who lived nearby and carefully monitored their development.

The year 1875 was a pivotal one for Miranda Venning. She had attended the Institute for Colored Youth up to that point, but that year her parents sent her to live in Cambridge, Massachusetts, where she attended the predominantly white Washington grammar school for two school years. This was a sacrifice for her mother, Julia Venning, who had two infants and two primary-school-age children. Just at the age when Miranda could have been a great help with childcare, Julia chose to give her oldest daughter an opportunity to complete her grammar school education at an elite institution. This sacrifice was possible because the family was close with the family of Harriet Jacobs, the author of *Incidents in the Life of a Slave Girl* (1861). In 1875, Eleanor Jacobs, Harriet's sister-in-law, lost her husband. She was running a boardinghouse in Cambridge; Harriet and Louisa Jacobs were running a boardinghouse a few blocks away.[34] Miranda boarded with Eleanor Jacobs, who doubtless kept a close eye on the young girl as she adjusted to attending a predominately white school. The Jacobs family provided Miranda with invaluable mentorship as she came to the end of her girlhood.[35]

During her final semester in Cambridge in 1877, Miranda collected autographs. This part of her album is a snapshot of her last season of girlhood; when she returned in Philadelphia in the fall of that year, she attended Roberts Vaux High School, an academically rigorous Black school, in preparation for applying to the all-white Girls Normal School. The album begins with the signature of her father's brother, Richard DeReef Venning, who was teaching at the ICY in 1877; he bought the album for her. That act indicates that he anticipated that Miranda would become friendly enough with her white classmates to ask some of them for their autographs. The next day, Miranda asked Flossie Lewis. Flossie was likely a friend from the ICY, for she was knowledgeable about literature. She quoted Lord Byron: "If it were not for Hope where would the future be?" She may have been Florence Lewis, a nineteen-year-old young Black woman who also lived in the Third Ward.[36] Miranda waited three months before she began to ask her white schoolmates at Washington Grammar School for their signatures, but after that she seems to have had no hesitation. At least 35 percent of the signatures she collected in 1877 were from her white classmates. As Miranda was leaving Cambridge, she collected the signatures of Harriet and Louise Jacobs. Louise wrote, "Precept is good but example is better."[37]

As Harriet Jacobs considered what to write in the album of the fifteen-year-old Black girl she had become friendly with, she likely cast her mind back to 1828, when she herself was fifteen. That year Harriet Jacobs was trying to avoid the sexual advances of her owner, who refused to leave her alone. Jacobs writes about this difficult decision in her *Incidents in the Life of a Slave Girl*: "I was struggling alone in the powerful grasp of the demon Slavery." She continues, "I was a poor slave girl, only fifteen years old."[38] Harriet Jacobs must have felt satisfaction and pleasure to see fifteen-year-old Miranda preparing for a future by developing her intellectual capacities instead of trying to stop a sexual predator or manage pregnancy and childbirth against her will. Jacobs writes in Miranda's album, "Trust and be hopeful."[39] This message has profound implications.

Surely Miranda had read *Incidents in the Life of a Slave Girl* and had thought of her own grandmother, who had faced the same situation as Jacobs at the age of fifteen. And surely Miranda must have been mindful of the many contrasts between her girlhood and the girlhoods of her grandmother, Sarah Martha, and Harriet Jacobs. The calculations and choices Miranda made about her future were so different from the ones her grandmother and Jacobs were forced to make. So when Harriet wrote of being hopeful in Miranda's album, she was transmitting the power of Black women's persistence and determination to young Miranda Venning.

Miranda Venning fulfilled the expectations of her grandmother, Aunt Cordelia, her mother Julia Venning, and her mentors Harriet, Louisa, and Eleanor Jacobs. Although segregation limited her to the "colored" schools, she became a teacher in the Philadelphia school system. Miranda traveled over nine miles one way to reach the schools where she taught in Germantown.

Unwilling to accept that predominately black schools should offer less, she went to night school to learn what was then called "modeling," a precursor of industrial design, so she could teach it to her students. When the city began offering night schools for workers in public schools, Miranda made sure her school was included.[40]

An accomplished musician who played a prominent role in the music ministry of her church, Miranda brought music to her students.[41] She was involved in musical initiatives and performances throughout Philadelphia. At the age of nineteen, Miranda was listed as Assistant Director for Church of the Crucifixion's Annual Concert on December 26, 1881.[42] When Miranda was twenty-one, she participated in the closing ceremonies of the Quaker City Recital as a piano soloist.[43] Miranda Venning eventually became the principal of the Joseph E. Hill School. She died in 1900 at thirty-eight years old.

By the time Sallie, Miranda's younger sister, was ready to start school, financial circumstances had changed for the family. In 1875, when the Vennings sent Miranda to Cambridge, Edward Venning had been earning an income as a carpenter. But by 1880, the year Sallie started school, it is likely that consumption had made it difficult for him to work full time. That illness cost him his life four years later.[44] In 1879, Cordelia Sanders, who had married and borne two sons, had died of consumption. Her death was mourned intensely by family and friends, and her widower, William Chew, was uncertain how to care for his young sons and earn a living.[45] When Julia returned to the house she co-owned with her brother Robert Sanders, she was available to care for the two Chew boys while their father worked as a barber. Thus, in 1880, the household included Robert Sanders and his wife Martha; William Chew and his son Charles; and Edward and Julia and their children Miranda (age eighteen), Julia (fifteen), Oliver (eleven), Sallie (eight), George (six), and Louisa (two).[46]

During Miranda's young girlhood, the Vennings had lived with Edward's parents, Edward and Elizabeth Nixon Venning, at 910 Rodman Street in the Seventh Ward. The Institute for Colored Youth was just two blocks away—an easy walk for a little girl. But, Julia and Edward Venning had moved their family into 1116 Fitzwater by 1880. That meant that Sallie was living in a different ward from the ICY. In Philadelphia it was illegal for children to attend a public school outside their ward, but Philadelphia's schools were deeply segregated. Sallie and her cousins Charles and Richard Chew, who also lived at the house on Fitzwater Street, were caught in the racist practices of a city that was rapidly closing doors to Black people.

The move to 1116 Fitzwater combined with the segregation of Philadelphia's schools meant that, at the age of eight, Sallie and her cousin Charles Chew were told that, due to their race, they could not attend the all-white Primary

School on Catharine Street, which was located two blocks from their home.[47] Sallie's uncle, William Chew challenged the Philadelphia school board with a lawsuit. On September 3, 1880, he enrolled the children in the school anyway and accompanied them on the first day of school. According to an article in the *Philadelphia Inquirer*, students at the school treated Sallie with "freezing indifference."[48] Thus, the beginning of Sallie's schooling was traumatic. There must have been many discussions around the dinner table about the importance of a good education even when every day was difficult. Yet, for the Venning family, freedom meant access to the same rights and public goods as whites. It was natural for Julia Venning to insist on an education for her daughter, Sallie. This fighting spirit was instilled by her mother, Sarah Martha Sanders, when Julia was a young girl in Charleston, South Carolina. This family had been imagining freedom for decades.

Sallie eventually adjusted to school. Her album, which commemorates the end of her education in the eighth grade, is filled with affectionate greetings from her friends. By linking the names of classmates who signed Sallie's album in 1886 with the 1880 manuscript census, I determined that at least 35 percent were white, mostly the children of immigrants. The content of their inscriptions indicate that Sallie was truly friendly with them. "L. Koeneman," likely Louisa Koeneman, the daughter of a Prussian father and a German mother who lived just blocks from 1116 Fitzwater, wrote, "Leaves may wither, Flowers may die, Friends may forget you, But never shall I." Maggie Morrison, the daughter of Irish immigrants who lived seven-tenths of a mile from Sallie, penned, "Remember me in friendship, remember me in love, remember me dear Sallie, when we meet above." On March 31, 1886, another schoolmate, Alice McCluskey, recorded, "When the golden sun is setting, / And your heart from care is free / When of others you are thinking, / Will you sometimes think of me." On December 9, 1886, E. Hickey wrote, "What is home, / Without its joys / What are the girls / Without the boys." On December 21, 1886, another friend, Stella, inscribed, "To Sallie: When you are old, / And cannot see, / Put on your specks / And think of me." In the same month on December 22, 1886, another friend, E. Schitt included a familiar poem: "Roses are red / Violets blue / Sugar is sweet / And so are you."[49] That these white classmates chose to inscribe sentimental lines in Sallie's album when they could have just signed their names indicates warm feelings toward her.[50]

Extended Black Girlhoods

Graduation was likely an anxious rite of passage for Sallie. By 1886, Edward Venning had died, and the family no longer had his income. Miranda was earning a beginning teacher's salary, and her older sister Julia was likely earning some money as a dressmaker in Robert Sanders's tailoring business. Julia still had two school-age children to support. It is unlikely there was money to give Sallie the kind of education that Miranda had. Sallie ended her education in the eighth grade. Nonetheless, she enjoyed an extended girlhood after graduation, continuing to live at 1116 Fitzwater Street with her mother, Miranda, her Uncle Robert, and his wife, Martha.[51] Due to the money Miranda and Julia Venning earned, Sallie did not have to work at the age of fifteen, which likely occurred with many of her girlhood friends in Philadelphia's Black community. When Miranda was sick, Sallie sometimes taught school in her place. Sallie took sewing, tailoring, and millinery classes and worked in the family tailoring business to earn money. She was also active in her church.[52] Yet, as her diary entries from 1890 to 1892 indicate, Sallie also had a robust social life. She spent summers with her friends, playing cards or going to the beach or the theatre. Thus, by the end of the nineteenth century, the family had achieved a freedom for Sallie Venning that gave her options and time to make careful decisions as her girlhood came to a close. That they were able to do this as racial boundaries grew more restrictive speaks volumes about the determination of the women in the Sanders-Venning family to expand what freedom meant with each decade. Sallie took her time selecting a partner. When she was thirty-one, Sallie Venning married William B. Holden on October 28, 1903. Census records indicate that Sallie worked as a dressmaker and a homemaker.[53]

During Miranda's and Sallie's girlhoods, the economic opportunities available to Black people in Philadelphia shrank. The hope that Miranda's mentors spoke of in the 1870s was not realized. By 1890, only 10 percent of Black men and 6 percent of Black women had jobs in manufacturing. The vast majority of the city's Black women (92 percent) crowded into jobs in the census category of domestic and personal service. The majority of Black men worked in either domestic and personal service (66 percent) or in transportation as porters on railway cars (22 percent).[54] W. E. B. Du Bois was one of the first scholars to note that the industrial revolution did not benefit Philadelphia's Blacks. He wrote in 1899 that "most people [in Philadelphia] were willing and many eager that Negroes should be kept as menial servants rather than develop into industrial factors."[55]

Miranda witnessed the effects of white employers slamming doors against Black workers in her school. In 1884, nearly a hundred students enrolled in the Haines Street school where she taught, but the average daily attendance reached only thirty-eight, and twenty-one students left during the year. Poverty forced Black children into the labor force when they should have been getting an education. Miranda toiled as the only teacher at that school for six years. She did not receive an assistant until 1889.[56] Yet, Julia Venning

Figure 13. Sallie Venning (b. 1872) in the 1890s, Shaw's Stereotype Photograph Gallery, Atlantic City, NJ, Stevens-Cogdell/Sanders-Venning Collection, The Library Company of Philadelphia.

and Cordelia Chew encouraged Miranda to take advantage of every educational opportunity available, including attending elite schools. The family envisioned a freedom for their daughters that ignored racial barriers. In the 1880s, when barriers appeared, Julia and William Chew, Cordelia's widower, showed Sallie how to oppose them. Louisa Jacobs wrote to a friend that William Chew's challenge to segregation in Philadelphia schools reflected "just what our dear Delie would have liked him to do."[57]

It is rare to witness written evidence of Black girls' expressions of joy and friendship in the 1880s. The Venning autograph albums are refreshing reminders that Black girls engaged in youthful practices. The albums reveal that the Venning girls forged friendships, replicated popular nineteenth-century norms and practices, and found their own expressions within rigid social expectations. Inscriptions in nineteenth-century autograph albums teach us about Black girls' networks and early alliances. They show us where Black girls traveled, with whom they communicated, and how they practiced freedom on their own terms. Autograph albums are overlooked sources that contribute to recovering the rich history of Black girls' lives from the archives.

Notes

1. The Black girl as "not-yet" draws from Spillers's explanation of the captives of the Middle Passage, who were removed from the indigenous land and culture, and who are "not-yet 'American'" in their movement across the Atlantic, but are suspended on a body of water and "were also nowhere at all." See Hortense Spillers, "Mama's Baby, Papa's Maybe: An American Grammar Book," in *Within the Circle: An Anthology of African American Literary Criticism*, ed. Angelyn Mitchell (Durham: Duke University Press, 1994), 455. Nazera Sadiq Wright, *Black Girlhood in the Nineteenth Century* (Urbana: University of Illinois Press, 2016), 10.

2. We know Sarah Sanders's birth year because her age was recorded on her death record. Death record for Sarah Sanders, September 21, 1850, South Carolina, Death Records, 1921–1965, Charleston, 1850, 66, Ancestry.com. In death, Richard gave her his last name; she is listed as "Sarah R. Cogdell."

3. Michael Trinkley, Debi Hacker, Nicole Southerland, Sarah Fick, and Julie Poppell, "Youghal: Examination of an Eighteenth and Nineteenth Century Plantation, Christ Church Parish, Charleston County, South Carolina," *Research Series* 65 (Chicora Foundation, Columbia, S.C., 2006):19.

4. H. M. Henry, *The Police Control of the Slave in South Carolina* (PhD diss., Vanderbilt University, 1914), 177.

5. Will of Sabina Hall, Charleston, June 15, 1821, South Carolina, Wills and Probate Records, Wills, Volume 36, 1818–1826, 187–189, Ancestry.com.

6. Death record for Sabina Hall, January 9, 1827, South Carolina Death Records, 1821–1849, Charleston, 1827, Ancestry.com.

7. Trinkley et al., "Youghal," 32.

8. Michael Trinkley, "A Historical and Archaeological Evaluation of the Elfe and Sanders Plantations, Berkeley and Charleston Counties, South Carolina," *Chicora Foundation Research Series* 5 (Chicora Foundation, Columbia, South Carolina, May 1985): 45; Eric C. Poplin and Michael C. Scardaville, "Archaeological Data Recovery at Long Point Plantation (38CH321), Mark Clark Expressway (I-526), Charleston County, South Carolina" (Brockington and Associates, 1991): 154–155.

9. Trinkley et al., "Youghal," 19.

10. John Hope Franklin and Loren Schweninger, *Runaway Slaves: Rebels on the Plantation* (Oxford: Oxford University Press, 2000), 400n5.

11. Bill of sale between Thomas D. Condy and R. W. Cogdell, February 23, 1830, South Carolina Estate Inventories and Bills of Sale, Bills of Sale 1773–1843, Volume 5K (1829–1832), 285, https://www.fold3.com/image/269306484.

12. Robert Sanders, Martha's first child, was born in March 1832, so he was likely conceived in June 1831. Amrita Chakrabarti Myers, *Forging Freedom: Black Women and the Pursuit of Liberty in Antebellum Charleston* (Chapel Hill: University of North Carolina Press, 2011), 152.

13. Tradd Street, located just a block from the harbor, was a mixed residential and commercial street. Judges lived there, but it was also the street where everything "from a two pence ribbon to the whole scale of plantation and household commodities" could be purchased. Charles Fraser, *Reminiscences of Charleston* (Charleston, S.C.: John Russell, 1854), 17, quote on 12–13. For the racial makeup of Ward 1, see John P. Radford, "Race, Residence, and Ideology: Charleston, South Carolina in the Mid-Nineteenth Century," *Journal of Historical Geography* 2, no. 4 (1976): 320–346.

14. Richard's brother, John S. Cogdell, the president of the Bank of South Carolina from 1835 to 1846, lived at the corner of Tradd and Market Streets. Washington Augustus Clark, *The History of the Banking Institutions Organized in South Carolina Prior to 1860* (Columbia: Historical Commission of South Carolina, 1922), 186; John S. Cogdell in U.S. City Directories, 1822–1925, 1830, Charleston, South Carolina, 101, Ancestry.com.

15. Myers, *Forging Freedom*, 157.

16. Myers, *Forging Freedom*, 150, 153–155, 163.

17. Death record for Sarah Sanders. This record lists the cause of death. Puerperal fever is an infection of the uterus that develops within three days after childbirth and often led to septicemia in the nineteenth century. Mortality rates from this disease were typically very high. Christine Hallett, "The Attempt to Understand Puerperal Fever in the Eighteenth and Early Nineteenth Centuries," *Medical History* 1, no. 49 (2005): 1–28.

18. Sarah Sanders, cemetery subscriptions, 1843, Box 8, Folder 4, Stevens-Cogdell-Sanders-Venning Collection, Library Company of Philadelphia (hereafter SCSVC).

19. Myers, *Forging Freedom*, 163.

20. John Cogdell's will noted that Richard was in "easy circumstances." Will of John S. Cogdell, March 1, 1847, South Carolina, Wills and Probate Records, 1670–1980, Charleston Wills, Vol. 44–45, 1845–1851, Ancestry.com.

21. Although a state law outlawing education for Blacks had been on the books for many years, in 1834, the state legislature passed a new law making it illegal for Blacks to even learn to read. Myers, *Forging Freedom*, 157, 160–161; Jane H. Pease and William Pease, "Social Structure and the Potential for Urban Changes: Boston and Charleston in the 1830s," *Journal of Urban History* 8 (February 1982): 187.

22. Katie Ann Stojsavljevic, "Housing and Living Patterns among Charleston's Free People of Color in Wraggborough, 1796–1877" (PhD diss., Clemson University, 2007), 10.

23. Stojsavljevic, "Housing and Living Patterns," 20.

24. The earliest evidence of the Sanders siblings in Philadelphia is the fact that Cordelia and Sarah Ann Sanders visited Charlotte Forten at home in March 1858. Mary Maillard, ed., *Whispers of Cruel Wrongs: The Correspondence of Louisa Jacobs and Her Circle, 1879–1911* (Madison: University of Wisconsin Press, 2017), 158n4. Racial composition of Fitzwater Street derived from U.S. Federal Census, Philadelphia Ward 3, 408–416, Ancestry.com, accessed September 8, 2018. Only a few households were headed by Blacks.

25. The occupations of the heads of the households in the blocks surrounding 1116 Fitzwater included hardware dealer, grocer, superintendent, watchman, physician, type founder, stove maker, merchant, and manufacturer. 1860 U.S. Federal Census, Philadelphia Ward 3, 408–416, Ancestry.com, accessed September 8, 2018. Only a few households were headed by Blacks.

26. Robert Sanders in 1860 federal census, Philadelphia, 3rd Ward, 188, Ancestry.com

27. R. W. Cogdell in 1860 federal census, Philadelphia, 8th Ward, 333, Ancestry.com.

28. Maillard, *Whispers of Cruel Wrongs*, 4.

29. Maillard, *Whispers of Cruel Wrongs*, 22.

30. The Institute for Colored Youth was at 715–718 Lombard Street.

31. Maillard, *Whispers of Cruel Wrongs*, 22; *Annual Report of the City Superintendent of Schools of the Consolidated City of Brooklyn for 1863* (Brooklyn: George C. Bennett, 1863), 87, 95, 122, 129; *Manual of the Common Council of the City of Brooklyn* (Brooklyn: The Council, 1865), 345; *Manual of the Common Council of the City of Brooklyn* (Brooklyn: The Council, 1867), 147; *Manual of the Common Council of the City of Brooklyn* (Brooklyn: The Council, 1869), 269.

32. Marriage record for William Chew and Cordelia Sanders, May 25, 1870, Pennsylvania and New Jersey, Church and Town Records, 1669–2013 (hereafter PNJCTR), Philadelphia, Crucifixion Episcopal Church, Ancestry.com; death record for Sophia E. Sanders, September 8, 1865, PNJCTR, Philadelphia, Crucifixion Episcopal Church, Ancestry.com.

33. Death record for Sarah Ann Sanders, 1116 Fitzwater Street, August 21, 1871, Philadelphia, Pennsylvania Death Certificates Index, 1803–1915, Ancestry.com.

34. Mrs. Harriet Jacobs and Eleanor Jacobs, widow of John, U.S. City Directories, Cambridge, Mass., 1875, 229, Ancestry.com; Myers, *Forging Freedom*, 37.

35. Myers, *Forging Freedom*, 182n1.

36. Florence Lewis in 1870 federal census, Philadelphia, 3rd Ward, 146, Ancestry.com.

37. Miranda Venning Autograph Album, Box 4, Folder 1, SCSVC.

38. Harriet Jacobs, *Incidents in the Life of a Slave Girl* (New York: Oxford University Press, 1988), 84.

39. Miranda Venning Autograph Album, Box 4, Folder 1, SCSVC.

40. "Special Notices," *Philadelphia Times*, October 3, 1884, 3; "Germantown Schools," *Philadelphia Times*, December 9, 1888, 13.

41. "To Teach Teachers: A List of Those Who Will Attend the Saturday Class in Modeling," *Philadelphia Inquirer*, February 11, 1886, 2.

42. Announcement, "We take great pleasure in announcing to our friends and the public generally that the Young People's Musical and Literary Association of the Church of the Crucifixion has secured Musical Fund Hall, Locust Street, between 8th and 8th Streets, for their Annual Concert . . ." Scrapbook Materials, SCSV Box 6 Folder 14.

43. Announcement, "You are cordially invited to the Closing Exercises . . ." Scrapbook Materials, Scrapbook Materials SCSV Box 6 Folder 15.

44. Death announcement of Edward Y. Venning, *Philadelphia Inquirer*, July 29, 1884, 3. The announcement listed the cause of death and noted that "for several years he took an active part in every movement affecting the colored people of this city."

45. Maillard, *Whispers of Cruel Wrongs*, 20, 56, 61.

46. Although the 1880 census, which was taken in June, records Edward as living with his parents at 337 Dean Street and Julia and the children as living several houses away at 357 Dean, by the beginning of September the Vennings had moved to 1116 Fitzwater. Edward Venning, Julia Venning, and William Chew in 1880 federal census, Philadelphia, Pennsylvania, 90B, 102A, and 481A, respectively, Ancestry.com; "Blacks in a White School," *Philadelphia Inquirer*, September 3, 1880, 1. William Chew's older son, Richard, was living in Trenton, New Jersey, with William's mother, Charlotte Henson Chew. After Cordelia's death, a family friend wrote "Poor Deley's death made a big change in domestic matters." Maillard, *Whispers of Cruel Wrongs*, 177n13.

47. "The Chew Case," *Philadelphia Inquirer*, September 9, 1880, 3.

48. "Blacks in a White School," 1 September 3, 1880

49. Sarah "Sallie" Venning Autograph Album, Box 4, Folder 1, SCSVC.

50. One example is *One Thousand Popular Quotations Comprising the Choicest Thoughts and Sayings of Eminent Writers of All Ages . . . Suitable for Writing in Autograph Albums* (New York: J. S. Ogilvie, 1884).

51. Sallie Sanders diaries, 1890–1892, Box 4, Folder 3, SCSVC; Sallie Sanders in 1900 federal census, Philadelphia, 3rd Ward, page 89A, Ancestry.com.

52. Sallie Sanders diaries, 1890–1892.

53. Marriage certificate of William B. Holden and Sallie S. Venning, October 20, 1903, PNJCTR, Philadelphia, Church of the Crucifixion, Ancestry.com.

54. Author's calculations from Department of Commerce and Labor, *Special Report: Occupations at the Twelfth Census* (Washington, DC: Government Printing Office, 1904), Table 43, pages 672–678.

55. W. E. B. Du Bois, *The Negro in Philadelphia* (Philadelphia: University of Pennsylvania, 1899), 126.

56. *Annual Report of the Board of Public Education, First School District of Pennsylvania, Comprising the City of Philadelphia* for 1883–1889 (Philadelphia: Burke and McFetridge, 1883–1889).

57. Maillard, *Whispers of Cruel Wrongs*, 68.

CHAPTER 8

"The Girl Who Is to Die at the Rope's End"

The 1892 Execution of Milbry Brown and Definitions of Childhood in South Carolina Courts

CYNTHIA R. GREENLEE

At 11 a.m. on October 7, 1892, twenty observers congregated inside the Spartanburg, South Carolina jail enclosure.[1] Many more milled outside the jail waiting for the rare spectacle of a double execution. Some likely came to see a specific hanging: that of Milbry Brown, a girl whose age was variously reported as anything from the early teens to sixteen.[2] A Black domestic servant from the nearby mill town of Gaffney, Brown had allegedly poured the caustic household cleaner carbolic acid into the mouth of the one-year-old daughter of her employers, the Carpenter family. According to most newspaper reports, the poison had been Brown's vengeful comeback for the white "missus" scolding her for sweeping too slowly.[3] The girl supposedly confessed before a panel of white male inquisitors that she intended only to burn the child, a comment that galvanized supporters who claimed she was malicious but unable to understand the seriousness of her actions. Young Geraldine died in about twenty hours.[4] Four months later, Milbry Brown paraphrased an old hymn—"I'm going home to glory to die no more"—and was hanged along with a Black man who had accidentally killed the mayor of Spartanburg.[5]

Far from an open-and-shut case, legal and community stakeholders did not automatically define Brown as an adult woman or reflexively push for her death. Milbry Brown's case and that of Axey Cherry, another Black South Carolina girl accused of child poisoning years earlier, exposed how in flux ideas about childhood and its implications were in the late nineteenth century, a time that was simultaneously the nadir of African American history and the formative moment for both the concept of "protected childhood" and the stirrings of juvenile justice.[6]

Specifically, the trial of Milbry Brown illustrated the pitched battles over what age, race, gender, and perceived disability or "mental dullness" should mean in a capital case. Advocates for Milbry Brown—including one of South Carolina's most influential newspaper editors—applied notions of childhood ungovernability; ideas of female emotionality; racially paternalistic beliefs about Black ignorance; and supposed cognitive impairment to argue that Brown should not be held accountable for her alleged actions. A few argued for leniency because white people accused of similar crimes were unlikely to be sentenced to death or severe punishment. On the other hand, Brown's "law and order" detractors also deployed essentialized arguments. They labeled her a fiendish virago who strayed monstrously from the norms of femininity and youthful innocence. In their eyes, her age and gender identities served as aggravating, not mitigating, factors in legal proceedings.

October 7, 1892, earned Spartanburg and South Carolina a dubious distinction. On that day, a total of four South Carolinians—three Black residents and one white wife murderer—were executed in different locales in what *The State* newspaper labeled "the hangman's harvest."[7] And Brown was not the only female prisoner to be executed on that day.[8] About sixty miles away in rural Newberry County, the sheriff also hanged a young Black female, nineteen- or twenty-year-old Anna Tribble. A farm laborer, Tribble had been convicted of killing her newborn infant by exposure.

Brown and Tribble's executions were graphic proof of the punitive turn in Southern penal systems that, after the Civil War, jailed more Black women and girls than ever before.[9] Female executions have been infrequent in the United States, with less than 600 occurring from the late seventeenth century to the early 2000s.[10] But in the 1890s Carolinas, executions picked up pace, especially for young Black women. Caroline Shipp had been hanged for infanticide in the North Carolina border town of Dallas eight months earlier than Brown and Tribble; her hanging drew thousands of tourist-witnesses.[11] The executions of Brown, Tribble, and Shipp represented a troubling and unusual cluster of female hangings in the region, all for crimes against children.

Milbry Brown is known only by a crime, her death, and a few paltry details referenced in newspapers and broadsides by crusading journalist Ida B. Wells.[12] Even her name is something of a mystery; she is referred to as Milbry most often, but also Milbrey, Mildrey, or Mildred. Her surname is also reported as Smith, not Brown.[13] Census records suggest that Milbry Brown's seemingly full-time work was relatively unusual among her community's Black girls. Though many may have done sporadic or part-time domestic work, relatively few were acting as nurses like Milbry Brown, suggesting that she lived in economic precarity that necessitated full-time work and likely co-residence with her employers.

In contrast to Milbry's fragmentary documentary trail, the Carpenter family for whom she worked left deep archival footprints. The Carpenters were economically privileged enough to employ Milbry, a nanny, and a cook.[14] The family patriarch, William Carpenter, ran the successful general store, Carroll and Carpenter.[15] His wife, née Carrie Brown, was a Confederate blueblood; her father, Major John Brown, mustered a Civil War company, and when that company refused to fight, so goes the local tale, he signed up with another group.[16] Milbry Brown likely had a connection to the Carpenter family that preceded her arrest by many years. In the 1880 census, the dwelling adjacent to the Brown home where ten-year-old Carrie—later, Milbry's "missus"—resided was occupied by forty-year-old cook Amelia Mitchell, daughter Soffia, and a two-year-old daughter, "Milberry," whose age in 1892 would place her within the possible age range.[17] Furthermore, in Gaffney, the distinctive name Milbry could easily be found in Carrie Brown Carpenter's family tree. According to online records, a white Milbry Jane Brown (known as Miss Jane or Janie), died suddenly after several days of illness.[18] While this white Milbry's precise relationship to Carrie Brown Carpenter remains unclear, it's certain she was a relative (perhaps a young aunt) and that she died the same month as the toddler Geraldine in June 1892. The white Milbry Jane Brown thus shared both her first name and a surname with Milbry Brown, a Black girl accused of murdering one of her kin.[19]

Newspaper reports and legal documents observed or presumed the absence of a Black family or kin group for Milbry Brown.[20] A newspaper claimed that "Mrs. Brown raised the girl" (the Mrs. Brown was Carrie Carpenter's mother) suggesting that the relationship between the Carpenters and Milbry Brown was a long, complex one that may have been predicated on, but not entirely limited to, employment.[21] As scholars Thavolia Glymph and Rebecca Sharpless have demonstrated, Milbry Brown's workplace was simultaneously a home and site of simmering interracial conflict.[22] It may also have been Milbry Brown's only home if the Carpenters had assumed responsibility for the girl after her mother's death or other family separation. Mrs. Brown's supposed rearing of a young Black servant seemed a benevolent gesture, but one that also potentially captured Brown's labor in a de facto apprenticeship with no end and translated into a lack of recourse in disputes.[23] And for pundits who followed the girl's trial, the Carpenters' guardianship transformed Milbry's alleged offense into the ostensible betrayal of a particularly ungrateful servant taken into the family fold.[24]

Brown's alleged crimes required intimacy and access. Both arson and poisoning had been considered common offenses of bondswomen during slavery, and they continued to be associated with African Americans after emancipation.[25] The location of the Black female cook or nanny within the home established, in white minds, a durable connection between female servants and poisoning. Brown's case echoes that of twelve-year-old Axey Cherry of Barnwell County. In 1887, Cherry had been pressed into a live-in domestic service job by her family.[26] She was accused of fatally poisoning the small child of her employers, the West family, with concentrated lye. According to witnesses, she had been heard grumbling that she wasn't going to "bother with that baby" much longer. She bolted and was caught only when the child's father chased and tackled her into submission.[27]

Nineteenth-century media routinely described the physical attributes of crime suspects and, with African Americans particularly, reinforced the idea that competence and criminality were discernible. One report described Axey Cherry as a "pure-blooded Negress, black as coal and with a very stupid expression."[28] Before the widespread use of the mugshot and racial typologies that purported features could predict criminality, Cherry's race, dark complexion, and facial features were interpreted as visual clues to her ostensibly poor intellect and penchant for misbehavior. Furthermore, said the writer, Cherry's eyes had abnormally large whites, which resembled those of an excited beast.[29]

But descriptions of the young woman vacillated between the monstrous and those that played up her childish qualities. As Robin Bernstein has noted, childhood innocence is often "raced white" and personified by characters like *Uncle Tom's Cabin*'s Little Eva, whose blonde hair, fondness for wearing white apparel only, and angelic personality obviously signaled a distance from the knowing, frequently violent ways of the world, adults, and African Americans.[30] The same wild-eyed Axey Cherry was also the Axey Cherry who "cried for her father" at trial.[31] Reports that Cherry twirled and laughed in her jail cell, longed to play outside, and tried to dart out of the local jail during mealtimes effectively emphasized both childishness and "simple-mindedness" for the courtroom audience. They also framed her as a more sympathetic character than Milbry Brown, whom newspapers quoted as spitefully saying she would have poisoned the entire Carpenter clan if only she had known carbolic acid could kill.[32]

Long and fatal though Cherry's life sentence was—the governor reversed the decision committing her to death—her lesser sentence demonstrated that even the most inflammatory cases didn't always garner capital punishment. A York County case showed that even Black female adolescents had social networks from which to draw when they faced criminal charges.

When fourteen-year-old domestic servant Anna Belle Jones was convicted of attempted homicide by poisoning in 1891 and sentenced to ten years in prison, "nearly every lady in Yorkville" vouched for the girl in a letter to the governor, drowning out dissenting male voices who dismissed their petition as women's irrational and ill-informed patter. "We believe her to be innocent," the women wrote. "She has been employed in many families in Yorkville as a nurse and had the confidence of all her employers and the affection of the children she nursed."[33] Other correspondence to the governor indicated that "the prisoner belongs to a numerous and influential family of Negro's [*sic*] in this community."[34] A disproportionate number of Black girls' purported crimes stemmed from their labor in white homes, but connections borne of work and white benefactors sometimes paid off.

The dearth of primary sources doesn't shed light on whether Milbry Brown had social capital or support from people who actually knew her. Her first execution date—during which she received a last-minute respite—was attended by many Black upcountry residents and a few whites.[35] To ward off conflict, real or imagined, the sheriff cut holes in the execution enclosure and stationed guards armed with Winchesters at each opening. There was no disturbance, but the newspaper noted considerable comment on Brown's case and varied sentiment among Black residents, some of whom it claimed had a "hang them all" mentality.[36] But it's likely that the crowd included people who knew the girl, those who were outraged at the execution, others who clamored for or approved of Brown's punishment, and many more who were simply interested in the spectacle.

"The criminal is nothing more than a child"

When it became apparent that Milbry Brown was a suspect, Axey Cherry's case provided a template for the efforts to save the Gaffney girl's life. Most notably, Cherry's case had attracted the attention of James C. Hemphill, the prominent editor of the Charleston *News and Courier* newspaper. Hemphill personally wrote or signed off on editorials that questioned Cherry's execution. "She undoubtedly killed the child," an opinion piece wrote, "but whatever the motive that led to the killing, the murderer is but a child herself" while being "so low on the scale of humanity."[37] While expressing its concern that the girl did not have any conception of her supposed crime, the article did not support an outright pardon. Its unnamed author, possibly Hemphill, instead pontificated on "one of the most troublesome features of the Southern problem," that "the lower order of negro criminals" seemed not to fear retribution for misdeeds, suffered from a supposedly characteristic lack of foresight, and pursued pleasure at all costs.[38] Warming to the topic, the editorial writer warned parents to be more careful about entrusting their little ones to untried Black hands.

The *News and Courier* published remarkably similar sentiments five years later, this time in reference to Milbry Brown. "The criminal is nothing more than a child . . . a half-grown girl! . . . Imprisonment is as severe a penalty as the public sentiment of the state and country will tolerate in her case. It would be a crime to hang her, when a white girl would not certainly be hanged."[39] Hemphill's advocacy kept Milbry Brown's case in the spotlight but, in the context of the state's fractious and perpetually feuding Democrats, also damaged her prospects among his political foes. The *News and Courier*'s forthright criticism of a state that would execute children was just the latest volley in its sometimes issue-specific and boisterous opposition to the administration of Governor Benjamin Tillman, the one man with the power to change Brown's fate. The Columbia-based *State* newspaper rebutted the claims of racial bias, saying that Hemphill's publication's claims "that a white woman would not have been hung for a similar crime" were hysterical and unfounded. Such atrocious crimes were not the province of white women and families, whom another article depicted as victims compelled to commit their helpless infants to the care of inhuman nurses.[40]

Also at issue was whether Milbry Brown, as a girl, could be held legally responsible for poisoning Geraldine Carpenter. Following English common law, the state of South Carolina held that the age of full criminal culpability—at which time youth could be treated like adults—was age fourteen.[41] But the law allowed for judicial discretion. As James Aldrich, the presiding judge at Brown's trial, would later write, under seven years of age a child was considered incapable of committing crime; between seven and fourteen years of age was the debatable period, the presumption being that a child under fourteen is incapable of committing crime. Still those standards could be rebutted by evidence showing ability and intent to conceive and commit a crime.[42]

If the law did not dictate precisely how jurists should deal with children, neither was Milbry Brown's age entirely clear. Parties who represented the state or were called to help with the pardon decision were far more likely to use the oldest age estimates. Aldrich continued in his letter, "As I remember the evidence on the part of the state, Milbry Brown was sixteen years old." Thus, he recommended no changes to the execution plan. As Brown's case traveled to the governor for reconsideration, the lawyer enlisted to independently review the case repeated that Brown's age was sixteen and she was therefore wholly accountable for murder.[43] Advocates for mercy typically cited a younger age, as did Converse College President B.F. Wilson (identifying Brown as "about fourteen years old"). But despite cross-county petition campaigns and calls on the governor in Columbia, there appears to have been no effort to verify her age.[44]

More debate, however, centered around Milbry Brown's mental and intellectual faculties beyond the issue of age. White commentators characterizing her as too "dull-witted" for real accountability were pitted against others arguing that she was competent enough to stand trial. Multiple explanations for her compromised decision-making capacity included her youthful immaturity, lack of adult ratiocination, or apparently nonexistent education.[45] Pleaders for condemned girls' lives tried to leverage the evolving metaphorical power of childhood and to frame governors as states' premier benevolent patriarchs. When Axey Cherry was sentenced to death, a writer, who identified herself as a twelve-year-old from Oneida, New York, wrote South Carolina Governor John Peter Richardson, "I know how I would feel if I were to be hung. Please, sir, if you have a little child, girl or boy, think how you would feel if she or he were doomed to die." The letter writer called on Richardson "to start up all your manly feelings" and noted that up north, "they would not dare do such a thing." Signed "your little friend, Agnes Reynolds," the missive spoke to the idea of children as moral and political actors.[46]

Little Agnes Reynolds' letter also showed how far and how fast news could travel, and Milbry Brown's execution reached the ears of Black progressive and muckraking journalist Ida B. Wells. Wells recycled the story of Brown's execution in two of her most circulated speeches and broadsides including "The Reason Why the Colored American Is Not in the World's Columbian Exposition." Wells saw Milbry Brown's execution not as a symbol of the girl's depravity but as a sign of the South's own sectionally specific brand of sin. Wells recast Milbry Brown's execution as a "legal hanging" that was more akin to a lynching than a product of due process. She wrote:

> So great is Southern hate and prejudice, they legally(?) hung poor little thirteen-year-old Mildrey Brown at Columbia, S.C., Oct. 7, on the circumstantial evidence that she poisoned a white infant. If her guilt had been proven unmistakably, had she been white, Mildrey Brown would never have been hung. The country would have been aroused and South Carolina disgraced forever for such a crime. The Afro-American himself did not know as he should have known as his journals should be in a position to have him know and act.[47]

Popular press around the country similarly viewed the case as proof that the South was distinctly un-Reconstructed.

Within South Carolina, journalists also understood criminal-justice treatment of children to be a key barometer of a civilized society, and they debated the case as a referendum on the perennial topic of lawlessness in the state. Multivalent in meaning, lawlessness was popularly used to describe widespread societal violence and, more specifically, lynching. But in regard to the convicted girl, lawlessness took on other definitions. Hemphill, the Charleston editor and Brown's most vocal advocate, saw her death sentence as the ultimate sign of a law gone so astray that it was an affront to moral principles and colorblind justice.[48] Predictably, Brown's detractors had a quite different read. They registered Brown's crime as an undeniable marker of lawlessness; though children often shot and maimed each other accidentally in the state, the specter of a young girl coolly poisoning a smaller child symbolized a culture more inclined to chaos than order.

Childhood and femaleness were not universally understood as mitigating circumstances in South Carolina courts. Milbry Brown was caught in a war of petitions that dueled about whether her age and girlhood were enough to preserve her life. Lawyer Charles Barrett presented a petition urging a commutation based on "her tender age and sex" and signed by about thirty of the upcountry's "very best men," captains of industry and education: Dr. James Wofford, president of Wofford College; D.D. Converse, the president of the Clifton and Glendale textile mills; and George Cofield, president of the National Bank of Spartanburg, among others.[49] A second petition followed with hundreds of signatures, many this time from women, a few African Americans, and residents of the "rural suburbs" outside Spartanburg.[50] But a counterpetition urging Brown's execution attracted hundreds more signatures than Barrett's first petition, and it bore the signatures of scores of men who identified themselves as carpenters, clerks, jewelers, and farmers—a snapshot of the working and agricultural classes that Tillman was busy co-opting into a white-supremacist power bloc.[51]

The counterpetition took aim, first, at the idea that gender should affect her execution: "The law makes no distinction between male and female. An argument in this Case based upon the sex of the convict is based upon a sentimentality and does not appeal to the principal [*sic*] of the law." Indeed, it argued that "the facts that such crimes are so rarely committed at this age, and are more rarely committed by a female at this age, prove, if they prove anything, that this person is depraved, mentally and morally," to a degree which fully justifies the full penalty of the law: death.[52] With a few drops of poison, Milbry Brown had ventured so far outside the boundaries of acceptable child and feminine behavior that she was considered irredeemable.

In comprehensive fashion, the counterpetition addressed and dismissed a third concern: that Milbry Brown was mentally disabled: "There was no proof of want of mental development at the trial." Charles Petty, editor of the *Carolina Spartan* newspaper and a commutation advocate, had indeed chimed in on this point, saying "I learn from those who knew her well that she is very dull in mind and never had any opportunity for the improvement of mind or morals." James B. Cleveland, who had never met Milbry, noted "she was not a bright girl, much below the average in intelligence, this fact alone it seems to me should have great influence."[53] Convicting Judge Aldrich spoke his piece, recalling that Milbry Brown did not testify on her behalf but that others said she had "good sense" and was chronologically old enough to face her sentence. Milbry Brown's competence was gauged by hearsay and a cadre of white men with substantial influence but no experience in the nascent science of psychiatry and little confidence in Black intellectual capacity.

Since retrospective diagnosis is not possible, reports of Milbry Brown's diminished mental faculties should be handled with special care. Milbry Brown may have indeed had a mental or emotional deficit, though contemporaneous assessments of her capacity consisted of run-of the-mill statements that were ascribed to many Black people accused of crimes. Brown lived in a time when chronic masturbators, epileptics, and others now recognized to have underlying health conditions were labeled deviant and sometimes routed to lunatic asylums.[54] Furthermore, the racialized theories of intellectual development and the hierarchy of species proliferating in the late nineteenth century relegated Blacks to the bottom of civilization's ladder. After the Civil War, the forerunners of modern psychiatric medicine observed what seemed to be spikes in Black mental illness—interpreted as confirmation that freedom had harmful effects—and identified Black madness as qualitatively different and more violent than whites' melancholy-prone insanity.[55]

As the execution date approached, residents of Gaffney and Spartanburg waited to hear whether Gov. Ben Tillman would favorably hear Brown's request for clemency. Tillman had respited Brown's case once, leaving her literally standing on the gallows in a suspenseful act of political theater. Hopes for a pardon were slim. To her grudging supporters, Milbry Brown was an ignorant delinquent at best, but there was no reformatory for Black girls to house her. To those who wanted her executed, she was a dangerous "defective." Assuming that media reports that she had entered the Spartanburg jail without loved ones were not true, would those people have stood by her if she had exited the jail alive? Her notoriety would, no doubt, have dwindled her prospects for employment and post-release life in the South Carolina upcountry. In some states, Black women were leased out to private households for domestic work as a condition of parole.[56] This seemed a far-fetched option for Milbry Brown. Accused and convicted of a serious crime committed at the workplace and against her prominent white employers, who would be willing to take her on as a living, breathing community-based rehabilitation project in exchange for labor?

Despite the best efforts of Charleston newspaper man James Hemphill and his last-ditch telegram pleading for her life, Milbry Brown was hanged and was pronounced dead from a broken neck nine minutes later.[57]

The debate surrounding Milbry Brown's fate reflected conflicting yet convergent societal notions. Ideas about children, women, and Black Americans as dependents prone to emotion and violence co-existed with discourses that elevated motherhood and, increasingly, childhood. South Carolinians wrestled with the role such identities should play in sentencing, especially in capital cases where so-called crimes *against* nature (here, offenses against children) were also crimes *of* female, youth, or Black nature. The toxic combination of different narratives that argued for or against Black, female, and youth ignorance led white South Carolinians to agree that some punishment was in order for Milbry Brown. She could both exemplify the extremes of youth, femininity, and blackness gone ungoverned and still access the emerging idea of minors' innocence. In Milbry Brown's case, there was no automatic promotion from Black girlhood to Black adulthood in the criminal justice system. She did not need to be framed or tried as an adult to be hanged. Milbry Brown was equally the immature child who did not consider consequences, the malevolent teen whose actions proved her deviance, and a surly Black citizen whose ignorance or lack of reason killed the ultimate innocent: a white babe in arms entrusted to her care. She lived—and died—at a dangerous intersection.

Notes

1. By the late nineteenth century, most Southern states had passed measures outlawing public executions and moved hangings into walled or enclosed jail yards, as in the Milbry Brown execution; South Carolina changed its law in 1878 in An Act Regulating the Mode of Conducting Capital Executions (March 1, 1878). Also see Michael A. Trotti, "The Scaffold's Revival: Race and Public Execution in the South." *Journal of Social History* 45, no. 1 (Fall 2011): 195–224.

2. A September 6, 1892 newspaper article listed Brown as fifteen. See "Executive Clemency," *The* [Charleston, S.C.] *News and Courier*, 1. A September 27 article suggested that Brown might be younger. "Mildrey Brown, Again," *The News and Courier*, 4. Its biggest journalistic competitor, *The* [Columbia, S.C.] *State*, said that Brown was fourteen. "Mildrey Brown Respited. The Governor Will Likely Commute the Child's Death Sentence," *The State*, September 7, 1892, 8. A day before her state-sponsored killing, *The State* published her age as fourteen. "The Fatal Gallows Tree," *The State*, October 6, 1892, 8.

3. "The Fatal Gallows Tree," *The State*, October 6, 1892, 8. A few accounts suggest the conflict was between Brown and the male head of household, W.C. Carpenter.

For an example of that slight variation, see "Hangman's Day," *The Bay City Times of Michigan*, October 8, 1892, 4.

4. "The Grim Work of the Gallows, *The State*, October 8, 1892, 1.

5. Brown's last words appear to have been an adaptation of "Gloryland," one common version of which says, "I'm going home / Up there we'll die no more / No coffins will be made up there." John Williams, hanged on the same day as Brown, killed Spartanburg Mayor John Henneman, when Henneman intervened in a domestic dispute. "The Spartanburg Hanging," *The News and Courier*, September 10, 1892, 1.

6. For discussions of protected childhood, see Barbara Nelson, *Making an Issue of Child Abuse* (Chicago: University of Chicago Press, 1984); Viviana Selizer, *Pricing the Priceless Child: The Changing Social Value of Children* (New Haven: Princeton University Press, 1994); Steven Mintz, *Huck's Raft: A History of American Childhood* (Cambridge: Harvard University Press, 2004); and Michael Grossberg, "A Protected Childhood: The Emergence of Child Protection in America," in *American Public Life and the Historical Imagination*, eds. Wendy Gamber, Michael Grossberg, and Hendrik Hartog (Notre Dame, IN: University of Notre Dame, 2003), 213–239. More recent texts have specifically addressed ideas about how Black women writers, sociologists, policymakers, "child savers," and Black girls themselves have viewed protection of Black girls and young women. See Marcia Chatelain, *South Side Girls: Growing Up in the Great* Migration (Durham, NC: Duke University Press, 2015); Monique Morris, *Pushout: The Criminalization of Black Girls in Schools* (New York: The New Press, 2015); LaKisha Simmons, *Crescent City Girls: The Lives of Young Black Women in Segregated New Orleans* (Chapel Hill: University of North Carolina Press, 2015); and Nazera Sadiq Wright, *Black Girlhood in the Nineteenth Century* (Champaign: University of Illinois Press, 2016).

7. "The Fatal Gallows Tree," *The State*, October 6, 1892, 8.

8. "Women on the Gallows," *The State*, September 6, 1892, 8. The quoted phrase in the title comes from this article.

9. See Nicole Hahn Rafter, *Partial Justice: Women in State Prisons*, 1800–1935 (Boston: Northeastern University Press, 1985); and Anne M. Butler, "Still in Chains: Black Women in Western Prisons, 1865–1910," *Western Historical Review* 20, no. 1 (February 1989): 18–35. Rafter's work underscores the general pattern that while Black women were incarcerated at lower rates than either Black or white men, they consistently made up a larger proportion of the female population than either male group.

10. David Baker, "Black Female Executions in Historical Context," *Criminal Justice Review* 33, no. 1 (March 2008): 64–88.

11. "Carolina Shipp, Last Woman Hanged in N.C., wrongful?" *The* [New Bern, N.C.] *Sun Journal*, February 11, 2017, http://www.newbernsj.com/news/20170211/caroline-shipp-last-woman-legally-hanged-in-nc-wrongful.

12. Ida B. Wells, "The Reason Why the Colored American Is Not in the World's Columbian Exposition," 1893, chapter 3, https://digital.library.upenn.edu/women/wells/exposition/exposition.html

13. The State of South Carolina v. Milbry Brown/Smith, (1892). Spartanburg Court of General Sessions, indictments, box 3, folder 15, South Carolina Department of Archives and History (henceforth SCDAH).

14. The State of South Carolina v. Milbry Brown/Smith.

15. John Belton O'Neal Landrum, *History of Spartanburg County: Embracing an Account of Many Important Events* (Atlanta: The Franklin Printing and Publishing Co., 1900), 580–582.

16. Landrum, *History of Spartanburg,* 578–579.

17. U.S. Census Bureau, 1880 U.S. Census, Gaffney City/Limestone Springs Township, Spartanburg, South Carolina, roll 1240, page 271B, enumeration district 144. Last accessed December 30, 2019 via Ancestry.com.

18. A profile for Milbry Jane Brown is available at https://www.findagrave.com/memorial/48389449/milbry-j-brown. She is buried in the family plot in a Gaffney city cemetery and may be the sister of Carrie Brown Carpenter's father, though the findagrave.com years for Major John Brown's birth are inconsistent with his ability to serve during the Civil War.

19. For a discussion of naming conventions postemancipation, see Elizabeth Regosin, *Freedom's Promise: Ex-Slave Families and Citizenship in the Age of Emancipation* (Charlottesville: University of Virginia Press, 2002), 54–78.

20. "A Harvest of Hangings," *The Observer*, October 8, 1892, 1.

21. "The Fruit of the Gallows," *The News and Courier*, October 8, 1892, 1.

22. See Thavolia Glymph, *Out of the House of Bondage: The Transformation of the Plantation Household* (Cambridge and New York: Cambridge University Press, 2008) and Rebecca Sharpless, *Cooking in Other Women's Kitchens: Domestic Workers in the South, 1865–1960* (Chapel Hill: University of North Carolina Press, 2010), xxii, 87, 102, 58.

23. This may bear some similarity to a historical and contemporary Brazilian labor practice called *criacao*, by which mostly Black women are "adopted" by white families and expected to contribute their unpaid labor to the family or household. See Elizabeth Hordge Freeman, "Family Bonds and Bondage: Unpaid Servitude in Salvador, Bahia," (unpublished paper presented at the 2010 National Conference of Black Political Scientists, Raleigh, North Carolina).

24. Eugene Genovese and Elizabeth Fox-Genovese noted that slaves becoming "quasi-kin" was part of the ideological imperative of the chattel culture and system. See their *Fatal Self-Deception: Slaveholding Paternalism in the Old South* (New York: Cambridge University Press, 2011), 25. For a discussion of this language in Milbry Brown's home region in the textile country of the Carolinas, see Jacquelyn Dowd Hall, James Leloudis, Robert Korstad, Mary Murphy, Lou Ann Jones, and Christopher B. Daly, *Like a Family: The Making of a Southern Cotton Mill World*, 2nd ed. (Chapel Hill: University of North Carolina Press, 2000), xxii-xxiv.

25. For varied accounts that posit arson as intentional or unplanned parts of enslaved uprisings or urban crises, see Afua Cooper, *The Hanging of Angélique: The Untold Story of Canadian Slavery and the Burning of Old Montreal* (Toronto: Harper Collins, 2006); Don Gerlach, "Black Arson in Albany, New York: November 1793,"

The Journal of Black Studies 7, no. 3 (March 1977): 301–312; and Jill Lepore, *New York Burning: Liberty, Slavery, and Conspiracy in Eighteenth Century Manhattan*, 1st ed. (New York: Alfred A. Knopf, 2005). For two important takes on poisoning and the enslaved in diasporic perspective, see Sasha Turner Bryson, "The Art of Power: Poison and Obeah Accusations and the Struggle for Dominance and Survival in Jamaica's Slave Society," *Caribbean Studies* 41, no. 2 (July-December 2013): 61–90; and Glenn McNair, "Slave Women, Capital Crime, and Criminal Justice in Georgia," *The Georgia Historical Quarterly* 93, no. 2 (2009): 135–58.

26. "To Save a Child from Hanging," *The Observer*, July 23, 1887, 1.

27. "South Carolina News," *The* [Augusta, Georgia] *Chronicle*, July 19, 1887, 3.

28. "A Case without a Parallel," *Kansas City Times*, August 1, 1884.

29. "A Case without a Parallel."

30. Robin Bernstein, *Racial Innocence: Performing American Childhood from Slavery to Civil Rights* (New York: New York University Press), 4–5.

31. "South Carolina News," *The Chronicle*, July 19, 1887, 3.

32. "A Child Criminal," undated newspaper clipping (likely from *The Charleston Post*), Axey Cherry pardon file, Governor John Peter Richardson papers, petitions for commutation of sentence, Barnwell County, box 1, folder 7, SCDAH.

33. Letter to Governor Benjamin Tillman, Dec. 23, 1891. Anna Bell Jones file, Governor Ben Tillman papers, petitions for pardons, York County, box 10, folder 11, SCDAH.

34. Letter to Governor.

35. "Only Two Got Away: Governor Tillman Spoils a Quadruple Hanging," *St. Louis Republic*, September 10, 1892, 7.

36. "Only Two Got Away," 7.

37. This passage was excerpted in "To Save a Child from Hanging," *The Chronicle*, July 23, 1887, 1.

38. "To Save a Child from Hanging," 1.

39. "She Should Not Be Hanged," *The News and Courier*, September 5, 1892, 8.

40. "A Proper Thought for the Babies," *The State Newspaper*, October 8, 1892, 4.

41. This schema of age and culpability is generally ascribed to British jurist William Blackstone. See his *Commentaries on the Laws of England: In Four Books*, Vol. 4, "Public Wrongs," 22–24.

42. James Aldrich letter to Governor Benjamin Tillman, September 9, 1892. Governor Tillman papers, petitions for commutation, Spartanburg County, box 59, folder 15, SCDAH.

43. Schumpert comments in petition for pardon, September 6, 1892, Governor Tillman papers, petitions for commutation, Spartanburg County, box 59, folder 15, SCDAH.

44. B.F. Wilson letter to Gov. Ben Tillman, September 7, 1892, Governor Tillman papers, petitions for commutation, Spartanburg County, box 59, folder 15, SCDAH.

45. James Bomar Cleveland letter to Gov. Ben Tillman, August 24, 1892, Governor Tillman papers, petitions for commutation, Spartanburg County, box 59, folder 15, SCDAH.

46. Agnes Richardson letter to Governor John Richardson, petition for commutation files, Barnwell County, box 10, folder 11, SCDAH.

47. Wells, "The Reason Why the Colored American Is Not in the World's Columbian Exposition," available online at https://digital.library.upenn.edu/women/wells/exposition/exposition.html. Last accessed October 18, 2021.

48. "Do Not Begin With That One," *The News and Courier*, September 8, 1892, 4.

49. Charles Barrett letter and petition to Gov. Ben Tillman, September 6, 1892. Governor Tillman papers, petitions for commutations, Spartanburg County, box 59, folder 15.

50. Petition of September 1892 (no date or primary author). This petition may be associated with a September 7 letter from Converse College president B.F. Wilson, who was asked to write a letter supporting commutation. Governor Benjamin Tillman papers, petitions for commutation, Spartanburg County, box 59, folder 15.

51. "Want Mildrey Brown to Hang," *The State*, September 21, 1892, 5. This typed petition is undated and not obviously linked to a particular author or organizer. The original petition is also located in the Governor Tillman petition papers, Spartanburg County, box 59, folder 15, SCDAH.

52. "Want Mildrey Brown to Hang," 5.

53. James Bomar Cleveland letter to Gov. Ben Tillman, Aug. 24, 1892. Governor Tillman papers, petitions for commutation, Spartanburg County, box 59, folder 15, SCDAH.

54. April R. Haynes, *Riotous Flesh: Women, Physiology, and the Solitary Vice in Nineteenth-Century America* (Chicago: University of Chicago Press, 2015); Charles Arthur Mercier, *Text-book on Insanity* (London: Swan Sonnenschein and Company, 1902) 187–189.

55. Martin Summers, "'Suitable Care of the African When Inflicted with Insanity': Race, Madness and Social Order in Comparative Perspective," *Bulletin of Medicine* 84, No. 1 (Spring 2010): 67–75.

56. In a notable recent example, Sarah Haley writes about this practice, which she calls the domestic carceral regime, in *No Mercy Here: Gender, Punishment, and the Making of Jim Crow Modernity* (Chapel Hill: University of North Carolina Press, 2016), 175–189. See also Talitha LeFlouria, *Chained in Silence: Black Women and Convict Labor in the New South* (Chapel Hill: University of North Carolina Press, 2015), and Ann Butler, *Gendered Justice in the American West: Women Prisoners in Men's Penitentiaries* (Champaign: University of Illinois Press, 1999), 191–192. Butler notes the impressment of Black female incarcerated people for such private-household domestic labor outside an Arkansas prison.

57. "The Fruit of the Gallows," *The News and Courier*, October 8, 1892, 1.

CHAPTER 9

"Racial Hauntings" and the Complexities of Afro-German Women's Kin(d)ship

VANESSA D. PLUMLY

Within the German context, blackness occupies heterogeneous and often ambiguous positionings both from within and without.[1] Overtly racist and infantilizing terms became popular parlance in dominant media and everyday discourses throughout twentieth-century Germany.[2] Through their labeling of Black Germans as eternally juvenile, white Germans nodded to their fear of miscegenation, which further hinged on the stereotype of blackness as hypersexual. White Germans' efforts to make Black Germans less "threatening" to the national body rendered Black Germans small and prepubescent.

With the publication in 1986 of the seminal text *Farbe bekennen: Afro-deutsche Frauen auf den Spuren ihrer Geschichte* (translated as *Showing Our Colors: Afro-German Women Speak Out* in 1992), members of the Black German community created the self-designations Afro-German and Black German. Afro-German designates a German individual who has a white German parent (often the mother) and a Black parent (often the father). Black German is broader in its usage, embracing German citizens who have common experiences of racism and discrimination. This includes any person of color, such as Turkish-Germans or Asian Germans.[3] Moreover, this volume laid the foundation for the Afro-German women's movement, taking shape in the mid-1980s. Under the guidance of Caribbean American author, lesbian, mother, warrior, and poet Audre Lorde, who spent many years in Berlin (1984–1992) as a guest lecturer at the Free University and later as a visitor, the movement evolved out of an international and intersectional feminism.[4] With Lorde's encouragement, Afro-German women, many for the first time, narrated experiences from their childhood and later life in *Showing Our Colors*. Several accounts document their childhood with white families and their socialization as white. Some women recount narratives of their adoptive parents; a few discuss their extended kinship networks.[5] As a result of this volume, its impact, and the Black German movement's evolution within a predominantly female and lesbian community,[6] women initially directed autobiographical writing in the Afro- and Black German context.

What I refer to as kin(d)ship in this chapter is the German national form of concretizing blackness as child- or *Kind*-like in order to structure a denial of kinship and belonging to the supposedly mature white German national community; as such, white Germans withhold Black Germans' membership in the imagined community of German kin on a macro level. At the same time, Black Germans actively demonstrate their own agency in determining and articulating their positionalities from within German society; their kin(d)ship in this case is embodied in the childhood kinship bonds they established within their white German families that contributed to their belonging on a micro level. They narrate these from the present as adults in autobiographical works. As such, Black German women's autobiographical writing defies the imposition of an endless child-like status and detaches them from Black Germans' discursive exclusion from without. Their coming of age may be a non-normative process due to racist and sexist structures, but it transpires in spite of its repudiation. Resisting the trope of perpetual youth, Black German women engender their national belonging in writing, giving birth to a multiracial German nation and leaving a legacy for the next generation of Black Germans to come. They radically re-envision the reproduction of the nation through matrilineal bonds from within.[7]

A genre that details one's life, autobiography best lends itself to an analysis of childhood—here, girlhood—and kin(d)ship. I interpret three Afro-German women's autobiographies, including Marie Nejar's 2007 autobiography *Don't Make Such Sad Eyes Because You're a Little Negro* that details her survival under the National Socialist regime and her later life and career; Ika Hügel-Marshall's 1998 autobiography *Invisible Woman: Growing Up Black in Germany*, which is one of the first comprehensive Afro-German autobiographies to be published and recounts her quest to find her African American father; and Jennifer Teege's 2013 autobiography *My Grandfather Would Have Shot Me: A Black Woman Discovers Her Family's Nazi Past*, written in conjunction with journalist Nikola Sellmair.[8] While the former two autobiographies are prominent early examples of the genre, the third work is a more recent New York Times and international bestseller. Notably, Teege's is not explicitly an Afro-German autobiography since she does not identify politically as a Black German. Nevertheless, her mother is a white German and her father is Nigerian.

Each of these Afro-German women authors hails from a different generation, coming of age in distinctive socio-historical contexts: Nejar during the Third Reich; Hügel-Marshall in the post-WWII era; and Teege in the second generation of the post-WWII era. Furthermore, all of the women have unique positionings vis-à-vis the Afro-German diaspora. Nejar's father is Ghanaian (though her mother, too, was Afro-German), Hügel-Marshall's father is African American, and Teege's is Nigerian. These women's individual positionalities indicate the heterogeneity existing within the Afro-German diaspora. Although generalizing Afro-German experiences is impossible, making assertions about points of commonality is important and inevitable. In this chapter, I assess the overlap in these women's autobiographical reflections on their childhood and the kin(d)ship bonds they established to their white German family members as well as how both their own and structurally imposed lenses shaped these bonds.

Theoretical Framework

Historically, structural and racist policies expelled the fathers of Afro-Germans through temporal limitations placed on the length of post-WWI and post-WWII occupation, governmental regulations placed on visas and marriages, and more. Some mothers, though by no means all, gave Afro-German children up for adoption, put them into foster care, or sent them to children's homes in the post-WWII era.[9] Even today, Afro-Germans grow up in an overwhelmingly white German environment. How, then, and with whom did Afro-German women produce kinship connections in their accounts of childhood? The white German maternal grandmother haunts these selected life narratives as the common specter.[10] She functions as provider, protector, and/or caregiver, inhabiting both text and image. Often, though not always, she contrasts with the mother who does not fully identify with her daughter, rejects her due to white German society's own ostracizing of her, or does not want to be her mother. Fundamental differences across intersectional divides including racial, maternal, and generational complicate Afro-German women's kin(d)ship and belonging.

Complicated kin(d)ship reveals itself in the form of racial hauntings in Afro-German women's autobiographies. Both text and image transport the cumulative elements of the "affective filter."[11] The affective filter in my iteration contains three macro lenses (at the structural level),[12] each of which impact on micro levels (at the individual level). The three macro lenses I delineate are: Apparatuses, Apparitions, and Apprehensions. *App*, as a prefix, derives from the Latin *Ad*, meaning "toward." Thus, it establishes orientation, which is tied to one's positionality. Blackness, just like whiteness, is orientated in time and place and in the past, present, and future.

1. Apparatuses.

An apparatus organizes and can be politically constituted. One example is a country's governing bodies. A device or mechanism that humans use is also an apparatus. In terms of apparatuses I address, I specifically deal with institutions of kinship,[13] race, and gender. I am also concerned with the camera as a physical apparatus that captures and conveys affective kin(d)ship bonds through photos.[14] These apparatuses complicate belonging through their intersections and through their framing.

2. Apparitions

An apparition can be defined as the appearance of a dead spirit. For this lens, I focus on ghosts, real and imagined hauntings, and generations as phenomena. Building on existing scholarship,[15] I probe what haunts these autobiographies at the level of the image or photograph and the text.[16]

3. Apprehensions

Apprehensions are understood mostly as detainment, anxiety about the present or future, and the ability to comprehend something. Here, I center the concepts of racial miscegenation and transformation. Photographic images of Afro-Germans arrest the historical reality of interracial relations in time. As a result, white German anxieties incite what sociologist Avery Gordon refers to as haunting producing "a something to be done" about race and racism but also about society.[17] Taken together, these three macro lenses or *apps* orient Afro-German women in the narration of their life experiences and kin(d)ship.

In her chapter "Everyday Matters: Haunting and the Black Diasporic Experience," Kimberly Alecia Singletary draws on the work of Gordon to argue that American blackness haunts the capacity and existence of Black Germanness, oftentimes erasing the very fact of German blackness through its dominant positioning in the white German imaginary. Singletary writes, "Haunting often refers to the physical absence of matter that is physically felt. It is the impact on our mental state that makes haunting such a powerful act."[18] In Afro-German girlhood narratives, white German *Omas*/grandmothers embody both this absence and presence. They often occupy the status and position of the missing mother, are a further generation removed—haunting the present from an irretrievable, lived past—and are a jarring white presence across which filial bonds are established. The grandmother's whiteness haunts the blackness of Afro-German girls. At times, it displaces that very blackness to emphasize the granddaughter's belonging and her kin(d)ship connection. This is because the granddaughter's Blackness also haunts the imagined white German (national) family that denies her belonging. Read in conjunction with one another, the text and images in Afro-German women's autobiographies represent the reality of multiracial German families and counter attempts at erasure of these established filial bonds.

By seeping into the narrative and lived experiences, the grandmother's whiteness also permeates the boundaries of the apprehended and visually framed kin(d)ship bonds. Text and image become unbound; they offer not only complex narratives of family and national history, but also childhood desires or projections and lived realities of acceptance and belonging. This represents what feminist memory studies scholar Marianne Hirsch articulates as photographs occupying a "space of contradiction between the myth of the ideal family and the lived reality of family life. Photographs can more easily show us what we wish our family to be, and therefore what, most frequently, it is not."[19] Thus, kin(d)ship is established via family bonds and disrupted through exclusion from the imagined white German national community. The affective filter both produces this contradictory kin(d)ship and has the power to be potentially drawn upon to comprehend and rectify it.

Marie Nejar

Don't Make Such Sad Eyes Because You're a Little Negro details Marie Nejar's survival as a child actress cast in minor roles in Nazi German cinema, her work at a cookie factory until the end of World War II, as well as her careers as a singer and nurse. After bearing a white German child out of wedlock and being cast out of her family, Nejar's grandmother married a Caribbean man and gave birth to two Afro-German children; Nejar's mother was one. Though Nejar never knew her grandfather, her grandmother served as her sole and primary caretaker and died when Nejar was eighteen. She and her mother never maintained a close relationship. Nejar's father was Ghanaian, and he and her mother had a fleeting relationship. Although he visited her occasionally, she never developed a deeper connection to him. Nejar recounts a time when her grandmother showed her a picture of her father and his family; she could not identify with them.[20] Of her mother, Nejar writes that she "appeared every week at my grandmother's, where I lived and often brought me gifts, but I never got along well with her. . . . For me, my grandmother was my mother. She was the one who took care of me, put food on the table for me, and made sure that I felt at home."[21] Despite this clearly articulated emotional and maternal attachment to her grandmother, Nejar remains critical.

Nejar notes her white grandmother's misjudgment of the effects of racism. As a result of her whiteness, she dismisses the embodied racial differences between herself and her granddaughter. Questioning her grandmother about derogatory comments other youth made, Nejar wonders if her blackness is a punishment for misbehaving. Her grandmother silences her, tells her she will make certain she behaves and to stop saying such things. Her Oma takes the position that racism can be brushed off and/or hardened against. To this Nejar rejoins: "My grandma could easily speak. She possessed a 'pure,' white skin. These derogatory remarks had, in any case, really impacted me."[22] In this statement, Nejar highlights her grandmother's adherence to a doctrine of colorblindness, one her grandmother employs to protect Nejar from white children's racist taunts. However, this colorblind stance only served to perpetuate racism, leaving a further imprint. According to Richard Delgado and Jean Stefancic, colorblindness "stands in the way of taking account of difference in order to help those in need."[23] While white German *Omas*, such as Nejar's, wished to protect their granddaughters from internalized destructive thoughts, their solutions often resulted in treating their blackness as equivalent to whiteness.

Nejar also reflects on the time directly before WWII broke out. Once, she was sick, and their Jewish family doctor declared that she "actually" needed to go the hospital. Her grandmother questioned the doctor: "What do you mean by 'actually'?" He then explained that German doctors would likely sterilize Nejar according to National Socialist German race laws and doctrine. To this, Nejar's grandmother retorts: "That is not even a possibility. . . . They can sterilize cows but not my granddaughter. She is not livestock."[24] This is one realization, alongside others, that her white grandmother has of the macro level impact of racism and sexism's intersections. Nejar's grandmother comprehends Nejar's racial difference in the eyes of white German society and repeatedly seeks to protect her from the fascist Nazi regime. In the chapter titled "A Young Girl Like All the Others?," Nejar clearly conveys how she "felt secure" with her grandmother. "Grandmother and I were an official team, we lived in our 'two-person' family. For me, she was one-of-a kind."[25] However, the unbridgeable racial gap between her grandmother and herself remained across micro and macro levels.

Given the sense of belonging her grandmother produces for Nejar, it is not surprising that the first image the reader confronts aside from the cover image is a portrait of Nejar's grandmother as a young woman. The reader stumbles upon another image of her grandmother later in the text, this time with Nejar as a young girl also present.[26] But here the image appears manipulated, as if something was removed or cut out; there is white space between the two of them. Was this image taken from a scrapbook? In what ways does it evoke the familial and maternal bond between grandmother and granddaughter? What do we make of the visible gap? What should actually fill the space but is absent? Her mother? Does it evince race (here, whiteness as void) as an unbridgeable divide? Is it a generational gap? Or perhaps all of the above? The image draws the two together in the unity of an oval or even a heart and articulates that they are close, even if not completely touching or bound by the same frame.

In her monograph, *Image Matters: Archive, Photography, and the African Diaspora*, Tina Campt asserts that with photographs, "given their context, the home and everyday life, their primary register is clearly that of the family. But this register is not merely descriptive, for such photographs do not record simple relations of kinship or genealogy."[27] They are also "objects that catalyze affect and make affect register." [28] These images no doubt establish kin(d)ship connections and attachments to the textual narrative, serving as one mode through which affective filial bonds in multiracial families are filtered to the reader. However, the image remains ambivalent. It is presented as if this is as close as the two might actually ever come.

Ika Hügel-Marshall

Ika Hügel Marshall belongs to the generation of so-called "occupation children" or, as this generation has coined for itself, "children of liberation."[29] She is one of about 3,000 mixed-race children born in the postwar period to African American GI fathers and white German mothers.[30] At the young age of seven, Hügel-Marshall's mother sent her to a Protestant institution, God's Little Cabin, at the behest of the racist German youth services. Many whites at the time deemed a strict upbringing of utmost importance to a Black child living in Germany.[31] Her family's white social worker feared youth pregnancy and sexual deviancy, as did a sister working at the Protestant children's home.[32] Although Hügel-Marshall writes fondly of her family, expressing love for both her mother and grandmother, the decision to send her to a home created a rift in her childhood and family life. Still, she withholds judgment, asserting her mother's love for her. According to Hügel-Marshall, she made this decision with her best interests in mind. Alongside her mother, Hügel-Marshall mentions her grandmother in the first pages. She, like Nejar's *Oma*, features not only in the narrative but also in the images in the autobiography.

The opening pages describe Hügel-Marshall's family situation and the lack of a person of color as an attachment figure in her life: "There was only one world, one culture—the white one—and that is the world I was born into. No Black culture existed and I had no Black father, no Black grandmothers, no Black siblings, and no Black neighbors in my environment."[33] Hügel-Marshall's words emphasize her desire for a positive point of reference for her blackness, a lens that is missing.

In the pages that follow this brief description, Hügel-Marshall stresses her white family members and the efforts they undertook to defend and protect her in a racism-riddled society:

> Every time Herr Siebert from Youth Services comes to visit, I hide. . . . The first time he met me, he greeted me by stroking my hair, as if we were well acquainted. He gave me chocolates and asked if I had playmates and whether my mother liked them. . . . And the next time he comes, . . . I don't want to answer his questions. Perhaps it's because I've heard my grandmother tell him, more than once: "Take your hands off my granddaughter, please. And give your bonbons to another child. We have plenty of our own here."[34]

Such instances detailed at the beginning of her autobiography highlight the important role her grandmother played as someone unwilling to accept the differential treatment her granddaughter received because of her blackness and likely also her gender. Hügel-Marshall describes this moment and her grandmother's reaction as one that "will leave such lasting impressions on me—impressions I will only later be able to understand."[35]

And yet unlike Nejar's narrative that focuses solely on her white German grandmother as the source of acceptance and deeper connection, Hügel-Marshall documents her emotional and filial attachment to her mother: "I knew that she had in some way sacrificed her standing in the community on my behalf. Though her sacrifice was not something she ever explicitly made me aware of, it created a powerful bond between us."[36] Hügel-Marshall's mother loved her and left a positive impression tied to fond memories rather than aversion.

Directly following the comments about her mother, Hügel-Marshall returns to her grandmother and writes:

> She was there for me, cared for me, played with me, and protected me from adults and children alike. I was her granddaughter, and she never shrank from being seen with me in public. . . . She refused to be insulted. . . . And to me she was the dearest, most courageous grandmother in the world.[37]

Her white grandmother gave her a sense of belonging: "She let me know that I was her favorite grandchild, and I suffered greatly when she died at ninety years of age."[38] Similar to Nejar's own response to the death of her grandmother, Hügel-Marshall alerts the reader to her heartbreak upon losing her.

In the photographic images present in Hügel-Marshall's autobiography, her grandmother appears in three. Hügel-Marshall stands front and center in the cover image of the English translation from 2008, perhaps because she holds a bike, her white grandmother, mother, and little sister frame her in the

Figure 14. Ika as a child with her grandmother, used with the permission of Ika Hügel-Marshall, from Ika Hügel-Marshall. *Daheim unterwegs. Ein deutsches Leben.* (Berlin: Orlanda Frauenverlag, 1998), 142.

Figure 15. Ika pictured with her grandmother on the left and her mother beside her grandmother, used with the permission of Ika Hügel-Marshall, from Hügel-Marshall *Daheim*, 145.

background; this image can also be found inside the German version of the autobiography. In the other images (from both language versions), Hügel-Marshall is physically connected to her grandmother. Arms outstretched as a toddler, she holds her grandmother's hand in an image that depicts their filial bond (figure 14).The two appear to maybe even be dancing, given the blurred motion of her grandmother's left hand. In the next image, the viewer sees Hügel-Marshall and other women in her family. In it, she stands at her grandmother's side. One hand of her Oma is visible and on her lap. The other, we assume, is behind Hügel-Marshall's back (figure 15). The bond the two share solidifies through touch in these images. Hügel-Marshall's representation of her family in post-WWII Germany summons an intact conjugal family unit; her grandmother and mother's relationship is amenable, and she has a father figure present in her life, albeit her white stepfather. Importantly, he appears in an image below the second image that orders a matriarchal lineage.

What haunts the myth of "the familial gaze" that these family photos capture, however, is the fact that the text provides us with information that calls into question what Hirsch terms an "embeddedness in familiality".[39] Since Hügel-Marshall spent much of her childhood in an institution, her blackness relegated her to a space outside of the domestic family frame at the same time that the autobiography's images depict her as an integral part of it. As a result of white German fears of miscegenation and blackness, Black German children in the post-WWII era haunted the nation's self-image. What haunts these selected images in Hügel-Marshall's autobiography, then, is a whiteness that makes the knowledge of exclusion invisible without the (con) text. It is an embedded whiteness that her family members also structured. What are the implications this has for understanding Hügel-Marshall's narrative as bridging the Nazi regime's downfall on the one hand and the postwar second-generation's conflict with their parent's generation on the other?

Jennifer Teege

Jennifer Teege grew up as a second-generation post-WWII child. When she was a baby, her mother gave her up for adoption. A white German family in Munich took her in. Her adopted mother was "amazed at how 'happy and mature' Jennifer was. She had been expecting a shy, traumatized, institutionalized child."[40] Although Teege briefly maintained contact with her mother and grandmother, her adoptive family cut off their communication to prevent her from feeling torn. Teege articulates this move as affecting her relationship to her grandmother: "When I was seven and my adoption became official, my adoptive parents broke off all contact with my mother; they thought that it would be best for me. With that, my grandmother also disappeared from my life. She left behind a gap, I missed her."[41] Years later, at the age of forty, while searching a library for books on depression, she found one with her mother's image on it. On that day, she learned she was not only the daughter of a Nigerian student with whom her white German mother had maintained a secret relationship but also the daughter of Monika Goeth—*the* Monika Goeth, the daughter of the notorious mass murderer Amon Goeth (the real-life man portrayed in Steven Spielberg's *Schindler's List*). Following World War II, he was hanged. During the Holocaust he served as commandant of the Płaszów camp in Poland and was responsible for the death of over 6,000 Jews. Teege's autobiography details the uncovering of this family and national history and presents an extremely complicated bridging of maternal, racial, and generational divides structured through the three macro lenses of the affective filter.

In *My Grandfather Would Have Shot Me*, Teege thematizes her childhood as fraught with a search for hidden (hi)stories. She writes that her "adoptive parents thought it was best to act as if I really was their own child." While both she and her adoptive parents wanted "a normal family,"[42] this attempt to normalize also meant a colorblind approach taken to her identity. It left no room for its complexity to unfold. Describing her youth, Teege explains, "Early on, I knew I was different." She narrates how other children called her "'Black boy'—mistaking me for a boy due to my height and short, curly hair. I would quickly retort, 'I am a mixed-race girl!'"[43] Positioning herself, Teege's resistance counters this misreading of her identity.

Following the discovery of her complicated family history, Teege dedicates an entire chapter to her grandmother,[44] bearing the title "The Commandant's Mistress: My Grandmother Ruth Irene Kalder." Attempting to come to terms with her haunted past, Teege grapples with her love for her grandmother while acknowledging her complicit bystander status during the Nazi regime. She wonders whether her grandmother was

> "not just blinded by love but deafened by it too? Where was my grandmother's compassion? People were dying a few hundred yards away. . . . My grandfather has long been dead, but I knew my grandmother. When I was a small child, she was the person who mattered most to me. I had little, if anything, to hold on to. She liked me, and that meant a lot. To me, she radiated kindness. Whenever I think of her, I feel safe and secure again."[45]

Teege counters her grandmother's documented cruelty with personal experiences. A stark contrast and contradiction exists between the personal and political contexts. Teege's blackness further confounds this, in addition to her studies in Israel. She has nurtured close friendships with many second-generation Holocaust survivors.

Teege highlights the power of images in establishing and disrupting kin(d)ship connections and familial/national lineage:

> For all these years, I've had only one photograph of my grandmother. It shows her wearing a long, flowery dress, her hair combed into a beehive, the golden bangle on her arm twinkling in the sun. . . . Now I am finding very different pictures of her, posing with a dog that would attack people on Goeth's command—it is unbearable; it is too upsetting.[46]

These two competing images are *unheimlich* (uncanny), registering the haunted nature of their socio-historical existence and breaking Teege's positive frame of reference for her grandmother from childhood. These images expose Hirsch's assessment that "[t]he referent is both present (implied in the photograph) and absent (it has been there but is not here now). The referent haunts the picture like a ghost: it is a revenant, a return of the lost and dead other."[47] Here, there is a double haunting: the dead grandmother and the dead others of which Teege might easily have been a part in the past 'there.' Notably, Teege is not present in either of the provided images of her grandmother in her autobiography, though the attack dog that is white with what appear to be black spots is.[48] Her mother's decision to give her up for adoption erased Teege's existence from her biological family's national genealogy.[49] Further, the authority of whiteness in National Socialism that both her grandmother and grandfather personified and executed, and of which her mother had to carry the inherited historical baggage, also haunts Teege.

Weighing her memory and these captured, material, and tactile moments arrested in time, Teege writes,

> I cannot reconcile these pictures of her with my image of her. I do not grieve for my grandfather, but I do for my grandmother. I grieve for the person she never really was. She was always good to me, which is why I always thought of her as a good person. As a child, you cannot imagine that the person you love could have another side, a darker one.[50]

In Teege's case, as in Nejar's and Hügel-Marshall's, she comprehends the complexity of humans and their inability to be judged through a lens that is merely black or white because of one's own relationship to that person and her/his/their own rose-tinted glasses. Still, the structural macro lenses conflict with the individual micro one. Rather than trying to defend her position in relation to her grandmother, Teege states her experience: "I still feel close to my grandmother. I will not try to justify the fact; I won't explain it either. That's just the way it is. When I was a little girl, she made me feel that I wasn't alone. I will always remember her for that."[51] These words are stated as a matter of fact. They do not conceal their difficult and historically violent potential. If anything, they acknowledge that even the closest of relationships can be some of the most complicated and inexplicable.

The affinity of gender and the desire for maternal nurturing and kinship connections affected the relationships these Afro-German women forged to their racially and generationally removed white German grandmothers.[52] They bridged, while not effacing, existing racial (and, at times, generational) divides that haunt both text and image in their autobiographical accounts of childhood. The apparatuses of race, gender, nation, kinship, and history leave their imprint on both the texts and the camera's captured images embedded in these works. The familial and generational apparitions that permeate the written narrative and become arrested in the images disrupt the apparatuses functioning in the service of a hegemonically conceived white German nation. Apprehensions that white Germans have about "racial mixing" are transformed in these works through Gordon's "something-to-be-done" about race and racism that the autobiographies bring into the picture. Moreover, these autobiographies capture how Afro-Germans establish their own means of belonging through kin(d)ship. Afro-German women's girlhood narratives uncouple national reproductive modalities from heteronormative contexts. They achieve this through the constitution and apprehension of multiracial, matrilineal familial bonds that normalize at the micro level their non-normatively construed childhoods at the macro level via the act of writing. In this sense, they queer belonging and ethnicity.[53] The three *apps* I delineate position the reader in relation to the narrated subject. Dismantling and deconstructing white Germans' mythical, racialized pathologies of blackness through Afro-German narratives facilitates a transformative acknowledgment of the complexity of Afro-German women's kin(d)ship, envisioning and archiving multiracial bonds within the German nation.

Notes

I would like to thank Tiffany Florvil and Deyanira Rojas-Sosa for providing feedback that greatly improved this piece, as well as Silke von der Emde for her input when I presented an earlier version of it at Vassar College. Thanks also to Cori and Kisha for the organization of the conference that led to this volume and Ika Hügel-Marshall for permission to reprint the images in this chapter.

1. Michelle M. Wright, *Becoming Black: Creating Identity in the African Diaspora* (Durham, NC: Duke University Press Books, 2004), 190.

2. Monikers white Germans bestowed upon Afro- and Black Germans include: "Rhineland Bastards," a pejorative labeling used in the post-World War I era, referring to mixed-race children born to white German mothers and French colonial troops; "brown babies," "occupation children," and "Mischlingskinder," used in the post-World War II era to refer to children of white German mothers and African American soldiers; and "GDR children," used to refer to Namibian youth brought to East Germany in a solidarity initiative during the Namibian fight for independence.

3. See Opitz (Ayim), May, et al, *Showing Our Colors: Afro-German Women Speak Out*, trans. Anne V. Adams (Amherst: University of Massachusetts Press, 1992), xxii.

4. See Peggy Piesche, ed., *Euer Schweigen schützt euch nicht. Audre Lorde und die Schwarze Frauenbewegung* (Berlin: Orlanda, 2012), and Tiffany Florvil, *Mobilizing Black Germany: Afro-German Women and the Making of a Transnational Movement* (Urbana: University of Illinois Press, 2020).

5. Angelika Eisenbrandt recalls her white German grandmother's desire to prevent her from wearing the color red and her proclamation that she and her brother could not be immunized due to their "different blood." Later she asserts "I think our grandmother loved us, but she had difficulties with our being different" (Eisenbrant 192). Eisenbrandt, Angelika, "All of a Sudden, I knew what I wanted," in *Showing our Colors: Afro-German Women Speak Out*, May Opitz (Ayim), et. al., eds., trans. Anne V. Adams (Amherst: University of Massachusetts Press, 1992), 191–195.

6. Peggy Piesche, "Inscribing the Past, Anticipating the Future: Audre Lorde and the Black Women's Movement in Germany," in *Audre Lorde's Transnational Legacies*, ed., Stella Bolaki and Sabine Broeck (Amherst: University of Massachusetts Press, 2015), 223.

7. This is significant given patrilineal German citizenship laws that inherited nationality through the father unless the child was illegitimate. Deniz Göktürk, et al., eds., *Germany in Transit: Nation and Migration, 1955–2015* (Berkeley: University of California Press), 154.

8. Nejar's autobiography has not been translated into English. All translations are my own. The original title is *Mach nicht so traurige Augen, weil du ein Negerlein bist*. It references childhood and smallness in the use of the *-lein* form. My use of negro in the translated title is insufficient, as it derives from African American historical, cultural, and political contexts. Hügel-Marshall's translated English title renders a different interpretation than *Daheim unterwegs: ein deutsches Leben*. Jennifer Teege's title in German is *Amon: Mein Großvater hätte mich erschossen*, which provides no reference to her blackness in the original but does in translation. That the autobiography centers on the Nazi past in its English iteration is also stressed in the English title. Marie Nejar, *Mach nicht so traurige Augen, weil du ein Negerlein bist: Meine Jugend im dritten Reich* (Hamburg: Rohwohlt, 2007); Ika Hügel-Marshall, *Invisible Woman: Growing Up Black in Germany* (1998; New York: Peter Lang, 2008); Jennifer Teege and Nikola Sellmair, *My Grandfather Would Have Shot Me: A Black Woman Discovers Her Family's Nazi Past, trans. Carolin Sommer* (New York: The Experiment, 2015).

9. Opitz (Ayim) et al. *Showing Our Colors,* 94.

10. Other Afro-German works feature white German grandmothers in both image and dialogue/text. See Mo Asumang, *Roots Germania* (Perf. Mo Asumang. MA Motion, 2007); Samy Deluxe, *Dis wo ich herkomm: Deutschland Deluxe*, 2nd ed. (Hamburg: Rowohlt Taschenbuch, 2010).

11. H. Dulay and M. Burt, "Remarks on Creativity in Language Acquisition," in *Viewpoints on English as a Second Language*, ed. M. Burt, H. Dulay and M. Finnochiaro (1977), 95–126. Dulay and Burt coined the term "affective filter." I use the

term affective filter in an anxiety-related context but in conjunction with the affective notion that the "work of emotion involves the 'sticking' of signs to bodies." Sara Ahmed, *The Cultural Politics of Emotion*, 2nd ed. (New York: Routledge, 2014), 13.

12. In photography, macro lenses allow the photographer to capture small objects with greater focus.

13. Vern L. Bengtson and Petrice S. Oyama, "Intergenerational Solidarity and Conflict," in *Intergenerational Solidarity* (Palgrave Macmillan, New York, 2010), 35–52, https://doi.org/10.1057/9780230115484_3; Maria A. Monserud, "Intergenerational Relationships and Affectual Solidarity between Grandparents and Young Adults," *Journal of Marriage and Family* 70, no. 1 (2008): 182–95.

14. Tina M. Campt, *Image Matters: Archive, Photography, and the African Diaspora in Europe* (Durham, N.C.: Duke University Press Books, 2012).

15. Roland Barthes, *Camera Lucida: Reflections on Photography* (New York: Hill and Wang, 1980). Avery Gordon, *Ghostly Matters: Haunting and the Sociological Imagination* (Minneapolis: University of Minnesota Press, 1997).

16. W.T.J. Mitchell refers to this interplay as imagetext. Mitchell, "What Do Pictures 'Really' Want?" *October* 77 (1996): 71–82.

17. Gordon, *Ghostly Matters*, 183.

18. Kimberly Alecia Singletary, "Everyday Matters: Haunting and the Black Diasporic Experience" in *Rethinking Black German Studies: Approaches, Interventions, Histories*, ed. Tiffany Florvil and Vanessa Plumly (Oxford: Peter Lang Press, 2018) 144.

19. Marianne Hirsch, *Family Frames: Photography, Narrative, and Postmemory* (Cambridge, Mass.: Harvard University Press, 1997), 8.

20. Marie Nejar and Regina Carstensen, *Mach nicht so traurige Augen, weil du ein Negerlein bist: meine Jugend im Dritten Reich* (Reinbek bei Hamburg: Rowohlt Taschenbuch, 2007), 62.

21. Nejar and Carstensen, *Mach*, 62.

22. Nejar and Carstensen, *Mach,* 30.

23. Richard Delgado and Jean Stefancic, *Critical Race Theory*, 3rd ed. (New York: New York University Press, 2017), 145.

24. Nejar and Carstensen, *Mach*, 89.

25. My translation, Nejar and Carstensen, *Mach*, 35, 37.

26. Nejar and Carstensen, *Mach*, 11, 59.

27. Campt, *Image Matters*, 9.

28. Campt, *Image Matters,* 9.

29. Marion Kraft, ed., *Kinder der Befreiung. Transatlantische Erfahrungen und Perspektiven Schwarzer Deutscher der Nachkriegsgeneration* (Münster: Unrast, 2015).

30. Fehrenbach, *Race after Hitler: Black Occupation Children in Postwar Germany (Princeton: Princeton University Press, 2005), 2, 74.*

31. Ika Hügel-Marshall, *Invisible Woman: Growing Up Black in Germany*, trans. Elizabeth Gaffney, New edition (New York: Peter Lang Inc., International Academic Publishers, 2008), 7, 11.

32. Hügel-Marshall, *Invisible,* 8, 42–43

33. Hügel-Marshall, 4–5.

34. Hügel-Marshall, 7–8.

35. Hügel-Marshall, 8.

36. Hügel-Marshall, 22.

37. Hügel-Marshall, 22.

38. Hügel-Marshall, 22.

39. Hirsch, *Family Frames*, 11.

40. Jennifer Teege and Nikola Sellmair, *My Grandfather Would Have Shot Me: A Black Woman Discovers Her Family's Nazi Past*, trans. Carolin Sommer, Reprint edition (New York: The Experiment, 2016), 116.

41. Teege and Sellmair, *Grandfather*, 67, 123.

42. Teege and Sellmair, *Grandfather*, 123.

43. Teege and Sellmair, *Grandfather*, 123.

44. This chapter also introduces the reader to her adoptive grandmothers and briefly to her Nigerian grandmother.

45. Teege and Sellmair, *Grandfather*, 59.

46. Teege and Sellmair, *Grandfather*, 64.

47. Hirsch, *Family Frames*, 5.

48. Teege and Sellmaier, *Grandfather*, 63.

49. Teege and Sellmair, *Grandfather*, 11. "The book about Monika Goeth mentions the year 1970, the year of my birth. There is not a word about me; my mother pretends I don't exist."

50. Teege and Sellmair, *Grandfather*, 65.

51. Teege and Sellmair, *Grandfather*, 95.

52. See Monserud, "Affectual Solidarity"; Bengtson, "Intergenerational Solidarity".

53. Fatima El-Tayeb, *European Others: Queering Ethnicity in Postnational Europe* (Minneapolis: University of Minnesota Press, 2011).

INTERLUDE

Wholly

NAJYA A. WILLIAMS

On what girlhood means to me as a writer. . . .

Black girlhood is the whisper of accountability we avoid. Black girlhood is the flash of hope in the midst of unbelief. Black girlhood is the embrace of love we don't recognize. Black girlhood is the superhero painted villain right before the revolution.

My writing is an attempt to capture the weight of existence etched beneath my chest. My writing is the gentle caress of spirit and flesh and bone and life our society has ignored. My writing is a war cry for the little Black girl within and beyond.

THANK YOU

To a body long forgotten. To a body long stretched plucked pulled.
To a body long

abandoned.

To a body never forgiven. To a body often criticized. To a body
discarded. To a body thick like molasses. To a body distorted. To a
body well traveled. To a body invaded. To a body degraded.

To a body.
To my body.

I offer a prayer
of thanks.

Thank you for touching the <**sky**> when my spirit clawed at the
earth.

Thank you for not buckling under the weight of hate's sovereignty. Thank you for writing your own roadmap to divinity along my thighs and tummy.

Thank you for counseling me on the power of beauty rooted by intimacy. Thank you for the dark hues that envelop me. Thank you for illustrating adequacy in hidden crevices I've never seen.

Thank you for protecting the truth I am manifesting. Thank you for growing and shrinking so effortlessly. Thank you for swallowing the worst of me.

Thank you for gracing the horrors in me. Thank you for walking me toward freedom when I couldn't even recognize it. Thank you for forgiving me even as I condemned myself through eternity. Thank you for modeling the maturity I never knew I needed.

Thank you for accommodating the entirety of me. Thank you for being
what I need you to be.
Thank you for being
what I didn't want you to be.
Thank you for

taking

up

space

so that I can just be me,
wholly and unequivocally.

ON MOTHERING

The calm in the eye of every storm. The cloak of protection in the midst of darkness. The hope in the face of fear.

With all the magic wrapped in her palms, Mama is everything everywhere at every moment.

Mamas are warrior legends we have the chance to learn about long after they've earned their stripes. Long after they've won impossible battles. Long after life turned them upside down. Mamas are a window into a solar return near and far. A path to the righteousness sitting beneath our noses. A vessel of communion with the vapors of life we cling to. Mamas are international museums, overflowing with artifacts. Bursting with the wisdom of ancestral guides. Doling out the love every inner child needs.

And even still, 'mama' is too small to hold her mothering. Too narrow to fit all the tools of her nurturing in its verbiage. Too claustrophobic to encompass the breadth of her reach.

For who can truly name the soul who holds God, the world, and herself simultaneously?

MY PORTION

If someone would have told me I'd be standing in love five years ago, I would have laughed. Love . . . the elusive partner that soothes and sabotages as quickly as lighting strikes the skin of this earth. Love . . . a volatile vehicle headed straight toward the deep of self. Love . . . the death-defying magician that always leaves me breathless with fear and curiosity.

Love was never meant for me. Nothing more than a cartoon fantasy painted onto my TV. But love . . . love took me by the horns and humbled me. Brought my spirit down to its knees and reminded me of what it means to have intimacy. A spiritual reckoning of more than what time can keep.

And as I stare into the eyes of heaven's gates, hand in hand with God's promise to me, I can only remind myself that this is only the beginning. Of undoing. Unraveling. Unfurling. The chains that once shackled the affection laced through my body.

I now know love was never meant for me. Not because I am unworthy. Love was never meant for me because the flicker of intimacy is revolutionary.

FIND ME

Home is where the heart is, but what happens when you don't know where the heart is? What happens when the heart is nothing more than love's vestibule on hate's altar? What happens when the heart is nothing more than a pagan sacrifice made holy on ashen ground? What happens when the heart is nothing more than Sunday morning worship under the blood moon's shadow?

Home is where the heart is, but what happens if the heart was never there? What happens if the heart was coaxed from its cage to be shackled once more? What happens if the heart was carved from the souls of feet stomping across my cracked concrete streets? What happens if the heart was drowned in a river of words left unsaid?

Home is where the heart is, but who needs a heart when a heart can be broken? Who needs a heart when love's waiting at home, sleeping past midnight in the whisper of a haunted past? Who needs a heart when the vultures have already bled me dry?

Home is where the heart is. Home is where the hurt is. Home is where the pain is. Home is where the grief is. Home is where the resentment is. Home is where the loss is. Home is where the salve is. Home is where the joy is. Home is where the power is. Home is where the hope is. Home is where the healing is. Home is where the truth is.

Home is where I'm not.

THE LAST TIME

I remember it like it was yesterday. The clouds had returned to their homes for the night. The sun hung up its blue collar. The stars shed skin to make ours glow. And the only thing standing between us, is the moon and her Child galaxy and her lover darkness. Slow dancing in front of our faces, brushing by our bodies without care or concern.

And as we lay here on this grass, not looking at each other, I can't help but to feel, but to feel you, but to feel we, but to feel it all on the line. Trying to figure out what the hell went wrong. To make your spirit cower in my presence instead of entangling with the web of my own. We aren't the same, the ones we used to be, but it feels like you've been using me, using this dream to paint your reality a bit differently than we imagined it would be.

I spent too much time asking you why you left. Why you left the pieces of our love on the ocean floor. Why you left me wondering if somehow, I could do just a little bit more. But the hourglass is finished now. The moon and her child galaxy and her lover darkness keep rhythm, drowning out the evidence of ours. These days, our two-part harmony feels more like a single instrument misstrung in the caught breath of a connoisseur.

I think I smothered you. I tossed you into my wings, carrying you wherever I flew just to make sure we could share even half the view. Yet somewhere along the way, you were the one trying to carry me. I knew you, your glass laced fragility was no match for the fullness of me, but I trusted you anyways because our love would fill the gaps where you never could. Or perhaps would. I just didn't know that it'd be only my love doing the work of two hearts, pumping desperately against a rib cage made stone.

The grass is itching, the moon and her child galaxy and her lover darkness have grown tired of our intrusion, and this is supposed to be the last time. You won't remember this in your memory made of self and you and only you and no truth, perhaps a little obtuse, but I'm going to take this leap, just to make myself clear, to you, for you. I'm sorry. And I mean, truly from the depth of myself sorry, because there's no reason I should have expected more from you. More from us, a collision course doomed from the beginning. I've survived a lifetime of love long lost, far away from even my eyes' reach, so what exactly made this any different? I'm sorry I assumed different . . . I'm sorry I bothered you . . . I'm sorry I believed in you and me more than you believed in we. I was dead wrong, to even expect anything outside of a whirlwind brush with forever before a forever fall into a whirling pain. That's my fault and I won't make that mistake again.

BIRDS WITH BROKEN WINGS

Birds with broken wings tend to land on my windowsill. I don't know what it is about my house that's so appealing but they land here. Well, maybe that's a bit disingenuous because every time I see them hobbling too close to the edge, I can't help but to lean out the window myself, even if it means I fall with them. I never thought me and those birds had much in common until I stood in front of the mirror one day. And just looked. And looked again. And looked a bit harder. And saw the shards of myself I kept hidden in fancy words and shrouded creativity. And saw the small scars on my skin hiding the scar right beneath the surface. And saw the weights in my brain dropping down to the souls of my feet. And saw the broken ends of my hair so distant from my thickened roots. It made me wonder how long my wing had been broken. How many doorsteps I flew to just to be noticed by a warm soul waiting to invite me in. How long I teetered close to the edge wanting someone to dive out the window and save me. How many days I'd go until I got my wing set. How many months I'd go before flying back to the nest. How many years I'd go before doing it all over again. Birds with broken wings tend to land on my windowsill. Now I know why.

PART III

Global

CORINNE T. FIELD AND
LAKISHA MICHELLE SIMMONS

Introduction: What Is Global about Black Girlhood?

Olive Morris was born in 1952. She spent her young girlhood in Jamaica and moved to London at nine years old to be with her immigrant parents. In London, Morris faced discrimination in school and left high school at age sixteen, without a diploma. By the time she was seventeen years old, Morris joined a chapter of the Black Panther Youth League, where activists read Black theorists and protested police brutality. On November 15, 1969, London police officers harassed, brutalized, and arrested a group of young activists, including Morris. Olive Morris became well known in her community, as one classmate remembered: "Olive and I went to the same school. Even then she had that streak in her—in school, they would have called it rebelliousness or disruptiveness, but it was really a fearlessness about challenging injustice at whatever level."[1]

Morris's work as a young activist expanded over the next few years; she protested evictions, fought for squatter's rights, and by her mid-twenties co-founded the Organization of Women of African and Asian Descent (OWAAD).[2] The OWAAD brought together Black teens and young women from a variety of different backgrounds living in England; the young women in the group had family from the Caribbean, Africa, South Asia, and multiracial backgrounds. Yet the group imagined a connection under the identity of Black. One of the other co-founders, Stella Dadzie, recalled, "[OWAAD] brought together a plethora of groups with all kinds of different backgrounds and histories and origins and it was that very diversity that was both our strength and our Achilles heel."[3] Dadzie, Morris, and other young activists began exploring what it meant to be part of a larger Black feminist community, united by anti-Black and anti-imperialist oppression. They engaged in conversation influenced by Black feminists across the globe, and they reimagined liberation from the vantage point of young women who had entered activism as teenagers. As Dadzie explained, this global imagining helped different groups of women highlight the international contours of anti-blackness in England and in the rest of the world. At the same time, Dadzie noted that their differences as Black women from different places, classes, and backgrounds was OWAAD's "Achilles' heel" because they did not spend as much time thinking through internal disputes and privileges (class privilege, biracial privilege, colorism).

Scholars of the African diaspora have long been interested in Black internationalism. They have studied the ways in which Black political actors see their own experiences of discrimination as tied to global systems of power: colonialism, postcolonialism, transnational slavery, and global capitalism. Scholars studying Black internationalism have focused on transnational rights movements, intellectual history, and cultural studies. They have highlighted the elite of the African diaspora and travelers with transnational networks, most often men: intellectual giants such as W. E. B. Du Bois, bands of dockworkers traveling from place to place, or male writers moving from the United States or the Caribbean to Paris and London.[4] Contributors to this section seek to identify the shared characteristics of Black girlhood that traveled transnationally, the ideas, feelings, and experiences that defined "being a Black girl" in Africa, Europe, and the Americas. By centering the words and actions of Black girls themselves, these chapters highlight how Black girls created internationalism, engaged in youth activism, or imagined connections to girls in other parts of the world by articulating a global community.

Recently, historians interested in Black internationalism have highlighted how Black women built the networks and ideological justifications that sustained a global movement for racial justice from the sixteenth century to the present. Tracking Black women's physical and imaginative travel between the Americas, the Caribbean, Europe, Asia, and Africa, historians identify how Black women's vision of internationalism often differed from the goals of their male peers.[5] Girls also had their own dreams of a global community, envisioning connections to other young people that might facilitate rebellion against older women or help them define the experience of being part of a generational cohort distinct from their elders. While some Black girls traveled (by choice or compulsion), many others stayed put, imagining a global community from within the confines of their homes, schools, and community centers. By listening to both those who saw the world and those who merely dreamed it, we can begin to recover how Black girls defined global Black girlhood on their own terms and for their own purposes.

Even as Black girls articulated and performed a shared identity recognizable regardless of location, local communities exerted a strong pull toward particularity. Adults made very different demands on Black girls in the United States than they did in Jamaica or Haiti, for example, and those expectations changed over time. Contributors to this section thus seek to identify how local relationships at the level of neighborhood, state, and region functioned to limit Black girls' dreams of global empowerment. Further, girls themselves sometimes chose to emphasize their unique family or regional heritage in articulating identities as the representatives of their families or nations. Patriotism and loyalty offered possibilities for Black girls who emphasized the local over the global.

In 1945, nine schoolgirls, daughters of the Haitian elite, performed the roles of militant revolutionaries in a staging of Jean F. Brierre's play *Famous Women in Haitian History*. This ephemeral performance, captured in photographs and remembered by the now adult daughters of the students who took part, expressed a creative, playful, celebratory understanding of the diasporic dimensions of Black girlhood. The girls took evident pleasure in their ability to perform history, creating connections across time and embodying female heroines celebrated by Black people on both sides of the Atlantic. Katharine Capshaw argues that this performance offers evidence for how empowered engagement with Black girls' history has been passed down through generations.

The Haitian schoolgirls used history to express pride in Black identity, a strategy that took center stage and received a clarifying label in the global Black Power movement of the late 1960s and 1970s. Dara Walker explores how high school students in 1970s Detroit fought to make Black girls' history part of their official curriculum. These girls mounted a twofold fight against Eurocentric curricula taught in classrooms, on the one hand, and white beauty standards celebrated in popular media, on the other. These young leaders convinced administrators to offer classes on Black history and literature. Their ability to see themselves in relation to global ideas about Black beauty in turn facilitated very personal struggles for self-determination. Their experiences suggest that the Black Power movement's resistance to white supremacy and its embrace of a Black aesthetic offered Black girls something that the civil rights movement's focus on desegregation did not: a vision of the self as whole.

Shani Roper turns attention to how class and color distinctions trap girls in intersectional binds even in majority Black contexts where race is not always the most salient factor. Between 1869 and 1937, the Jamaican government funded a Reformatory and Industrial School that offered an alternative to the criminal justice system for girls charged with crime or vagrancy. Many of the adults in charge of this effort were themselves Black, but they adopted colonial understandings of working-class Black girls as a problem in need of reform. Even when their intentions were to help girls, they employed harsh methods to change and correct them. Working-class Black families preferred keeping Black girls within their communities, and the fragmentary records reveal that judges remanded girls back to their communities more often than boys. The state, communities, and girls themselves thus defined the possibilities for girls both by adapting colonial institutions and maintaining local cultural practices, thus putting Jamaican Black girls in a particular relation to the global construction of juvenile justice.

The section ends with a roundtable discussion among four Black woman activists—two from South Africa and two from the United States—recorded at the Global History of Black Girlhood Conference held at the University of Virginia in the spring of 2017. Participants reflect on why they became politically active early in life, how their youth framed understandings of justice, and how understandings of Black girls' history facilitated or frustrated alliances across generation. This section will offer a primer for activists interested in exploring the history of Black girls as a means of strengthening global and local movements for Black Liberation.

Notes

1. Beverly Bryan, Stella Dadzie, Suzanne Scafe, and Lola Okolosie, *The Heart of the Race: Black Women's Lives in Britain* (London: Verso Books, 2018), 154.

2. For more on Olive Morris and the OWAAD see, Bryan et al., *The Heart of the Race: Black Women's Lives in Britain* (London: Verso Books, 2018); Tanisha Ford, *Liberated Threads: Black Women, Style, and the Global Politics of Soul* (The University of North Carolina Press, 2015) Chapter 5; Tanisha Ford, "Finding Olive Morris in the Archive," *The Black Scholar* 46. no. 2 (2016): 5–18; Tracy Fisher, *What's Left of Blackness: Feminisms, Transracial Solidarities, and the Politics of Belonging in Britain* (New

York: Palgrave Macmillan, 2012), 77–90; Rashida L. Harrison, "Movement Makers: A Historical Analysis of Black Women's Magic in Social Movement Formation," in *Black Girl Magic Beyond the Hashtag: Twenty-First-Century Acts of Self Definition*, ed. Julia S. Jordan-Zachery and Duchess Harris (Tuscon: University of Arizona Press, 2019), 41–59; Amie Tsang, "Overlooked No More: How Olive Morris Fought for Black Women's Rights in Britain," *The New York Times*, October 30, 2019, sec. Obituaries, https://www.nytimes.com/2019/10/30/obituaries/olive-morris-overlooked.html.

3. Stella Dadzie, interview by Rachel Cohen, video, June 2, 2011, "Sisterhood and After: The Women's Liberation Oral History Project," The British Library, London, http://www.bl.uk/learning/histcitizen/sisterhood/bioview.html#id=144062&v=true&id=144062.

4. Paul Gilroy, *The Black Atlantic: Modernity and Double Consciousness* (New York: Verso, 1993); Brent Hayes Edwards, *The Practice of Diaspora: Literature, Translation, and the Rise of Black Internationalism* (Cambridge: Harvard University Press, 2009); Kevin K. Gaines, *American Africans in Ghana: Black Expatriates and the Civil Rights Era* (Chapel Hill: University of North Carolina Press, 2012).

5. Keisha Blain and Tiffany Gill, *To Turn the Whole World Over: Black Women and Internationalism* (Urbana: University of Illinois Press, 2019).

CHAPTER 10

Haitian Girls Perform Resistance in the Wake of U.S. Occupation

Jean F. Brierre's *Famous Women in Haitian History* and Diasporic Girlhood

KATHARINE CAPSHAW

Nine Port-au-Prince schoolgirls took the stage on June 26, 1945, to perform a version of the Haitian Revolution. Unlike most accounts of the revolution circulated in narrative, image, song, and performance, their rendition was resolutely female, insistently youthful, and intrinsically rebellious against the currents of history. Performing Jean Brierre's *Famous Women in Haitian History*, these girls embraced women's political action, a potent agential statement in the wake of United States occupation of Haiti (1915–1934). Reflecting on the traces that remain of this performance, we must consider the possibilities open to scholars in reconceiving Black diasporic girlhood. The pursuit of a revivified perspective on Black girlhood demands that we eschew any pressure on historical completeness, and that we embrace the shards of history and memory that remain. For while literary history has traditionally neglected texts for young people, the literature and life of children in the Caribbean and especially of the most understudied—Black girls—provide a new perspective through which we can value the stories that have mattered within Black communities for generations. To understand Black girlhood, we must grapple with contexts. In order to see those nine animated girls in Port-au-Prince, we must understand the investments that framed their performance and enabled their feminist statement and critique of conventional historiography.

The play script itself remains in memory because of its American publication. In facilitating transnational exchanges for Black girlhood in the first half of the twentieth century, the independent Black press offered American child readers a range of radical perspectives on colonialism and race. For example, the children's periodical, *Our Boys and Girls* (1919–1920)—edited by Anselmo R. Jackson, a Virgin Island immigrant to New York, and supported by a group of radical West Indian thinkers, including Arturo Schomburg, Hubert Harrison, and Claude McKay—offered searing critiques of U.S. imperialism in the Caribbean and highlighted the failures of America to make good on its promise of racial equality. Soon after *Our Boys and Girls*, W. E. B. Du Bois launched the children's arm of *The Crisis* magazine; titled *The Brownies' Book* (1920–1921), Du Bois's monthly magazine included his column "As the Crow Flies," which offered finely tuned anti-colonial interpretations of current world events. During the same period, Carter G. Woodson, the father of Black history, founded a scholarly journal for adults, *The Journal of Negro History* (1916-present), and after developing Negro History Week in 1926, he extended his commitment to educating communities by initiating a journal for children and teachers, the *Negro History Bulletin* (1937–present). The very name of the journal suggests its mediation between past and present, yoking the perspective of history with the urgency of a news bulletin. As a children's journal, the *Negro History Bulletin* also published stories, plays, and poems, sometimes with a diasporic sensibility. It was in Woodson's publication that Black American children would read this forceful argument for Black girl heroism: Jean F. Brierre's *Famous Women in Haitian History* (1944).

Brierre's play valorizes the women who contributed to the Haitian revolution and its aftermath and urges contemporary girls and women to imagine themselves in political and military roles. By publishing the play within a Black American periodical, Brierre and Woodson insist on the relevance of female revolutionary action for Black children in the US as well as the Caribbean. As Dara Walker argues in her essay in this volume, educators and Black girls in the United States decades later would similarly intervene in accounts of Black cultural identity, taking a political stand in revising biased high school curriculums. With Walker's context in mind, we can see that the transformational project of curricular reform that later erupted with the Black Power movement began with educators in the 1920s and 1930s.

In terms of the subject of Haiti, Black and white audiences in the United States had been captivated by the country for decades. For theater, Leslie Pinckney Hill published his play *Toussaint L'Ouverture* (1928) with the intent of redressing global inattention to Black accomplishment, especially among child audiences: "The Negro youth of the world has been taught that the Black race has no great traditions, no characters of world importance, no record of substantial contribution to civilization."[1] Other productions included Shirley Graham's opera *Tom-Tom* (1932) and Josephine Baker's role in the French film *Zouzou* (1934). Other Black artists, including W. E. B. Du Bois, Jacob Lawrence, and Langston Hughes, focused on Black masculine militancy as the value of Haitian history.[2] With his friend Arna Bontemps, Hughes also published a children's novel, *Popo and Fifina: A Story of Haiti* (1934).[3] For white audiences, attention to Haiti in the period around U.S. occupation brought representations that reified stereotypes of exoticism and sensuality. For instance, Eugene O'Neill's *The Emperor Jones*, first staged in 1920, appeared on film in 1933 with Paul Robeson as the title character. Orson Welles staged his *Voodoo Macbeth* in 1936 through the Federal Theatre Project. In these versions of Black identity, Haitian military history and revolutionary figures embodied hyper-masculinity, a degree of savagery, and desire for revenge.[4]

Given the era's emphasis on masculine accomplishment—whether as icon of nationhood for Black writers or symbol of virility for white artists—the publication by schoolteachers of several U.S. children's plays about heroines in Haiti by women playwrights (even before Brierre's *Famous Women in Haitian History*) appears quite courageous. Helen Webb Harris's *Genifrede: The Daughter of L'Ouverture* (1922/1935) and May Miller's *Christophe's Daughters* (1935) are exciting examples of resistant counter-narrative. Significantly, both of these plays were issued by Carter G. Woodson's Associated Publishers in the volume *Negro History in Thirteen Plays* (1935), edited by Miller and playwright Willis Richardson. Through this publication we witness Woodson's sustained commitment to reinstating suppressed histories of women's involvement in the Haitian revolution.[5] As Samantha Pinto argues, "Drama, then, stands as a medium of critique of ideals of racial community and of the uneven reproduction of historical narratives that refuse Black women subjects entry into the ongoing complexity of diaspora narratives of racial belonging."[6] Through *Famous Women in Haitian History*, we see a profound challenge to traditional diasporic narratives of Haitian heroism, especially as they were configured on the U.S. stage.

Although shared with American audiences, Brierre's play has deep Haitian roots. While extant production histories of Harris's and Miller's plays are incomplete,[7] Brierre's play was first staged at a girls' school in Port-au-Prince, Haiti (Lycee des Jeunes Filles) in the early 1940s, and then translated into English by Mercer Cook (the ambassador and son of composer Will Marion Mercer Cook). Brierre originally issued the play in Haiti in French, the English translation appearing in *The Negro History Bulletin* in 1944. A dual-language pamphlet was published in 1950 in Haiti with a cast list from the June 26, 1945, performance. Brierre's play brings into relief several of the challenges of studying global Black girlhood. How do we contend with the elisions of history in order to speak about the performance of the play? How do we locate Black girlhood within a political and economic landscape that has elided childhood entirely as a subject of discourse and of academic study?

In order to engage these questions, I deploy a metaphor offered by Angela Sorby in reference to Black American childhood of the nineteenth century. Sorby posits that Black authors writing for young people often had to "conjure" readership imaginatively, to call into being in their minds the young people who would engage their texts. She says, "To conjure a child reader is . . . to create—partly through practical measures and partly through the imagination—the conditions that make literate agency possible."[8] Brierre did not have to "conjure" the girls to whom he wrote, since he wrote for girls in a particular school, but considering our position in the twenty-first century, we may attempt to summon the past, as far as we can discern and imagine it, when engaging the text. With indebtedness to Sorby, I use the term "dream" instead of conjure, since Brierre's play—and Brierre himself as a poet—exercises the framework of the "dream" in order to imagine the connections between the girls in the play and history, and between Haitian artists and Black American intellectuals.[9] How do we dream these girls in 1940s Port-au-Prince? How do we dream their revolutionary performance? How do we dream its impact on their lives?

The political alliances of the play's author offer one context for imagining the performance of *Famous Women*. Brierre is best known by scholars in the United States for his participation in the Haitian negritude movement and his poem *Black Soul* (1947). During his lifetime in Haiti, Brierre was a vital political figure. In the 1930s, he was a fierce opponent of the U.S. occupation of Haiti and was jailed by President Sténio Vincent from 1932–1934 (the year the occupation ended) over editorials in the newspaper Brierre founded, *La Battile* (Jean Brierre: l'homme et l'oeuvre).[10] In 1942, Brierre spent a year at Columbia University, where he met and became friends with Langston Hughes, who may have put Brierre in contact with the community in Washington, D.C, where Woodson lived and worked. Hughes had long been invested in Haiti; in addition to his plays and a children's book, Hughes authored the scorching "People without Shoes" after his visit to the nation in 1931. Published in *New Masses,* the piece argues, "All of the work that keeps Haiti alive, pays for the American Occupation, and enriches foreign traders—that vast and basic work—is done there by Negroes without shoes."[11] Hughes and Brierre became lifelong friends, in large part because of their shared Marxist, populist vision and their commitment to youth. When Brierre returned to Haiti in the summer of 1943, he became supervisor of schools in Jérémie until he published another editorial critical of the government and was fired. An article on Brierre in Woodson's *Negro History Bulletin* of March 1946 explains that after losing his post, "to make ends meet, he practiced law in Jeremie, and tried his hand at business, but the urge to serve the younger generation was uncontrollable. . . . [He] wrote playlets to acquaint Haitian schoolchildren with their ancestors' sacrifices and accomplishments. One of these playlets told of King Christophe's daughters. A second was entitled 'Famous Women in Haitian History.'"[12]

From this brief outline, we can see a bit about the exchange between the negritude movement through Brierre and the Black American intellectual community. Friends with Hughes, Brierre also worked closely with his translator Mercer Cook, a professor at Howard and Atlanta Universities and eventual diplomat, who also taught at the University of Haiti during the time of the play's production (1943–45).[13] Cook and Woodson collaborated in the 1940s; Woodson's Associated Publishers issued Cook's *Five French Negro Authors* (1943), and in 1948 Cook joined the editorial board of Woodson's planned Encyclopedia Africana. We have to move through these multiple connections in order to understand the statement of affinity Brierre and Woodson offered in issuing *Famous Women in Haitian History* to Americans. Brierre himself envisioned a kinship between Harlem and Haiti, writing several poems about their like-mindedness in the face of racism, and as J. Michael Dash suggests, "The euphoric celebration of an embattled fraternity inspired Jean Brierre to conceive of kindred cultures 'dreaming the same dream.'"[14] By publishing *Famous Women in Haitian History* in *The Negro History Bulletin*, Woodson enables a glimpse of the kind of resistant work Brierre facilitated among Black girls. Brierre holds faith with the girls at the Lycee des Jeunes Filles, as they work together in solidarity to animate a vision of Black female heroism; this cross-generational collaboration anticipates the Black teachers in Walker's essay in this volume who engaged students, churches, and community groups in order to build a new vision of diasporic education.

The term "dream" follows the emphasis and content of Brierre's play, which describes two girls walking in the mountains above Jérémie in the south of Haiti. They fall asleep on the hillside but will themselves to dream of the female heroes of the Haitian revolution. After talking about the beauty of nature, Marie says to Lucienne, "I believe in the miraculous, I do. This morning, for example, I should like to meet on the scene of History the great men who founded the nation."[15] Lucienne replies with a critique of education: "There is something unjust about the teaching of history in Haiti. As teacher was saying yesterday, they always talk about the men and forget about the women, just as if the men could have founded the nation all by themselves."[16] This scene initiates the play's emphasis on the physicality of the female body, one which becomes later infused with revolutionary power. The girls first imagine the "venerable Ancestresses who have woven with their courageous and untiring hands the glorious colors of our flag."[17] The girls thus start the play by imagining the hands that bring the flag, and the nation, into being. Marie says to Lucienne, "In the name of all little Haitian girls, let us try, with all our heart, to call to those century-old women who are like mothers that have long been lost and whom we miss."[18] The stage directions tell us "There is a deep silence," and the girls sleep. Dreaming becomes a means of access, a vision and act of imagination that results in connection rather than invention. The girls imagine an embodied connection between mothers and daughters, across time, as a means to bring the past into the present.

The women they resurrect move from conventional depictions of gender roles to more extreme assertions of Black female militarism. The play resembles a pageant, in which each figure appears, gives testimony of her life and accomplishments, and then exits. Operating teleologically, the play begins with moderate perspectives and culminates with figures who offer the most radical, interventionist perspectives on women's agency. Sainte Belair, a fighter, is the first to appear, and when the children ask her what they should learn from her example, she replies: "To know how to share worthily the ideal of one's mate. Like Charles Belair, the uncompromising fugitive slave who steadfastly refused to bow his head before the arrogant and tyrannical planters, I owe my reputation to the fact that I too was an uncompromising leader of the insurgents."[19] While Sainte Belair encourages the girls to follow a husband's model, she becomes her own form of "leader" in the revolution, dynamically challenging the status quo. She is armed, possessing a combative power typically denied to women.[20] Her language echoes the embodied presence of women through the form of hands; she says, "If the very cradle of our nation is bloodstained, it is because our hands, our poor Black, mashed, mutilated, our tired hands have never stopped bleeding."[21] Most radical is her statement about the voices absent from accounts of the revolution. She says, "You know my story. You know my name, but there are thousands upon thousands of other women who were just as great, just as courageous as Sainte Belair."[22] If the girls' teacher at school reminds them that history elides female revolutionaries of record, the heroines themselves draw attention to the multitudes of brave women who remain nameless. Their bleeding hands experienced the "unspeakable torture"[23] of enslavement and responded with rebellion.

The spouse of Toussaint L'Ouverture—certainly the most famous Haitian historical figure—follows Sainte Belair and comments on the upending of gender offered by Belair's example. Suzanne Simon says, "The fortitude with which she braved death has stood as an example not only for the women but also for the men of Saint Dominigue. In Sainte Belair, my children, you must salute a great *man*."[24] The figuration here is perplexing because the woman who advises to "share worthily the ideal of one's mate" becomes both an example for men and a "great *man*" herself. The italicization of "*man*" suggests something about the way history works through hagiography, offering the great man model as historical legibility and investing Sainte Belair with that status. Suzanne also offers a model that focuses on the domestic sustenance that women offer their spouses. She explains:

> You see, children, when Touissant Louverture would come home, he was no longer General Louverture, but a man who often was tired, and who sometimes needed to be understood, encouraged, loved. That powerful brain which conceived the greatest dream that has enlightened the world since Bethlehem: the emancipation of the Black Race, that broad brow of a determined thinker and patriot sometimes found repose on a woman's shoulder.[25]

Her perspective relocates L'Ouverture, shifting our perspective on him from visionary and public figure to a man in need of comfort within the domestic sphere. This moment is akin to the move of establishing Sainte Belair as a model for men; just as Sainte Blair's meaning shifts from following one's mate into combative power and historical legibility, women again move into visibility as Suzanne offers psychological strength and comfort to the most famous of Haitian revolutionaries, a hero who retreats into dependence on his wife.

The radical women of the second half of the play foreground the role played by the female body in revolution. The next figure who appears onstage invokes the fallen woman. But Brierre reclaims Black female sexuality as politically powerful, resisting its dismissal and stigmatization. Henriette St. Marc enters, a Haitian woman who seduced French officers in order to steal munitions to give to the revolutionaries. Popular renditions of St. Marc figure her as a prostitute, though Brierre does not explicitly categorize her as such. Instead, he emphasizes identification rather than stigmatization. St. Marc's first statement aligns her body and those of the girls she addresses: "Children, I was beautiful and young as you are, and seductive, too."[26] The "too" is ambivalent, for it might be additive to "beautiful and young," distinguishing St. Marc from the girls, or it might suggest their kinship in embracing a seductive sexuality. She explains her mobilization of that power: "My role was to provide the insurgents with gunpowder and bullets that I would take from the white officers who made love to me."[27] Eventually she is discovered and says: "They led me to the gallows, but at the very instant when they beheaded me, I experienced the inexpressible joy of hearing my bullets, my shells explode under the feet of the planters and on Rochambeau's palaces."[28] In addition to the striking embrace of sexuality as a weapon, St. Marc's descriptions of the revolution are resolutely violent and embodied; she calls Rochambeau, the French general, "that monster who required each day wagon loads of corpses and buckets of blood."[29] Paired with the description of planters blown from their fields, we see here the girls (both audience and players) are not sheltered from the expediencies of revolution, and are encouraged to consider the material potential for political power, and for violence and loss, inhabiting the Black female body.

The final two figures culminate the play's emphasis on embodied resistance. Marie Jeanne fought in the battle of Crête-à-Pierrot and, before that, was a freedom fighter. She proclaims, "In the great decisive hours of a nation's existence, there is no difference in sex, dresses to one side and trousers to another. There are simply men resolved to sacrifice their all in order to merit the name of men."[30] As in the case of Sainte Belair, the embrace of militancy renders the woman a great "*man*" of history. The hyper-masculinization typically associated with Black nationalism, as well as with depictions of Haiti onstage in U.S. adult theater of the 1930s, gets controverted, transmuted, and appropriated within these children's plays about revolutionary women. Marie Jeanne explains that history might be "amazed" at her work as a soldier, but she contends that "[her] presence in the fort seemed quite natural to the . . . other Haitian heroes who fought beside [her]." She goes on, "I was not a woman; I was a comrade, a soldier, an insurgent, struggling for independence. And so, my children, do not forget that you must be courageous in soul, in spirit, and at heart."[31] Embodiment again comes to the fore: the activist, militant Black body is de-gendered here, moving away from the delimiting cultural designation of "woman" and into a state of personhood, comradeship, courage, and alliance.

The play culminates with a staggering figure: "Enter an old lady; her arms are folded as though she were carrying something."[32] Crazy Défilée then takes the stage. Known in life as Dédée Bazile, Crazy Défilée is the figure who gathered up the dismembered body of Jean-Jacques Dessalines in October 1806 when no other person would go near the remains. Dessalines, as the girls know, was the first leader of the independent nation. In the play, Défilée carries the dismembered body of Dessalines in her arms, explaining to the girls: "They mutilated him, children, they mutilated him. And I am carrying his sacred remains back to the earth that he bequeathed to us."[33] Importantly, the three characters that dominate the conclusion of the play are not members of the Haitian elite. They are not privileged economically, and although Henriette St. Marc is remembered as a "mulatto" in some accounts, within the world of the play these are the outcasts, the marginal, the renegades who recall the legacy of French colonial devastation. Not only do their bodies conjure the history of enslavement and exploitation, but also by calling Crazy Défilée "crazy," Brierre evokes the tradition in folklore of imagining her insanity as resulting from being raped by her master as a child.[34] Violent, rebellious, and uncontainable, these women are called up by the girls' dream. These are the models the girls have dreamed back into being.

The frame narrative establishes these militant women as patterns for action in the world, as models for the young to embody in the present. When the girls climb the mountain over Jérémie in the opening scene, they look down at the remnants of U.S. Occupation, which become picturesque from a distance.[35] They begin as spectators; they end by waking from the dream and quoting the words of the most provocative figure from the revolution, one who is mislabeled as crazy; Lucienne channels Défilée, concluding the play by stating "in truth, children" she tells us, "there was only one sane person, and that was Crazy Défilée. The others were criminals and fools."[36] Brierre linked the occupation with continued American economic imperialism in Haiti, writing in January 1946, "But the American danger is not only in the threat of warships. It is above all in the action of the American dollar in commerce and finance. The bank is in American hands."[37] For Brierre, and for the girls in the play, continued resistance to U.S. dominance over Haiti is the impetus for staging Black feminism, a feminism that has national, political, and economic implications. Clare Corbould has detailed the uses of American-based Haiti plays during the occupation as a mode of resistance: "Denouncing their homeland as an imperial overlord, not so different from the European imperial states Americans so often defined themselves against, Black Americans instead pledged their allegiance to Haitians, and by extension, with other colonized people around the world."[38] Through Brierre's play, we discover in Haiti that performance aimed to galvanize Black communities in order to advance economic and social autonomy and to resist U.S. imperialism. The girls are figured as the freedom fighters who can dream the past in order to forge a resistant future.

Who were these girls proclaiming revolution, describing battlefield carnage, carrying Dessalines's dismembered body? At this point, dreaming history required me to consider the site of the performance, the Lycee des Jeunes Filles in Port-au-Prince, and to hope to find records of the play and its actresses.[39] Unfortunately, no such official information exists at the school. Woodson's *Negro History Bulletin*, however, contains images of the cast, its author, and the school in a 1946 article about Brierre and in a 1949 essay on the "Negro Little Theater Movement." The photographs document the performance of June 26, 1945.[40] These images depict a group of teenagers taking great pleasure in their accomplishment. The details of the costumes, the smiles on their faces (especially the young woman playing Crazy Défilée), the oversized bows in the girls' hair, signifying youth—all these aspects speak to the care they took with the production (see figure 16). Reflecting on how these girls may have inhabited the performance space, offering their bodies as scripts marking the beauty, courage, and determination of historical figures, one might recall Uri McMillan's theory of "performing objecthood":

Figure 16. Full Cast, used with the permission of the Association for the Study of African American Life and History.

Figure 17. Brierre and Main Characters, used with the permission of the Association for the Study of African American Life and History.

"Becoming objects . . . proves to be a powerful tool for performing one's body, a 'stylized repetition of acts' that rescripts how Black female bodies move and are perceived by others."[41] Although separated by decades, these girls' inspiring physical articulation of heroism anticipates the feeling of cultural pride performed during the Black Power movement through hair, dress, and language. Since the Brierre play resembles a pageant, with figures standing somewhat like a *tableau vivant*, the young people's bodies themselves rescript revolutionary possibilities for Black girls. In their physical presentation, the girls' bodies offer a palimpsestic articulation of activist connection and political potential, pointing backward across time and forward into the actresses' futures (see figure 17). Their production resembles what Daphne Brooks calls the "embodied insurgency"[42] of Black performances in the early twentieth century.

The Lycee des Jeunes Filles served the children of the elite, those who could afford education and whose social events made the society pages.[43] How much more striking, then, that they would stage a play that celebrates seductresses, female soldiers, and the poor. As S.R. Riley argues of depictions of the Haitian Revolution in the United States, "to the degree that the plays and performances depict racial pride, they do so not as an effect or expression of a pre-existing homogenous group formation but rather as part of the very mechanism (an affective mechanism- . . .) for forging a more inclusive category."[44] While Riley is concerned with the way the revolution enabled a mixed-race identity, I see this production emerging from the Haitian elite as a profound political gesture in terms of negritude; this was a period in which the more progressive, leftist members of the elite (like Brierre) sought common cause with the lower classes in rejecting the class stratification that facilitated United States economic imperialism. As Corbould notes, this moment was a turning point: "Whereas elite Haitians had previously disdained 'peasant culture,' they now revered it in their efforts to demonstrate a cultural national sovereignty in the face of an attack on their political sovereignty."[45] Brierre himself was involved in the 1946 revolution that did just that: it ousted the successor to Sténio Vincent and attempted to erect a more egalitarian, autonomous government.

The French pamphlet version of the play includes a cast list and a moving dedication, which gives some sense of Brierre's motivation:

> To my mother and to my wife,
> And through them,
> To the Haitian woman,
> Courageous and strong,
> Worthy of civil
> And politic rights.[46]

Brierre here recognizes the importance of women in Haiti during the period, and also the need for greater civil liberties and social recognition. Additionally, the dedication makes present the influential women in Brierre's life. McMillan argues that "performance is intrinsically linked to memory and history" and explains that "performances are not simply the residue of past events but closer to, in Joseph Roach's words, 'restored behaviors that function as vehicles of cultural transmission.'"[47] In addition to honoring the women he depicts, Brierre's dedication configures the play as a tribute to and an extension of the women in his life; they all layer upon each other to reveal the very idea of Haitian womanhood, a "cultural transmission" alive in the female body on stage at a girls' school in Haiti as well as in the roles those bodies enact. In addition, while Brierre is not known for a feminist investment across his work, he emerged as a writer at the same time as the first Haitian women novelists, such as Cléante Desgraves Valcin and Annie Desroy, who were similarly motivated to write in the wake of U.S. occupation.[48] Brierre was part of a milieu that pressed for the political rights and cultural visibility of Haitian women.

But what of the girls themselves? The cast list also names actual people involved in the play, and while marriage often erases the maiden names of young girls for record keeping, two of the young women moved to the United States and became more locatable. Denise Wolff Dallemand, who played Crazy Défilée, passed away in 2018 at ninety-two years old in Albany, New York. According to her daughter, Karine Lataillade, Denise and her husband immigrated to the United States in 1967 where Denise spent her career as an export agent. The cast member who played Lucienne, one of the little girls who witnesses the ancestresses, was Elza Thomas Bréa, an immigrant to the United States who passed away in 2012 at eighty-four years old (see figures 18 and 19). Her daughter, Reverend Myrna Bernadel-Huey, describes Bréa as a member of the economic and social elite who fled Haiti with her family in 1965, the year after François Duvalier took the title of "President for Life." Bréa worked as a clinical pathologist with Wyeth Pharmaceuticals for nearly twenty years. Her daughter explains, "In terms of feminism and work, this was the thing that blew my mind, the idea in the 1970s of the empowerment of women: I *never* had the sense that I wasn't empowered. The expectation was that I was to go to school, do really well, and become a responsible, professional woman. My family's dinner conversation was always about politics—what was happening in Haiti, the politics there. There was always this sense of pride and tremendous resentment about the U.S. occupation." Bréa raised her daughters to be forces in the world, to see in themselves the potential for transformative social change. Daphne Brooks argues that Black performance can "defamiliarize the spectacle of 'Blackness' in transatlantic

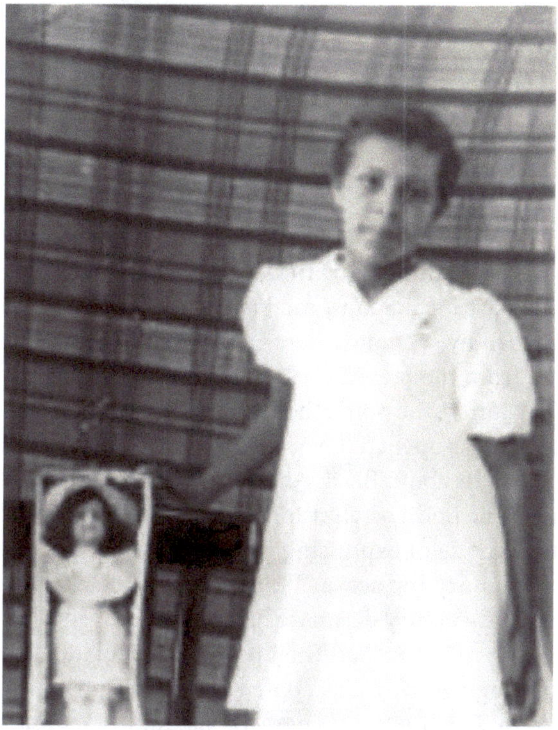

Figure 18. Bréa in 1939 in Haiti, collection of Reverend Myrna Bernadel-Huey.

Figure 19. Bréa as an Adult, collection of Reverend Myrna Bernadel-Huey.

culture."[49] These Haitian girls in 1940s Port au Prince certainly defamiliarized Black history. By reinventing, resurrecting, and dreaming a new version of revolution, the girls at Lycee des Jeunes Filles contacted and created Black female revolutionary role models that would serve them in Haiti and in their adulthood abroad.

As one of the most provocative pieces of diasporic children's literature, *Famous Women in Haitian History* comments on the failures of historiography and claims the terrain of the past for Black women and girls. The fact that this play, as well as those written by schoolteachers Helen Webb Harris and May Miller, has disappeared from the record speaks of the sexist and racist currents of cultural memory. More to the point, those currents also submerge Black girlhood. In their day, dramas opened the space for Black girls to come into focus; Kyra D. Gaunt's insights about Black American girls also apply to the young actresses in Haiti: "The bodily stylizations that assert 'somebodiness' have remained a critical mode of expressing our inalienable rights to freedom embodied as social memory and action."[50] For us looking backward, the girls' performances bring mid-century diasporic Black girlhood—in all its creativity, playfulness, and resolve—into relief. Their physical articulations of "somebodiness" allow us to recognize the radical potential of Black girlhood. Brent Hayes Edwards asserts in *The Practice of Diaspora: Literature, Translation, and the Rise of Black Internationalism* that an international perspective does not imply a "premeditated 'solidarity' but a hard-won project only practiced across difference, only spoken in ephemeral spaces."[51] Performance is by definition ephemeral, but by immersing ourselves in a dream of Haitian girlhood, we can begin to witness its courage and accomplishment.

Notes

1. Leslie Pinckney Hill, *Toussaint L'Ouverture: A Dramatic History* (Boston: Christopher Publishing House, 1928), 7–8.

2. Shannon Rose Riley, *Performing Race and Erasure: Cuba, Haiti, and US Culture, 1898–1940* (New York: Palgrave, 2016), 175–76; Stephanie Leigh Batiste, *Darkening Mirrors: Imperial Representation in Depression-Era African American Performance* (Durham, NC: Duke University Press, 2011), 74.

3. In addition to an adult novel about revolutionary Haiti, *Drums at Dusk* (1939), Bontemps also produced an unpublished children's work entitled *Tom Tom Treasures* (1938).

4. Batiste, *Darkening Mirrors*, 73.

5. Woodson has been known for being personally difficult and perhaps unsupportive of women writers, as evidenced by W.E.B. Du Bois's statement: "He had no conception of the place of woman in creation" (Dagbovie 83); however, his efforts in terms of supporting "Negro History Week" involved many women, both in terms of book publication through his Associated Publishers and through the *Negro*

History Bulletin. See Katharine Capshaw Smith, *Children's Literature of the Harlem Renaissance* (Bloomington, IN: Indiana University Press, 2004), "Chapter 4: The Peacemakers." See Pero Gaglo Dagbovie, *The Early Black History Movement, Carter G. Woodson, and Lorenzo Johnston Greene* (Urbana, IL: University of Illinois Press: 2007), chapter 4.

6. Samantha Pinto, *Difficult Diasporas: The Transnational Feminist Aesthetic of the Black Atlantic* (New York: New York University Press, 2013), 79.

7. The Howard Players in May of 1922 produced "Genifrede," and the Morgan College Dramatic Club presented "Christophe's Daughters" in 1935. See Shannon Rose Riley, *Performing Race and Erasure: Cuba, Haiti, and US Culture, 1898—1940* (New York: Palgrave Macmillan, 2016), 176–77.

8. Angela Sorby, "Conjuring Readers: Antebellum African American Children's Poetry," in *Who Writes for Black Children?, African American Children's Literature before 1900* (Minneapolis: University of Minnesota Press, 2017), 6, http://www.jstor.org/stable/10.5749/j.cttlpv88xm.4.

9. See J. Michael Dash, *Haiti and the United States: National Stereotypes and the Literary Imagination* (New York: Palgrave Macmillan, 1997).

10. http://lenouvelliste.com/lenouvelliste/article/79992/Jean-Brierre-lhomme-et-loeuvre. Accessed 11 April 2021.

11. Langston Hughes, "People without Shoes," in *The Collected Works of Langston Hughes, Vol. 9: Essays on Art, Race, Politics, and World Affairs*, ed. Christopher C. De Santis (Columbia and London: University of Missouri, 2002), 12.

12. Mercer Cook, "Jean F. Brierre, Poet and Hero," *Negro History Bulletin* 9, no. 6 (1946): 127. The children's play about Christophe's daughters has not survived.

13. Cook would also translate the works of negritude writer and eventual Senegalese president, Léopold Senghor.

14. Dash, 61.

15. Jean F Brierre, *Les aïeules(Famous women in Haitian history): sketch en un acte présenté pour la 1ère fois au Lycée des jeunes filles le 26 juin 1945* (Port-au-Prince, Haïti: Editions Henri Deschamps, 1950), 36.

16. Brierre, 36.

17. Brierre, 36.

18. Brierre, 36.

19. Brierre, 38.

20. Brierre, 36.

21. Brierre, 38.

22. Brierre, 38.

23. Brierre, 38.

24. Brierre, 15.

25. Brierre, 38.

26. Brierre, 38.

27. Brierre, 38.

28. Brierre, 38–39.

29. Brierre, 38.

30. Brierre, 39.

31. Brierre, 39.

32. Brierre, 39.

33. Brierre, 39.

34. See Jana Evans Braziel, "Re-membering Défilée: Dédée Bazile as Revolutionary Lieu de Mémoire," *Small Axe*, 9.2, (September 2005), 57–85.

35. Brierre, 36.

36. Brierre, 39.

37. Quoted in Cook, "Jean F. Brierre, Poet and Hero," 141.

38. Clare Corbould, "At the Feet of Dessalines," in *Beyond Blackface: African Americans and the Creation of American Popular Culture, 1890–1930*, ed. W. Fitzhugh. Brundage (Chapel Hill: University of North Carolina Press, 2011), 259, https://doi.org/10.5149/9780807878026_brundage.17.

39. Wendel Octa, a university student and associate of the Haitian Education Leadership Program, kindly assisted me by visiting the school and conducting interviews. Unfortunately, Wendel discovered that all of the records of the early years of the school were destroyed in the 2010 earthquake. Wendel pursued interviews in order to find out more about the performance, but nothing concrete surfaced regarding the play or the student actors. I am grateful for his tremendous efforts.

40. Because the cast photograph in the 1946 periodical is the same as that which appears in the 1950 bilingual pamphlet published in Haiti, we can assume that the images represent the performance named in the pamphlet: June 26, 1945.

41. Uri McMillan, *Embodied Avatars: Genealogies of Black Feminist Art and Performance* (New York: New York University Press, 2015), 7.

42. Daphne A. Brooks, *Bodies in Dissent: Spectacular Performances of Race and Freedom, 1850–1910* (Durham, NC: Duke University Press Books, 2006), 3.

43. For example, the actress who played Crazy Défilée is mentioned in the *Haiti Sun* for throwing an Easter gathering for her classmates: "Miss Georges Dallemand's residence in Ruelle Roy was the scene of a gay party Thursday evening marking the end of the Easter holidays for the Jeune filles 'Class II' of the Sacre Coeur" (9). Bernard Diederich, "Haiti Beach Comber," *Haiti Sun*, April 20, 1952: 9. Denise Wolff's marriage to Georges Dallemand in 1951 also made the society page.

44. Riley, *Performing Race and Erasure: Cuba, Haiti, and US Culture, 1898–1940*, 178.

45. Corbould, "At the Feet of Dessalines," 272.

46. Brierre, *Les aïeules (Famous women in Haitian history)*, 3.

47. McMillan, *Embodied Avatars*, 15.

48. Myriam J. A. Chancy, *Framing Silence: Revolutionary Novels by Haitian Women* (New Brunswick: Rutgers University Press, 2007).

49. Brooks, *Bodies in Dissent*, 5.

50. Kyra D. Gaunt, *The Games Black Girls Play: Learning the Ropes from Double-Dutch to Hip-Hop* (New York: New York University Press, 2006), 5.

51. Brent Hayes Edwards, *The Practice of Diaspora: Literature, Translation, and the Rise of Black Internationalism* (Cambridge, MA: Harvard University Press, 2003), 186.

CHAPTER 11

Moving Beyond the "Dark Africa" Narrative

Black Girls, Black Power, and the Battle for a Culturally Relevant Curriculum

DARA WALKER

In the fall of 1970, members of Detroit's Cass Technical High School's Black Student Caucus (BSC) organized a sit-in to demand Black Studies courses. From the students' perspective, much of the content taught in history courses at Cass Tech depicted the African continent through the lens of "dark Africa." This version of African history argued that Africa was a lost continent that had failed to contribute to the development of human civilization. Similarly, the school's literature and English courses emphasized the literary contributions of European thinkers and writers. African American student activist Jametta Lily noticed similar problematic treatments in the school's performing arts curriculum. While Plato and the Greek Arts received great coverage, students rarely learned about Black cultural figures like Amiri Baraka or the African American dancer and anthropologist Katherine Dunham. Like much of the high school curriculum that students encountered across the United States, Detroit's program failed to address the culture and histories of Black youth. As many African American students came of age in the era of African liberation movements, they found this pedagogical approach to teaching American life and history inexplicable. Lily's friend and fellow Cass Tech activist Shirikiana Aina thought to herself, "How could this happen in Detroit, a Black place? Why don't we look at some of the accomplishments and some of the histories and cultures of our variety of population?" These questions led students to actively seek alternatives to the district's culturally *irrelevant* curriculum. Organizing sit-ins that occupied the "vein of the school," or the fourth floor of the racially diverse institution, Black girls like Lily and Aina laid claim to both physical and intellectual spaces that had questioned their very presence. Through their organizing and with community support, Cass Tech's adolescent activists successfully pushed school administrators to hire two educators to teach Black History and Black Literature courses.[1]

The struggle at Cass Tech was one of many in the movement for Black Studies and Black community control of schools. Students at Cass Tech would ultimately reap the benefits of the seeds that the prominent historian Carter G. Woodson had planted several decades before.[2] While national civil rights leaders largely fought for school integration during the first half of the twentieth century, African American communities pushed the movement to address local control of educational institutions by the end of the tumultuous 1960s. High school students were among some of the fiercest advocates and leaders in this movement. The most prominent of these battles was the fight to uproot the culture of American schooling from its Eurocentric moorings and to decolonize public education. With the mass exodus of whites and capital from Detroit, a process that began during the 1950s but accelerated after the rebellion of 1967, Detroit's population was majority African American by 1968. Consequently, African American communities believed that a predominantly Black city should have institutions and elected leaders that spoke to their needs. In the case of the school curriculum, the city had to address the pedagogical needs of Black students.[3]

While the struggle to make the curriculum culturally relevant to their lives was a political project, African American girls had a personal stake in this battle as well. For much of the 1950s and 1960s, they encountered stereotypical images of Black women and girls as a social problem in the popular media and in public policy debates. As a case in point, in 1965, Daniel Patrick Moynihan's *The Negro Family: The Case for National Action* argued that female-headed households and gendered disparities in educational attainment were among the many causes of poverty in African American communities. The gender disparity between Black girls and Black boys was just the beginning of the cycle of a Black matriarchy, which the Moynihan study identified as the root of the "tangle of pathology." The Moynihan report informed many of the policies and programs that emerged out of the War on Poverty.[4]

Moynihan was also concerned about Black girls' sexuality, namely, that unwed teenage mothers would become dependent on the welfare state. Moynihan represented a larger trend in social science research that suggested to Black girls that they should not be too sexually active or too smart. Since Moynihan took much of his interpretation from Black sociologist E. Franklin Frazier's work on Black youth and family life, Moynihan's report should be read in the tradition of what historian Rebecca de Schweinitz has termed "youth-centered racial liberalism" that fixated on the personality development of African American youth. Moynihan explained,

> The disorganized families have failed to provide for their emotional needs and have not provided the discipline and habits which are necessary for personality development. Because the disorganized family has failed in its function as a socializing agency, it has handicapped the children in their relations to the institutions in the community.[5]

While African American female migrants came to Detroit in search of better jobs, their daughters and granddaughters became the ire of policymakers.

Although African American girls may have encountered such images and policies, they created alternatives. Much like the Haitian schoolgirls featured in Katharine Capshaw's "Haitian Girls Perform Resistance in the Wake of U.S. Occupation," who turned to performance art as a means of crafting a diasporic consciousness, African American girls coming of age during the 1970s turned to nontraditional sites of education to explore alternative ideas about blackness, and subsequently, Black girlhood. In Malcolm X's speeches, high school youth found a history of African and Asian nations that sought to break the stronghold of colonialism and imperialism. For example, students often turned to Malcolm X's "Message to the Grassroots" where he encouraged activists to consider the Bandung Conference of 1955 as a model for gaining Black political power. Representatives from several African and Asian nations attended the conference—including leaders from Ethiopia, Egypt, Iran, Iraq, Liberia, Libya, and Thailand—in hopes of building economic, political, and social sovereignty and collaboration among formerly colonized peoples.[6] African American youth who witnessed struggles for independence also learned a great deal about these movements from African theorists and activists. From Amilcar Cabral's writings, they discovered a history of the African Party for Independence of Guinea and Cape Verde (PAIGC)'s struggle to achieve liberation from Portugal. Black high school student activists took the ideas and histories that animated decolonization struggles into their communities and school hallways using mimeographed newspapers that they self-published. For example, the editors of Highland Park High School's *Black Student Voice* presented a brief history of PAIGC's movement in its fourth issue, and asked students to consider the methods Cabral and the PAIGC used to "defeat Portugal's white domination."[7] The tumultuous global 1960s presented a world of possibilities for Black girls to connect with histories and cultures that, for decades, had been absent in their textbooks. The speeches and writings of such prominent diasporic thinkers ultimately helped to expand African American girls' diasporic imaginations and their ability to envision their path to this world of possibilities. Engaging in the process of self-discovery against the backdrop of liberation movements offered them a great sense of self-pride and a desire to learn about their relationship to the African diaspora.

For African American girls who were politically active in the Black Power movement (1965–1975), formal and informal education along with beauty culture became two critical sites of struggle that offered a window into the possibilities of a diasporic Black girlhood. Each arena provided Black girls the space to consider their relationship to the African Diaspora. While education presented them with the opportunity to explore their relationship to the continent as historical actors and change agents, their engagement with Eurocentric beauty culture promised to create alternative images of Black girlhood and Black womanhood that relied on American understandings of blackness, Africa, and notions of beauty. In waging struggles for a culturally relevant curriculum at schools like Cass Technical High and against Eurocentric beauty standards, Black adolescent female activists revealed the possibilities of a diasporic Black girlhood.[8]

When African Americans arrived in Detroit during the second Great Migration (1945–1965), they imagined a world with schools that would prepare their children for a life independent of the sharecropping system that was the cornerstone of the southern economy. Although African American women did not always explicitly discuss the futures of Black girls, Black women's escape from violence in southern households suggests that they envisioned a life for their daughters that freed them from domestic and workplace violence. And yet, the children of migrants would encounter draconian dress policies, a curriculum that embraced ideas about Black racial inferiority, and social policies that depicted them as a social problem as they came of age during the 1950s and 1960s. Nevertheless, carrying forward the tradition of political struggle, African American girls went on to organize against these measures and to craft a vision of Black girlhood that encapsulated their desires for self-determination and self-discovery as movement activists. As members of high school organizations such as the Black Student United Front (BSUF), the student component of the Detroit-based League of Revolutionary Black Workers, the Black Panther Party, and independent student groups, African American girls organized political education classes in freedom schools and liberation schools, led walkouts in high schools, and created community organizations. The Black Power movement's commitment to developing a new Black aesthetic that valued the experiences and culture of the African diaspora greatly informed Black girls' politics and activism and helped to reshape the world they had inherited from their parents. [9]

While many proponents of Black Power asserted Black racial manhood, the movement's battles to revise the Euro-centric curriculum, beauty standards, and school governance simultaneously presented Black girls with a new conception of blackness and Black girlhood. By the end of the 1960s, Black girls saw women like high fashion model Joanna LaSane wear natural hairstyles on the cover of *Jet Magazine*. This era also brought the emergence of powerful Black anthems such as James Brown's "Say It Loud—I'm Black and I'm Proud" (1968), Nina Simone's "To be Young, Gifted and Black" (1969), and Aretha Franklin's "Respect" (1967).[10] With the tools provided by the Black Power movement's Black aesthetic, Black female high school activists constructed an image of Black girlhood that uprooted and complicated popular conceptions of Black girls' lives.

Jametta Lily drew upon the movement's commitment to a Black aesthetic in her battle to make the high school curriculum more relevant to her life. When she urged the administration at Cass Technical High School to include the Katherine Dunham dance technique in the curriculum, Lily called for the decolonization of American ideas about the Black body. According to the scholar and choreographer Ojeya Cruz Banks, Dunham used her expertise as an anthropologist and choreographer to introduce dance as a form of liberation. Banks writes, "As a choreographer, she brought movement and parts of the body not activated by European dance to the American stage; and as a dance researcher and educator she discovered important knowledge embedded in African dance of the diaspora to foster self-knowledge in African American communities and her students." She continues, "The purpose of her dance education was about returning dance to 'its roots in communal loving' . . . and drawing from the historical and cultural knowledge embodied in dance." Turning towards Dunham and away from the Eurocentric stylings of ballet and the Eurocentric curriculum, Lily's demands created a space for Black girls to locate themselves within the African diaspora through dance.[11] Though separated by space and time, it would seem that the Haitian schoolgirls of the 1930s who appear in Katharine Capshaw's study and the African American female youth activists of the 1970s created a kind of transhistorical diasporic Black girlhood and consciousness though their demands for and embrace of embodied performances.

While Black girls' demands for opportunities to center Black art and the possibilities for embodied performance provided a space for them to discover their relationship to the African diaspora, so too did the collective, informal educational spaces that were a hallmark of the Black Power movement. When the high school curriculum failed to address the lives of African American girls, and their personal and political concerns, these adolescent activists turned to consciousness-raising groups and political education classes. According to Shirikiana Aina, the high school activist who participated in the Cass Tech building takeover, these groups helped her identify herself as a member of the African diaspora. For Aina, self-discovery was especially important to her ability to navigate her biracial identity. In co-ed reading groups with friends, she read Adelle Davis' *Let's Eat Right to Keep Fit* and works by Amilcar Cabral, Malcolm X and Eldridge Cleaver. According to Aina, the 1960s and 1970s created an environment in which "self-discovery was mandatory." She explains:

> It was a grounding for everybody to find out 'yeah well this little stuff in my hair is okay, that the way that I talk, that our street talk is not because we don't know English. It's because it has a relationship to African languages. There's nothing more wholesome than to realize that you are not wrong, that everything about you is not wrong; that it simply has a relationship to Africa.

For Aina, these consciousness-raising groups ignited a life-long process of resolving global issues and of envisioning her contributions to larger political struggles. Engaging in this kind of self-discovery as a Black girl in the era of the War on Poverty, the War on Crime, and the Moynihan report empowered Aina and others like her to see their place in the world, not as a problem, but as change agents who possessed roots in Africa.[12]

The process of self-discovery was especially important for Black girls who had to navigate the residual effects of the 1940s "All-American boy" and "All-American girl" in popular U.S. culture. According to the first issue of the citywide *Black Student Voice*, "The All-American . . . is white, has crew-cut hair, is on the football, basketball, baseball and/or swim team, is on honor roll, in the student council, and in the R.O.T.C. or its equivalent." The editors described the image of the All-American girl as "white, has bouncy blond hair, is healthy and carefree, is as 'American as Apple Pie,' loves America, hates communism, and 'some of her best friends are 'Negros,' or more common none of her friends are 'niggers.'" These "All-American" tropes characterized white boys and girls with blond hair and letterman's jackets as the model American adolescent. The Black Power movement and the Black Arts movement pushed back against this version of white supremacy and socialization of Black and white youth. In their own lives, Black youth activists offered a critique of sentimentalized adolescence as the first step in their efforts to advance an alternative vision of Black girlhood.[13]

The Black Power movement challenged Eurocentric notions of beauty that had animated many of the core beliefs of white supremacy, while the Black Studies movement contested long-held beliefs about the educational value of Black cultural productions. The redefinition of Black beauty offered by both movements was especially important to African American girls who came into their adolescence just a decade after youth became a targeted group for the advertisement industry. During the 1950s, advertisement agencies viewed youth as the largest group of consumers of music, clothes, and beauty products. The Black Power movement's reconceptualization of beauty standards was especially impactful for Black girls because of the ideas about gender, race, and girlhood they encountered in school hallways and in popular culture.[14]

African American girls who organized alongside the League of Revolutionary Black Workers also gained access to alternative images of Black girlhood and the possibilities of Black womanhood from many of the organization's adult female members. As a case in point, Marian Kramer, a former member of the Student Nonviolent Coordinating Committee (SNCC) and founding member of the League, facilitated discussions about gender exploitation with male and female high school students who joined the Black Student United Front. She used readings such as *No More Fun and Games: A Journal of Female Liberation* to help students develop an analysis of the conditions that shaped African American women's exploitation and the important role of capitalism in crafting that exploitation. The journal addressed topics such as "Female Liberation as the Basis for Black Women's Liberation" and "What Do Women Want?"[15] These debates allowed male and female student activists to study and recognize gender oppression, lessons that they did not likely encounter in the traditional high school classroom. Furthermore, they revealed the long history of women's political activism to African American girls who would not wait to carry forth the tradition as adults; they had decided to wage political struggle as fourteen-, fifteen-, and sixteen-year-old activists.

As foot soldiers and theorists in the movement for the development of a culturally relevant curriculum, African American teenagers joined the ranks of Black teachers who began these struggles in previous years. Throughout the 20th century, progressive and radical educators demanded revisions to textbooks that depicted African Americans as racially inferior, that claimed enslaved communities did not resist, and that supported the view that "slavery was benign." In their classrooms, they confronted a curriculum which suggested that African Americans had had not made contributions to world history. These educators proclaimed that "American education was a partner in the perpetuation of racism."[16] In Detroit, Black teachers worked alongside local activists to create alternative models of education. One such organization, the Black Teachers Caucus, emerged out of a collaboration between the Black Church and young, Black teachers from Detroit's public schools. As a subcommittee of the Shrine of Black Madonna's Action Council, the caucus sought to harness the Black Church's power and Black Nationalist philosophy in its protracted struggle for the minds of Detroit's youth. According to the Caucus' objectives, "Every action by Black teachers must be designed to prepare Black children to participate in the liberation struggle and achieve self-determination for the Black community." The pedagogical aims of these teachers' organizations sometimes reflected the patriarchal ethos of the broader society. For example, the caucus argued that "anything that weakens the struggle is immoral (the dream of integration is therefore immoral, while an ADC family which relates children meaningfully to the liberation struggle is moral in a profound sense which transcends the question of a child's 'legitimacy or illegitimacy')."[17]

Lessons from the Shrine's Summer School examined Black family life through the prism of Black Christian Nationalism. In-class questions asked students to consider what constituted a family. Some questions explored topics like who the head of the household should be, "what makes a Black family weak or strong, and what factors demonstrate if a family is 'together' or 'not together.'" The lesson plan also featured a "NO NO" chart for the Black family, which included illustrations of white Christ, interracial married couples, a Black woman emulating white women's culture, and a drug scene. The questions outlined in the curriculum revealed the school's conception of an authentic Black family as one that worshipped a Black God, embraced a Black beauty aesthetic, and believed in only marriages between Black people. While it is not clear what African American girls thought of these images and ideas about family, the curriculum offers a window into the ideas educators who attended this program likely brought into their classrooms.[18]

However, African American girls also likely encountered Black educators who compared the conditions of African Americans to the struggles of communities fighting for independence in Africa and Asia. The African American Teachers Association (AATA), a national organization which formed in 1964, explained its concerns in "Mandate for Community Action in School Crisis." The organization wanted to see concepts like "self-control, self-determination, and self-defense" practiced in the realm of Black education, and they sought an end to school segregation, which they defined as a means through which outsiders exploited and controlled educational institutions. Black educators, according to the mandate, "wanted an end to this form of colonialism, an end to this brand of absentee ownership, an end to this form of educational imperialism and the beginning of self-control and self-determination for Black and Puerto Rican people."[19] African American educators, and the informal and formal educational spaces they created, had far-reaching effects that emerged beyond the classroom.

The personal revealed that the political mattered to adolescent activists because the political shaped their personal lives at every turn. The Black Studies movement, which was born out of resistance to Eurocentric educational models, was a part of a global battle against white supremacy. With the emergence of a new Black aesthetic that eschewed Eurocentric notions of beauty, Black people's physical bodies became sites of this struggle. Black girls best embodied the birth of this aesthetic. African American girls who were of a darker hue, like Cassandra Ford, a founding member of the Black Student United Front, exposed just how deeply personal the political struggle for culturally relevant curriculum was to African American youth. Ford spent much of her childhood in the home her grandmother purchased in a predominantly white neighborhood. As a child, Ford viewed fashion models as role models but quickly learned that Black girls like her had limited examples to look up to for inspiration. Ford explains,

> As a child, I looked at models, but I always knew that I couldn't be one. I used to always think that was just so wonderful to be able to do that, for a whole lot of reasons. I figured that I couldn't be that because I was Black, number one. And at that time, most of them were all white.

While dark-skinned girls like Ford came of age with African American female celebrities like Nina Simone and Cicely Tyson, Ford suggested that she had very few role models to whom she could relate. The desire to see herself, as a little Black girl, in the popular images of Black women shaped much of her childhood and later informed her fight for culturally relevant curriculum.[20]

With the Black Arts Movement and Motown taking center stage in American popular culture, the ability of Black girls to see themselves as connected to a global cultural phenomenon expanded. In 1968, just one year after the Detroit Rebellion, soul and funk artist James Brown released "Say It Loud—I'm Black and I'm Proud." When Brown crooned, "Say it louder, I'm Black and I'm proud," teenaged girls like Ford and Toni Jones found a counter narrative to what they had been taught and heard about dark-skinned girls in school. Ford states,

> Because I was dark skin, I was always teased about being Black. And then James Brown came out with *I'm Black and I'm Proud*. Hey! Say it loud. Choo choo. And all of that affects you. I think I was doing it [organizing] because of that too. I don't think you should have to be talked about or be teased because of the color of your skin.[21]

The association between dark skin and Africa as the "Dark Continent" absent of culture and civilization was a common one.[22] And yet, Ford saw in soul music a path from the teasing of her peers to student organizations that sought to exorcise such ideas from the curriculum. According to Jeffrey Ogbar, "Soul music was a very common, somewhat generic, term for phenomena that reflected the unique qualities of 'blackness.' For many black artists, its overtly black style safeguarded it against white cooption, unlike jazz and rock and roll." The genre "reflected the new black mood of resistance and self-determination that pervaded black communities after 1966."[23] While Brown's own politics may not have aligned with the movement's politics often, Ford saw that song, and soul music more broadly, as an accessible way for rethinking the meaning and possibilities of blackness and Black girlhood.

Jones, who was not a member of the League but had participated in student protests for a short period, shared a similar experience. Before Brown released the song, Jones disliked her brown skin so much that she tried to brighten it with bleaching cream as a teenager. Part of Jones' contempt for her skin color was informed by comments made by family members and experiences with Black boys who preferred to dance with light-skinned girls at junior high school dances. For these Black girls, the Black Power movement, and its influence on popular culture, gave them the space to re-conceptualize blackness and Black girlhood. They were no longer the negative alternative to the "All-American Girl" or evidence of Black dependence upon the state; rather, they were a part of the Black experience that was worthy of celebration.[24] Furthermore, it suggested that popular culture was itself an educational force.

African American girls turned to cultural icons and popular ideas about Africa to make sense of their relationship to blackness and to the African diaspora. When James Brown released "Say It Loud—I'm Black and I'm Proud," Toni Jones looked at herself in a different way. Not only did she feel pretty, but she also loved the "nappiness" of her hair, which, she joked, girls with straight hair couldn't achieve. As a pre-teen, Jones hated swim class for many reasons. One of her principal concerns was that the water caused her hair to curl up into its natural state since her mother pressed her hair often. Conversations with friends about hair were a constant presence in Toni's life. They considered "nappy" to be bad but viewed wavy or fine hair as good. Most of her friends had long hair, but in Toni's words, she had "bad" hair. She and one of her best girlfriends gave each other perms. Once she started to attend Mumford High School, however, she began to wear her hair in an Afro. Jones' mother resisted this change with great persistence. But Jones continued to wear her Afro, except for the times her mother pressed her hair for prom, senior pictures, and graduation. Most of her friends wore Afros, though not as consistently as she had. When they began to wear afros, they often discussed preferences for certain hair oils and sprays like Carson's Ultra Sheen. Another young activist named Jeri Love found herself, like Toni, at the intersection of hair politics and Black Power politics. Love's decision to grow her hair natural developed out of her interest in Maasai women's culture. As a teenager, Love cut her hair in the spirit of the Maasai women who she believed wore their hair short in support of Maasai men and to show that they, too, were indigenous warriors.[25]

As Black adolescents found their voices in political organizations and underground presses, the Black Power movement's demands for community control and self-determination permeated their personal lives. As such, parents, teachers, and community activists sought to instill in Black youth a positive self-image and conception of blackness. Black popular culture icons also asserted claims that Black was beautiful and that it was a great achievement to be "Young, Gifted, and Black."[26] In daily life, Black youth demonstrated their pride in Black culture through hair and language. Their experiences suggest that the Black Power movement's resistance to white supremacy and its embrace of a Black aesthetic offered Black girls something that the civil rights movement's focus on desegregation did not: a vision of the self as whole, as a being connected to the larger African diaspora.[27] As the relationship between Black youth's sense of self and their fight for culturally relevant curriculum strengthened simultaneously, African American culture played an integral role in the construction of personal politics. Black cultural productions of music and art—the Black aesthetic that was at the heart of the movement—provided Black girls with a language to articulate their own conceptions of Black girlhood and to envision their relationship to the African diaspora. They resisted Eurocentric notions of beauty as they amplified the Black Power movement's calls for self-determination. And as activists, they found the political to be liberating in their personal lives, even when the political became complicated by the movement's internal gender politics.

In their collective study communities, in their engagements with the speeches and writings of Black diasporic thinkers, and in their embrace of Black popular culture, African American female activists of the 1960s and 1970s imagined themselves to be a part of a global Black community, not as passive youths but as active political thinkers. Even though they had yet to travel to the countries they encountered in these sources, they found a world beyond the limitations that their grandmothers and grandfathers encountered as migrants to Detroit decades before.

By using the tools of social history and Black feminist thought, we can explore Black girls' diasporic imaginations within a local context. Social history reveals the role of high school youth's familial and community networks and their inner lives in the development of Black youth politics, which made liberatory education possible. Black feminist thought provides a window into social movement pedagogy as constitutive of the many forms that education took in the daily lives of Black youth, from popular culture to the street corner.[28] Furthermore, using Black feminist thought's focus on embodied discourse, intersectionality, and the "everydayness" of Black women's resistance, this study illuminates the political experiences that shaped the high school movement, as well as how the personal and gendered politics of hair, dress, and love animated demands for liberatory education. Together, these frameworks reveal Black girls' own conceptions of a global Black girlhood that is grounded in the everydayness of young people's lives.

Future research may address how the tools of historical anthropology might enrich our understanding of Black girls' ideas about cultural or regional kinship and their process of self-discovery. Furthermore, scholars may explore how other histories will become legible when they begin to read artifacts of the Black aesthetic from the perspective of Black girls. For Black girls like Aina, Ford, and Jones, the struggle for a culturally relevant curriculum was much more than another site of struggle for the Black Power movement. It was also the means through which they could articulate and realize their own conceptions of blackness, beauty, and power. In an era where movement spaces abounded for women's liberation and Black power, Black girls accessed an intersectional approach to their activism in and beyond the schoolyard.

Notes

1. Portions of this chapter were included in my dissertation, Dara Walker, "Black power, education, and youth politics in Detroit, 1966–1973," (PhD diss., Rutgers University, 2018); Shirikiana Aina, interview with the author, September 11, 2010, in the author's possession; Jametta Lily, interview with the author, November 3, 2015, in the author's possession.

2. Pero Dagbovie, *The Early Black History Movement, Carter G. Woodson, and Lorenzo Johnston Greene* (Champaign: University of Illinois Press, 2007).

3. Ibram Rogers, *The Black Campus Movement: Black Students and the Racial Reconstitution of Higher Education, 1965–1972* (New York, Palgrave Macmillan, 2012); Donna Murch, *Living for the City: Migration, Education and the Rise of the Black Panther Party in Oakland California* (Chapel Hill: The University of North Carolina Press, 2010); Martha Biondi, *The Black Revolution on Campus* (Berkeley: The University of California Press, 2012); Jon Hale, "'The Fight Was Instilled in Us': High School Student Activism and the Civil Rights Movement in Charleston," *South Carolina Historical Magazine* 114, no. 1 (January 2013): 4–28; Jeanne Theoharis, "'W-A-L-K-O-U-T!': High School Students and the Development of Black Power in L.A," in *Neighborhood Rebels: Black Power at the Local Level*, ed. Peniel Joseph (New York: Palgrave Macmillan, 2010), 107–130; Dionne Danns, "Chicago High School Students' Movement for Quality Public Education, 1966–1971," *Journal of African American History* 88, no. 2 (2003): 138–149; and Rebecca De Schweinitz, *If We Could Change the World: Young People and America's Long Struggle for Racial Equality* (Chapel Hill: University of North Carolina Press, 2009). For the historiography on Detroit's postwar urban crisis, see Thomas Sugrue, *Origins of the Urban Crisis* (Princeton: Princeton University Press, 1996) and Heather Ann Thompson, *Whose Detroit?: Politics, Labor, and Race in a Modern American City* (Ithaca: Cornell University Press, 2001).

4. Daniel P. Moynihan, "Chapter IV: The Tangle of Pathology," in *The Negro Family: The Case for National Action*, Washington, D.C., Office of Policy Planning and Research, U.S. Department of Labor, 1965.

5. For more on "youth-centered racial liberalism," see Rebecca de Schweinitz, *If We Could Change the World: Young People and America's Long Struggle for Racial Equality* (Chapel Hill, N.C.: The University of North Carolina Press, 2009); Moynihan, "Chapter V: The Case for National Action."

6. Malik Yakini, interview with the author, July 23, 2010; *Malcolm X Speaks: Selected Speeches and Statements*, edited by George Breitman (New York: Grove Weidenfeld, 1990), 3–17; The Ministry of Foreign Affairs, Republic of Indonesia (Ed.). *Asia-Africa speak from Bandung* (Djakarta: 1955), 161–169, https://www.cvce.eu/en/obj/final_communique_of_the_asian_african_conference_of_bandung_24_april_1955-en-676237bd-72f7-471f-949a-88b6ae513585.html

7. Aliou Ly, "Revisiting the Guinea Bissau Liberation War: PAIGC, UDEMU and the Women's Rights and Emancipation Question, 1963–1974," in *Portuguese Journal of Social Science* 14, no. 3 (2015): 361–377; Highland Park High *Black Student Voice* 1, no. 4 (2/13/70), General Gordon Baker's Personal Collection, in the author's possession.

8. For more on gender relations in the Black Power movement, see Robyn Spencer, *The Revolution Has Come: Black Power, Gender, and the Black Panther Party in Oakland* (Durham: Duke University Press, 2016) and Ashley Farmer, *Remaking Black Power: How Black Women Transformed an Era* (Chapel Hill: The University of North Carolina Press, 2017).

9. Darlene Clark Hine, "Black Migration to the Urban Midwest: The Gender Dimension, 1915–1945," in *The Great Migration in Historical Perspective*, ed. Joe William Trotter (Bloomington: Indiana University Press, 1991). Annelise Orleck, *Storming Caesar's Palace: How Black Mothers Fought Their Own War on Poverty* (Boston: Beacon Press, 2005). For more on Black girls' experiences during the Great Migration and Jim Crow, see Marcia Chatelain, *South Side Girls: Growing Up in the Great Migration* (Durham: Duke University Press, 2015), Lakisha Simmons, *Crescent City Girls: The Lives of Young Black Women in Segregated New Orleans* (Chapel Hill: The University of North Carolina Press, 2015), and Paula C. Austin, *Coming of Age in Jim Crow DC: Navigating the Politics of Everyday Life* (New York: New York University Press, 2019).

10. "Cover," *Jet Magazine*, Johnson Publishing Company, November 10, 1966, https://books.google.com/books?id=jLgDAAAAMBAJ&printsec=frontcover&source=gbs_ge_summary_r&cad=0#v=onepage&q&f=false; James Brown, "Say It Loud—I'm Black and I'm Proud," Vox Studios, 1968; Nina Simone, "To Be Young, Gifted and Black," Stroud Productions, 1969; and Aretha Franklin, "Respect," Atlantic Records, 1967.

11. Ojeya Cruz Banks, "Katherine Dunham: Decolonizing Dance Education" in *Education as Liberation: African American Educational Thought and Activism*, eds. Noel S. Anderson and Haroon Kharem (Lanham: Lexington Books, 2009), 121–137.

12. Shirikiana Aina, interview with the author, September 11, 2010; Adelle Davis, *Let's Eat Right to Keep Fit* (New York: Signet Books, 1970); Eldridge Cleaver, *Soul on*

Ice (New York: Ramparts Press Inc., 1968). For more on teenagers and consciousness-raising groups, see Kera Lovell, "Girls Are Equal Too: Education, Body Politics, and the Making of Teenage Feminism," *Gender Issues*, vol. 33 (June 2016): 71–95.

13. *Citywide Black Student Voice* 1/1970, General Gordon Baker, Personal Collection, in the author's possession; For an excellent study of the Black Arts Movement, see James Smethurst, *The Black Arts Movement: Literary Nationalism in the 1960s and 1970s* (Chapel Hill: University of North Carolina Press, 2005).

14. Lizabeth *Cohen, A Consumers' Republic: The Politics of Mass Consumption in Postwar America* (New York: Vintage, 2004).

15. Gregory Hicks, interview with the author, July 2017; *No More Fun and Games: A Journal of Female Liberation* 1, no. 1, Women's Liberation Movement Print Culture Digital Collection, Duke University Libraries.

16. For recent historical scholarship on Black teachers' resistance to the traditional curriculum, see Jarvis Givens, *Fugitive Pedagogy: Carter G. Woodson and the Art of Black Teaching* (Cambridge: Harvard University Press, 2021); Detroit Federation of Teachers, "Proposed Conference on Negro History," 1967, AFT: Human Rights and Community Relations Department Collection, Box 1, Folder 12, Archives of Labor and Urban Affairs, Wayne State University; Detroit Board of Education, "Selection of Textbooks," June 25, 1968, Detroit Board of Education/Detroit Public Schools Collection, Box 35, Archives of Labor and Urban Affairs, Wayne State University; "Teaching Negro History in Detroit Schools." *Detroit Schools*, March 12, 1968; Detroit Board of Education/Detroit Public Schools Collection, Box 88, Folder 4, Archives of Labor and Urban Affairs, Wayne State University; "Educators Plan More Action on Racism in Classroom Textbooks." *Detroit Schools*, October 29, 1968, Detroit Board of Education/Detroit Public Schools Collection, Box 88, Folder 4, Archives of Labor and Urban Affairs, Wayne State University.

17. Black Teachers Caucus, reel 16, Albert B. Cleage Jr. papers, Bentley Historical Library, University of Michigan. ADC refers to Aid to Dependent Children, a means-tested federal program to provide financial support to children in low-income families.

18. Black Teachers Caucus, reel 16.; Shrine of the Black Madonna Summer School of Black Studies (1970), roll 17, Albert B. Cleage Jr. Papers, Bentley Historical Library, University of Michigan.

19. "Mandate for Community Action in School Crisis," roll 16, Albert B. Cleage Jr. Papers, Bentley Historical Library, University of Michigan.

20. Cassandra Ford, interview with the author, August 5, 2010.

21. Cassandra Ford, interview with the author, August 5, 2010.

22. Z.O. Ekimwere, "Exploring a paradigm shift: The New York Times' framing of sub-Saharan Africa in stories of conflict, war and development during the Cold War and post-Cold War eras, 1945–2009," PhD diss. (University of South Carolina, 2013). Retrieved from https://scholarcommons.sc.edu/etd/2618.

23. Jeffrey Ogbar, *Black Power, Radical Politics and African American Identity* (Baltimore: Johns Hopkins University Press, 2004), 110.

24. Toni Jones, interview with the author, July 10, 2010.

25. Toni Jones, interview with the author, July 20, 2010; and Jeri Love, interview with the author, October 20, 2015.

26. James Brown (1968) and Nina Simone (1967).

27. Shirikiana Aina, interview with the author, September 11, 2010.

28. For more on movement pedagogy, see Russell Rickford, *We Are an African People: Independent Education, Black Power, and the Radical Imagination* (Oxford: Oxford University Press, 2016); Daniel Perlstein, "Freedom, Liberation, Accommodation: Politics and Pedagogy in SNCC and the Black Panther Party," in *Teach Freedom: Education for Liberation in the African American Tradition*, eds. Charles M. Payne and Carol Sills Strickland (New York: Teachers College Press, 2008), 75–94.

CHAPTER 12

A Disciplined and Sweet Environment

Girls' Work and Lives at the Government Reformatory in Jamaica, 1869–1937

SHANI ROPER

Children's voices are rare in the traditional colonial archives of the Caribbean. For example, in 1877, the colonial government instituted a commission of inquiry investigating the juvenile population but failed to interview any young people. Instead, adults spoke extensively about the misbehavior of Black working-class children and juveniles throughout the country. Given this silence within the archive, Jamaica's industrial schools provide a unique space to investigate the inner workings of colonial institutions for children and especially in relation to the experiences of Black girls.[1] Though Black boys outnumbered girls in these institutions, the archive provides us with some information about the daily lives and experiences of Black girls. In this chapter, I explore how Black girls lived while institutionalized in Jamaica's Government Reformatory and Industrial School (GRIS) between 1869 and 1937. The GRIS records give some insight into how colonial reformatories functioned and into the everyday lives of Black girls living there.[2] I argue that the industrial school archive reveals that very few Black girls were institutionalized because colonial government was more interested in crafting Black male laborers and citizens. While Black girls' labor was valuable to the school administrators, ultimately, financial concerns outweighed the Jamaican colonial government's commitment to providing Black girls with access to an industrial education.

As the oldest government run children's institution at the time, the GRIS admitted both boys and girls from 1869 until 1937 when the girls' institution closed. It provided the most expansive industrial education programme in Jamaica. An industrial education focused on agriculture and skills such as baking, tailoring or dressmaking, blacksmithing, carpentry, and laundry work—all the skills deemed important to sustaining a labor-based economy. Similar institutions during this period employed variations of the GRIS educational programme.[3] Consequently, there exists an extensive archive on policies, programmes, and the care of children living in the institution. Given the paucity of court records, this archive provides useful insight into attitudes towards children, enabling us to speak about their daily lives and speculate about their experiences.

Reformatories and Industrial Schools emerged within a larger context where newly freed Black Jamaicans exercised their right to move, build homes away from former slave masters, and control their children's labor. This social and economic independence threatened the white hegemonic community's sense of economic well-being, as the island's economy was dependent on cheap Black labor. As a form of vagrancy legislation, Jamaican authorities used reformatory legislation to police and control the movement of Black working-class children.[4] The Reformatory and Industrial Schools Act targeted children between the ages of five and sixteen years who were convicted of crimes or found begging, orphaned, and abandoned without evidence of parental support or a place to live. Officials argued that Black families were unstable and that their poverty resulted from laziness and immorality. Unstable Black families, they argued, created lazy and immoral children. Newspaper accounts reinforced this perception, pointing to unruly behavior among Black boys such as stone throwing, indecent language, drunkenness, and fighting in the streets.[5] Colonial officials and elites identified industrial schools and reformatories as the ideal space to reform youth, especially boys in conflict with the law.[6]

The majority of the Jamaican children housed in state run institutions or reliant upon poor relief were Black. Institutionalized children were classified by ethnic, religious, and socio-economic groups. Within this context, blackness in Jamaica was a social category mediated by class, access to education, economic mobility, and religion. In fact, records only mention a child's ethnic, class, and/racial composition when it was the exception to the rule, which was to be Black and poor. Separate institutions housed children of different religious groups and those of higher economic standing. The Wortley Home (established 1923) in St. Andrew was created for girls of Indian descent and more "respectable" classes. Alpha Cottage (established 1881, and later called Alpha Industrial School) catered to children from a Catholic background. Children of Indian descent, who fell under the Board of Immigration until 1917, were specifically consigned to the Lyndale Home or the Swift Home in the parishes of St. Mary and Portland respectively if orphaned or in need of care. The Government Reformatory and Industrial School, however, was a non-denominational institution that catered to the Black majority. All girls sent to the GRIS were of African descent unless the record explicitly stated otherwise.

Gender as well as race also informed colonial policies. The state invested more resources in boys' industrial education during this time as it regarded boys as future citizens who could contribute to economic and cultural production. This may have exacerbated the fact that boys outnumbered girls five to one at the institution. Administrators at the GRIS argued that an industrial education could benefit girls as well as boys, but judges and colonial officials focused more attention on the rehabilitation of boys. Whenever possible, judges sent Black girls back to their communities. This gender disparity allows for two possibilities. The first is that the pathologization of the Black family did not create a policy framework identifying Black girls as being permanently tainted by criminality or destitution. Or, it may be that the colonial state did not deem Black girls' potential as workers and citizens to be a valuable investment. What we do know, however, is that institutionalization of Black girls was the exception to the rule. Many Black girls reintegrated into their communities after being brought before the courts while boys were institutionalized under the control of a state intent on shaping their future citizenship. My focus here, therefore, is the small group of girls housed at the institution during the period under review.

The Early Years 1857–1889

When the Government Reformatory and Industrial School opened in 1869, it inherited the administrators, students, and educational programme of its predecessors, the Kingston and St. Andrew Reformatory for Girls (established 1857) and the St. George's Home and Reformatory for Boys (established 1858), which were managed by the Ladies Reformatory Association and a general management committee, respectively. Children convicted of crimes and those orphaned and destitute lived together in both institutions until 1868, when financial insolvency forced the colonial government to assume full oversight of both the boys' and the girls' institutions.[7] One-hundred-and-sixty-eight boys and seventy-one girls moved to the new Stony Hill location in October and November of 1869, respectively. Our focus, therefore, begins with these seventy-one girls whose time at the original reformatory would inform their experiences at the new institution.

The original goal of the 1858 girls' reformatory was to bring forth "a class of servants who have been trained in the principles of the word of God."[8] Their education emphasized religious instruction as well as basic vocational training in the areas of starch-making, straw hat making, weeding, and preparing the grounds for a small garden.[9] All girls received training as domestics by working in the kitchen and the laundry room. More importantly, they washed laundry from the community to raise funds to supplement subscriptions from several societies in London including the Ladies Negro Education Society and the Society of Friends.[10] Growing and ginning cotton as well as washing clothes kept the girls busy all year. Several of them received training as seamstresses.[11] They attended a day school while at the same time taking turns in the duties of housekeeping and cooking. The Managing Committee tried to place girls to work with "respectable families" as domestics. Of the five girls that left the institution between 1861 and 1862, two girls were dismissed from their employment for suspected wrongdoing such as stealing.[12] The Managing Committee withdrew their support from those who failed to live up to their training after leaving the reformatory.

Their lives, however, changed once they moved to Stony Hill. Between 1869 and 1877, the governor convened two commissions of inquiry to investigate rumours of disfigurement, abuse, and debility at the institution. The 1875 Inquiry included the testimony of three boys—Francis Grant (institutionalised 1868–1873), Edward Sims (institutionalised 1870–1875) and a current inmate, Alexander Berry—which revealed details of daily life for both boys and girls.[13] Girls lived in the South Barracks, which housed the laundry, while the boys resided in the North Barracks. Administrators considered the socializing of boys and girls a severe crime, but the inmates managed to interact with each other. The record indicates that they wrote letters, and there is evidence of some level of physical interaction, sexual violence, and intimacy. Grant and Berry were beaten severely by Superintendent Melville for "holding intercourse" with the girls based on a letter found in a girl's clothing in the laundry. The girl, whose name was never mentioned, was also punished for participating in the subterfuge.[14]

Examples of the silencing of Black girls' voices within the institution can be found. In 1877, several girls reported an incident of potential sexual violence to the Board of Visitors. The Board of Visitors inspected the institution more than twice a year to ensure that the administrators ran it efficiently and that the children were not subject to abuse. On December 10, 1877, several girls accused a boy, described as a "hermaphrodite," of "lecherous conduct and attempt at assault" the night before. A physical examination by Dr. Campbell and Mr. Phillippo, a member of the Board of Visitors, found that the inmate was actually male but "with organs so underdeveloped as to render him incapable of distinctly criminal assault."[15] Though the adults dismissed the girls' claims, they had a very clear definition of assault that had nothing to do with the size of a male's organ. The incident hints that the administration may not have been as effective at maintaining the boundaries between both groups given that the indecent exposure occurred at night. It also reveals that some individuals did not fit easily into the gendered binary established by the institution. The lack of records, however, prevents us from accessing the administrators' or the juveniles' own interpretation of gender roles and sexual intercourse.

Fears about intimacy among inmates may have contributed to school administrators' belief that the girls suffered in both their education and socialization by being institutionalized with boys at Stony Hill. After the 1877 inquiry, the Board of Visitors recommended the removal of the girls to Admiral's Pen, in Kingston, a decision which received support from Governor Sir Anthony Musgrave and Mr. Shaw, Inspector of Prisons. They believed that the move would enable a visiting committee of women from Kingston to see the girls more frequently and provide moral influence.[16] The potential for increased interaction between female inmates and women of the elite reflected reformers' cultural preoccupation with socializing girls to be good mothers and wives. In 1882, the girls were transferred to a new institution across from the Union Poor House in Admiral's Pen, and administrators converted their recently vacated dorms to accommodate boys. However, the numbers of girls institutionalized fell over time, and school administrators believed that it would be more financially prudent to return the girls to Stony Hill in 1899. The financial costs outweighed any benefits they gained by being in Kingston.

Why were so few Black girls institutionalized? Children entered industrial schools through the courts or the poor relief system. Unfortunately, the paucity of court records prevents us from making definitive conclusions about judges' perceptions about Black girls brought before the courts. The little we know is based on the lists of juvenile offenders brought before the court in 1931, 1932, 1934, and 1935, which included includes the age, gender, offence, and sentence received by the juveniles. In 1934, approximately 504 children and youth ranging from as young as three years to fifteen-and-a-half years came before the courts.[17] Of that number, only eighteen were girls. Further assessment of the 1931, 1932 and 1935 lists reveal similar figures. Very few girls were brought before the courts, and this had a direct impact on the demography of the GRIS population.

During the period 1869 to 1937, girls constituted 13–23 percent of an approximate population of 400 inmates residing at the Government Reformatory and Industrial School. Boys outnumbered girls five to one. In fact, during their tenure at the Admiral Pen location from 1882 to 1899, the number of girls fell to an all-time low of thirty-seven inmates in residence. It is possible to speculate that Black girls were kept close to home and were less likely to be in public spaces, but given the absence of corroborating evidence, this would be difficult to argue.[18]

The institution's annual reports provide a breakdown of the age and categories under which the girls were admitted. Throughout this period, most of the girls residing at the institution were between the ages of twelve and sixteen, with roughly half convicted of a crime and the rest destitute. For example, in 1878 out of a total of forty-two girls, thirty-five were between twelve and sixteen years and twenty-five of this number were categorized as criminal. Thirty-two years later, in 1910, forty-five girls lived on the compound, and of this number, forty-three were twelve to sixteen years old. Girls over twelve sometimes outnumbered younger inmates by a ratio of two to one.[19]

Over time, the overall number of girls at the reformatory declined from sixty-four in 1888 to thirty-seven in 1893. More significantly, the proportion of orphaned and abandoned girls increased while the number institutionalized for crimes decreased. In 1895, the editor of *The Gleaner*, Kingston's leading newspaper, noted that the police and the courts increasingly released girls into the care of the community rather than institutionalize them in the Reformatory. Most girls who entered the institution came through the poor relief infrastructure. Writers to *The Gleaner* protested this shift. They complained that sending girls back into their "unstable" home environments not only denied the girls access to an industrial education but also limited the possibility of utilizing these girls as laundresses and dressmakers. Several writers advocated the tightening of vagrancy laws and urged increased collaboration between the courts and the police to ensure that girls were institutionalized. The editor agreed. "While it is difficult to eradicate hereditary impulses of evil," he wrote, "a few years of discipline in a sweet environment must leave its trace on the natures of girls."[20] Hon. A. H. Alexander, Inspector of Prisons and Reformatories, posited that the "Reformatory and Industrial School can and does reclaim a great many from this class from ever becoming the reputed thief or constant inmate of a prison."[21] Similarly, Director of Prisons Mr. L.F. Knollys in his 1889 report reiterated this commitment to the re-socializing power of labor by arguing that the training that the girls received was likely to be of significant value to them when they reintegrated into society.[22] Both administrators and writers to *The Gleaner* pathologized the Black family and promoted institutionalization to access Black girls' labor.

A Sweet Environment: Girls' Lives and Work 1869–1937

Girls living at the institution were subjected to a regimented system of labor that emphasized agricultural work or skills associated with women's professions such as sewing, washing, and cooking. School administrators depended on children's labor as essential to the overall running of the institution. According to government reports, between 1869 and 1879, both boys and girls performed manual labor five to seven hours each day. No more than two to three hours on alternate days were spent in the classroom learning to read and write with five hours in recreation and eating. Children received free time on Saturday afternoons when friends and family visited between noon and 4:00 p.m. While the boys spent time in the fields, girls washed, sewed, and mended clothes.

Prior to their removal in 1882, the girls' activities centred in the laundry as the boys cooked, baked, farmed, and performed carpentry and mason work on the girls' buildings. Boys cultivated over fifty acres of farmland in a variety of foodstuff, which provided produce for the institution and for sale. Symbolically, this dynamic reflected Victorian ideas of gender roles that placed women as caretakers of the home and men as providers, thus reinforcing women's dependency on men. This dichotomy in the division of labor also occurred in response to the demography of the institution. Boys outnumbered girls, therefore, administrators invested less in girls' education. Short-changing their education, however, stood in opposition to Afro-Jamaican working-class community values. In working-class communities, Black women divided their attention between the home and the market, contributing equally with men to family support. In fact, Afro Jamaican women dominated the market system and were essential to food security within the island.

The girls' labor was of more value to the survival of industrial schools than to the wider public or to the girls' themselves. Girls' work in the 1880s contributed £476 to the institution account, thus lowering the cost of maintaining each child, which varied each year depending on the number of children living on the grounds. In 1883, the girls sewed 1,700 pieces of clothing, mended 6,750, and washed 21,881. By the 1890s, girls provided laundry services to the Jamaica Female Training School at Shortwood in the parish of St. Andrew, to the Immigration Department, and to private citizens. Throughout this period, administrators repeatedly expressed concern about the poor quality of education that the girls received in relation to the boys, but very little was done to rectify this problem. In fact, the girls remained in the shadow of the boys throughout the institution's existence.

This was exceptionally clear in the late 1920s and 1930s when investment in girls' education declined further and administrators did little to alter the girls' curriculum. The girls sewed for the school, did laundry work, and cooked. In April 1934, a company of Girl Guides formed. The island's Secretary, Mrs. K.H. Bourne, supported this effort, initiating a hobby class where girls learned to crotchet and make hats from banana trash. By July, Superintendent James Mair reported that the Girl Guides attended the Rally at Kings House and won the hat-making competition while earning second place in the Games.[23] Women of the Victorian League of Jamaica hosted a Christmas Dinner for the girls. Despite these efforts, the girls' education continued to pale in comparison to boys.

The boys' curriculum was far more diverse. The skills taught to boys at Stony Hill included carpentry, blacksmith, tailoring, masonry, cooking, and baking, as well as general agricultural work. Boys engaged in work for the institution, for the Girls' Department (until 1935), and for the general public. In March 1932, Superintendent James Mair reported that thirty-six boys learning carpentry repaired buildings on the institution as well as making, repairing, and polishing a variety of furniture for the general public. In June 1932, the twenty boys in the Mason's Department built a new kitchen for the Girls Department and converted an old school room into a dining room.[24]

The boys displayed their work at fairs and participated in competitions and national events such as the All Jamaica Exhibition in 1932.[25] In February 1934, they sent their handiwork to the Jamaica and Empire Trade Exhibition and Fair.[26] The Boy Scouts attended the Farewell Rally to outgoing governor Sir Edward Stubbs while the Band participated in the Welcome Rally for new governor Sir Ransford Slater.[27] In December 1933, the boys' choir entered and won the elementary schools competition while the older group came second to Calabar College in the Secondary Schools Competition.[28] All of these opportunities prepared boys to become future citizens, both laborers and producers of Jamaican culture. The girls, in contrast, learned little beyond domestic work.

Closing of the Girls Industrial School 1935–1937

As the number of girls at the state-run reformatory declined in the 1930s, the Director of Prisons argued that the girls' department of the Industrial School had been underutilized. For the system to work, he suggested that all members of the judiciary and poor relief administration should cooperate to send "neglected" girls to the institution early, before they became young delinquents.[29] Colonial officials thus continued to insist that destitution was the precursor to delinquency and that an industrial education was an important rehabilitative force. Members of the Jamaican judiciary, however, regarded delinquency and destitution as Black urban male problems. Judges regularly institutionalized Black boys while releasing Black girls to their communities whenever possible. In the parish of Trelawny, for example, three girls ages eight, nine, and eleven were brought before the court and admonished for throwing stones. The judge released them to their families.[30] The acting Resident Magistrate for the parish of St. Thomas reported that first time juvenile female offenders were often released to a "responsible relative or friend willing to care for the child." He posited that "in Kingston and Saint Andrew where [there] is a large criminal population localized in a comparatively small area it is far more difficult to rescue the child from her undesirable environment." The courts and poor relief institutions in Kingston sent more girls to the school than any other parish. The limited records available suggest that judges, especially those outside of Kingston, chose to release Black girls to their communities even as colonial officials continued to advocate industrial education.[31]

In 1935, concerns about the quality of education of the inmates and the underutilization of the girls' dorms forced the Governor to convene an inquiry into the running of the Government Industrial School. The number of girls fell to forty-eight inmates, and administrators concluded that the space would be more effectively used as a Junior School for boys under ten years old. The committee recommended they close the school entirely as a means of freeing the inmates from the stigma of being in a reformatory.[32] The Governor and Director of Prisons immediately closed the girls' section.[33] They relocated the girls to other institutions such as the Alpha Cottage, the Lyndale Home, and the Salvation Army Rescue Home.[34] Efforts were also made to secure employment for older girls in government institutions such as hospitals. Miss Symons, former headmistress for the girl's department, remained to work with the boys in the new department.[35]

Several complications occurred during the closure of the school. The Industrial Schools Law allowed the Governor to discharge inmates from the school but did not permit him to further detain inmates in an institution that was not an industrial school such as the Salvation Army Home. In addition, only a child below the age of twelve years could be transferred from one institution to another.[36] Other institutions such as the Lyndale Home did not have the proper facilities to accept "incorrigible" children as defined by law. These legal issues had to be addressed before any child could be transferred from the school.

Three cases illustrate these complications. Melvina Davis, aged twelve years, was transferred from the GRIS to the Lyndale Home in St. Mary. Once transferred to Lyndale, Melvina absconded from the Institution after stealing several items. The Resident Magistrate for St. Mary refused to recommit her to the Lyndale Home but desired to send her to an Industrial School.[37] None at the time existed because the GRIS had been closed. In another instance, two girls returned to Stony Hill requesting assistance after they were released to their families. Inez Fairclough stated that her guardians were unkind to her and falsely accused her of stealing on a regular basis. The Superintendent allowed Inez to stay with a staff member until alternate arrangements could be made for her. Another former inmate, Elsie Hillerie, wrote administrators stating that her mother died a few weeks after she was discharged. As a result, she was now homeless with no one to "take interest in her."[38] Eventually both Inez and Elsie were transferred to the Alpha Industrial School in Kingston.[39] These experiences reveal that there was little provision for aftercare when discharged children could not reintegrate into their communities. Despite the low occupancy of the girls' department and the underlying class- and race-based ideological framework of the educational programme, the institution made an important intervention for those girls who lacked community support.

Conclusion

Concerns about accessing and controlling the potential labor of children were the main reasons for the development of industrial schools for both Black girls and boys in Jamaica. Administrators justified access to children's labor by arguing that unstable Black family life created a class of children convicted of crimes or left destitute. The Jamaican state created an infrastructure targeting Black children based on the pathologization of the Black family. Colonial officials believed that developing an industrial education programme that emphasized agricultural labor would be rehabilitative and prepare children to be first laborers and later citizens. The state, however, always invested more in boys than in girls.

The GRIS, established in 1869, was the oldest institution and by the 1930s, the most advanced in educational offerings for boys. Throughout the institution's history, boys outnumbered girls sometimes as high as five or six to one. Low admittance rates to the institution as well as concerns about the quality of the girls' education led to the relocation of the girls' institution from Stony Hill in 1882 and its return to Stony Hill in 1899 when the cost of maintaining a small number of girls became prohibitive. The continued sparse numbers of girls at the institution deterred investment in their education.

The Jamaican colonial state failed to develop a clear policy framework to educate girls admitted to the GRIS. Girls' daily lives were spent at work sewing, laundering, and feeding themselves and other residents at the school. The school program devoted more resources to shaping the masculinity of boys rather than defining girlhood. By the 1930s, officials concluded that the girls' institution was underutilized and that their dorms would be better used to house boys under ten years of age. Low admittance rates proved detrimental to the expansion of educational programme for girls at the GRIS. While there is little evidence explaining why so few girls were brought before the courts or admitted to the institution, the archive suggests that cultural practices of reintegration as well as the judiciary's view of juvenile crime as being a Black urban male phenomenon effectively undermined the expansion of girls' institutions in Jamaica. The judiciary often opted to admonish and release girls rather than incarcerate them.

The case of Jamaica reveals that it is important to expand our understanding of how colonial institutions and legislation targeted children. The state's approach to criminality and destitution among Black girls was shaped and ultimately undermined by cultural practice, financial concerns, as well as the demographic profile of inmate populations. In the end, colonial administrators and school officials invested little in developing industrial school curricula for Black girls, choosing to focus instead on the potential of boys as future citizens.

Notes

1. Cecilia Green's investigation of the treatment of juvenile offenders and the incarceration of women in Barbados argues that the Barbadian colonial government focused on shaping masculinity because it was believed that women could only be reformed through the rehabilitation of the Black male. This is a simplification of Green's argument, which theorizes and explores the underlying economic, class, and gender-based factors that resulted in higher levels of incarceration of women and the excessive policing of juvenile crime among boys in Barbados. The Barbadian judiciary incarcerated far higher numbers of women aged twenty years and older and whipped more boys fourteen years and younger than anywhere else in the Anglophone Caribbean between 1875 and 1929. See Green, "Disciplining Boys: Labor, Gender, Generation and the Penal System in Barbados, 1880–1930," *Journal of the History of Childhood and Youth* 3, no. 3 (2010): 374–75; Cecilia Green, "'The Abandoned Lower Class of Females': Class, Gender, and Penal Discipline in Barbados 1875–1929," *Comparative Studies in Society and History* 53 no. 1 (2011): 144–179; Cecilia Green, "Local Geographies of Crime and Punishment in a Plantation Colony: Gender and Incarceration in Barbados, 1875–1928," *New West Indian Guide* vol. 86, nos. 3–4 (2012): 263–290, 263–4.

2. Using the legislation that guided colonial policy on juvenile crime, this paper defines a child as anyone between the ages of five and twelve years of age and youth as persons aged twelve to sixteen years. The legislation also defines an adult as anyone over the age of sixteen years. The laws that governed the treatment of children before the courts include The Reformatories and Industrial Schools Law (1881), The Juvenile Offenders Law (1896), and the Young Criminal Punishment Law (1904).

3. An example of this is the Alpha Cottage, which housed girls on the same com-

pound with boys; Shortwood Industrial School specifically catered to girls and Hope Industrial School to boys.

4. Patrick Bryan, *The Jamaican People: Race Class and Social Control* (Barbados, Jamaica, Trinidad and Tobago: University of the West Indies Press, 2000), xi. Patrick Bryan argues that there were two Jamaicas. One where the white minority emulated European, more specifically, Victorian ideals and values, while Afro-Jamaicans created a hybrid culture that combined both European and African traditions and practices. Throughout the nineteenth and early twentieth centuries, white hegemony maintained social, economic, and political domination over the Black majority laboring population by controlling "land resources."

5. *Report of Commission upon the Condition of the Juvenile Population of Jamaica* (Government Printing Establishment, 1879) Appendix A, 92, Appendix B "Evidence Taken at Montego Bay Falmouth and St. Ann's Bay," 10.

6. In her examination of regional attitudes toward juvenile crime in the Caribbean, Sheena Boa concluded that scarce financial resources and a general lack of commitment to social reform limited the expansion of these institutions in the Caribbean. More importantly, she argued that the general absence of institutions for girls reflected a belief that girls were irreparably damaged once exposed to negative influences. Sheena Boa, "Discipline, Reform or Punish? Attitudes towards Juvenile Crimes and Misdemeanours in the Post-emancipation Caribbean, 1838–1888," in *Contesting Freedom: Control and Resistance in the Post Emancipation Caribbean,* ed. Gad Heuman and David Trotman (United Kingdom: Macmillan Caribbean, 2005), 65–86, 74–75. Other authors writing on this issue include Juanita De Barros, "Metropolitan Policies and Colonial Practices at the Boys' Reformatory in British Guiana," *The Journal of Imperial and Commonwealth History* 30, no. 2 (2002): 1–24; Green, "Disciplining Boys."

7. Prior to 1869, the colonial state avoided assuming direct responsibility for children by allowing the church and other philanthropic organisations to engage in the practice of welfare. Jamaican administrators expected Parochial Boards and City Councils to be financially buoyant and by extension families and communities to support those who were in need.

8. The National Archives (TNA) Colonial Office (CO) 137/366/10 Fourth Annual Report of the Girl's Reformatory (Kingston, Jamaica: M. De Cordova Printers and Company, 1862).

9. TNA CO 137/337 [#63] "Half Yearly Report of the Ladies Reformatory Association."

10. TNA CO 137/353/6 "The Third Annual Report of the Kingston and St. Andrew Reformatory and Industrial Association for Girls," 1861.

11. TNA CO 137/390/1 Rev. Watson, Kingston, to the Governor and the Executive Committee, Spanish Town, January 19, 1864; "The Girl's Reformatory," *The De Cordova's Advertising Sheet* April 8, 1867.

12. TNA CO 137/366/10 Governor Edward Eyre to the Duke of Newcastle 8 May 1862. Appended Fourth Annual Report of the Kingston and St. Andrew's Reformatory and Industrial Association for Girls.

13. Witness testimony is found in TNA CO 137/482 no. 222, 22 December 1876 Grey to Carnarvon. Also includes correspondence from the District Medical Officers Cargill, Wethered and Steventon; Enclosed "Fortnightly Report of Dr. Cargill on the Government Reformatory," Stony Hill 3rd Dec 1870; "Report of the Reformatory Committee," 10th September 1875. For more information on the commissions of inquiry See Shani Roper, "Punishment, Discipline and Agency in the Government Reformatory in Colonial Jamaica 1869–1885," *Journal of Caribbean History* 50, no. 2 (2016): 200–221.

14. TNA CO 137/485/12 Sir Anthony Musgrave, Jamaica, to Lord Carnarvon, Secretary of State for the Colonies 10th December 1877. Appended Report of the Board of Visitors inspection of the Reformatory.

15. TNA CO137/485/12 Sir Anthony Musgrave, Jamaica, to Lord Carnarvon, Secretary of State for the Colonies 10th December 1877. Appended Report of the Board of Visitors inspection of the Reformatory.

16. TNA CO 137/488 #234 Sir Anthony Musgrave to Sir M. G. Hicks Beach, 4 December 1878, Appended Mr. Shaw, Inspector of Prisons and Reformatories to the Colonial Secretary, Kingston, 3 December 1878.

17. JA 1B/5/77/58 (1934), "Statistics of all cases of Juvenile Offenders brought before the Courts of the Colony during the year 1934."

18. "Government Reformatory and Industrial School" in Charitable and Literary Institutions *Blue Books of Jamaica 1878,* (Jamaica: Government Printing Office, 1879).

19. "Report of the Industrial School and Reformatory for the year ended 31 March 1910," in the *Departmental Reports of Jamaica 1909–1910* (Jamaica: Government Printing Office, 1912), 21.

20. *The Gleaner,* January 11, 1895.

21. "Report of the Government Reformatory and Industrial School," November 1882 in *Blue Books and Departmental Reports 1881–1882.*

22. "Report of the Government Reformatory and Industrial School," November 1889 in *Blue Books and Departmental Reports 1889–1890.*

23. Jamaica Archives (JA) 1B/5/77/187 (1932), "Rodgers to Shillingford, 10 July 1934."

24. JA 1B/5/77/187 (1932), "James Mair to Shillingford, 7 July 1932."

25. JA 1B/5/77/187 (1932), "Mair to Shillingford, 6 October 1932."

26. JA 1B/5/77/187 (1932), "Mair to Shillingford, 4 April 1934."

27. JA 1B/5/77/187 (1932), "Mair to Shillingford, 7 January 1933."

28. JA 1B/5/77/187 (1932) "Mair to Shillingford 8 January 1934."

29. JA 1B/5/77/24 (1934), "Precis."

30. CO 137/813/11 C.C. Wooley, Office Administrator to W.G.A. Ormsby Gore, Secretary of State of the Colonies, 22 August 1936.

31. JA 1B/5/77/24 (1934), 'RM, St Thomas to the C. C. Woolley, 15th June 1937.'

32. JA 1B/5/77/628 (1935), "Minute."

33. JA 1B/5/77/24 (1934), "Souter, Secretary of the Board of Visitors, to the Colonial Secretary 22nd November 1935."

34. JA 1B/5/77/24 (1934) "Colonial Secretary to the Director of Education 27th November 1935."

35. JA 1B/5/77/24 (1934) "W. Shillingford to Colonial Secretary 3rd September 1935."

36. JA 1B/5/77/24 (1934), "Minute."

37. JA 1B/5/77/24 (1933), "Clerk, St. Mary to the Colonial Secretary, 14th January 1936."

38. JA 1B/5/77/24 (1934), "W. Shillingford to the Colonial Secretary, 8th October 1935."

39. JA 1B/5/77/24 (1934), "Dignum to W. Shillingford, 24th January 1936."

CHAPTER 13

Roundtable

Activists Reflect on Youth, Justice, and Girlhoods

This panel discussion took place during the Global History of Black Girlhood Conference, March 17, 2017, at the University of Virginia. Panel participants included: Janaé E. Bonsu, National Public Policy Chair of Black Youth Project 100 (BYP100); Beverly Palesa Ditsie, an artist, filmmaker, and founding member of GLOW, the first multi-racial LGBTI organization in South Africa; Phindile Kunene, a curriculum specialist based at the Tshisimani Centre for Activist Education, Cape Town, South Africa; and Denise Oliver-Velez, an Associate Professor at SUNY New Platz, former Minister of Economic Development for the Young Lord's Party and member of the Black Panther Party. Claudrena N. Harold, Professor of History, University of Virginia, moderated. The transcript has been lightly edited for readability.

CLAUDRENA HAROLD (CH): I feel so blessed and so lucky to be sitting with four transformative activists, scholars, and artists. I want to begin with a sort of general question that will provide you with an opportunity to talk about your political trajectory. When you got the invitation to come here, what did you think about the theme of Black girlhood within the context of your current work?

JANAÉ E BONSU (JEB): When I first got the invitation to come here, my initial thought was, "I don't know if I'm the right person to speak, because when I think about the point at which I was really politicized, or activated in an overtly political way, that didn't happen until grad school, really. I was twenty-three when I first joined BYP100 and that was my introduction into activism and political organizing. But the more that I thought about it, I reflected, "You know, I wouldn't be where I am if it wasn't for the compounded experiences of my entire life that led me to this point." Right? There was an experience that I needed to even choose the type of program that I chose, to end up in Chicago. So, I might have something to contribute to this conversation.

BEVERLY PALESA DITSIE (BPD): I got the invitation, and, I just went, "Ah, this is a joke." And I think it took about a week to go back to it because similarly I didn't see myself being an activist when I was growing up. I was just being me, being rebellious and doing what felt like needed to be done. And so, it didn't occur to me that this is some kind of big deal to be part of a kind of a brand-new organization and to be marching down the street. And—in fact at that very first Pride March, someone said, "You know this is the first LGB Pride in Africa?" And I'm like, "What?" So, you know, a lot of this stuff we were doing as young ones, for me, was just what needed to be done. And if not we, then who? Also, I was growing up in a very kind of politicized space, being from Soweto, and having been kind of influenced by this 1976 uprising even though I was only five years old then. I remember my mom kept saying, "It's the young people that are rising. It's the youth that are trying to change the system." And I understood a little bit of what that was because I was already living in a very kind of politicized home. I grew up in a maternal household where I was constantly questioning, and I was lucky that both my grandmother and my mother didn't hide things from me, so they would answer honestly whenever I asked, "Why are we in this situation? Why don't we have lights? Where's water?" You know, whatever it was, I kept getting honest answers. So, I grew up politicized, but I would never have said that then. I didn't know what that was then.

PHINDILE KUNENE (PK): I think that similarly to Janaé I worried first about legitimacy and credibility. I was, I think, politicized at eighteen or nineteen, my first year at university. A lot of my experiences before then I didn't consider necessarily political. The invitation came at a time when I started reflecting on my own political activism, so I thought it's an opportunity to actually start thinking more critically about what my role has been, to step back and think about how I understand my years before eighteen as political—or, whether I think about those years in different ways and in other terms.

DENISE OLIVER-VELEZ (DOV): When I got the email, I was like, "This is a conference with little girls? They don't want to hear from me; I'm seventy years old. I'm old." So, I didn't read it well. I just saw "Black Girls." And then I read it. And then I also understood that there were going to be people from South Africa, and I was thrilled, having grown up through the anti-apartheid movement. I have to say that my experience was very different. I was political from the time I dropped out of my mother's womb. Seriously, I grew up in a very political family. My grandfather identified himself as a "race man." And my father was a fellow traveler. All of my parents' friends were in a resistance tradition of being in the Communist party. And you know, when Paul Robeson comes and sings "Happy Birthday" to you when you are six years old, you grow up political. I didn't know that there was a world that wasn't political. And living in New York, there were Black intellectuals, and mostly non-practicing Jewish communist intellectuals, and you can throw in a few Puerto Ricans, and there were folk singers and union organizers. My grandfather was in the Sleeping Car Porter organizing with A. Philip Randolph. So, I didn't know that people weren't political, and it was later, moving out of that bubble, that I was just like—I went into complete and total catatonic shock, you know? In fact, I became a Panther because I was rebelling against my boring communist parents. If I had to read one more piece of Lenin, I was going to throw up. So, it was better, to be like, "Off the pigs! Let's get out in the street!" You know, and so that's why my perspective was a little weird.

CH: I guess the next question is how did that sort of politicization intersect with your feeling of being a girl? When were you conscious of being a Black girl, in all of the beauty and all the complexity that that entailed? Could you say a little more about your political becoming and the process of girlhood?

BPD: I was never aware that I was a girl until my early teens, when all of a sudden there's boobs, and there's bleeding and period pains. I wasn't aware that I was a girl. But, having said that, I was constantly being made aware that I was a girl by the different uncles and neighbors and all the different people that were trying to touch and that were trying to do more than just touch. But in my head, there was something wrong with them, not just because I was a child, but because I wasn't a girl. So that crisis culminated in my early teens when I came across the words that could identify me and "lesbian" was the closest thing because that was the only thing that existed. Gender fluidity and all these other words are very new. That is probably how I would have identified then had I known those words. But lesbian was the closest thing, and even that word was a crisis in a Black, very cultural, very religious home. And of course, my maternal grandmother—she's the love of my life—didn't want me hanging out with the boys. It was, on the one hand, "Oh, fantastic, because that means we're not going to have any pregnancy," but on the other hand, it was like, "Something's wrong, let's take her to, you know, traditional healers and all of that. Let's try to make sure that she grows up to be a girl." So, I feel like I was forced into awareness of being something that I didn't identify with for a long time, and by the time I started identifying with it, I started realizing that I didn't want to be that, because that just felt so powerless. But I think the confusion for me was also watching my grandmother be this powerhouse, this tower of strength, this person that just navigated my household and our entire neighborhood. And everyone who was in trouble came to my home, for whatever reason. So, I had to kind of lay in between that space where

I was, on the one hand, looking up to her and saying, "But women are powerful," and, on the other hand, "Am I a woman?" So those politics played themselves out for me through joining and being part of the LGBTI movement where, for the first time, I felt that I belonged and that meant something to me. But then I also had to fight within that space because the gay men were dominating, and according to them, being gay meant everything. It meant you were a woman, so it's the same issues, but they didn't even "see us as women," because again we didn't have language. The women and girls used to say, "We're all boys, girl," and vice versa, which was happiness, because they were recognizing me as a boy, and I would then identify them as a girl.

I think it was really when I started looking at myself being a girl at seventeen or eighteen, within the movement, that for the first time, I actually said, "I am a girl. And I have to identify and make sure that girl voices like mine are heard." If there is no lesbian standing up, then the myth continues that only gay men exist, and that there are no lesbians, because what is that? Plus, you're African, plus you're traditional—you know, that doesn't exist. So that became critical for me to then begin to identify as a lesbian for myself more than for anything else, but then it ended up being for everybody else that started coming out afterwards.

PK: If I'm to describe my experience of coming to realize I was a girl, it was this whole notion of a constant rehearsal of failure. Some of the words that I heard constantly growing up were, "Why do you look like a boy?" "Are you a boy or a girl?" "Why do you speak like a boy?" "Why do you keep the company of so many boys?" "Why are you not comfortable playing with other girls or doing the things that other girls do, appreciating the things that other girls do?" But there was a contradiction there because when it came to some of the roles that are associated with girls, I was very good at performing them. For instance, helping my mom to clean the house and to do all of those things, I performed quite well. But the source of a very strange relationship with my mom always came when it related to the performance of gender and me not fitting this mode of what a "normal girl" is supposed to do. I remember being bought a Barbie doll, this thin doll with very long hair. I think it was basically a way of my father winning my affection. He was separated from my mother at the time, so he bought us these expensive gifts. He bought my sister a different gift, but somehow chose a Barbie doll for me. Obviously, I couldn't care about this doll that didn't look like me or even reflect me in any way. I sort of left it neglected outside, and other kids found it. And then I was constantly reminded of this Barbie doll that I lost, which cost a hundred pence, slightly over $10 in today's denomination. That was a lot of money for my mom and I was constantly reminded of this doll that I lost. But I just couldn't understand what the big deal was because I didn't even enjoy playing with it.

Of course, most of these things changed with puberty. When I received my first menstrual period, I felt like the world was collapsing. The boobs came, and then the hips came, and all of a sudden there's this whole lot of attention—I was twelve at the time—a whole lot of attention from men, being sexualized and being seen differently. And I spent a lot of time hating that particular body, even though I thought maybe this body is a way of answering their question, "Why do you look like a boy?" because all of a sudden nobody was asking me why I looked like a boy anymore. I think that's sort of the conundrum that I'm still trying to resolve even now. So, the notion of being a girl comes with contradictions in my life, performing some gender roles perhaps better than my sister, and yet failing in other respects.

DOV: I want to separate the two things, because I think as a child, I was lucky that I didn't have parents that forced me into a girl role, because from the time I was three, I was like, "I want a dump truck." My aunt bought me these stupid Madam Alexander dolls. You have to be really old to know—they're made of porcelain, they have dresses. They have a whole museum full of them in Brooklyn. You couldn't play with them, because they were really expensive, and I thought, "This is really stupid. I want my dump truck." And I was allowed. I was born in 1947, so we're talking early 50s, and my mother would allow me to wear jeans. Nowadays, you all are used to women wearing pants. You can go to school and wear pants. That did not exist. You know, girls wore dresses and skirts, and my aunts were very upset that my mother put me in dungarees, in jeans, because, you know, "She's going to be strange if you allow her to dress in this nonconforming way." So, I was not good with this girl stuff. And then on top of it, growing up in the Black community and being around the Latino community, I weighed, like, seventy-two pounds soaking wet, and I was totally flat-chested. They called me "Olive Oyl," like from Popeye, because my last name is Oliver, or they'd say, "Denise is a pirate's treasure, she's got the sunken chest." This came from girls. And it did not make me very happy with girls. I did not have [a] chest, nor ass, nor thighs, nor hips, nor big legs—none of the stuff you're supposed to have. And it was said to me, "Oh, you look like Twiggy." I was like, "Great, I have to go be White." It was very difficult being a girl, and then on top of it being a Black girl and being very militantly Black. And then colorism came in. I was raised in a family that was very proud of being Black and then all of a sudden, Black artists were what came along. I was working as a teenager in the Truth Coffee Shop in Harlem and all starry-eyed because there was Amiri Baraka, and he had just changed his name from LeRoi. All the writers and poets and playwrights came to that cafe. And I was just thrilled because this was really Black. And then this lunatic was like, "We've got to get you half-breed bitches out of Harlem." I'm a teenager and he started picking on me. He would come and order, "I didn't order that. It's not hot. Take it back to the kitchen." He picked on me, and he kept referring to my skin color. And that was more what was going on at that period in time. To be Black, you know. I was Black—but they're telling me I'm not. Finally, I got so tired of him, he ordered chili, and I took that bowl of chili and dumped it in his damn lap. But I shouldn't have done that. He ran out and he came back with a gun to kill me. He was going to shoot me. And there were these two really nice gentlemen who I used to serve tea to, and they used to play chess because it was one of those coffeehouses where intellectuals play chess. One taught martial arts, and the other one was somebody I didn't know. He had sort of freckles. And that other guy got up and stepped right in front of the gun. And I peed on myself because I thought I was dead. I had urine trickling down my leg. This man said, "Brother, Blackness has nothing to do with skin color." And the other turned white and spun around and ran out the door with his gun. And I went back to the owner, and I said, "Who is that guy with the freckles?" And he said, "Girl, you dumb. That's Minister Malcolm!" And I was like, "Oh." I didn't know what he looked like. I didn't know he had freckles. I just knew he was a nice man who played chess and ordered tea and was very polite—always said thank you. But that was the end of my, "Do not tell me I am not Black, okay? I don't want to hear it, because Minister Malcolm said so."

JEB: So Black girlhood for me was a combination of distinct experiences that are separate but very much tied up with my body and sexuality. I mean the times when I would visit my dad. I was born in Brooklyn and raised in South Carolina. My mom, when I was about five years old, said she wanted a different "quality of life" to raise me and so we moved to South Carolina where my maternal grandparents are. My dad still lived in Brooklyn and so I would visit him in the summers. He was a single Black bachelor with this little girl every summer. He didn't know what to do with my hair. He didn't know what to do. We were on the way to Harlem on 125th Street so I can get my hair braided, and he'd just be talking shit, like, "Man I wish you was a boy, I could just take you to the barber shop." Aside from the shade that he threw me every summer from there, my cognizance of my girlhood was really when I began to develop a body. So, I had the opposite problem you had, Denise, you said you didn't have enough—I had too much, too early. I started puberty at nine years old, right? You know, I had boobs and hips and butt in elementary school. And so definitely experienced unwanted male attention and just this objectification and fetishization. It was like not being seen as a person, just as body parts. When I had my first girlfriend, I had all my classmates telling me that I was too cute to be gay.

Then in terms of just blackness, the first time that I was called a nigger was on a playground in elementary school by someone—I remember his name too, Jameson. He was comfortable enough to call me a nigger to my face. But then there was not being Black enough for my neighborhood friends. I lived in Columbia, South Carolina, in an all-Black neighborhood and the school that I was going to I guess wasn't a quote "good school," relative to the school that I would be in zone for if I lived with my grandparents. So, my mom did illegal stuff, had my grandparents' address as our residence so I could go to the better school, which of course was the white school, right? So, I've always been a nerd, I've always loved reading, had a vocabulary that was relatively bigger than my peers, and I guess I spoke a certain way that was not Black enough for my neighborhood friends. Whatever "Black enough" means, right?

And so, from 9:00 to 5:00 or 7:00 to 4:00, whatever times we were in school, I'm in this, like, lily-white environment, where I'm like the Oreo crumb in the cup of milk, and then I go home, and it's just, "Oh, you know, you ain't nothing but a white girl in a Black girl body." You know? And so really, my questions were, "What does it mean to be Black? What is blackness?" Because I know my maternal grandmother was born on a plantation and worked as a sharecropper from the time she was five years old, and my paternal grandmother is Ghanaian, lives in Ghana right now. I'm literally African American, and you're telling me I'm not Black enough? What does that mean, right? So, having those questions, having my blackness questioned, what it meant to have someone not be interested in talking to me until after I pass them and they saw how big my booty was, you know? Those things, like the intersection of my sexuality, my gender, and just my blackness, and what that means for how people respect me or not, how people talk to me, how I'm just able to engage with the world. Yeah, it's a spectrum of experiences that inadvertently or not, definitely shapes me—how unapologetic I am when I say I'm a Black queer feminist today.

CH: The thing that I appreciate about all of you is that you're activists rooted in organizations, and I think sometimes young Black girls—and young people in general—really struggle to navigate organizations and an activist life. In, the Young Lords, the average member was seventeen, I think.

DOV: Mm-hm. And we had one or two who were twelve.

CH: So, I wonder if you could talk about activism and the importance, for a lot of young people out there, of organization.

JEB: I think organization is super important. Black Youth Project 100 is a research initiative started by Cathy Cohen at the University of Chicago—y'all don't know Cathy Cohen, look her up, she's a super dope political scientist. In the field of political science, at that time, around 2004, no one was really checking for the attitudes, experiences, beliefs, et cetera of young Black people. That was what Cathy was trying to combat and disrupt with the Black Youth Project. There was an advisory council that was made up of some young people that she was working with. Fast-forward to 2012 and they have the idea to convene young activists, artists, writers, tech folks, and just young Black folks from across the political spectrum and from across the country to come together in the same room to talk about, "What does mobilization look like beyond electoral politics?" After a year of planning, in July 2013, what was called the Beyond November Movement convening happened, right outside of Chicago. I don't believe in coincidences, so I can't say that it was a coincidence—I believe it was fate that that same weekend was when the George Zimmerman verdict was announced in the killing of Trayvon Martin. So, we learned that the verdict was going to be announced, and people decided to experience that verdict together. And when it came down "not guilty," when he was acquitted, as you can imagine a room full of about 100 young Black people experiencing this collective heartbreak, this collective trauma, this collective reinforcement of the devaluation of Black life in America—it was an agitational moment and everyone responded in different ways. That moment was a catalyst to not just movement building broadly—that same week was when the Black Lives Matter hashtag was created—but when BYP100 as an organization was agitated into existence. And so now almost four years later, it's a national organization with eight chapters across the country and growing.

I tell this story of its founding all the time like I was there, but I actually wasn't. I came into BYP100 about six months after that founding moment. It being so early in the organization's history, we were still figuring a lot of things out—we're still figuring a lot of things out. Being an organization that is comprised of and led by young Black people, we didn't have a handbook for what it means to be trying to build an organization and a movement at the same time, because that's hard, right? Organizations are important because they're spaces for political education, they're containers for leadership development, for base building, for bringing other people into the movement. It's one thing to have a rally or a protest and be like, "Yeah, fight the power." And everybody goes home with no action items. Organizations help keep momentum going. That's the difference between mobilizing and organizing.

I remember the first mobilization that I had ever attended. I was nine years old; it was 2000 MLK weekend. Being in South Carolina, the Confederate flag was flying over the state house unapologetically. That mobilization brought thousands and thousands of Black people into Columbia—I didn't even know there were that many Black people in South Carolina. And I was just like, "Man, this is beautiful! Like, this is great! Like, we're all coming together for this common goal to get this

White supremacist oppressive symbol off the state house." And then after that, there was nothing. There was no follow-up. And that was disheartening. So, I see organizations as way to combat that, as a way to really sustain a movement. When you're trying to do that, you also have to be attuned to the fact that the revolution will not be funded. You've got to fundraise; you've got to create structure to bottom-line things. You know, you can have all these action items, but if you don't know how to delegate, if there's not people in formal roles, you won't continue—there's just so much to organization and movement-building that is very difficult but it's necessary. That's not to say that people's only entry point or contribution to movement has to be within the context of an organization, because that's not the case. But I don't think movements can be sustained without it.

DOV: Yeah, I agree. There's nothing wrong with demonstration—I don't care if you riot, you know? But I don't see us progressing and moving forward without structure and without organization. And I've had young people say to me, "Oh, who funded you all? Did you all have grants?" Grants for the Black Panther party, right? It is so key to have structure. One of my biggest critiques as an older person looking at things—because we are allowed to criticize. You know, we're not going to take over, we are not going to tell you what you have to do, because that's your stuff. But we can criticize. I looked at this insanity of—what was it—Occupy Wall Street? "Mic check! Mic check!" Yeah, okay. And what did they accomplish? They were telling people, "Don't vote." Excuse me? People in my family died to bring you the vote. They died. And I take that very seriously. And I'm not saying that only electoral politics is the solution, because you have to have multiple approaches. But ultimately, permanent change tends to get made in this country through judicial and legislative kind of action. So, we cannot afford to ignore that. I was in St. Louis, and I went to see the statue of Dred and Harriet Scott. And I'd like to bring up Harriet, they only just talk about Dred, you know, but it's Dred and Harriet Scott. We need to keep that in mind. Yes, that's history, but the Supreme Court is quite capable of making another one of those kinds of decisions. And we have to be very, very careful. And we have to be very, very organized. And I sat on a panel in Minnesota recently with some young people who were saying, "All of y'all don't vote because you won't achieve nothing. It won't get you anywhere." And I interrupted and said, "That's bullshit." They looked at me, you know, on the panel because, I'm sorry, there are multiple approaches, but one of them is you must be organized. I went to Raleigh, North Carolina and there were 80,000 people marching in Raleigh. This was two years ago. Yet do you ever see anything in the media about what is going on there? They have organized, led by Reverend William Barber, an evangelical minister who supports LBGTQ issues, environmental justice, reproductive justice, voter registration, prison enfranchisement. All of those issues, yet we don't hear about that. And the reason that they've been successful is that they are organized. And they have some old-time civil rights organizers in their organization. They also have vibrant young people—fifteen, sixteen, seventeen, eighteen years old—who are organizing. They have youth training sessions so that they mobilize and organize. And how many of you knew there were 80,000 people marching in Raleigh? I see three hands. Four hands, okay. Figure out why you don't know this is happening.

BPD: You know, working in media and seeing what is being reported and what isn't, I feel your distress. I'm from a country that has experienced what is supposed to have been a miracle transition. And that miracle transition is bullshit. Anybody now who comes to me with some Mandela-esque, "Oh wow, how wonderful rainbow nation"—bullshit. What you're not seeing in the media—and when they tell you about white genocide, when 88% of the country is still being owned by the same white people who owned it pre-apartheid—is Black rage. It is anger. And a lot of what is called the heightened violence of South Africa—it's rage. We are angry. And what you're not seeing in the media is the organizing. What you're seeing is the mediocrity. You see an incompetent president; you see incompetent ministers; we have structures right now that have no leaders. There literally is no CEO for the South African broadcasting. There's no CEO or MD or anything for the rail services. There's no MD or CEO for the social services. The Grant Sassa has no leader. There are no leaders in about seven different national institutions right now. So, this thing that we fought for has all gone down the drain. But when you look at who's benefiting, when you literally look at this transition, and the handshake and who's benefiting, it's quite scary, because you then realize that we were sold out. And unfortunately, the lack of organization has a lot to do with people being disillusioned by the fact that we actually had amazing structures at one point, and that people believed so strongly in these structures. I personally could not belong because, even though many of us who were growing up under apartheid already knew that there were structures and organizations that you could join, because just literally every street had to have a street committee, that had to have, you know, membership within this political party or that political party, but mostly we're talking about the ANC, which is the governing party. Although I'm from a Biko conscious point of view, which is very much Black power and Black consciousness. But I think having grown up in a situation where everyone belonged, I struggled with this particular belonging as not just Black, but Black conscious, and would just not follow the rhetoric, but also being queer and very aware that I am different in pretty much every single aspect. And so, seeking out an organization or at least loosely a group of people that

I could identify with, and then finding a movement that seemed to encompass all of me. You know intersectionality—we knew then that we would be a non-racist, non-sexist, non-discrimination-of-all-sorts type of organization. And it was the first time that I found belonging.

Around the time—this is 1988, 1989—the euphoria in the country was already palpable because people knew that apartheid government was coming to an end; they could not sustain themselves anymore. And so, it was perfect timing for all the different kinds of organizations to emerge. A lot of those who had survived until the new constitution was drafted and adopted were organizations that were very clear about what their mission and agenda was. Unfortunately post that, everyone relaxed. And what that did was it almost created a backlash. I think your Obama backlash might be similar—like, you've got this amazing achievement, and then everybody thinks, "Okay, now we can focus on the individual and live." And besides, there was what we call in South Africa "struggle fatigue," where people had been activists and activisting for all their lives—your parents and your grandparents and your great-grandparents before you. Finally, there was a moment and a time where we could now begin to relax and start to focus on career, individual. And everyone is aspiring to the pseudo-middle classness that you now have, everyone is just, "Oh, you know, the richer you are the more important you are," that type of thing. The aspiration to capitalism, which is also—now we're all realizing is a problem on its own. Because now the richer people get, the handful of people, the majority are in desperate need in South Africa right now. And so now I'm beginning to see again a reemergence of organizing. Because now people are realizing that without belonging to structures where you can begin to implement some of the vision that is emerging, we can't do it as individuals. So even some of us—like myself in particular who wasn't part of any movements for the last ten years as I've been "individualizing my life for filmmaking"—are now beginning to go back into communities, and beginning to get together and organize. Because without these structures, there are no follow-ups, because you can't just march. I mean we've been having all these marches in South Africa, "March against corruption, yay!" And then what? You know, there's so many different efforts that need to be done, to make sure things happen. So, without structures, without organizing, we can have our own individual contributions, but I think we are stronger organizing as large groups of people with the same vision. And I think the vision for all of us is some kind of measure of body autonomy and freedom to just be, right?

PK: Thanks for that. I think for me, mass politics and mass organizations are particularly important for acting out one's politics. An organization which for many Black people has been the traditional organization of choice is an organization that people actually consider their own or talk about it in a way that is both personal and political. So, the African National Congress, the ANC, despite its challenges, it's highly organized. There isn't a part of South Africa where you won't find an ANC member or, on any random day, find someone wearing an ANC t-shirt. It's an organization, it works, it functions. It's one thing to stand outside and be critical of those politics. It's another to actually look at the ANC and the way it organizes and the ways it's been able to sustain itself with all the challenges, and actually draw some lessons from it. I think one of the critical things that holds the organization together is that whole notion that organization supersedes individuals. So even when it's messy and it's dirty, you still have people who are setting themselves and saying, "But the ANC's bigger than Zuma, so we must get Zuma out or there is still space at the grassroots level to contest that." Um, I don't believe that anymore, but there's still a significant number of people that believe in that. The second thing is that if you are not linked to organizations, your views about politics are sometimes divorced from popular sentiment. It's one thing to criticize people for still believing in a particular project, it's another to understand the reasons why they still believe in that particular project. So, for instance, I listen to a lot of young people in South Africa today saying things like, "Oh, the people continue to vote for the ANC because they think the ANC liberated them and they're so grateful to the ANC." That's not the case. With many people that I speak to, people in my family, people who are my friends—there are different reasons, one of them being that people actually feel that it's *their* organization. So, they may not be card-carrying members of that organization, but they see the organization as a critical part of their history, their trajectory, and all of that, and that's what defines them. So being close to an organization allows you to get into the head of what people think, and all of that. There are issues that organizations are also not paragons of virtue, right? It's a space to do collective work and to experiment with a whole lot of things. But organizations do become stifling at times. They do undergo challenges. Democratic impulses do get suppressed, sometimes. And where there's involvement of money, where there are positions, where there's proximity to state power, you do have politics getting quite diluted. But the critical thing to also remember is that all organizations are contested. At whatever time, there's always different, contending ideas within organizations. And whenever there's still space to wage a fight back, I'd say stay and wage the fight back, but sometimes the space is completely closed; some of the organizations that I've been involved in where you actually get people being actively forced out of those particular organizations, when the space closes, then maybe it's time to experiment with other things and to look at other things. So, I think mass politics is very important for seeing the world beyond your immediate surrounding, for being involved in campaigns. I mean, the organization that I joined, the outcome is a fundamental reason why I identified with that organization, it's organized around issues that defined my life and existence. So, the basic necessities, public transport that is safe, that is portable, that is reliable; education that is public, that is free up to university level; free sanitary towels for young girls, and all of that. So those things in an organization you can shape actually the campaigns and the direction. But organizations are not paragons of virtue; sometimes you become really, really hurt and wounded in organizations. And the type of organizations that we've been involved in actually preclude us from talking about the hurt and the pain and victimization and the sexism and all of these other things.

JEB: I just want to say real quickly before we end, that organizations are essentially a laboratory for the type of world that you want to live in. When internal conflicts arise, when there are differences, whether it's sexism, misogyny, transphobia, homophobia, whatever within the organization, especially in political organizations where you're literally organizing for a better world, whatever better is for you—you have to create those structures and mechanisms to address the oppressor in all of us when it comes up in our organizations. You know, harm is just inevitable. Any situation where you have interpersonal relationships with people, harm is going to happen, and we never say, "Oh, this is a safe space." The safe space is a myth. It is a myth. We can't guarantee a safe space, but we can guarantee an accountable space. How do you hold people accountable? How do you respond to harm? How do you deal with that? Maybe it doesn't always look like a restorative or transformative justice process, but how do we do that? How do we address that in a way that doesn't replicate the systems that we're trying to tear down?

CONCLUSION

Divine Chaos Dear Homegirls

RUTH NICOLE BROWN

Oh divine chaos
I watch eyes wonder
and divert, who is gonna do it?
Yes, you. Shapers of edges,
keepers of margins,
who turn walking tours into
freedom trails
with Harriet sang Halo
spontaneity
roach-cricket hybrids
come also to
gather where there is water:
witness chorus
& we thought we knew our ABCs
transformed by
Alisha and Ashlyn's presence
history serious
about our work together
feed them
learn growth
long view body as demand
for readiness
and play among a few who don't really know
love
as respect as giving
and giving again is why it's a practice.
Schooled in distraction
what taught us to look away when we feel? Unlearn this

an Education
of I'll go first and let's go together
abolishing fear required reading
Black girlhood is so many
wrappers and so much butcher paper
and waiting among
all preferences and coded looks
already doing
from expanse to the smallest
of every living
being.

Dear Homegirls,

It is my pleasure to welcome you all! First, I want to thank and acknowledge those who taught us possibility stirring this moment into a sweet sweaty salty reality. Jessica, thank you so much for your diligent work and assistance with organizing. You all should know this week would not be possible without her efforts. What you will enjoy throughout the week is a trace of her brilliance as much as mine. So much will move effortlessly to appear as something you might take for granted. This is some solace. This is some audacity. Though in every part, there was a means I am asking you to not forget. Give thanks.

This week is filled with activity! Every time we think about doing less, somehow the will is there to push us to our limit. Here we are again with a very full schedule! I encourage you to bring a younger person with you to everything and participate as much as you can. Homebase is always the collective work with the girls. This week, we will spend much of our time in partnership with the school. This is very much a collaboration. Still, and as always, I'm expecting us to show up as we always do. I am so grateful to be a good steward of our ideas, funds, positive intentions, relationships, conversations, and yearnings, and I trust you'll do the same. As you prepare for our time together, please keep the following on your heart and mind:

1. Our time with Black girls is an honor and a privilege. When we arrive at the school until after we clean up, revere all you see, hear, and experience. Know that for many of us this collective work is sacred. We see ourselves transforming status quo conditions to actually open up skies for brilliance. Every time we are in session, feel it all. Know there is no one way to be a Black girl. Trust everything the girls say as truth and freedom strategy. Believe we have all we need to make this moment and our biggest dreams possible from 11:45 a.m. to 3:30 p.m.
2. Extend and enjoy yourself. No need to model roles. We show up, present and ready. I would like you to show the girls how we listen by extending their thoughts, ideas, and the moment, so that they feel the

celebration. To extend is to lead and this may also be called participation. Everyone who comes should be ready to participate, fully.

3. Be a bringer. Bring things you might anticipate we will need like a case of water, chips, paper plates, sound equipment, crystals, poetry, affirmations, fruit, salad, a warm-up exercise, incense, a lighter, candle, chalk and/or balloons. Any materials that inspire our collective health and creativity are welcomed. Do not expect the one who is perceived to hold the most power or has the most credentials or is the oldest to do the thing you know needs to be done. Act like you know this is about us all.
4. Have and hold yourself in the presence of homegirls who love you back. Many of us have worked together before and some of us are new to the space yet our time together is always a reunion. When we are together, I ask that you have each other's back like your life depends on it—because it surely does. Look each other in the eye. Meet that Black girl face to face. Do what you need to do beforehand: eat, hydrate, pee, meditate, all the things body and spirit demands so you won't focus on and cultivate fear. The time with girls is all we have and where the love comes to you like waves on the shoreline, go to meet it. Allow the girls to peep game, play in it, and fill it up in ways you didn't expect and can't imagine. This right here is what the week is all about. This is that politics. This is everything that ever matters. This energy is elemental, and we are the ones who shape it.
5. Remember, *homegirl* works as a title for how we call each other, and the function of what we call ourselves is revolutionary. This project is so much about finding a language that comes closest to how it is while we're together. We can't rest on assumed proximity or presumed affiliation. And so, taking that into account there and here, if the girl in home bothers you, well, let us know how you prefer to be called and it's all good, even as I ask you not to forget them. We also know, home can be unsafe.
6. Do read, review, and stay ready for the agenda that will follow. I think it's best to over-plan but remain flexible preknowing we won't get to it all. We go deep, and we always follow the lead of the girls. Be as inspired as you've been trained to be critical of the spaces we visit. This is our first time at this particular school, and hopefully, it will not be our last.

I could go on, but I'll stop here. It's a delicious delight to witness your shine and be in community with some of the dopest, most brilliant, spirit-called, and fantastically in touch, engaged beings of galactic imagination and blueprints that I've ever met. I'm so glad. Thank you.

SOLHOT 4 life!
Dr. B

TO DO LIST:

breathe
organize
strengthen the network
gather homegirls together
identify diverse talents and skills
meet a Black girl face to face
get her name right
plot and ruminate over who needs what
think about who can learn from whom
make sure homegirls can come back
bring curriculum
review curriculum
improvise curriculum
mind the archives
organize files
do the reading
ignore her well-intentioned words
rehearse and practice timing
make movement
create a schedule
order supplies
ask new homegirls how they feel
check the budget
comparison shop
listen to Sonia Sanchez
order food
call ahead
learn this policy
teach them how to read
buy plates napkins silverware
create permission slips
create flyers
post to social media
individually invite people
call on people to invite
send email
let people know
reserve the room
pay room reservation fee
arrange transportation
book hotel
book the flights
pick them up from the airport

pick the kids up from school
walk the block
meet the people
ask how you can serve
work for freedom
ask for a raise
eat
ask a homegirl to pick up food, coffee, bagels
order T-shirts order notebooks, order hoodies
find another designer
arrange childcare
check to see if folks filled out paperwork
pay the artists
resist institutionally induced competition
give them a funny look when they reduce humility to low self esteem
laugh when they call it unacademic
let them know where you from
don't answer the person uncalled for
negotiate time space
create PowerPoint
create brochure
present to administration
visit the schools
do radio
plug event on social media
dream about new collaborations new connections
feel the anticipation
respond to thoughtful texts of homegirls still with you
listen to the bird's song
send care to homegirls who made the moment possible and are no longer physically here
check in for encouragement
encourage yourself
deal with an issue the university bureaucracy created
trust the process
see that girl
get your hair done
prep your heart
choose seven dope outfits
train the homegirls
arrive at the school extra early
bring twenty pizzas with two hands
lug the supplies boxes equipment snacks
learn the names

teach the rituals
follow the agenda
trash the agenda
take questions, answer parental concerns
find the elder, say hello
find the youngest, get on their level
ask for more water
tell her yes, you can go to the bathroom
direct the homegirls
pause
collect yourself
improvise
greet the visitor. Did you
bring the candle?
ask who brought the lighter
wonder
dip out to answer daughter's call
stop at the store
serve the food
remember to eat
charge the batteries
clean up
answer a homegirl's question
remember who left and who needs to leave early
wait out the PA system announcement
get big group attention
hold their attention with love
check in on small groups
put out the fire
keep the spark
change the air
check in on the girl left alone
ask them if they're having fun
listen for desire
revise the plan again
ask if they remember your name
practice their names
listen
listen deeply
look her in the eye
challenge-praise yourself
challenge-praise her
remember.

Dear Homegirls,

We are right where we are supposed to be. This is good news.

I am so proud of our work! Nothing less than an ingenious spatial invention of new architecture is some of what it is. I don't know the all of it but that is the least of it. That we are moving into our third year is nothing short of sunshine nurturing our wildest dreams. Even still, I have threatened to pull out of this.

I have said rather boldly and with great sincerity that it does not have to exist anymore. The context in which we labor is beyond difficult and makes apathy attractive even to me. However, after some time away (but not really), I have come to realize that I am only ready to do away with it as we knew it. When I think about all the drama we've been through in the last couple of months, I realize that we are not at the end, rather quite the opposite. We are changing. I have felt the growing pains. While initially frustrating, I'm beginning to realize the possibility of this unorganized agony. I'm gaining direction about how we should go on and it feels more satisfying and less gloom and doom. This is the good news!

The satisfaction: We should celebrate ourselves because after three years we are coming to know something so profound about ourselves, each other, this place, the girls, and the world through our work. We have created words, images, actions, and performances to communicate to each other and everybody else what we know from our daily and nightly practice of celebrating Black girlhood in all of our/its complexity. Some of us for years. What we know is what we have created, a process of doing as the work claims. I love it when folks recognize this with the revelation, our talk is our walk. Black girlhood transforms it all as we knew it would.

The gloom and doom: I was quite ashamed of hiding behind academic expectations that presumed I was not after radical transformation with you all. I spent my family's money while allowing people to think it was coming from my research account (that does not run very deep!). I am an organizer who like so many before me have used personal money to fund this. And it's not just the money but also the energy expended at the expense of those who replenish me. What other insecurities have I kept silent fermenting fatigue? I will have to let these go if I am to keep going with it. Certainly, the distinction dealt with me during sleepless nights and overwhelming conversation and quietude. Now, it feels like a blessing. At the time, it felt unmovable.

Revolutionary collective work requires us to hold each other. This will require compassion. Disagreements are likely. And we should not shrink. We do have issues, very real issues between people and personalities, and we certainly have issues in our curriculum and practice. I'm not afraid of these issues. I am afraid of feeling like I have to solve them alone—that made me tired. I know in order to move with a greater sense of passion, enthusiasm, and justice we will have to think through how at least two explanations can both be heard and rethink recognition. We must all witness all explanations of the "problem" as ways to expose yet again violence at so many levels, the girls and ours. If we can expose it, we can also reveal the knowledge and spirit required to undo those situations not always of our own making, though they are likely expressed as such and also a denial of consequence to the girls.

Violence and militarization are endemic to our socialization, and as such, I'm not surprised that injury shows up. Because Black girls so readily identify as soldiers, I'm not surprised that we play war by attempting to take each other out. Can we understand those logics that make Black girls soldiers without resigning ourselves to what had happened? We could all have plausible reasons for how violence was done to us based on our different locations. We learn from being in relation to one another no matter how far the presumed distance or how different the presumed differences are because injury is not absolute nor definitive, and I want to believe we can become without the violence. How do we bring our bodies, problems, and ideas into conversation in ways that do not further perpetuate the worst of it? Our ideas and our bodies, on the grounds of specificity, will allow for some new questions of what it means to be and do in the name Black girlhood. I want the struggle to be worth the stress because it will reinvigorate us to keep working, though weary.

Because   , we should not be invested in kicking people out of SOLHOT—homegirl or girl. I don't care if they aren't authentically Black girls with a real Black girl consciousness though I recognize we are much too about it to be about it in those exact words. Let's celebrate who we are as "still here" for life and living. If someone walks into this collective work desiring to be down and they see something they want to be, we cannot police the borders. If we get into policing borders then we are doing the collective work of white supremacy operating as an extension of the state, completely complicit in every system we say we are working against.

Many of us are extremely preoccupied with questions such as:

Who belongs?

Who takes responsibility?

Who is rewarded?

What ideas circulate and how?

What is(are) our issue(s)?

What underlying logics operate to make possible the celebration of some Black girls and not others?

How do you know what you are seeing?

In what ways are we colluding with and resisting capitalism?

What is our issue, really?

Would I, or did I leave Harold?

Who are we?

What about us, as cause makes what we would rather look away from, worth the time and effort. Let's name it and address it all together. Because organizing information, knocking on doors, spreading the word, creating a way, incorporating the parents, creating a plan, being at other sites, increasing awareness, developing a website and newsletter, remaining in relationship, and building a campaign is more important than petty drama.

We were offered a radio show; it never happened. We could be at more schools, and we are not. We want to do more performances. We want to change school policies. We want our girls to live healthy. We want institutions accountable to us. These things weren't accomplished for multiple reasons. The primary problem restricting our effectiveness at this moment is all the ways we are not growing. We all want me tenured. I need to write another book. We need to present at conferences. We need to be with the girls. The girls want to be with you. We deserve to be at more sites, the girls want to travel, this collective work has to be funded, and our voices should be heard in different forms and formats. This can all happen if we don't hoard a good thing.

When I said you must bring your highest self to the collective work, I don't mean being someone you're not. But if you can't see that you bringing some real shady business in the door and you are not courageous enough to name your fears, then you need to be humble in the process of learning. Glimpse at least a part of yourself in the mirror and see love looking back—so that you can bring that. None of us are perfect. The same structures of power and domination we seek to resist invade our deepest sensibilities, so conflict, difference, and disorder is a part of it too. But you cannot lose sight of the goal. Just to reiterate: The goal is not academic. The goal is not fame or celebrity. The goal is our collective survival. I can absolutely guarantee that if you stayed committed and gave it your all, you would receive an education worth your time and mama's sacrifice.

Why? Because the questions and theories that mean something to any of us comes exactly out of this work. When the collective work we write and publish comes out of social movements and political organizing with people, it feels satisfying and you won't distract yourself with non-factors of professionalization. You will not be able to make sense of the academy or do the kind of scholarship you say you love without attempting to make spaces like this.

There are many ideas of success as there are also many questions about whether or not the academy is good or bad, which are distracting queries for me. The classroom and the subject are only relevant in a Black feminist kind of way if the issues you discuss are related to the people you love. You don't produce good scholarship solely in/through your head. The readings alone will not do it. The questions that keep me up come directly from the issues we struggle with collectively as we organize in daily practice. The answers become urgent and theory becomes important to explain our hardest dilemmas. Joy is all about coming to insight apart from the who and the where of the exact thing but is also not inseparable from us who were there to actually do the collective work and communicate the stories in all the ways we that allow us all to recognize each of our distinct inflections. We must not act of obligation. Let's move on homegrown desires.

Again, humility is so important. There is no room to be self-righteous in the struggle. We must think about how power structures, our different experiences, and the girls' experiences. In any case, our discussions of sexuality should not be rendered in binaries. Or better yet reduced to replicate binary thinking. The experiences and processes of sexualization and racialized gender as they have and do occur are complicated. Our explanations of the issues that arise should also be complicated.

One thing that is genius about this is that we have mastered tools that are available to organizers *and* academics. A few of us know how to time travel. We have other gifts too because we prioritize creativity and imagination. We have tapped into a Black girl logic. Others really sleep on our ability to make power. We are artists. Let's have some respect for our creative power and also for our interpretive authority.

You have to be there to learn and you have to be there over time to practice. You have to study to see it when it's happening. You are scholar/activist/artist when you can explain what we do in a way that is appreciated by those with whom you organized. You have to know that I am never one to punish critical thinking and praxis. Given that we have so much expertise that do our girls no justice, I thought that if we wanted to respond to the folks organizing differently who think we are wrong, we should. But only if we change the terms of the game. I am not playing.

What we have to say to those peoples, places, and ideas that seek to discipline and punish Black girls' bodies? What do we offer in return? You all made and shared power. You traveled space time. You became each other's strength. That is love. Let's build on it. In coalition with others who are antiracist, feminist, progressive, diasporic, and/or transnationally committed, we will do better. We have more to do and will do it. It is the most unlikely of alliances that I believe will provide us with greater resources to do what we love. This means we will be able to travel with our ideas and circulate a process we've put our own stank on as a part of advancing something we call Black girlhood celebration, which they might call something else.

This collective work is absolutely necessary. We are doing something incredibly important. I do think if we dedicate ourselves in the ways that we commit to other projects, we could be who and what we *really* want. You could really shine as you know you are capable. It's significant work. It's damn important. It's radical. It's also very fragile.

Thinking critically of her strength, our younger years, hard lessons learned, all we deserve, our children's children, and unlimited possibilities, I do not want to take any of this for granted. I do not want to take you all for granted. I do not want to take for granted, me. I terribly miss the presence of girls and homegirls who used to be with us. In that space, I am certain our time together is now. I do not want to take our efforts for granted. For that reason, you should know that revolution started a couple of months back, and it's on!

Love,
Dr. Brown

• • •

My study of Black girlhood emerges from fourteen years of practice, face-to-face conversations, rituals of dance and movement, and active relationship building with Black girls and women in Saving Our Lives Hear Our Truths, which we lovingly refer to by the acronym SOLHOT.

I wrote the poem, welcome address, list, position paper, and this reflection in central Illinois, where SOLHOT began. Located in the middle of the state of Illinois in the United States of America, this is a place I once attended college for four years, then left for over a decade, and returned to start my career as a professor. After fourteen years my children understand small college town living as their norm. Two hours away from my hometown where I was born and raised just south of Chicago, my family prefers to visit me down state for a slower pace and a different scene. In much this same way I offer poem, letter, list, and position paper as greener pastures from which to extend the audience to whom I wrote first. Now, SOLHOT exists in many places and it still the multi-functional and antithetical forms that keep us desiring to act and improve on the last SOLHOT thing we recently did with enough wonder for what we will make in the future.

Just as those who do SOLHOT, we most assuredly have our questions, differences, reflections, desires, and solidarities within this collection entitled *Global History of Black Girlhood*. There are old ways, new ways, and newer ways. Either way, we teeter totter the politics of translation. The ups of translating and the downs of keeping it between those in the know, or vice versa, I trust that you too have struggled with how structure formalizes feeling together and how much of that can be appreciated. I want you, as I do the homegirls, to want to jump in and believe you're already in it. Narrators of our work often ask about change predetermined by global racial capitalism, colonization, and white supremacy. We perform with heart and honest longings for a kind of impact that goes deep and leaves us not as dominant power would have us.

To write in whisper and share ideas to get us out of one moment to another, I have found aliveness by writing our own terms, and keeping lists so we don't forget the big and small tasks of creating revolution to uproot stately stated missions and shiny media posts. For me, sitting long enough to insight care, creativity, and connection inspired these documentations of the heart which required listening more deeply to the means by which Black girls gathered and assembled. I meant to convey that for a while we understood immediately, the relationship between history and peoplehood, blackness and time, space, and presence. In this work, I'm attempting a format that indexes the questions and affective aha's between fragility and transformation of making something dependent on Black girls' lives and livelihood. Girls and homegirls stay with SOLHOT through it all for varied reasons, many of which coalesce around an important question: Who do we determine we are?

Bloom. A place you can depend on to never count you out nor count you at all. Expected to show up without having to explain yourself, you feel like yes, I'm there. There is joy among those who chose to come, sometimes loud and sometimes quiet. You begin to trust your own intuitive guidance. You leave or decide to make audible a question. It's all about what you never seen her do and never did we not be us doing our thing. Witnessing yourself through the heart of someone strong enough to put everything else on hold for your presence. Transforming time and space requires you to present, wonder, wander, and announce yourself to yourself and chosen friends. To swear and side-eye. A mediation is necessary because liberation is not without conflict. To be a comedian when the entire world demands you be an activist is to be a part of the address and addressed.

For Black girl laughter to echo until it decides to fade means change occurred. Everything must now be accountable to how we move once it is felt. A part of it means our collective brilliance grows under assurance that we will fill ourselves up with the pleasures that emerge from our hands. Poems, letters, lists, position papers evidence how she planned, worked, missed lunch, heard you say love, fed herself well, to watch how it almost didn't happen, and she thought again about everything. Then she called a homegirl to learn she was not alone. The rules should change, and the injury must be abolished, if it is following the lead of Black girls' laughter.

Change begins when the girls who show up expect a wild routine though they aren't responsible for it so much as they can take over something better in its availability. Entire institutions start to crumble when the shoot emerges from dried leaves of advancement. If there is any debt, it is all what the homegirls give the girls and what the world misgave the homegirls. This much is energy, every time.

Evidence—which might be most satisfying to the skeptic, to philanthropy, to the foundation, to colleagues across disciplines—will not come through me, my voice, and point of view. I leave some room for leisurely conclusion beyond validation. Validation as empowerment only makes sense of the scales of legality that have already presumed us guilty. We aim for divine chaos, a freedom field of variation, where positive and/or negative valuations have no currency, and it is only for us to be and thrive past permission's gate.

Chaos, which many call transformation, often makes connections and emboldens the senses during the three o'clock early morning hour. I have to write it down and read it back to hear the actions and reverb of what occurred. I am reading, doing, and reading again. My hope is that someone writes back until they start to rewrite it all. In its attention to the particularities, I track what's actionable as help and assistance for future time. Of course, after receiving such summation of who we are, delete is always an option. But there is enough in and through these forms to create some texture, which, as you already know, is a favorite canvas to become ever more creative.

Divine bliss is turning to the homegirls to ask, do you know what just happened? Always followed with something akin to happiness signaled by a smile and expressed giggle, I just can't help myself. I feel it first then announce it again. Usually, those who were a part of it don't know what I mean to reference. You could call it the moment of empowerment, but I wouldn't. Some might even say transformation or achievement which too feels insufficient. The word "change," as previously mentioned, incapsulates the self-determined to self-determine. What I know is political theory, and that like before and after that moment, there are certain things that can't be said anymore. The distinctions between us become as evident as our power. That is all praxis and everythang's everything to be poemed, reflected on, listed, and lettered.

APPENDIX

For Black Girls

Creating Your Own Black Girlhood Archive, #GlobalBlackGirlhood

LAKISHA MICHELLE SIMMONS
AND CASIDY CAMPBELL

As seen in this anthology, scholars of Black girls' history have asked what it means to find Black girls in the archives.[1] Historical archives—libraries, museums, special collections, police records, government reports, and official school records—are most often collected and saved by those in power, saturated with the prejudices of dominant society's views about Black girls.

In this section we provide activities for Black girls, young women, and students to become their own archivists and historians. This process includes the following: creating content, saving content, and sharing stories that you create from the sources you've collected.

Becoming your own archivist and historian gives you control over the story that gets told about your community. These activities are just one starting place. Feel free to be creative; come up with activities that help you link the past to the present, make intergenerational connections, and document and collect the stuff of your own girlhood.

Activities

THE GAMES BLACK GIRLS PLAY

As musicologist Kyra Gaunt explains, "From backyards to schoolyards, [Black girls'] game-songs predate Emancipation. Their musical blackness has much to offer once we unpack the magic in the rhythms and rhymes that animate their torsos and release their tongues with laughter."[2]

Write down or record a game you've played with your friends. Next, learn a game your parents, family members, or friends played when they were younger. Do you notice similarities or differences in these games based on time or place? What do the games reveal in terms of girls' engagement with ideas about race, gender, sexuality, sense of place? What do the games show about Black girls' and LGBTQ youth's creativity?

RECORDING HAIR AND BEAUTY CULTURE

In your own community: Go to a salon or observe friends/family doing hair more informally. Write down, record, or take pictures of the sights, sounds, and stories found at that time.

- Observations: Notice the setting. Where is the salon located? What does the building look like? What objects are important to the space? What kind of conversation is going on? What nonverbal communication happens in the space (songs, dance, movement, hugs, and touch)? Carefully take notes of all that is going on. Are there any themes that emerge from your recordings?

ORAL HISTORIES AND INTERVIEWS

Interview elders in your community or your own friends and other young women.

- Ask elders in your community to share a story about their own girlhood. You may wish to record their answer on your phone. You might ask about a specific historical event, about their first date, their favorite toy or teacher.
- Place-Based Oral History: Have the interviewee talk and walk (or drive) through their old neighborhood. How does place matter to the story they are telling? What spaces brought them joy as Black girls? Which spaces remind them of racism or segregation?
- Food-Based Oral History: Spend time cooking or preparing food with an elder in your community. What do you learn about their childhood as you cook and talk?

Very Important Note: Be sure to get permission before you record; get permission to upload the story on the internet, if you decide to do that.

DIARIES AND SCRAPBOOKS

Go old-school and keep a diary, scrapbook, or planner with your daily activities, thoughts, dreams, and creative imaginings. These might include collages, drawings, sketches, or even notes from your friends.

LETTERS

Exchange letters with an older friend or family member. Ask them about events from their childhood, and share with them things that happen to you. Save the letters you receive.

RACE & PLACE AT SCHOOL AND COLLEGE

Collect stories and photographs from current and former students at your school or a school you used to attend. What is it like to be a Black girl or young woman at that school? What are the challenges you face? What are your successes? Ask former students to reflect back on their time as a student. How have things changed? How have they stayed the same?

You might also consider sharing some of your stories to create change. For example, in November 2013, students at the University of Michigan started a hashtag to share stories of what it was like "Being Black at Michigan." In 2020, current and former students from LaKisha's Catholic high school, Xavier College Preparatory in Phoenix, created Instagram and Facebook pages to share stories of racial bias and wrote a letter to the Roman Catholic Diocese of Phoenix, including student stories and concerns.[3]

POPULAR CULTURE

- Scholars of girlhood are always wondering what girls *thought* about the popular culture, mass media, and texts of the time. This is called "reception studies." Make your own collection of reviews of some of the most popular media. What do you and your friends think about the new album or music video by the biggest pop star? Who is a little-known artist that you love?
- Ask an elder LGBT person or woman to teach you dance moves from their youth. Make videos based on what you've learned.

CURRENT EVENTS

Scholars of Black girls' history often wonder what girls are thinking about politics, civil rights, and current events in their community. Here are some ideas for contributing to the historical archive on these topics.

- Write a letter to your mayor, governor, president, senator or local state officials (your city council members, state representatives, etc.). Let them know about your concerns regarding current events, your hopes for the future, and what you think of the job they are doing. You can save a copy for yourself in your own personal archive. Many letters sent to public officials also end up in the official archive after the public official retires.[4] Historians sometimes use these letters in their own research and writing.

- Create a zine or newsletter with your friends. What important information about current events, Black Lives Matter, or politics do you think is important to share with friends and other young people?
  - What is a zine? A zine is a self-made feminist magazine that explores your daily life, popular culture, and your own theories about the world around you. They often include images, drawings, collages. They can be serious, ironic, funny or all of these things all at once! They are a place for creativity and play.[5]
- Many feminist and anti-racist collectives and activist groups created their own newsletters. Consider creating your own, with news, research, and updates for your readers.[6]

FAMILY HEIRLOOMS AND MATERIAL CULTURE

Ask a family member or friend to share an object they still own from their own girlhood. Take a picture and write down the story of the object.

Do you have any objects or trinkets that were owned by family members you may not have met but want to learn more about? Keep these items in a special place and imagine what their childhood might have been like. How might they have made use of the object?

Identify one of your favorite objects. What makes it special? What is the story of the object?

PLACE OF WORSHIP

Collect stories from the women in your church, masjid, or place of worship. What was the worship space like when they were a child? How has it changed or stayed the same? How have women, girls, and LGBTQ folks been included or excluded over time?

Sharing what you've collected

DIGITAL MEMORIES—CREATING INSTAGRAM OR BLOG POSTS

Curate your items and collections by sharing them on a special social media account (such as Instagram, TikTok, WordPress, Weebly, Twitter, etc). For all of your activities, think about collecting a diversity of content: sound, video, photographs, handwriting, and drawings. Finally, write short stories or notes to go along with your collection.

Important: Make sure you have permission to share the content you are collecting. Also remember that digital memories sometimes do not last forever. Try to back up your favorite pictures and videos using an external hard drive, the cloud, and/or by printing and saving some.

Notes

1. This section is written for Black girls and young women to aid in the creation of their own Black girlhood archive. We encourage all girls to think about ways to create archives of girlhood in their own communities as well. Some activities may be different, some the same. Feel free to use this to brainstorm activities that make sense in your own communities.

2. Kyra Gaunt, "The Magic of Black Girls' Play," *The New York Times*, July 21, 2020, sec. Parenting, https://www.nytimes.com/2020/07/21/parenting/black-girls-play.html; Kyra D. Gaunt, *The Games Black Girls Play: Learning the Ropes from Double-Dutch to Hip-Hop* (NYU Press, 2006).

3. For BBUM see, Jennifer Preston, "On Twitter, 'Being Black at the University of Michigan,'" *The Lede* (blog), February 25, 2014, https://thelede.blogs.nytimes.com/2014/02/25/on-twitter-being-black-at-the-university-of-michigan/; Kellie Woodhouse, "Black Student Union on Talks with University of Michigan Administrators: 'This Is Not the End of the Road,'" *Mlive*, April 21, 2014, sec. Ann Arbor, https://www.mlive.com/news/ann-arbor/2014/04/black_student_union_on_talks_w.html; Remi Murrey, "4 Years Later, Reflections on a Generation of #BBUM," *The Michigan Daily*, accessed August 26, 2020, https://www.michigandaily.com/section/campus-life/4-years-later-reflections-generation-bbum; Lorna Brown, "BBUM: Our History," The Michigan Daily, March 12, 2018, https://www.michigandaily.com/section/mic/bbum-our-history. For more information on Xavier see, "Via Instagram, Catholic Colleges Face a Racial Reckoning," *National Catholic Reporter*, July 29, 2020, https://www.ncronline.org/news/accountability/instagram-catholic-colleges-face-racial-reckoning; "Effective Anti-Racist Education Requires More Diverse Teachers, More Training," *All Things Considered*, July 8, 2020, https://www.npr.org/sections/live-updates-protests-for-racial-justice/2020/07/08/889112818/what-it-would-take-to-get-an-effective-anti-racist-education; "Alumnae for Change," Alumnae for Change, accessed August 26, 2020, https://www.alumnaeforchange.org/.

4. See some examples of "Letters to the President" Lesson Plans at the Ronald Reagan Foundation. https://www.reaganfoundation.org/education/curriculum-and-resources/curriculum/letters-to-the-president/. Or from the Jimmy Carter library: https://www.jimmycarterlibrary.gov/assets/documents/Unit1.pdf

5. For more on zines, see the library of congress website Meg Metcalf, "Research Guides: Zines at the Library of Congress: Introduction," Research Guide, accessed August 27, 2020, https://guides.loc.gov/zines/introduction. See also Janice A. Radway, "Zines Then and Now: What Are They? What Do You Do With Them, How Do They Work?," *Reading the Readers*, 2011, https://www.scholars.northwestern.edu/en/publications/zines-then-and-now-what-are-they-what-do-you-do-with-them-how-do-; Janice Radway, "Zines, Half-Lives, and Afterlives: On the Temporalities of Social and Political Change," *PMLA* 126, no. 1 (January 1, 2011): 140–50, https://doi.org/10.1632/pmla.2011.126.1.140; Tomás Boatwright, "Flux Zine: Black Queer Storytelling," *Equity & Excellence in Education* 52, no. 4 (October 2, 2019): 383–95, https://doi.org/10.1080/10665684.2019.1696254; Melanie Ramdarshan Bold, "Why

Diverse Zines Matter: A Case Study of the People of Color Zines Project," *Publishing Research Quarterly* 33, no. 3 (September 1, 2017): 215–28, https://doi.org/10.1007/s12109-017-9533-4.

6. For an example see, Ashley Farmer, "The Third World Women's Alliance, Cuba, and the Exchange of Ideas," *AAIHS* (blog), April 7, 2017, https://www.aaihs.org/the-third-world-womens-alliance-cuba-and-the-exchange-of-ideas/. Read the 1970s newsletter, The Black Women's Manifesto online: Eleanor Holmes Norton et al., "Black Women's Manifesto," Duke Digital Collections, accessed August 27, 2020, https://repository.duke.edu/dc/wlmpc/wlmms01009.

Further Reading

Transatlantic and Global

Blain, Keisha, and Tiffany Gill. *To Turn the Whole World Over: Black Women and Internationalism.* Urbana: University of Illinois Press, 2019.

Charles, Carolle. "Being Black Twice." In *Problematizing Blackness: Self Ethnographies by Black Immigrants to the United States*, edited by Jean Rahier and Percy Hintzen, 169–80. Hoboken: Routledge, 2014.

Chatelain, Marcia. "International Sisterhood: Cold War Girl Scouts Encounter the World." *Diplomatic History* 38 (2014): 261–70.

Duane, Anna Mae, ed. *Child Slavery Before and After Emancipation: An Argument for Child-Centered Slavery Studies.* New York: Cambridge University Press, 2017.

Ford, Tanisha. *Liberated Threads: Black Women, Style, and the Global Politics of Soul.* Chapel Hill: University of North Carolina Press, 2015.

Hartman, Saidiya. "Venus in Two Acts." *Small Axe* 12, no. 2 (June 2008): 1–14.

Helgren, Jennifer, and Colleen Vasconcellos, eds. *Girlhood: A Global History.* New Brunswick, N.J.: Rutgers University Press, 2010.

Livesay, Daniel. *Children of Uncertain Fortune: Mixed-Race Jamaicans in Britain and the Atlantic Family, 1733–1833.* Chapel Hill: Omohundro Institute, University of North Carolina Press, 2018.

Palmer, Jennifer. *Intimate Bonds: Family and Slavery in the French Atlantic.* Philadelphia: University of Pennsylvania Press, 2016.

Weinbaum, Alys et al., eds. *The Modern Girl Around the World: Consumption, Modernity, and Globalization.* Durham: Duke University Press, 2008.

Africa

Amadiume, Ifi. *Male Daughters, Female Husbands: Gender and Sex in an African Society.* London: Zed Books, 1987.

Bridger, Emily. "Functions and Failures of Transnational Activism: Discourses of Children's Resistance and Repression in Global Anti-Apartheid Network." *Journal of World History* 1, no. 4 (December 2015): 856–87.

Bryant, Kelly M. Duke. "Changing Childhood: 'Liberated Minors,' Guardianship, and the Colonial State in Senegal, 1895–1911." *Journal of African History* 60, no. 2 (2019): 1–20.

———. "Runaways, Dutiful Daughters, and Brides: Family Strategies of Formerly Enslaved Girls in Senegal, 1895–1911." *Women, Gender, and Families of Color* 7, no. 1 (Spring 2019): 37–55.

Decker, Corrie. "The Elusive Power of Colonial Prey: Sexualizing the Schoolgirl in the Zanzibar Protectorate." *Africa Today* 61, no. 4 (2015): 43–60.

———. "Fathers, Daughters, and Institutions: Coming of Age in Mombasa's Colonial Schools." In *Girlhood: A Global History*, edited by Jennifer Helgren et al., 268–88. Rutgers: Rutgers University Press, 2010.

———. "School Girls and Women Teachers: Colonial Education and the Shifting Boundaries Between Girls and Women in Zanzibar." In *Gendered Lives in the Western Indian Ocean: Islam, Marriage, and Sexuality on the Swahili Coast*, edited by Erin E. Stiles and Katrina Daly Tompson. Athens, Ohio: Ohio University Press, 2015.

Duff, S. E. "The Jam and Matchstick Problem: Working-Class Girlhood in Late Nineteenth-Century Cape Town." In *Colonial Girlhood in Literature, Culture and History, 1840–1950*, edited by Kirstine Moruzi and Michelle Smith, 124–40. Basingstoke: Palgrave Macmillan, 2014.

George, Abosede. *Making Modern Girls: A History of Childhood, Labor, and Social Development in Colonial Lagos*. Athens, OH: Ohio University Press, 2014.

Halley, Meghan. "Sex and School on the Southern Swahili Coast: Adolescent Sexuality in the Context of Expanding Education in Rural Mtwara, Tanzania." In *Gendered Lives in the Western Indian Ocean: Islam, Marriage, and Sexuality on the Swahili Coast*, edited by Erin E. Stiles and Katrina Daly Tompson. Athens, Ohio: Ohio University Press, 2015.

Oyěwùmí, Oyèrónkẹ́. *Invention of Women: Making an African Sense of Western Gender Discourses*. Minneapolis: University of Minnesota Press, 1997.

Razy, Elodie and Marie Rodet, eds. *Children on the Move in Africa: Past and Present Experiences of Migration*. Rochester, NY: Boydell and Brewer, 2016.

Rodet, Marie. "'Under the Guise of Guardianship and Marriage': Mobilizing Juvenile and Female Labor in the Aftermath of Slavery in Kayes, French Soudan, 1900–1939." In *Trafficking in Slavery's Wake: Law and the Experience of Women and Children*, edited by Benjamin N. Lawrance and Richard L. Roberts, 86–100. Bloomington: Ohio University Press, 2012.

Thomas, Lynn M. "The Modern Girl and Racial Respectability in 1930s South Africa." In *The Modern Girl Around the World: Consumption, Modernity, and Globalization*, edited by Alys Eve Weinbaum, 96–119. Durham: Duke University Press, 2008.

Caribbean and Latin America

Diptee, Audra Abbe. "Imperial Ideas, Colonial Realities: Enslaved Children in Jamaica, 1775–1834." In *Children in Colonial America*, edited by James Marten, 48–60. New York: New York University Press, 2007.

Turner, Sasha. *Contested Bodies: Pregnancy, Childrearing, and Slavery in Jamaica*, 1st ed. Philadelphia: University of Pennsylvania Press, 2017.

Vasconcellos, Colleen A. "From Chattel to 'Breeding Wenches': Abolitionism, Girlhood and Jamaican Slavery." In *Girlhood: A Global History*, edited by Jennifer Helgren et al., 325–43. Rutgers: Rutgers University Press, 2010.

———. *Slavery, Childhood and Abolition in Jamaica, 1788–1838*. Athens: University of Georgia Press, 2015.

Europe

Bryan, Beverley, et al., eds. *The Heart of the Race: Black Women's Lives in Britain*. London: Verso Books, 2018.

Campt, Tina. *Other Germans: Black Germans and the Politics of Race, Gender, and Memory in the Third Reich*. Ann Arbor: The University of Michigan Press, 2004.

———. *Image Matters: Archive, Photography, and the African Diaspora in Europe*. Durham and London: Duke University Press, 2012.

Donaldson, Sonya. "'How Does It Feel to be a Problem?': Black German Girlhood and the Historical Entanglements of Nation." *Women, Gender, and Families of Color* 7, no. 1 (Spring 2019): 12–36.

Fehrenbach, Heide. *Race After Hitler: Black Occupation Children in Postwar Germany and America*. Princeton and Oxford: Princeton University Press, 2005.

———. "Narrating 'Race' in the 1950's West Germany: The Phenomenon of the *Toxi* Films." In *Not So Plain as Black and White: Afro-German Culture and History, 1890–2000*, edited by Patricia M. Mazón and Reinhild Steingröver, 136–60. Rochester: University of Rochester Press, 2005.

Fenner, Angelica. *Race Under Reconstruction in German Cinema: Robert Stemmle's Toxi*. Toronto: University of Toronto Press, 2011.

Fisher, Tracy. *What's Left of Blackness: Feminisms, Transracial Solidarities, and the Politics of Belonging in Britain*. New York: Palgrave Macmillan, 2012.

Ford, Tanisha C. "Finding Olive Morris in the Archive." *The Black Scholar*, Special Issue: *On the Future of Black Feminism* 46, no. 2 (Summer 2016): 5–18.

Harrison, Rashida L. "Movement Makers: A Historical Analysis of Black Women's Magic in Social Movement Formation." In *Black Girl Magic Beyond the Hashtag: Twenty-First-Century Acts of Self Definition*, ed. Julia S. Jordan-Zachery and Duchess Harris. Tucson: University of Arizona Press, 2019.

Muniz de Faria, Yara-Colette Lemke. "Germany's 'Brown Babies' Must Be Helped! Will You?": US Adoption Plans for the Afro-German Children, 1950–1955." *Callaloo* 26, no. 2 (Spring 2003): 342–62.

Oguntoye, Katharina, May Ayim, and Dagmar Schultz. *Showing Our Colors: Afro-German Women Speak Out*. Amherst: University of Massachusetts Press, 1992.

Rudolph, Nancy. "Black German Children: A Photography Portfolio." *Callaloo* 26, no. 2 (Spring 2003): 383–400.

United States History

Agyepong, Tera Eva. *The Criminalization of Black Children: Race, Gender, and Delinquency in Chicago's Juvenile Justice System, 1899–1945*. Chapel Hill: University of North Carolina Press, 2018.

Baumgartner, Kabria. *In Pursuit of Knowledge: Black Women and Educational Activism in Antebellum America*. New York: New York University Press, 2019.

Bernstein, Robin. *Racial Innocence: Performing American Childhood from Slavery to Civil Rights*. New York: New York University Press, 2011.

Berry, Daina Ramey. *The Price for Their Pound of Flesh: The Value of the Enslaved, from Womb to Grave, in the Building of a Nation*. Boston: Beacon Press, 2017.

Bynum, Tara. "Phillis Wheatley on Friendship." *Legacy: A Journal of American Women Writers* 31, no. 1 (2014): 42–51.

———. "Phillis Wheatley's Pleasures," *Common Place* 11.1 (October 2010).

Capshaw, Katharine. *Civil Rights Childhood: Picturing Liberation in African American Photobooks*. Minneapolis: University of Minnesota Press, 2014.

Capshaw, Katharine, and Anna Mae Duane, eds. *Who Writes for Black Children?: African American Children's Literature before 1900*. Minneapolis: University of Minnesota Press, 2017.

Chatelain, Marcia. *South Side Girls: Growing Up in the Great Migration*. Durham: Duke University Press, 2015.

De Schweinitz, Rebecca. *If We Could Change the World: Young People and America's Long Struggle for Racial Equality*. Chapel Hill: University of North Carolina Press, 2009.

Devlin, Rachel. *A Girl Stands at the Door: The Generation of Young Women who Desegregated America's Schools*. New York: Basic Books, 2018.

Field, Corinne T., Tammy Charelle Owens, Marcia Chatelain, LaKisha Simmons, Abosede George, and Rhian Keyse. "The History of Black Girlhood: Recent Innovations and Future Directions." *Journal of the History of Childhood and Youth* 9, no. 3 (2016): 383–401.

Field, Corinne T., and LaKisha Michelle Simmons, eds. "Special Issue: Black Girlhood and Kinship." *Women, Gender, and Families of Color* 7, no. 1 (Spring 2019).

Hartman, Saidiya. *Wayward Lives, Beautiful Experiments: Intimate Histories of Social Upheaval*. New York: W. W. Norton, 2019.

Hodgson, Lucia. "Infant Muse: Phillis Wheatley and the Revolutionary Rhetoric of Childhood." *Early American Literature* 49, no. 3 (2014): 663–82.

Ibrahim, Habiba. *Black Age: Oceanic Lifespans and the Time of Black Life*. New York: New York University Press, 2021.

Jones, Catherine. *Intimate Reconstructions: Children in Postemancipation Virginia*. Charlottesville: University of Virginia Press, 2015.

Jones, Lindsey Elizabeth. "'The most unprotected of all human beings': Black Girls, State Violence, and the Limits of Protection in Jim Crow Virginia." *Souls: A Critical Journal of Black Politics, Culture, and Society* 20, no. 1 (2018): 14–37.

King, Wilma. *African American Childhoods: Historical Perspectives from Slavery to Civil Rights*. New York: Palgrave Macmillan, 2005.

———. "'Prematurely Knowing of Evil Things': The Sexual Abuse of African American Girls and Young Women in Slavery and Freedom." *The Journal of African American History* 99, no. 3 (2014): 173–96.

———. *Stolen Childhood: Slave Youth in Nineteenth-Century America*. Bloomington: Indiana University Press, 2011.

Ladner, Joyce. *Tomorrow's Tomorrow: The Black Woman*. Reprint Edition. Lincoln: University of Nebraska Press, 1995.

Lindsey, Treva, B. *Colored No More: Reinventing Black Womanhood in Washington, DC*. Urbana: University of Illinois Press, 2017.

Maddox, Lucy. *The Parker Sisters: A Border Kidnapping*. Philadelphia: Temple University Press, 2016.

Mitchell, Mary Niall. *Raising Freedom's Child: Black Children and Visions of the Future after Slavery*. New York: New York University Press, 2008.

Mitchell, Michele. *Righteous Propagation: African Americans and the Politics of Racial Destiny after Reconstruction*. Chapel Hill: University of North Carolina Press, 2004.

Moss, Hilary. *Schooling Citizens: The Struggle for African American Education in Antebellum America*. Chicago: Chicago University Press, 2009.

Phillips, Michelle H. "The Children of Double Consciousness: From *The Souls of Black Folk* to *The Brownie's Book*." *PMLA* 128, no. 3 (2013): 590–607.

Schwartz, Marie Jenkins. *Born in Bondage: Growing Up Enslaved in the Antebellum South*. Cambridge, MA: Harvard University Press, 2000.

Simmons, LaKisha Michelle. *Crescent City Girls: The Lives of Young Black Women in Segregated New Orleans*. Chapel Hill: University of North Carolina Press, 2015.

Stevenson, Brenda. *The Contested Murder of Latasha Harlins: Justice, Gender, and the Origins of the LA Riots*. New York: Oxford University Press, 2013.

Sundue, Sharon. "'Beyond the Time of White Children': African American Emancipation, Age, and Ascribed Neoteny in Early National Pennsylvania." In *Age in America: The Colonial Era to the Present*, edited by Corinne T. Field and Nicholas Syrett, 124–47. New York: New York University Press, 2015.

Webster, Crystal Lynn. *Beyond the Boundaries of Childhood: African American Children in the Antebellum North*. Chapel Hill: University of North Carolina Press, 2021.

———. "The History of Black Girls and the Field of Black Girl Studies: At the Forefront of Academic Scholarship." *The American Historian*. March 2020.

Wright, Nezera. *Black Girlhood in the Nineteenth Century*. Urbana: University of Illinois Press, November 2016.

Contemporary Black Girlhoods

Brown, Ruth Nicole. *Black Girlhood Celebration: Toward a Hip-Hop Feminist Pedagogy.* New York: Peter Lang, 2009.

———. *Hear Our Truths: The Creative Potential of Black Girlhood.* Urbana: University of Illinois Press, 2013.

Brown, Ruth Nicole and Chamara Jewel Kwakye. *Wish to Live: The Hip-Hop Feminism Pedagogy Reader*. New York: Peter Lang, 2012.

Butler, Tamara. "Black Girl Cartography: Black Girlhood and Place-Making in Education Research." *Review of Research in Education* 42, no. 1 (2018): 28–45.

Carroll, Rebecca. *Sugar in the Raw: Voices of Young Black Girls in America*. New York: Three Rivers Press, 1997.

Cox, Aimee Meredith. *Shapeshifters: Black Girls and the Choreography of Citizenship.* Durham: Duke University Press, 2015.

Crenshaw, Kimberlé, Priscilla Ocen, and Jyoti Nanda. *Black Girls Matter: Pushed Out, Overpoliced, and Underprotected*. African American Policy Forum, 2015. https://www.atlanticphilanthropies.org/wp-content/uploads/2015/09/BlackGirlsMatter_Report.pdf.

Epstein, Rebecca, Jamilia J. Blake, and Thalia González. "Girlhood Interrupted: The Erasure of Black Girls' Childhood." Washington, DC: Georgetown Law Center on Poverty and Inequality, 2017. https://www.law.georgetown.edu/poverty-inequality-center/wp-content/uploads/sites/14/2017/08/girlhood-interrupted.pdf.

Gaunt, Kyra D. *The Games Black Girls Play: Learning the Ropes from Double-Dutch to Hip-Hop*. New York: New York University Press, 2006.

———. "YouTube, Twerking & You: Context Collapse and the Handheld Co-Presence of Black Girls and Miley Cyrus." *Journal of Popular Music Studies* 27, no. 3 (2015): 244–73.

Gillam, Reighan. "Representing Black Girlhood in Brazil: Culture and Strategies of Empowerment." *Communication, Culture & Critique* 10, no. 4 (Dec 2017): 609–25.

Halliday, Aria S., and Nadia E. Brown. "The Power of Black Girl Magic Anthems: Nicki Minaj, Beyoncé, and 'Feeling Myself' As Political Empowerment." *Souls: A Critical Journal of Black Politics, Culture, and Society* 20, no. 2 (April-June 2018): 222–38.

Ibrahim, Habiba. *Troubling the Family: The Promise of Personhood and the Rise of Multiracialism*. Minneapolis: University of Minnesota Press, 2012.

Jarmon, Renina. *Black Girls Are from the Future: Essays on Race, Digital Creativity, and Pop Culture*. Washington, DC: Jarmon Media, 2013.

Jordan-Zachery, Julia S., and Duchess Harris. *Black Girl Magic Beyond the Hashtag: Twenty-First Century Acts of Self-Definition*. Tucson: University of Arizona Press, 2019.

LaBennett, Oneka. *She's Mad Real: Popular Culture and West Indian Girls in Brooklyn*. New York: New York University Press, 2011.

Ladner, Joyce. *Tomorrow's Tomorrow: The Black Woman*. Garden City, NY: Doubleday, 1971.

———. "Tomorrow's Tomorrow: A Twenty-Five-Year Retrospective," in *Tomorrow's Tomorrow: The Black Woman*, reprint ed. Lincoln: University of Nebraska Press, 1995.
Lindsey, Treva B. "'One Time for My Girls': African American Girlhood, Empowerment, and Popular Visual Culture." *Journal of African American Studies* 17 (2013): 22–34.
Love, Bettina L. *Hip Hop's Li'l Sistas Speak: Negotiating Hip-Hop Identities and Politics in the New South*. New York: Peter Lang, 2012.
Morris, Monique W. *Pushout: The Criminalization of Black Girls in Schools*. New York: The New Press, 2016.
———. *Sing a Rhythm, Dançe a Blues: Education for the Liberation of Black and Brown Girls*. New York: The New Press, 2019.
Noble, Safiya. "Google Search: Hyper-Visibility as a Means of Rendering Black Women and Girls Invisible." *Invisible Culture: An Electronic Journal for Visual Culture* 29 (October 2013).
Owens, Tammy C., Durell M. Callier, Jessica L. Robinson, and Porshé R. Garner, "Towards and Interdisciplinary Field of Black Girlhood Studies." *Departures in Critical Qualitative Research* 6, no. 3 (Fall 2017): 116–32.
Shange, Savannah. *Progressive Dystopia: Abolition, AntiBlackness, and Schooling in San Francisco*. Durham: Duke University Press, 2019.
Stack, Carol. *All Our Kin: Strategies for Survival in a Black Community*. New York, Basic Books, 1983.
Stokes, Carla. "Representin' in Cyberspace: Sexual Scripts, Self-Definition, and Hip-Hop Culture in Black American Adolescent Girls' Home Pages." *Culture, Health, and Sexuality* 9 (2017): 169–84.
Thomas, Ebony Elizabeth. *The Dark Fantastic: Race and the Imagination from Harry Potter to the Hunger Games*. New York: New York University Press, 2019.
Waters, M. Billye Sankofa, Venus E. Evans-Winters, and Bettina Love, eds. *Celebrating Twenty Years of Black Girlhood: The Lauryn Hill Reader*. New York: Peter Lang, 2018.

Queer Black Girlhoods

Ekine, Sokari, and Hakima Abbas, eds. *The Queer African Reader*. Dakar: Pambazuka Press, 2103.
Green, Kai M. "In the Life: On Black Queer Kinship." *Women, Gender, and Families of Color* 7, no. 1 (Spring 2019): 98–101.
Imma, Z'étoile. "(Re)visualizing Black Lesbian Lives, (Trans)masculinity, and Township Space in the Documentary Work of Zanele Muholi." *Journal of Lesbian Studies* 21, no. 2 (2017), 219–41.
James, Adilia E. E. "Queer Like Me: Black Girlhood Sexuality on the Playground, Under the Covers, and in the Halls of Academia." *Journal of Lesbian Studies* 15, no. 1 (2011): 41–48.
Matebeni, Zethu. "Intimacy, Queerness, Race." *Cultural Studies* 27, no. 3 (2013): 404–17.

Matebeni, Zethu, Surya Monro, and Vasu Reddy, eds. *Queer in Africa: LGBTQI Identities, Citizenship, and Activism*. New York: Routledge, 2018.

Munro, Brenna M. "States of Emergence: Writing African Female Same-Sex Sexuality." *Journal of Lesbian Studies* 21, no. 2 (2016): 186–203.

Shange, Savannah. "Play Aunties and Dyke Bitches: Gender, Generation, and the Ethic of Black Queer Kinship." *The Black Scholar* 49, no. 1 (2019): 40–54.

Snorton, C. Riley. *Black on Both Sides: A Racial History of Trans Identity*. Minneapolis: University of Minnesota Press, 2017.

Wallace, Anya Wallace. "Sour Apple Green: A Queer Memoir of Black Family." *Callaloo* 37, no. 5 (Fall 2014): 1042–50.

Contributors

CORINNE T. FIELD is an associate professor in the Department of Women, Gender, and Sexuality at the University of Virginia. She is currently completing a monograph titled *Grand Old Women: How Abolitionists and Feminists Transformed Aging in America*. She is the author of *The Struggle for Equal Adulthood: Gender, Race, Age, and the Fight for Citizenship in Antebellum America* (2014) and co-editor (with Nicholas Syrett) of *Age in America: Colonial Era to the Present* (2015). Field is the cofounder of the History of Black Girlhood Network, an informal collaboration of scholars working to promote research into the historical experience of Black girls. She was the co-organizer of the Global History of Black Girlhood Conference held at the University of Virginia in April 2017.

LAKISHA MICHELLE SIMMONS is associate professor of History & Women's and Gender Studies at the University of Michigan. She is the author of *Crescent City Girls: The Lives of Young Black Women in Segregated New Orleans* (2015), which won the SAWH Julia Cherry Spruill Prize for best book in southern women's history and received Honorable Mention for the ABWH Letitia Woods Brown Memorial Book Award for the best book in African American women's history. Simmons has written about Black girlhood and historical method in the *Journal of the History of Childhood and Youth*; about Black college students and sexual cultures in the 1930s for *Gender and History*; on southern Black girl writers in *Tulsa Studies in Women's Literature*; and on Black motherhood and infant loss in *Signs: Journal of Women in Culture and Society*. She is currently working on a book called *Labor, Love, & Loss: Black Women, their Children, and the Ancestors*.

JANAÉ E. BONSU (she/her) is an activist researcher and licensed social worker from Columbia, SC. Bonsu's activism and research are grounded in both her personal experiences as a survivor of violence and commitment to an abolitionist praxis that does not rely on policing for safety. Bonsu received her PhD from the University of Illinois-Chicago where her research focused on the intersection of interpersonal and institutional violence among Black people of marginalized genders, and the impact on survivors' safety-related empowerment. Bonsu currently works as the Director of Advocacy, Research and Evaluation at the National Black Women's Justice Institute.

RUTH NICOLE BROWN is the inaugural chairperson and professor of African American and African Studies at Michigan State University. In 2006, Brown created Saving Our Lives, Hearing Our Truths (SOLHOT) to celebrate Black girlhood by meeting Black girls face to face and heart to heart. She's authored two books, *Hear Our Truths: The Creative Potential of Black Girlhood* (2013) and *Black Girlhood Celebration: Toward A Hip-Hop Feminist Pedagogy* (2009) and co-edited several anthologies.

TARA BYNUM is an assistant professor of English and African American Studies at the University of Iowa. Her current monograph, *Reading Pleasures*, examines how eighteenth-century enslaved and/or free men and women feel good or experience pleasure despite the privations of slavery, "unfreedom," or white supremacy; it is forthcoming in fall 2022 from the University of Illinois Press New Black Studies Series. *Reading Pleasures* is part of a larger, ongoing project that thinks deeply about how Black communities in the early republic made and shaped the very meaning of nation-building in the greater New England area and beyond. Related essays have appeared or are forthcoming in: *Early American Literature, Common-Place, Legacy, J19, Criticism, American Periodicals,* and *African American Literature in Transition.*

KATHARINE CAPSHAW is professor of English and affiliate in Africana Studies at the University of Connecticut, where she also serves as associate dean for Diversity, Equity, and Inclusion. She is the author of *Children's Literature of the Harlem Renaissance* (2004) and *Civil Rights Childhood: Picturing Liberation in African American Photobooks* (2014), both of which won "best scholarly book" from the Children's Literature Association. With Anna Mae Duane, Capshaw edited *Who Writes for Black Children? African American Children's Literature before 1900* (2017). Capshaw is developing a book about Black children's theater in the 1970s and co-hosts the childhood studies podcast "The Children's Table."

CASIDY CAMPBELL is a PhD candidate in the Department of American Culture with certificates in Women and Gender Studies and Digital Studies at the University of Michigan Ann Arbor. Her research is focused on fullness of black girls' personhood and seeks to understand how black girls use the same digital technologies that often efface them to assert their quotidian perspectives. She is a 2021 Community of Scholars Fellow at the Institute of Research on Women and Gender, a DISCO (Digital Inquiry, Speculation, Collaboration, and Optimism) Network Graduate Scholar, and current member of the Digital Inequality Lab. She formerly chaired the African American Caucus and was a co-founder of the Black Research Roundtable. Campbell was a Mellon Mays Undergraduate Fellow at Emory University where she completed her BA in African American Studies and sociology.

BEVERLEY PALESA DITSIE is a human rights activist, musician, writer, and filmmaker. As an activist, she was a cofounder of GLOW, the first multi-racial LGBTI organization in South Africa. Her award-winning documentary film *Simon & I*, co-directed and produced by Nick Newman, is a personal tale of her coming of age as an LGBTI activist alongside Simon Nkoli.

S.E. DUFF teaches African and World History at Colby College in Maine. She is an historian of modern South Africa, with particular interests in histories of age and gender. Her first book is *Changing Childhoods in the Cape Colony: Dutch Reformed Church Evangelicalism and Colonial Childhood, 1860–1895* (Palgrave, 2015), and she is currently at work on a history of sex education in twentieth-century South Africa. Before moving to the United States, she held positions at Goldsmiths, University of London, and at Stellenbosch University and the University of the Witwatersrand in South Africa.

DR. CYNTHIA R. GREENLEE is a North Carolina-based historian and journalist. Her work focuses on Black girlhood and law in the late nineteenth-century U.S. South and on reproductive history. Her writing has appeared in the *Journal of Women's History* and media including *Longreads*, *The Nation*, *The New York Times*, *Smithsonian*, *Vice*, *Vox*, and *The Washington Post*, among others. She won a 2020 James Beard Foundation Award for excellence in food writing. Greenlee is also lead editor of *The Echoing Ida Collection*, an anthology of Black people writing about reproductive justice (2021). Follow her at www.cynthiagreenlee.com or @CynthiaGreenlee on Twitter.

CLAUDRENA N. HAROLD is professor of history at the University of Virginia. She has published *The Rise and Fall of the Garvey Movement in the Urban South, 1918–1942* (2007); *New Negro Politics in the Jim Crow South* (2016); and *When Sunday Comes: Gospel Music in the Soul and Hip-Hop Eras* (2020). She has coedited *The Punitive Turn: New Approaches to Race and Incarceration* (2013) and *Charlottesville 2017: The Legacy of Race and Inequality* (2018). She has an ongoing research project on the history of Black student activism at UVA, including eight short films that have been screened internationally.

ANASA HICKS is assistant professor of Caribbean history at Florida State University. Her research focuses on the intersection of race, gender, and labor in twentieth-century Cuba. Her book, *Hierarchies at Home: Domestic Service in Cuba from Abolition to Revolution, is forthcoming with Cambridge University Press.* Anasa's research has been supported by such institutions as the Ford Foundation, the Institute for Citizens and Scholars, the Florida Education Fund, and the Schomburg Center for Research in Black Culture.

LINDSEY ELIZABETH JONES is a historian studying African American education, Black women's intellectual history, and Black girlhood in the twentieth century U.S. South. She is writing *Common Prey: Wayward Black Girls in the Old Dominion, 1900–1954*, a book examining southern Black girls' experiences of education, incarceration, racial uplift, and Progressive social welfare reform using the case of Virginia's state reformatory for delinquent colored girls. She currently lives in Southside Virginia with her daughter.

PHINDILE KUNENE holds an MA in history from the University of the Witwatersrand in Johannesburg. Her research explores the history of the local state in South Africa, youth political activism, apartheid forms of co-option, and youth political demobilization. She has also researched post-apartheid forms and repertoires of collective action and protest. An activist herself, she has been involved in youth and student movements and trade unions. She currently works as an educator and curriculum specialist in service to activist organizations.

DENISE OLIVER-VELEZ is a feminist, activist, scholar, and former member of the Young Lords Party and the Black Panther Party. She is an adjunct professor of anthropology and women's studies at SUNY New Paltz and is a contributing editor for the progressive political blog *Daily Kos.*

JENNIFER L. PALMER is a historian of race and gender in the early modern Francophone world. Her book *Intimate Bonds: Family and Slavery in the French Atlantic* (2016) won the French Colonial Historical Society's Boucher Prize. She is currently working on a monograph, "Possession: Gender, Race, and Property in Atlantic France," which shows how property ownership became a form a white privilege. Palmer received a joint PhD in history and women's studies and has studied law. She is an associate professor at the University of Georgia.

VANESSA D. PLUMLY is an ACM Andrew W. Mellon Faculty Fellow and assistant professor of German Studies, as well as affiliate faculty in Ethnic

Studies at Lawrence University. Plumly holds a PhD in German Studies from the University of Cincinnati and an MA from the University of Kentucky. She is co-editor of the volume *Rethinking Black German Studies: Approaches, Interventions and Histories* (2018) and is an editor of the series *Imagining Black Europe* with Peter Lang. She is the author of numerous articles and book chapters on Black German cultural productions and political interventions in post-war and post-Wall Germany.

SHANI ROPER, PhD is curator of the University of West Indies Museum. Her research interests include histories of Caribbean childhood, museum educational practices, public history, and pedagogical approaches to the study of histories of trauma. She has published on Afro Jamaican childhood, gender, and poor relief policies in the *Journal of Caribbean History*, *Caribbean Studies* and the *Journal for the Study of Childhood and Youth*.

SA SMYTHE is a poet, translator, and scholar of Black European literary and cultural studies, contemporary Mediterranean studies, and Black trans poetics. Smythe's scholarship and political investments are broadly about otherwise Black belonging beyond borders and what they term "a nonbinary approach to black study." They study literature and other cultural responses to racial capitalism and border regimes in the wake of self-initiated migration crises and anti-Black, colonial, and xenophobic violence across Europe (in particular, Italy), East Africa, and the Mediterranean. Smythe also theorizes Black trans poetics as both practitioner and student. Smythe is an assistant professor in the Departments of Gender Studies and African American Studies at UCLA.

NASTASSJA E. SWIFT is a multi-disciplinary artist holding a BFA from Virginia Commonwealth University. She works with fiber, audio, performance, and film within her studio practice, speaking to Black femininity, spirituality, history, and place in relation to the body. Nastassja is the recipient of a 2021 Dr. Doris Derby Award, the Art Matters 2021 Fellowship Award, and the Virginia Commission of the Arts Fellowship in Craft for the 2020 cycle. Her work is permanently displayed at The Colored Girls Museum in Philadelphia and has been acquired into the Grace Linton Battle Memorial Fund for the Arts Collection, as well as Quirk Hotel in Charlottesville. Nastassja is currently living and working in Virginia.

DARA WALKER is an assistant professor of African American Studies, history, and Women's, Gender, and Sexuality Studies at Penn State University. She holds a PhD in History from Rutgers University. Dara is currently revising her book manuscript, *High School Rebels: Black Youth Politics, Organizing, and Education in the Motor City, 1966–1973*, which examines the role of

Detroit's high school organizing tradition in the development of Black Power politics. Her research has been funded by the Ford Foundation's Dissertation Fellowship and the NAEd/Spencer Foundation Postdoctoral Fellowship

CRYSTAL LYNN WEBSTER is assistant professor of history at the University of British Columbia. Her research interests lie at the intersection of race, gender, and age. Her book, *Beyond the Boundaries of Childhood: African American Children in the Antebellum North* (UNC Press, 2021), is a social history of African American children and foregrounds their lives as fundamental to the process of the North's prolonged transition from slavery to freedom. She is currently researching and writing her second book, tentatively titled *Criminalizing Freedom: African Americans and the Making of Criminal Reform in Early America*. Her research has been supported through grants from the Gilder Lehrman Center for the Study of Slavery, Resistance, and Abolition and the Andrew W. Mellon Foundation.

Born and raised in "Chocolate City," NAJYA A. WILLIAMS (she/her) is a writer and artist who is passionate about Black women, health, and equity. Her work has appeared in multiple publications, including *Black Youth Project*, *We are the 94 Percent*, and *Black Girl in Om*. In 2017, Najya released her debut poetry chapbook, *Cotton*. In 2020, Najya produced three original short films—*MORE LIFE, ALL GRAY,* and *BURN*—which can be viewed in her virtual gallery alongside her spoken word album, *mad black woman*. Looking ahead, Najya hopes to continue changing hearts and minds, one word at a time.

NAZERA SADIQ WRIGHT is associate professor of African American and Africana Studies and English at the University of Kentucky. Her book, *Black Girlhood in the Nineteenth Century* (2016), won the 2018 Children's Literature Association's Honor Book Award for Outstanding Book of Literary Criticism. Her current research explores the history of libraries and African American women writers of the eighteenth and nineteenth centuries. Her research has been supported by grants from the Ford Foundation, the National Endowment for the Humanities, and the Andrew W. Mellon Foundation.

Index

The University of Illinois Press
is a founding member of the
Association of University Presses.

University of Illinois Press
1325 South Oak Street
Champaign, IL 61820-6903
www.press.uillinois.edu

FSC
www.fsc.org
MIX
Papier | Fördert
gute Waldnutzung
FSC® C083411

Zeitfracht Medien GmbH
Ferdinand-Jühlke-Straße 7
99095 Erfurt, Deutschland
produktsicherheit@kolibri360.de